Scripture Made Easy

Polly Gwinn

Bloomington, IN   authorHOUSE®   Milton Keynes, UK

AuthorHouse™
1663 Liberty Drive, Suite 200
Bloomington, IN 47403
www.authorhouse.com
Phone: 1-800-839-8640

AuthorHouse™ UK Ltd.
500 Avebury Boulevard
Central Milton Keynes, MK9 2BE
www.authorhouse.co.uk
Phone: 08001974150

This book is a work of non-fiction. Unless otherwise noted, the author and the publisher make no explicit guarantees as to the accuracy of the information contained in this book and in some cases, names of people and places have been altered to protect their privacy.

First published by AuthorHouse   9/26/2006

ISBN: 1-4259-6180-0 (sc)

Printed in the United States of America
Bloomington, Indiana

This book is printed on acid-free paper.

This book is dedicated to the Believers: Carolyn, Cindy, Marie, and Stephen

Contents

Part VII Why, Where, and How

Part VIII God Uses People

Part IX Listen Up

Part X Balance

Part XI Good, Better, Best

Part XII Facts

Part XIII Life and Death

Part XIV Happy Ending

Part I – The Father

1. Believers/Christians/God/gods

In the beginning, there was One God, and in the beginning, there were believers. Even Lucifer believed in God; however, he believed he would make a better one. In my mind, this was the beginning of the "other gods." Lucifer set himself up to be worshipped above God, and some fell for it and some are still falling. The Israelites believed in One God, but other religions in the ancient world recognized a number of different gods. When the Israelites entered Canaan, they came into contact with the various gods of their neighbors. The Law of Moses commanded God's people to remain loyal to the One True God, who led them out of slavery and into the Promised Land (Ex. 20:1-5). Once in Canaan, they were tempted to follow idol worship, and often drifted away from Yahweh.

One of the most common names for "god" was El. The Canaanites did not believe that El was the only god, but they did believe that El was the one who ruled over all the other gods. They believed El was the creator of the universe, and the kind, compassionate father of the whole human race. El was worshiped in Palestine before the Israelites took over the land. In the Jewish scriptures, "El" also frequently refers to the God of Israel. This could have been the cause of some of the confusion among the new members of Canaan. Yamm was the god of the sea, Mot the god of death, and Leviathan the sea monster is said to be slain by the True God "in that day" (Isa. 27:1). Baal, which means "master," "husband," and "lord," was the most popular name for the god in the ancient world. Baal was worshiped as a god of fertility, who ensured good and abundant crops, and was connected with the storms that watered the crops. Some believed that parts of nature were filled with godlike spirits, so they worshiped things like trees, rivers, fountains, and caves.

Asherah was known as the mother of the gods, and identified as the wife of El. Manasseh, a king of Judah, had a carved image of her placed in the temple of the Lord in Jerusalem. The term *Asherah* referred also to the sacred poles that were erected for worship (2 Kings 21:2-5). Anat was famous for performing acts of violence against those who opposed her, putting us in mind of the queen Jezebel. The name of the city Anathoth is derived from her name, meaning she was probably worshiped in this city at an earlier time. The Philistine's chief god was Dagon (1 Sam. 5:1-5) and when they captured the Ark of God, they took it and set it beside the idol in his temple. The next day, Dagon had fallen on his face before the Ark of the Lord. Each time they would put Dagon back in his place, the next morning they would again find him on his face before the Ark of the Lord. Did this cause the Philistines to see the light and worship the true God? Well, they called a committee meeting and decided to have the Ark of the Lord moved out of their city, to another city, and to another city, and to another city, and finally, they sent it back to Israel. They did not want that crazy box that held the afflictions of God if they worshiped other gods. Do you move the box in order to do as you please (Judges 21:25)?

Astrology, the belief that the sun and the stars control human life, came out of Babylon, and had a great influence throughout the Greek and Roman empires. The people of Israel rejected this belief and believed that God created the sun, moon, and stars (Gen. 1:14-19, Ps. 8:3, 147:4). Along with believers in gods and idol worshipers, there was a string of philosophers who hinted at the belief in God, but still spent their lives trying to discover what the world was made of (according to Socrates). Plato taught that reason was the nature of the universe, controlling things from within. He believed that the human soul was immortal, and that the soul is superior to the body. Aristotle taught that the knowledge of a thing requires an understanding of what caused it. He did, however, believe that the only true form that caused matter to move was God. The list of gods, idols, and philosophers goes on and on, and they have probably not all been named in research to date.

In the centuries before Jesus was born, the number of religions, cults, and forms of philosophy in the ancient world had grown rapidly. The letters of the New Testament provide glimpses of how various religious teachings opposed Christian followers; 1 Corinthians 8 warns about eating food sacrificed to idols and becoming a stumbling block to those who do not understand. In Galatians 1:6, Paul is astonished that the One who called the people by grace was being deserted to turn back to a different gospel, while 1 John 2:26-28 talks about counterfeit anointing and those trying to lead you astray. Christianity came into being as one among many religions and philosophies spread around the ancient world by merchants and soldiers.

Although there have always been believers in God, Acts 11:26 tells us that the disciples were called Christians first at Antioch. Both the Old and the New Testament contain direct and indirect references to these other forms of belief. They have not all faced away, and it is a sad fact that more are being added with each generation. It is, therefore, important to become aware of (but not obsessed with) these other beliefs in order to understand the Bible more fully. Check everything against the Word of God, testing the spirits to see whether they are from God (1 John 4:1-6). "If anyone comes to you and does not bring this teaching, do not take him into your house or welcome him" (2 John 10, New International Version). The teaching spoken of here is, of course, acknowledging Jesus Christ as coming in the flesh. Do not imitate what is evil but what is good. Anyone who does what is good is from God (3 John). "These commandments I give you today are to be upon your hearts. Tie them as symbols on your hands. Write them on the doorframes of your houses and on your gates" (Deut. 6:6-8; Ps. 119:97 New International Version).

2. Just the Facts, Ma'am! Just the Facts!

I don't know if any of you remember the old TV show, *Dragnet,* with Jack Webb continuously saying, "Just the facts, ma'am." This also reminds me of a story about the little first-grade boy asking his mother where he came from. Mother went into a long and drawn-out explanation of the facts of life. When she was finished, a not-too-interested little boy said, "Well, a new boy moved here today from Iowa, and I was just wondering where I came from!" This happens all too often when we try to explain the Bible. If we could only stick to the facts and leave out the stories and personal opinions of why things in the Bible happened, perhaps there would be less confusion.

The most difficult question any Christian has ever been asked is, "Where did God come from?" The fact is in the book of John. "In the beginning was the Word and the Word was with God and the Word was God" (John 1:1). We find in the book of Genesis that God created man out of dirt and woman from the rib of the man. All through the Old Testament, the Messiah was talked about by the prophets, but not until the New Testament was He delivered by His Virgin Mother (Matt. 1:18-21). "All this took place to fulfill what the Lord had said through the prophet. 'The Virgin will be with child and they will call Him Immanuel—God with us'" (Matt. 1:22-23). The book of Luke is usually used to read about the birth of Jesus, because it includes that Mary gave birth in a stable, wrapped the baby in cloths, and placed Him in a manger because there was no room at the inn (Luke 2:4-7). The announcement of Baby Jesus by the angels to the shepherds is very exciting to the Christian (Luke 2:8-20), and each of us has at one time wished we could have been among the first to see this baby Savior.

Why was this baby born? "God loved the world so much that He gave His one and only Son so that whoever believes in Him may not be lost, but have eternal life" (John 3:16). Jesus said that the ones His Father gave Him [saved] He would not lose (John 6:39-51), and they would live forever with Him in heaven (John 14:1-3). How do we know that this man was Jesus? Jesus Himself asked, "Why is my language not clear to you?" (John 8:43). The fact is that you accept Jesus as your Lord and Savior, then you will know the truth, and the truth will set you free from all doubt about who Jesus is and keep you from sinning with the world (John 8:31-47). All scripture is inspired by God and written by men who were filled with the Holy Spirit; the words are trustworthy and true and they are the true words from God (Rev. 19:9, 21:5; 2 Tim. 3:16). The fact is that Jesus is the way, the truth, and the life that leads us to eternal life with Him in heaven (John 14:6). He was conceived by the Holy Spirit, born of a virgin, preached here on earth as a man, died on the cross for our sins, and rose again to live on the right hand of the Father in heaven. We are saved by grace through faith, and without faith, it is impossible to please God (Heb. 11:6), because anyone who comes to Him must believe that He exists. "Now faith is being sure of what we hope for and certain of what we do not see" (Heb 11:1).

We must be convinced that Christ Jesus is able to guard our salvation until His return to earth (2 Tim. 1:12) and see to it that none of us have unbelieving hearts that turn against God (Heb. 3:12). It is a fact that Jesus died once for all (Heb. 9:12), and it is a fact that all humankind will die once and after that, face judgment (Heb. 9:27). The number one fact that all need to understand and believe is that the saved will live forever and the second death (hell) has no power over them (Rev. 20:6). The second death is the lake of fire that the unsaved, at the time of Christ's second coming, will be thrown into and be tormented day and night forever and ever (Rev. 20:10, 14-15). The facts that are repeated over and again in the scriptures need to be repeated over and again to the world around us. "Everyone who believes in Him may have eternal life (John 3:15), whosoever believes in Him shall not perish (John 3:16), whoever believes in the Son has eternal life but whoever rejects the Son will not see life (John 3:36), whosoever believes and is baptized will be saved (Mark 16:16), he who believes has everlasting life (John 6:47), he who believes in Him receives forgiveness (Acts 10:43), and salvation for everyone who believes (Rom. 1:16, 10:9).

Jesus tells us in John 6:44 that no one can come to Christ unless the Father, who sent His Son, draws him. He continues: "I tell you the truth [fact], he who believes has everlasting life" (John 6:47). The Spirit of God gives life (John 6:63), He convicts the world of sin (John 16:8) and lives within the born-again Christian. Our minds are controlled by the Spirit and we have peace and life. The sinful mind [controlled by Satan] is hostile to God and cannot please God (Rom. 8:5-17). The wicked will not inherit the Kingdom of God [live eternally in heaven] (1 Cor. 6:9-10). Flesh and blood cannot inherit the Kingdom so all of us Christians will be changed to immortality when Jesus comes again (1 Cor. 15:50-56) through the victory of Jesus Christ. God anointed us, set His seal of ownership on us, put His Spirit in our hearts as a deposit and a guarantee that we have eternal life coming (2 Cor. 1:22). He chose us before the creation of the world, and in Him we have redemption through His blood and forgiveness of sins (Eph. 1:4, 7). It is by grace we are saved, through the blood of Christ (Eph 2:8, 13).

There is a fact that some are hesitant to believe and that is, yes, there is a devil. Another fact is that this devil does not have a forked tail and a red suit. Read Ezekiel 28:12-17 about Satan and find out what a beautiful creation he was. He was the model of perfection, full of wisdom, and perfect in beauty, and every precious stone adorned him. These stones, settings, and mountings were prepared for him the day he was created. He walked among the fiery stones, meaning he walked before God, and was blameless. The scripture says that he fell from heaven, but it does not say that his appearance has changed. He can make sin beautiful and desirous. He has access to and from heaven and earth (Job 1:7, 1 Pet. 5:8) and comes and goes into the presence of the Lord (Job 1:12). He is the accuser of men and never lets up (Rev. 12:10). Daniel 7:25 tells us that he will get worse in the end times and wear out the saints. In Zechariah 3:1, Satan stands before God, accusing Joshua of wearing filthy rags and not being worthy of having his prayer answered. In Luke 22:31, Satan asked Jesus if he might sift Peter, trying to kill, steal from him, and destroy him, just as he has come to do (John 10:10). The good news is that Jesus prayed for Peter, and the other good news is that Jesus prayed for you and me (John 17:20-26).

The fact is that God wants all men to be saved and come to the knowledge of the truth of the Gospel (1 Tim. 2:3). God keeps His Word and is patient, wanting everyone to repent and be saved (2 Pet. 3:9). However, His Spirit will not always strive with man (Gen. 6:3) and He will come like a thief, and we should make every effort to be found spotless (2 Pet. 3:10, 14). There are some most encouraging facts found throughout the Bible for believers, as we wait for that great day of Christ's coming. It is true that while living here on earth, we will have troubles, but God promises to deliver us from them (Ps. 34:19). He will make our steps firm, and if we should fall, He will catch us with His right hand (Ps. 37:23). There is a praise and worship song entitled "Fear Not" that the youth love to sing. The words come from Isaiah 43:1-2, but do not include the most beautiful words of this scripture. "Since you are precious and honored in my sight and because I love you." God speaks to us, telling us the right way to go (Isa. 30:21), giving us His Spirit for accomplishment (Zech. 4:6-9). Like Romans 8:31 says: "If God be for us then who can be against us?" Everything is possible to him who believes (Mark 9:23), God gives the strength to do all things (Phil. 4:13), and He leaves us peace (John 14:27).

The facts in a nutshell are: There is a heaven and there is a hell, and each person will spend eternity in one or the other after our physical death. You will go to heaven if you accept Christ as your Savior, and if you do not accept Him, you will spend eternity in hell. One day, every knee will bow in heaven and on earth and under the earth, and every tongue will confess that Jesus Christ is Lord (Phil. 2:10-11). The glorious fact is that we cannot comprehend what God has prepared for the ones He loves and who love Him (1 Cor. 2:9). The want-to, could-be-if-you-want-it-to-be, and should-be fact is that every household should declare that they will serve the Lord (Jos. 24:15). Read more facts in God's bestseller. The Bible tops the bestseller list every year. Nothing beats it. More than 100 million copies are sold yearly. This book will convince you of the number-one fact that Jesus lives!

3. *Does God Still Speak?*

A little five-year-old girl called my prayer line and asked how God speaks to us today. I told her that He comes into our hearts and lives and speaks to us through our spirit. Now you see, I don't "do" kids, so I thought I answered this as simply as I could, and prepared to hang up the phone. Then the little voice asked how God, majestic (her word) as He is could get in our little hearts. Then that other little voice (of God) spoke to me and said I had better pay attention and "let the little children come to me, and do not hinder them" (Matt. 19:14). I tried again, telling her that the part of God that lived in our hearts was the Holy Spirit, which she could not see but could feel around her, and He would tell her what to do. At this point, the little girl became the teacher and I the humble student. She compared the Holy Spirit to the wind that blew and "told" her when to go into the house. Also the wind blew in the snow, the leaves from the trees, etc., telling her when the seasons were changing. Or, as she put it, telling her when the old cold weather was coming. "From the lips of children and infants you have ordained praise" (Ps. 8:2). Here it got complicated! She informed me that a spirit was a ghost! After thirty minutes of talking, we finally came to an agreement. She knew where God lived, and decided that His Spirit was her friend, and I for sure had made a new little friend that day. Thinking all was well, I bid her good-bye, and just before hearing the click on her end of the line, the voice grew even smaller and she said, "Thank you and don't let that old holy ghost get you!"

So to answer the question, does God still speak today? He spoke to me loud and clear through that little girl. He told me I could not pick and choose to whom I witnessed, and that I should be prepared with an answer, in season and out (2 Tim. 4:2). He told me to take a walk and He would show me through nature how only He created us and the earth and the heavens and is showing Himself to me (Rom. 1:20). "Ask the animals and they will teach you. Or the birds of the air and they will tell you. Or speak to the earth and it will teach you. Or let the fish of the sea inform you" (Job 12:7-9). He reminded me of His Son taking the little children in His arms and blessing them (Mark 10:16). This is an example for me to take my grandchildren in my arms and say to them, *I love you and Jesus loves you too!* This works for your spouse and your grown kids also, provided you can still wrap your arms around them. If not, then a touch will do. Everyone loves to be loved, and God loves to love us. The Bible tells me so (John 3:16)!

God speaks through the Bible. "The Word was with God and the Word was God" (John 1:1). It is a sad fact that everyone does not have a Bible. It is an even sadder fact that some who have them seldom read them. I was asked why God didn't just send an angel to tell us about His plan for mankind, instead of expecting us to read about it through prophetic writings. NEWS FLASH! Scripture records approximately 104 cases, depending on the version of the bible you use, where angels have appeared before men. Why would we assume this appearance of angels would capture the attention of unbelievers today, any more than they did in biblical times? We know from Jesus's parable of the rich man and Lazarus that there were definitely those who did not believe. Scripture plainly states that the man was in hell, where he was in torment (Luke 16:23). Another news flash! Angels do appear today! We are told not to forget to entertain strangers, because they just might be angels (Heb. 13:2).

John the Baptist was sent to prepare everyone to accept Jesus, but there were those who only looked at the clothes he wore and paid no heed. John dressed in clothes made of camel's hair, with a leather belt around his waist (Matt. 3:4). He didn't mince words when condemning the Pharisees and Sadducees, calling them a brood of vipers (Matt. 3:7-9). He took no credit for his mission, even though some thought him to be Elijah or a prophet. His only answer was that he was the one calling from the desert and giving praise to the One that would come after him (John 1:21-27). I will bring your attention to the fact that the people had to go out to hear John preach. Since Christianity was not popular, some had to sneak around to hear the Word of salvation and hope that he brought. Most of us today do not have to go anywhere to hear a good sermon. With TV and tapes and radio, we can sit in comfort and hear a sermon each hour if we choose. For those who do not have freedom of religion, we have dedicated missionaries to carry the Word of God and hope around the world. It is made easier for some than others to hear God speak, but speak He does. "He who has ears let him hear" (Matt. 11:15).

Jesus walked on this earth for thirty-three and a half years, and many did not believe Him. Even the disciples thought they were seeing a ghost (Luke 24:36-49), and a couple of them did not recognize Him as He walked along beside them (Luke 24:13-16). And let's not forget that Jesus's own brothers asked Him to leave their town, for even His own brothers did not believe in Him (John 7:5). Jesus talked Himself right to the cross, trying to convince all men that salvation is found in no one else but Christ (Acts 4:12), but to no avail. Judas betrayed Him (Matt. 26:47-50) but still Jesus called him friend. Peter denied Him (Matt. 26:69-75) but Jesus reinstated him and filled him with the Holy Spirit to preach one of the most powerful messages recorded. They mocked Him, spit on Him, struck Him, and led Him away to crucify Him. Scripture records at least two who, in the final moments, believed that Jesus was the Son of God. The robber who asked Jesus to remember him, and watched Jesus die with the assurance of eternal life (Luke 23:42-43) and the centurion, seeing what had happened, praised God and said that surely He was the Son of God (Mark 15:39).

Jesus told the people that if they had believed Moses, they would believe Him, for Moses wrote about Him. But since they did not believe what Moses wrote, how then would they believe what Jesus had to say (John 5:46-46)? Nothing has changed today! If some will not believe the Bible, which is God's words, why expect them to believe an angel, which is God's creation and messenger (Luke 2:19, Dan. 9:21-23)? We Christians, and not just the disciples, were given the great commission to teach everyone to obey what the Bible teaches (Matt. 28:19-20). We ask, just as the Pharisees and teachers of the law, for a miraculous sign from God. The answer is the same today as it was then. A wicked and adulterous generation asks for a miraculous sign! But none will be given except the sign of the prophet Jonah (Matt. 12:38-40). We have been given a miracle in Christ, a Lamb without blemish or defect. Through Him we believe in God who raised Him from the dead and glorified Him and so our faith and hope are in God (1 Pet. 1:19-23).

Final note of encouragement! "Because you have seen me, you have believed; blessed are those who have not seen and yet have believed" (John 20:29). For you who are still insisting on hearing the voice of God before you make that important decision to follow Jesus, I urge you to listen more carefully. I urge you to use the resources that God has left us in the form of the Bible, preachers, friends, etc. to "hear and heed." If you still are waiting for God to speak in person, it is coming. "A time is coming when all who are in their graves will hear His voice" (John 5:28) and "every knee will bow before me" (Rom. 14:11). This is not the voice calling you to salvation but rather the voice calling you to judgment. Answer Him now while on this earth! When you hear that final call, it will be too late for salvation!

4. *The God Who Hears*

God inspired the psalmist to call Him *You who hears prayer* (Ps. 65:2, 34:17, 64:33) and in today's English, His name is *the One who heard prayer* (Prov. 15:29). The various names of God and the attributes which are found in these names are: El Elohe, the God of Israel, Most High; El Olam, the God of everlasting, the everlasting One; El Roi, the god who sees me; El Shaddai, God the Rock, the Provider; Yehweh Nissi, God is my banner; Yahweh Rapha, the God who heals; and Yahweh Shalom, the God of peace. We must believe through faith that God hears, because without faith, it is impossible to please Him. He rewards the ones of faith who diligently seek Him (Heb. 11:6). Before you can come to God, you must believe there is a God (1 Pet. 1:8) and that He will reward your faithfulness (Jer. 29:13). You must believe that God answers prayer by using your gift of faith. The gift of faith is a special gift, which is given supernaturally by the Spirit of God as He wills. Those who operate in this special faith, the gift of the Spirit, can believe God in such a way that God honors their word as His own, and miraculously brings to pass the desired results. It is impossible to approach God unless you believe that God answers prayer (Heb. 4:16); no one can be saved unless they believe that God answers prayer (Acts 2:21). No one can please God unless they believe God answers prayer (Heb. 11:6) and we must acknowledge that He is omnipotent (all-powerful), omnipresent (everywhere), and omniscient (all-knowing).

The heart of God's nature is to reveal His power (2 Cor. 12:9), His wisdom (Ps. 111:10), His grace and mercy (Ps. 18:50), and His love (John 3:16). Some claim that God used to answer prayer but not anymore. They are making God into a has-been, contradicting the scriptures that tell us God is the same yesterday, today, and forever (Heb. 13:8). James 4:2-3—among other places in scripture—tells us that we do no have it because we do not ask for it. A prayer-hearing God is a Living God, not an idol of wood or stone. In 1 Kings 18, when the priests of Baal cried out for their god to hear them and answer, there was no sound coming from the carved images. Elijah mocked them by telling them that perhaps their god was sleeping or busy. Perhaps you should shout louder, he jeered, so that they can hear you. The problem was, their god was merely an idol with eyes that did not see and ears that did not hear and a mouth that could not answer. A prayer-answering God is a God of mercy. God knows our past and He knows we don't deserve to have prayer answered. As sinners, we deserve to be forsaken and abandoned (Rom. 3:23), but God's mercy and love are boundless (Rom 5:20). God never commanded us to sing, preach, give, or work without ceasing. However, in 1 Thessalonians 5:17, God commands us to pray without ceasing! Let us pray!

5. *Does God Know You?*

Today, while listening to the radio, I heard the announcer address the men in his audience, saying, "Men! Women love roses, so remember to mention them once in a while." Amusing? Yes, when we are talking about roses that fade and die after a few days of bringing light into your life, but what about Jesus? He is the light of our life! We know others love Him, so we mention Him once in a while! For some, we have to mention Him in order for others to recognize that we actually know Him. For some, the way we mention Him causes doubt that we have ever known Him. We should be more excited from receiving Jesus into our lives than the joy we experience when receiving a dozen roses from a loved one. He is the God who gives life to the dead and calls things that are not as though they were (Rom. 4:17). If we stay totally filled with God's Holy Spirit, He will bring us from glory to glory. Just like seeing our reflection in a mirror, we reflect the glory of God to others (2 Cor 3:18). Do we need to get out the Windex and clean our mirrors? This man called Jesus bore our sins in His own body on the tree, that we, being dead to sin, should live unto righteousness, by whose stripes we were healed (1 Pet. 2:24). This is something to shout about! Christ died in our place, suffering the penalty God set upon human sin (Isa. 53:4-6), justified us by His grace (Rom. 3:24), became our Passover Lamb (1 Cor. 5:7), the One that had no sin was made sin for us (2 Cor. 5:21) and we were redeemed by His blood (1 Pet. 1:18-19). We sinners do not have to die for our sin but can trust Christ's sacrifice for us and we have no fear of death or judgment. This is the good news of the gospel that we are to proclaim and rejoice in (1 Cor. 15:1-8). Christ died and was raised again for us so that we, through faith in Him, might be delivered from eternal condemnation and might live eternally in His presence (Rom. 1:4, 4:25, 1 Cor. 15:20).

God is not an impersonal force like gravity, exerting influence in some mechanical, automatic way. He has personal characteristics, just as we do. God is living, working in His world, and relating to His people. He is aware of what is going on, relates to you through His Bible, and knows you. He created man in His own image (Gen. 1:27) and formed you in your mother's womb, so you are fearfully and wonderfully made (Ps. 139:13-14; Isa. 44:2). The meaning of God as your Father is shown in His personal concern for you, His protective watch care over you (Ps. 17:7-8, 57:1), in redemption (Col. 1:13-14), nurturing (Isa. 28:26), and discipline in your Christian life (Job 36:10-11). God's love is revealed in His actions (1 John 4:8), expressed through His mercy in forgiving sinners and in rescuing or blessing those who do not deserve His attention (Rom. 5:8). He knows you because you are one of His sheep, and as the Good Shepherd, the Son of God has laid down His life for you (John 10:15). Jesus said that the Father gave Him the sheep so that He might give them eternal life. He knows His sheep and they follow His voice (John 10:11-30). Believers' hearts affirm Jesus is the clearest picture of God the world has ever seen. Christians see in this one proper name, Jesus, a conjunction of God and man. The pre-existent heavenly Christ emptied Himself and became like you for your sake (Phil. 2:1-18). He is Emmanuel, God is with us (Matt. 1:23). The earliest Christian confession was when Peter stated that this was indeed the Christ, the Son of God (Luke 9:20; John 6:69) and Jesus is Lord (Rom. 10:9). Lord (Hebrew - *adonai*, Greek - *kurios*), was the term used in reverence to God when the Jews quit pronouncing the holy name Yahweh. *Lord* shows Jesus's worth as equal to God and our relationship to Him as His devoted servants. Because God exalted Jesus in the Resurrection, He is worthy to be called Lord (Phil. 2:6-11). Does He know that you know Him as Lord?

God will recognize you as His if you endure hardship like a good soldier and remain faithful to the gospel. Present yourself as a workman who does not need to be ashamed and who correctly handles the Word of truth. The Lord knows who are His, and those are the ones who confess the name of the Lord and turn away from wickedness. Flee the evil desires and pursue righteousness, faith, love, and peace, along with those who call on the Lord out of a pure heart (2 Tim. 2:1-24). Jesus tells us if we obey His commands, we will remain in His love, that His joy would be in us, and that joy would be made complete. Then He calls the ones who follow His commands His friends (John 15:10-14). What a privilege to be called the friend of the Savior! Jesus called John the disciple whom He loved, because John made an extra effort to always be close to Him (John 21:20). This is the effort that He expects from you and me, that we might be called His friend. The Bible teaches in various terms that we will be known by our fruit. Make a tree good and its fruit will be good, so says Matthew 12:33. This means that what a man stores up inside him, such as the Word of God, will overflow from the heart and out of the mouth. This also means that God cannot be fooled with your outer appearance. Jesus's parable of the fig tree, where it appeared green and fruitful from a distance, revealed on closer inspection that it had no fruit. Jesus withered the tree and said, "May you never bear fruit again" (Matt.21:19). There are several interpretations of this parable, but it reminds me of the Church of Sardis: "You have a reputation of being alive, but you are dead. Wake up! Strengthen what remains and is about to die" (Rev. 3:1-2). It is to God's glory that you bear fruit, much fruit, so that you show you are Jesus's and He knows you (John 15:8). The Great Commission is for us to go and spread the gospel worldwide (Matt. 28:19-20) and find that this gospel is bearing fruit and growing (Col. 1:6). We cannot do this unless we are known by God, since it is He that chose us and appointed us to go and bear fruit that will last

(John 15:16). If we do not remain in the Father and bear fruit, we will be pruned and/or cut off (John 15:1-6) and when withered, thrown away and burned in the fire.

Just like the rose, this world and its desires will pass away, but the man who does the will of God, the one whom God knows, lives forever (1 John 2:17). Does He know you well enough to free you from sin and make you a kingdom and priest to serve Him? Will you be given the right to eat from the tree of life and not be hurt by the second death? Will you receive the hidden manna and a white stone with a new name written on it? Will you be dressed in white, walk with God, and have your name in the Book of Life? Will you be kept from the hour of trial that is going to come upon the whole world? Will you have the privilege of sitting with Him on His throne or will you hear the dreaded, condemning words: "Depart from me, I never knew you" (Matt. 25:12, Rev. 20:15)? Our theme song should be; "Oh how I love Jesus, because He first loved me," being eager to make our calling and election sure, and receive a rich welcome into the eternal kingdom of our Lord and Savior Jesus Christ (2 Pet. 1:10). "Everyone who calls upon the name of the Lord will be saved" (Rom. 10:13).

6. *Are You One of God's Mighty Men?*

"All those who were in distress or in debt or discontented gathered around David, and he became their leader" (1 Sam. 22:2). Jesus seemingly followed David's lead when He invited all who were weary and burdened and He would give them rest. He asked that all take His yoke upon them and learn from Him, for He is gentle and humble in heart, and they could find rest for their souls. His yoke is easy and His burden light (Matt. 11:28-30).

In 2nd Samuel 23, we have a roster of David's mighty men, and this list is also included in 1st Chronicles 11. These are the men who joined David before he came to the throne as king over Israel. After David was anointed king by the prophet Samuel, there was a period of time before he was crowned king. During this period, there were times when he had to hide in the wilderness to escape the anger of King Saul. Saul was fiercely jealous because David had become an overnight celebrity and favorite son in Israel after he had killed the Philistine giant, Goliath. Although Saul had already been set aside by God as the rightful king of Israel, he had not yet been removed from the throne. During this time, when David was in disfavor within the establishment, many people joined him in the wilderness and became his army of loyal supporters. We read in 1ˢᵗ Samuel 22:2 that all those who were in distress or in debt or discontented gathered around David, and he became their leader. About four hundred men were with him. Some of these loyal followers of David accomplished great things on David's behalf, and they are registered as David's mighty men.

Why did God include such seemingly dry and barren name lists in the Bible? We can be sure that every catalog of names in scripture is there for a purpose. The Holy Spirit did not waste words. He did not inspire the biblical writers to include fillers to beef up the Bible. "All scripture is God-breathed and is useful for teaching, rebuking, correcting and training in righteousness so that the man of God may be thoroughly equipped for every good work" (2 Tim. 3:16-17). Romans 15:4 says that everything in the past was written to teach us, so that through endurance and the encouragement of the scriptures, we might have hope. What teaching and encouragement of the scriptures can we find from the list of David's mighty men? It indicates to us that God records our personal service also. All of your deeds will be brought into judgment, including every hidden thing, whether it is good or evil (Ecc. 12:14). If God kept track of David's valiant soldiers and their deeds, how much more does He keep track and reward the faithful servants of David's greatest Son? We will all appear before the judgment seat of Christ, and we will receive what is due us for the things done while in this mortal body, whether good or bad (2 Cor. 5:10). Other Christians may not be aware of your behind-the-scenes services for Christ, but God sees and knows you as an individual soldier, and will reward every act of faithfulness.

In many ways, King David portrays the coming Son of God, our Lord Jesus Christ. It is in his time of rejection that David particularly pictures Christ. As David was the anointed and rightful king but was unrecognized and rejected by the establishment, so Christ is the rightful King over mankind. He calls heaven His throne and the earth His footstool (Acts 7:49) but He is unrecognized and rejected by this world. Isaiah 53:3 and John 19:1-16 tells us that He was despised and rejected by men. Those who recognized David as king had to be willing to join him in the wilderness and share in his unpopularity and rejection. In the same way, we who recognize the Lord Jesus as King have joined Him outside the camp, bearing the disgrace He bore (Heb. 13:13). We can identify in a spiritual way with those who came to David in the wilderness in distress, needy and dissatisfied with the religious system. David's mighty men's feats portray the activities of believers who have made Christ their King (Acts 9:16; 2 Cor. 6:4-10, 11:23-33).

The actions of David's men on the battlefield, overcoming great odds, contain lessons for us about spiritual warfare. Eleazar (2 Sam. 23:8) stood and fought the enemy, even though his fellow soldiers had retreated. Even though he was at the point of exhaustion, he would not rest until the Lord brought victory. Spiritual warfare is very draining, but even though others throw in the towel, great victory comes to Christians who hang in there on the strength of God. We fight with weapons of righteousness in both hands (2 Cor. 6:7) and God gives us victory through our Lord Jesus Christ (1 Cor. 15:57). He stands at our side and gives us strength (2 Tim. 4:17) and the one that lives in us is greater than the one that is in the world (1 John 4:4). Shammah (2 Sam. 23:11-12) took his position in a lentil patch and defended the provisions of the Lord's people. The Lord is looking for the Shammahs of today who will defend the faith and be willing to go to contend for the faith that was once for all entrusted to the saints (Jude 3).

David longed for a refreshing drink from the well of his hometown, Bethlehem. This was not a military duty, and the men were not commanded to do this for David. However, out of love for their king, three of the men broke through the Philistine lines, drew water from the well, and carried it back to David (2 Sam. 23:15-16). Our worship of the Lord should not be performed as a duty, but as an act of devotion because we love our King. If we die to sin with Christ, we will also live with Him, and after enduring all this old world can throw at us, we will reign with Him (2 Tim. 2:11-12). Have you ever noticed how the devil tries to get in on every act of worship with our Lord and Savior? We must commit ourselves to time, effort, and sacrifice, and sometimes overcoming great barriers that are put in our path. The fact that David poured out the water (2 Sam. 23:16-17) makes it seem like the three were involved in a wasteful effort. David considered their act to be so significant that he honored it and elevated it by giving the water as a drink offering to God. Paul said that he did not run for nothing but was being poured out like a drink offering (Phil. 2:16-17). Our times of quiet meditation in worship of God may appear to some as a waste of time and effort. After all, thanking and praising God doesn't feed any hungry or provide care for the homeless. Do not let the devil control your thoughts during praise and worship; rather, follow the lead of the Holy Spirit, and God will feed the hungry and provide for the homeless through your faithfulness.

Benaiah went on to become the commander-in-chief of all Israel's forces under King Solomon (1 Kings 4:4). He was a valiant fighter who struck down two of Moab's best men, struck down a huge Egyptian, and went down into a pit on a snowy day and killed a lion (2 Sam. 23:20-23). In 1st Peter 5:8, Satan is pictured as a lion, called our enemy, that prowls around looking for someone to devour. Benaiah was not caught off guard but was on the offensive. He was not backed into a corner to fight his way out but met the lion in the middle of the pit and killed him. Are we that courageous? We are commanded to resist the devil and promised that in doing so, he will flee from us if we meet him head on (James 4:7). It has been stated by some writers that the full armor of God (Eph. 6:13-17) offers no protection for our backside. Using scripture from Isaiah 52:12, I must disagree with this statement. Isaiah tells us that the Lord goes before us and will be our rear guard. Maybe that is why God did not design us with eyes in the back of our heads, so that we would lean on His power and walk by faith.

The Moabites were physically related to Israel, yet as an enemy to Israel, they seemed to represent the flesh in terms of spiritual warfare. Flesh is closely related to every one of us, yet it is our deadly enemy, sometimes ruling our lives. Paul said that he didn't always do what he knew he needed to, but instead did what he did not want to do. He knew it was not him but sin living in him that caused these mistakes (Rom. 7:14-25). Sinful natural desires are in conflict with spiritual desires, and if we become might believers, we have the power of Christ to crucify the sinful nature within (Gal. 5:16-25). Benaiah showed no mercy to the Moabites, as we must show no mercy in overcoming the flesh. We must put to death whatever belongs to our earthly idolatry (Col. 3:5). Egypt was also an enemy of Israel, and is pictured in our spiritual warfare as the world. As God redeemed His people out of Egypt, so God has redeemed us out of this world (Deut. 15:15; Gal. 3:13). One of Israel's major problems was that they were still attracted to Egypt and the things that they remembered from living there. Sometimes they even wished they were still in Egypt, and often wanted to go back. If we are all honest, we will admit that the things of the world sometimes attract us, and every once in a while, way in the back of our minds, we want to go back to our old, not-caring lifestyle. We must continuously set our minds on things above, and not earthly things (Col. 3:1).

Not much is said about the rest of David's mighty men, but their names are recorded in 2 Samuel 23:24-39. Is your name recorded in God's list of mighty Christians? When the court is seated and the books are opened, will your name be there (Dan. 7:10)? When the scroll of remembrance is read, will your name be listed (Mal. 3:16)? Will your name be found written in the Book of Life (Rev. 20:12-15)? "Behold, I am coming soon! Blessed is he who keeps the Words of the prophecy in this Book" (Rev. 22:7).

7. *Walking in the Fear of the Lord*

In writing about the early church, Luke recorded that the church enjoyed a time of peace, was strengthened and encouraged by the Holy Spirit, and grew in numbers, living in fear of the Lord (Acts 9:31). Again, in writing to the church in Philippi, Paul told them to continue to obey the things that he taught them, working out their own salvation with fear and trembling (Phil. 2:12). Fear and trembling in connection with God is not a popular concept today. People prefer to hear about God's love, longsuffering, and mercy. Could this be why many Christians are apathetic in their service? Could it be we have forgotten whom we should fear if we are negligent in our service (Matt. 10:28)? In the next few pages, I hope to accomplish three things: Define the fear of the Lord, point out why the fear of the Lord is important to the Christian, and suggest how we can develop a healthy fear of the Lord without going to one extreme or the other.

The Hebrew word for fear is *yir'ah* and is used in the Old Testament to describe fear, terror, and an awesome, terrifying object, fear of God, respect, reverence, and piety. The Greek word is *phobos*, and it is used to describe fear, dread, and terror, or that which strikes terror. In connection with the fear of the Lord, it is often defined as reverence or awe. Though the terms *reverence* and *awe* imply a place for trembling, do most people make the connection? The fear of the Lord should include a place for trembling or being in the presence of the Lord. Just as one would likely tremble in the presence of one who could take our life, so Jesus taught us to fear the Lord for the same reason (Matt. 10:28). Trembling and quaking occurs when one knows he or she has offended God and has not obtained forgiveness (Heb. 10:26-27, 30-31, 12-28).

The importance of fearing the Lord can be found numerous times in the book of Proverbs. It is the beginning of knowledge (Prov. 1:7), causes us to hate evil (Prov. 8:13), will provide long life (Prov. 10:27), provides strong confidence, and is a fountain of life (Prov. 14:26-27). The fear of the Lord prompts one to depart from evil (Prov. 16:6), leads to a satisfying life, and spares one from much evil (Prov. 19:23). This same fear is also the way to riches, honor, and life (Prov. 22:4). Without the fear of the Lord, we close ourselves to the treasures of God's wisdom and knowledge, find ourselves flirting with evil and being corrupted by it. Our lives are likely to be shortened by our refusal to heed God's Word, such as suffering from sexually transmitted diseases because we did not heed His Word on sexual relationships. We will not come to know the love of God that gives us assurance and confidence of our salvation, and when fallen into sin, we will not be motivated to repent and turn to God. We will not feel the urgency to work out our salvation, and without fear, we cannot please God (Is. 66:1-2). Only the person who trembles at His Word has God's promise to receive His tender mercy (Ps. 103:17-18).

To develop a fear of the Lord, we must study His Word, gather and read this Word, so that you might learn the importance of reverent fear (Deut. 31:10-13; Rom. 2:4-11; 2 Pet. 3:7-14). The Word of God, properly used, will maintain a proper balance. We must read all of the words, and not only those portions that will reveal God's love and mercy. Many emphasize the fire, hell, and brimstone passages, and teach nothing of God's loving kindness. We must be careful how we use the Word of God, but use it we must. In teaching and hearing the message of the gospel, we must combine it with faith, or it will be of no value (Heb. 4:1-3). In reading, we must put the Words into practice and cleanse ourselves from all filthiness of the flesh and spirit, perfecting holiness in the fear of God (2 Cor. 7:1). Learning to fear God along with loving Him will keep your spiritual life in perfect harmony and save you from a world of disappointments.

8. Cooking up God's Word

This is not a cooking lesson, since I am the world's worst cook, but it came to me when I was trying to make a meatloaf. I have found that in order to make a decent meatloaf, you have to get your hands into the meat of the project. I will let you know later how it turned out, and if you don't hear from me…well….!! When cooking up a lesson or just needing a good meal of manna, you have to get your hands and mind into the meat of the Word of God. The scripture states that the Holy Spirit will remind you of everything that Jesus has said (John 14:26). However, in order to be reminded of something, you first have to have known it. Again, as in cooking, if you have never made a meatloaf, you might have trouble remembering what goes into the dish. Just as a cookbook guides you to a good and tasty meal, the Holy Spirit will guide you into all truth about God's Holy Word (John 16:13).

Ezekiel, John, and the psalmist all were served a delicacy of the sweetened Word, each being told that it would taste as sweet as honey (Ezek. 2:2; Ps. 19:10; Rev. 10:9-10). The Lord had instructions (recipes) for the water and food that Moses prepared for the escaping Israelites in the desert. The bitter water that the ungrateful people grumbled about needed just a piece of wood thrown into it to make it sweet (Ex. 15:22-25). God told the people that if they listened carefully to His voice and followed His instructions, they would not have any diseases. I would think that if you do not follow the instructions in cooking the meals in your own kitchen, you might expect a disease such as food poisoning. Just as some of us never learn to cook, the Israelites never learned to appreciate the food that God provided for them. Trust in the Lord was just not on their agenda. Remember that scrumptious meal of quail and bread that He sent each morning and each night? There was just one catch, and that was that they were to follow God's instructions and gather only what they needed for each day. However, some of them paid no attention to the directions, and their food spoiled.

Have you ever known someone who cooked without a recipe? You know, they just use a dash of this and a pinch of that. It somehow comes out edible and this is because they have made this dish time and time again, and the recipe is buried in their mind. That is what the psalmist says we must do with the Word of God. "I have hidden your Word in my heart that I might not sin against you" (Ps. 119:11). 2nd Timothy 3:16-17 tells us that the Word of God is useful for teaching, rebuking, correcting, and training in righteousness. We must add all the ingredients and not leave out verse 17, which says that we must be thoroughly equipped. To be thoroughly equipped in the Word is most helpful if you decide to go and remove a speck from your brother's eye (Matt. 7:5).

Handed-down recipes are common in families, but I caution you to write out the instructions given, lest you forget and subsequently place blame where blame is not warranted. The people in Ezekiel were blaming God for punishing them unjustly, saying that their suffering was because of their father's sins. They made up a proverb: "the fathers eat sour grapes, and the children's teeth are set on edge" (Ezek. 18:1-4). This false doctrine had just a kernel of truth in its teaching, so it seemed plausible. The righteous man is always careful to keep the right portions of the Word of God (Rev. 22:18-19), just as the third-generation cook keeps the original ingredients in the family-secret stew.

References to food and related themes appear in every book in the Bible, starting with Genesis 1 and ending in Revelation 22. Some of the best-known stories are those dealing with food, including Eve in the Garden of Eden, and Joseph saving his people and his estranged family from famine (Gen. 47). In the book of Ruth, Boaz found Ruth a tasty dish only after her mother-in-law got her hands into the meatloaf. She stirred up just the right combination of ingredients and let them marinate the appropriate length of time. The result of this carefully prepared wedding feast was Obed, the father of Jesse, and Jesse, the father of David and the rest is history. The lineage of our Lord and Savior, Jesus Christ, is listed in Matthew chapter 1. In 1st Samuel 17:17-18, Jesse tells his son and shepherd boy David to carry food to the battle grounds for his brothers. Notice that Jesse specified the exact amounts of each food to be taken to the brothers and an exact amount of cheeses to the commander. Later, when Abigail was bringing bribery food to David, she counted out exact amounts of each food. There is no pinching and dashing when your life depends on the recipe.

New Testament references to food are numerous, including Jesus turning water into wine, helping the disciples catch fish, feeding the five thousand with five loaves of bread and two small fish, and His last supper. Jesus also told parables which related to food, such as the parable of the sower, the weeds, the mustard seed, and the yeast. The disciples ate together in their homes with glad hearts, teaching us in-home hospitality, not just take-a-dish Christianity (Acts 4:26). If, from lack of food, you become malnourished, you would seek a doctor. If, from lack of the Word of God, you become spiritually malnourished, you should seek the great Physician, Jesus. He said that it was not the healthy who needed a doctor but the sick (Matt. 9:12). These sick persons to whom He referred were non-believers and scoffers, asking Him why He ate with sinners, not considering themselves sick with sin.

It is conveyed in the Word of God to nourish our inner man through the understanding or our rational mind, and is digested by our mental faculties so that we might grow spiritually. Have you known some who beg to be fed the Word of God? Well, beware! God will feed you, just as He did Ezekiel when He told him, "open your mouth and eat what I give you" (Ezek. 2:8, 3:1). This Ezekiel was given to eat was the word of judgment and he was told to go and speak God's Words to the House of Israel. If you want God to feed you, then you have to eat what is before you, digest it, and spew it out upon the unbelieving that God sends you to. Would you not rather eat the solid food that is for the mature in Christ (Heb. 5:14) than live on milk, being an infant and having someone always explaining and teaching the Word to you (Heb. 5:11-13)?

Jesus told the disciples that they had eaten the bread and had their fill, but they still did not realize that He was the bread of life (John 6:26-35) and the ones who come to Jesus will never go hungry. "Man does not live on bread alone but on every Word that comes from the mouth of God" (Matt. 4:4). God invites you to taste the goodness of the Lord (Ps. 34:8), to crave the Spiritual milk so that you might grow strong in your salvation (1 Pet. 2:2; 1 Cor. 3:2) and to treasure His Words in your mouth more than your daily bread (Job 23:12). Jeremiah stated that when God's Words came to him, he ate them and they were his joy and his heart's delight (Jer. 15:16). Let us open God's recipe book and stir up a great, nourishing meal that we can sink our teeth into and digest into our soul and experience the joy of the fullness of God's Word.

9. *God's Left Hand*

The Bible is the inspired Word of God. There are no idle words in the Bible. Each word reveals to us something about Christ. God created man in His own image (Gen. 1:27) for a purpose. God is Spirit but He made man in the flesh with workable, visible parts so we might be His physical being through mankind. We are meant to see in our weak, physical form, the attributes of God. He gives us in the physical realm, body parts in the likeness of His spiritual parts, so we can understand, through the scriptures, what God is able to do perfectly in the spiritual. We are given eyes to see, and Noah found grace in the eyes of the Lord (Gen. 6:8). James says to bridle your tongue (James 1:26) and if you have planned evil, clap your hand over your mouth (Prov. 30:32). Beautiful are the feet that bring the good news (Rom. 19:15). These body parts are all mentioned to show us how God wants His spiritual parts to be used.

In the Old Testament, stories will always point to the Birth, Resurrection, and the Second Coming or The End Times. In this story from Judges 3:12-31, we will find the meaning of a few commonly used words. "And the children of Israel did evil again in the sight of the Lord...and He strengthened Eglon, the king of Moab, against Israel....they smote Israel and possessed the city of palm trees [Jericho]." Remember in Joshua 6 when the Israelites fought the battle of Jericho and took the city? Does this story make you stop and wonder if evil in the sight of the Lord might cause you to lose something of value to you? The Children of Israel cried out just as we cry out when God brings discipline into our lives, and the Lord raised them up a deliverer just as He did for us (Matt. 11:28, John 3:16) by sending His Son to die for our sins. God gave the Israelites a left-handed man to send the king Eglon a present. Ehud, a left-handed judge, made the king a dagger which had two edges, meaning it represented the Word of God (Heb 4:12; Rev. 19:15). Ehud strapped the dagger to his right thigh under his clothing, carrying the name of the Lord with him (Rev. 19:16). And he brought the present to Eglon, king of Moab, and the scripture tells us that the king was a very fat man. When he heard that Ehud had a message for him from God, he assumed it was a favorable one, but it turned out to be a message of judgment, and Ehud pulled out the dagger with his left hand and killed the king.

A promise was sworn to by putting your hand under someone's thigh (Gen. 47:29), and blessings were given with the right hand (Gen 48:17-18). Perhaps this is why God chose a left-handed man to deliver not a message of blessing, but rather a message of doom and judgment. If blessings were given with the right hand, then it follows that judgment comes from the left hand. The belly which Ehud thrust his dagger into represents the serpent and the deceit in the Garden (Gen. 3:14). The belly also represents the flesh that will one day be destroyed (Gen. 3:15; Isa. 27:1; Rev. 20:2). Fat means they have a self-willed desire to indulge in human pleasure and human religion and cause division. Avoid them (2 Tim. 3:8; Rom. 16:17-18 KJV; Phil. 3:19 KJV; 1 Cor. 6:13 KJV), meaning not avoiding the overweight people but those with fat, egotistical minds, for they have perverted the gospel and their end is destruction. Remember the prodigal son, self-destructing from selfish ambition, longed to fill his belly with the pods (corn husks) that the pigs were eating (Luke 15:11-31). He was eating the corrupt flesh of the world, then remembered his father's bread and went home with a repentant heart and was served a banquet. Upon repentance of our own selfish ambition and turning away from the ways of the world, we too may eat of the Bread of Life (John 6:32-35).

John in Revelation was told to eat the little scroll of judgment, and in his mouth, it was sweet as honey, but turned sour in his belly. Sometimes sin is not only beautiful to our worldly eyes but sweet on the outside, but the truth of the gospel exposes the bitterness of flesh

(Rev. 10:8-10). After Ehud thrust the dagger into the king's belly the dirt came out, just as the Word of God, thrust into the belly of religious disobedience, will expose and drive out the sin from your heart (John 8:32). The right hand of God represents salvation (Isa. 45:17), saving power (Ps. 20:6), righteousness (Ps. 48:10), justice (Ps. 21:8), and victory (Ps. 98:1). We cannot appreciate the right hand of salvation, mercy, and grace, without believing God has a left hand of judgment. God is as powerful with His left hand as He is with His right, as He demonstrates with David and Saul (1 Chr. 12:1-2). Samson placed his right hand of obedience to God on one pillar, and his left hand of judgment on the other pillar, bringing total destruction to the Philistines (Judg. 16:26-30). Judgment of the sheep and goats is measured out with the left hand (goats) and the right hand (sheep) of God (Matt. 25:33-34). During the Crucifixion, the scripture does not tell us which criminal was on the left hand of God, but we can imagine it was not the one who was welcomed into Paradise with Jesus Christ (Matt. 27:38). Study the Word of God and believe every word written, because God Himself said that these words would never pass away (Matt. 24:35), He never changes His mind (Rom. 11:29), and what He has said, He will bring about (Isa. 46:11). Do not be deceived, for God will not be mocked (Gal. 6:7-10) and each of us will receive from His left hand or his right hand. Let us be standing on the right side when judgment comes!

10. *Questions and Answers*

Q: What does the Bible say specifically is the Father's business?

A: The Father's business spoken of in Luke 2:49 would be the reason that God sent His only Son, and that is to save the world from sin (John 3:16). By the time Jesus was twelve years old, He understood His mission on earth. Jesus drew a sharp distinction between His earthly mother and father and God, His true Father.

Q: What is the definition of a father? Is he one who you descended from or one who raised you?

A: Both definitions are correct, but must be separated and used in correct context. The Bible reveals God as the Lord of the Universe and calls Him Father in both the Old and the New Testament. We all need a caring human father in our lives to help us understand what God the Father is like as a person. If our earthly father is not a loving, concerned, involved father, then our Heavenly Father is always available to offer these characteristics (Hos. 14:3; Ps. 10:14, 27:10). The most wonderful aspect of being a Christian is that we all have a unique relationship with God, the Father of Jesus, and through faith, each one may call Him Abba, Father (Rom. 8:14-16). The scripture in Matthew 23:8-10, "and do not call anyone on earth father, for you have one Father and He is in heaven," has to do with the attitude of these Pharisee teachers wanting to put themselves above God in being honored (Matt. 23:5-7). Jesus is not forbidding us to call men fathers who actually are (literally or spiritually), but was warning against wanting to be worshiped as The Father in Heaven.

Q: When the scriptures tell us that the Lord searches the heart, what exactly is He searching for?

A: What God is searching for in our hearts is the truth of what we think (Pro. 23:7; Mark 7:21-23). He is looking for cleanliness inside and not clean appearances (Luke 11:39), checking that what you say with your lips is coming from your heart, and that you are speaking to glorify God (Matt. 15:8-9), since He knows all hearts (Ps. 44:21). He can look into the heart (1 Sam. 16:7), and searches for rebellion against His laws (Jer. 5:23) and a hard heart (Heb. 3:8). He is preparing the heart (Pro. 16:1) so we will be perfect (Matt. 5:48) and His peace will rule in our hearts (Ezek. 36:26-27).

Q: What makes God happy?

A: We make God happy when we live by His Word (Ps. 119:9) and promise to do what it says (Ps. 119:57, 145). When we have faith in God that He will do what the Bible says, then we make Him happy (Acts 27:25). We were chosen by Him and are precious to Him (1 Pet. 2:4) and He wants you to love Him as He does you (Mark 12:30).

Q: What does God think of His children, the Christians?

A: "God demonstrates His own love for us in this; while we were sinners, Christ died for us" (Rom. 5:8). He loved us so much that He gave His only Son to die for our sins (John 3:16-18). Is He ever disappointed in us? Most likely! But He never stops loving us.

Q: How is God described in the Psalms?

A: We must remember that 75 percent of the Psalms were written by David. David struggled with faith and feelings and fellowship on and off with God because of his continuous sins and shortcomings. Yet, because of his continuous repentant state, God called him a man after His own heart (1 Sam. 13:14; Acts 13:22). The most wonderful description of God is written in Psalm 23, where the psalmist and the king who was first a shepherd boy, David, compare the tender and continual care of the shepherd for his sheep to the tender and continual care of Christ the Shepherd to His flock, the Christians (John 10:1-18).

Q: What chapters and verses cover God's omnipresence throughout the universe?

A: Omnipresence is implicated throughout the scripture, but Psalm 139 is probably the most well-known description of God's omnipresence, showing us that He has access to all places and all secrets. Omnipresence is seen in healing from a distance (Luke 7:1-10). The fact that He can come and go into the heavens is stated in the Transfiguration (Luke 9:28-36). We cannot hide from Him (Amos 9:2-4), He fills the heaven and the earth (Jer. 23:23-24) and His eyes are everywhere (Prov. 15:3). The heavens cannot contain Him (1 Kings 8:27) and He is not far from each of us (Acts 17:27-28). He sits on His throne in heaven (Heb. 1:3) yet dwells among us (John 1:14).

Part II - The Son

1. Who Is Jesus?

Who does Jesus claim to be? What does the Bible say about Jesus? The Old Testament predicts the coming of the Messiah. Messiah or Christ, which in the Greek, means *anointed one*. The Old Testament says a lot about this man and what He would do. For example, Isaiah 9:6 says a lot about His characteristics and Isaiah 53 says He would be a suffering servant. Micah 5:2 tells us He would be born in Bethlehem, and all of these predictions and prophecies were fulfilled by Jesus and recorded in the New Testament.

In John 10:30, Jesus Himself tells us that He and the Father are one, but the Jews knew He was claiming to be God, for they picked up stones to throw at Him. They told Him they were not stoning Him for a good work but for blasphemy, and because He, being a man, made Himself out to be God. Jesus assured them that He and the Father were one by saying, "Believe Me that I am in the Father and the Father is in Me" (John 14:11). Jesus, as recorded in John 8:38, stated that before Abraham was born, He was. He used the phrase *I Am* just as it was used by God in Exodus 3:14 to describe Himself. God said that when He could swear by no other He swore by Himself (Ex. 20:2-3) meaning that He was the Most High, Jehovah, Elohim, Eternal, and the Creator. He has always been, He is, and will always be, and He created earth and all there is.

"And I appeared unto Abraham, unto Isaac and unto Jacob, by the Name of God Almighty, but by My Name Jehovah was I not known to them" (Ex. 6:3). God is testifying that He appeared unto Old Testament prophets by another name—God Almighty, El-Shaddi, the All Sufficient One, making many promises to them. He uses the name Jehovah, which means the self-existing one or eternal one who keeps covenant and fulfills promises. The name Jehovah was used from the beginning, but was not made known in fullness to men until it was time to fulfill the promises and covenant with Israel as a nation. In Exodus 3:11-15, when God said *I am that I am,* He was saying to Moses, *It's not about who you are, it's about who I am!* All they needed to know was that God sent Moses, and all Moses needed to know is that God was with him. Whatever God wants to be, He is, and whatever you need, He will be. God is the great Creator in Jeremiah 32:27, whether man acknowledged Him or not. This is the way He was from the beginning, and He will not change (Mal. 3:6).

Pilate went into the judgment hall again and asked Jesus where He was from and to what world did He belong. Jesus did not answer him, so Pilate took Him away and flogged and slapped Him; the soldiers struck Him with the palms of their hands, and the chief priest cried out, *crucify Him* (John 19:9; Isa. 53:3). The Word of God is loaded with questions posed to Jesus, and as much as we can relate to them, if we are born again, and believe that Jesus Christ is the Son of God and accept Him as our Lord and Savior, then we know where He came from and where we are going. We are of the Spirit of God, born from above and no longer of this world (John 5:1-5), called to go into all this world and preach the gospel to all nations and peoples, but not to be of this present world we live in (Matt. 28:18-20). If a "Pilate" should ask you where you came from, you should answer that as Jesus walked this earth, so do we, and just as He was resurrected to be with the Father, so will we who have accepted Him as our Savior.

2. Matthew

The story of Jesus's birth emphasizes His unique nature as human child and Son of God. The genealogy or list of human ancestors shows the human side of Jesus and connects Him, through Joseph, to David and Abraham, with whom God had special covenants, to achieve His redemptive purpose (Gen. 12:3; 2 Sam. 7:12). The virgin birth emphasizes Jesus's divine nature, since Mary was with child through the Holy Spirit (Matt. 1:18). Why does David's mane appear before Abraham's? Perhaps Matthew listed the name of David first because the king who would rule over the nation was to come through David (2 Sam. 7:12-17). Matthew gave Jesus's linage through His legal father, Joseph. Thus, this genealogy traced Jesus's right to the throne of David, which must come through Solomon and his descendants. Of particular interest is the inclusion of Jeconiah, of whom Jeremiah said, "Record this man as if childless" (Jer. 22:30). This relates to the actual occupation of the throne which Jeconiah's sons did not occupy. If Jesus had been a physical descendant of Jeconiah, He would not have been able to occupy David's throne. Luke made it clear that Jesus was a physical descendant of David through another son named Nathan (Luke 3:31), but Joseph, a descendant of Solomon, was Jesus's legal father, so Jesus's right to the throne was traced through Joseph.

Another interesting fact about Matthew's genealogy is the inclusion of four Old Testament women: Tamar, Rahab, Ruth, and Bathsheba. All of these women, as well as most of the men, were questionable in some way. Tamar and Rahab were prostitutes (Gen. 38:24; Josh. 2:1), Ruth a foreigner and Moabite (Ruth 1:4), and Bathsheba committed adultery (2 Sam. 11:2-5). Matthew may have included these women in order to emphasize that God's choices in dealing with people are all of His grace. Perhaps also in order to put Jewish pride in its place. Perhaps God included them to remind you and me that some of our actions are questionable, but God can and will use each of us in His plan. The fact that Jesus was born of Mary only (Matt. 1:16) demanded further explanation. Matthew's explanation can best be understood in the light of Hebrew marriage customs. Marriages were arranged by parents, and the couple were considered married and were called man and wife, although they did not live together for one year. This was to prove their faithfulness to each other. If she were found with child during this year, it would prove her impurity, and the marriage would be annulled. Joseph, therefore, had grounds to divorce Mary or put her away as the scripture calls it (Matt. 1:19), and she could be stoned to death (Deut. 22:23-24). Instead of exposing Mary to public scorn and stoning, Joseph was thinking about putting her away quietly (Matt. 1:19).

Maybe this was a test for Joseph, to see if he measured up to being the earthly father for our Lord and King. If so, he passed the test, because an angel of the Lord appeared to him in a dream and told him the child Mary carried in her womb was a unique child, for He would be a son whom Joseph should name Jesus, for He would save His people from their sins (Matt. 1:20-21). These words must have brought to Joseph's mind the promises of God to provide salvation through the New Covenant (Jer. 31:31-37). This was God's plan that the prophet Isaiah had declared 700 years before, that the Virgin will be with child (Matt. 1:23; Isa. 7:14). Knowing that there would be misunderstanding in the community and much gossip at the well, Joseph knew the true story of Mary's pregnancy and God's will for his life. When he awoke from the dream, he obeyed!

Tidbit: The woman's egg and the man's sperm have no blood in them. When they meet, the DNA and the blood type of the baby is determined at that time. Then, immediately, the placenta surrounds the fetus and not one drop of the mother's blood gets inside of the placenta or the baby. Therefore, it stands to reason that Jesus had only one blood type running through His veins, and that is the Blood of the Father God. Mary was only an empty vessel, not a co-producer. If Jesus had had one iota of a drop of man's blood in Him, it would have contaminated it, and it would have been futile for Jesus to shed that blood on the cross. It would not have washed away our sins (Pastor Jentezen Franklin).

Bathsheba was initially the wife of Uriah the Hittite (2 Sam. 11:3). David had her brought to him, even though inquiries disclosed that she was married to one of his top soldiers. When she became pregnant, David attempted to conceal his adultery by bringing her husband home. This plan failed when Uriah decided to stay with his troops instead of staying with his wife. David then ordered Uriah to the front lines, where he was to be killed, and then quickly married Bathsheba so the child would appear legitimate. Convicted of adultery and murder, David repented, and the death sentence was transferred to his son. David then became guiltless, and his marriage to Bathsheba was lawful, so the next child was legitimate and lived. This son was Solomon, who succeeded David on the throne, thus putting Bathsheba in the lineage of Jesus.

Rahab was a prostitute whose house adjoined Jericho's outer wall (Josh. 2:15). According to Joshua, the king of Jericho discovered that Joshua's spies were at Rahab's house, and ordered them to be brought out and killed. In return for Rahab's help, the spies agreed to spare Rahab's family in the coming battle. Later, at the Battle of Jericho, Joshua spared Rahab and her family, and she lived in Israel ever since, and appears in a list of heroes of the faith (Heb. 11:31). According to James 2:25, Rahab was justified by works because she welcomed the messengers and sent them out by another road. In both references, she is identified as Rahab the prostitute, the mother of Salmon and wife of Boaz (Matt. 1:5), and is the second woman mentioned in Jesus's lineage according to Matthew.

Ruth was a Moabite, traditional enemies to Israelites and corrupters of Israel. Moabites served other gods, and the Israelites are often troubled for mingling with the foreigners. However, God chose Ruth the Moabite to properly fulfill the obligations of the Jewish community. The community in Bethlehem prays a benediction for Boaz (not the same Boaz as in the story of Rahab), as he tells the people and elders of his plans to marry Ruth. In spite of the fact that Ruth is of a people who are considered to be noted enemies of Israel, Ruth and Boaz do build up the house of Israel and are the great-grandparents of King David. The book of Ruth has no named author, no named date of origin, and there is modern debate as to the purpose of the story except for the Davidic genealogy.

Tamar was the daughter-in-law of Judah (Gen. 38), given in marriage to Judah's firstborn son. Because he was wicked in the sight of the Lord, Er was killed by the Lord before he could sire a son (Gen. 38:7). Judah's next son is given to Tamar to perform the duties of Levirate marriage (Deut. 25:5-10) but he too was disobedient and the Lord killed him. Judah, having but one son left, refused to give him to Tamar. Tamar then saw to it herself that an offspring be raised up for her dead husband. Dressing as a harlot, she sat by the city gate, enticing Judah to sleep with her, and became pregnant, causing Judah to threaten to burn her as a harlot. When Tamar produced Judah's signet, staff, and cloak—convincing evidence that Judah was the father—he acknowledged that she was more righteous than he, since he himself had violated the Levirate requirements by refusing to give her his son. She gave birth to twins, Perez and Zerah, the former being a key ancestor of David (Ruth 4:12, 18). Tamar is one of the four women included in Matthew's genealogy of Jesus.

3. *The Blood of Jesus*

Have you ever heard someone pray the blood of Jesus? Have you wondered what this meant? Hopefully, these next pages will help you to understand this prayer and insert it into your prayers if you choose to do so. "This is the agreement I will make with them at that time," says the Lord. "I will put my teachings in their hearts and write them on their minds." Then He says, "Their sins and the evil things they do I will not remember anymore" (Heb. 10:16-19). Now, when these have been forgiven, there is no more need for a sacrifice for sins. So, brothers and sisters, we are completely free to enter the Most Holy Place without fear, because the Blood of Jesus shed upon His death.

According to scripture, there are seven places that Jesus's body bled when He was crucified. In the Garden of Gethsemane, His sweat was like drops of blood falling to the ground (Luke 22:44). Physicians say this is possible when you are dehydrated and under great stress. Fear opens up sweat glands and blood will seep out. Remember the prayer of Jesus? "Father, if you are willing take this cup from me, yet not my will but yours be done." He bled in the Garden, so that you and I can remain committed to the Father's will. God's will is not meant to pamper you physically, but to perfect you spiritually. Plead the blood of Jesus to remain committed to the will of God. This is a process of God moving you from the place you are to the place He wants you.

Jesus was taken from the Garden to Pilate's court. He was blindfolded, mocked, spit upon, and beaten (Luke 22:54-65). The soldiers were trained to hit with the fist, in order to inflict as much pain as possible. Some interpretations say the soldiers slapped him with the open hand (John 18:22). This was so that not one bone would be broken (John 19:36). His lips and eyes were burst open, and blood began to flow down His face. They plucked out His beard, causing more bleeding. "We who with unveiled faces all reflect the Lord's glory are being transformed into His likeness with ever-increasing glory, which comes from the Lord, who is the Spirit" (2 Cor. 3:18). The glory of God was on Jesus's face, and the devil was trying to slap it off, and is still trying to slap it off of Christians' faces today. To plead the blood of Jesus that came from His face is to change the appearance of your face, thus changing your countenance to let the glory of the Lord shine through.

They put a crown of thorns on Jesus (John 19:2) which they cut from a briar branch that grew over the courtyard wall. It was green and pliable, with thorns ranging from three to six inches long that were very sharp. They shaped a crown out of it and shoved it onto Jesus's head, with still no bones broken, but the skin around his head was torn. He bled from His head for a spiritual reason. "Cursed is the ground because of you. Through painful toil you will eat of it all the days of your life. It will produce thorns and thistles for you" (Gen 3:17-18). This crown of thorns represents curses put upon people who oppress, depress, and possess our minds. The devil tried to put this curse on Jesus's mind, but the cross broke all of the bonds of the curses away from us. "Do not conform any longer to the pattern of this world, but be transformed by the renewing of your mind" (Rom. 12:2). The scriptures mention scars on Jesus's hands and side, but never a scar around His head, because the curse has been broken by the Blood of Jesus once and for all.

Pilate had Jesus flogged, and handed Him over to be crucified (Mark 15:15), and He was pierced on the cross for our transgressions and crushed for our sins. The punishment that brought us peace He took upon Himself, and the wounds on His body have healed us (Isa. 53:4-5; 1 Pet. 2:24). Pray the Blood of Jesus that flowed from His back, and stop living with the pain and sickness in your body.

Jesus's feet were pierced with the Roman nails so that we might have the good news (Rom. 10:15, 16:20) and the God of peace will soon crush Satan under our feet. When you picture Jesus being lifted up onto the cross, remember John 8:28 and put your faith in Him.

The dagger was thrust into His side (John 19:34) between the third and fourth rib on the left side. Read the book of Leviticus to find the exact directions on how to prepare a sacrifice to the Lord. Water and blood ran out of the side of Jesus that was pierced. The only water that could have run out was in the cardiac sac around the heart, and with the blood, this represented the twofold witness of Jesus. "This is the one that came by water and by blood, Jesus Christ. He did not come by water only, but by water and blood" (1 John 5:6). This water and blood washes away all iniquity and cleanses us from our sin (Ps. 51:2).

Seven places from where the Blood of Jesus flowed: In the Garden from His sweat that we may commit to the Father, from His face that we might receive the closeness of His glory, from His head so we might break this worldly curse from our mind, from His back in order that we might be healed, from His hands so we can share the anointing and authority, from His feet to bring us the good news of the gospel, and from His heart to give us compassion for the lost. Jesus gave us the power to pray through His Blood, and we must use that power to bring the gospel to the world (Matt. 28:18-19).

4. Ten Things We Should Know about Jesus

a. The Bible declares Jesus to be God's One and only Son (John 3:16), still Jesus had to ask His disciples who men said He was (Matt. 3:17). They stumbled around for the right answer, some saying John the Baptist, some Elijah, and others Jeremiah or one of the other prophets (Matt. 16:13-14). The people were willing to believe that Jesus was some prophet raised from the dead, or Elijah returned from heaven, but because He came as a humble teacher, without the pretense and pomp of a ruler, not many were willing to accept Him as the Son of God, the Savior of men.

b. The relationship Jesus had with God is found in John 10:30: "I and the Father are one."

c. How the Apostle John described this relationship is found in John 1:1 and 14: "In the beginning was the Word, and the Word was with God and the Word was God. And the Word was made flesh and dwelt among us." The Greek word translated the Word means *the thought of God expressed*. At times, it is difficult to tell whether it is speaking of the Father or the Son. Christians gladly accept the definition of Moses in Deuteronomy 6:4 that the Lord is one Lord, but cannot fully explain how the Father and Son are one God.

d. Christ's existence before He was born in human flesh can be found in Micah 5:2, stating that His goings forth have been from of old, from ancient times. In John 17:5, Jesus tells us that He had been with the Father before the world was and His pre-existence is most definitely taught from John 6:38: "I came down from heaven."

e. Christ had a part in the work of creation and forming the universe (Heb. 1:1, 2). All things in heaven and on earth, whether we can see them or not, were created by Him, and without Him there would be nothing that was made (Col. 1:16; John 1:1-3).

f. The birth of Jesus was supernatural by the Virgin Mary, who conceived through the Holy Spirit (Isa. 7:14; Matt. 1:18).

g. Jesus had to struggle with temptation as we do, but was still without sin (Heb. 4:15).

h. What did Jesus's death accomplish for us? We were sinners saved by grace and through the shedding of His Blood (Rom. 5:8; Matt. 26:27-28).

i. Jesus has the keys of death (Rev. 1:17-18), He is the first and the last, He died that we might live, and He now lives forevermore. The Resurrection of Jesus is a doctrine that distinguishes Christianity from all other religions. Jesus alone points to an empty tomb as evidence of divine power and of His conquest over death.

j. If the Resurrection of Jesus were not a fact, how would that affect us? Our faith is in vain, our sins are still on us, and those who died in hopeful faith will perish (1 Cor. 15:17-18).

Jesus rose a victor over death, thus providing assurance of our resurrection from the grave!

5. *How to Get Jesus to Touch You – Points of Contact*

There are different points of contact that God uses and teaches us how He can touch us and we can touch Him to get our miracle, deliverance, or healing. There are people now who need healing and a miracle in their life. Jesus Christ of Nazareth is the master miracle worker. He is God and He does do miracles today, as He did in Biblical days, and He will touch your life. However, there is something you must do. I truly wish that the Bible was written to say that if God will draw near to you, then you will draw near to Him, but that is not what scripture says. You must draw near to God first, and then He will draw near to you (James 4:8). I wish God would move first, then we would know for sure what direction to follow, but God says that we must let Him see our faith. Make a move, do something radically abnormally faith-filled, and then God moves on our behalf (Luke 4:38-39, 5:12-13, 7:9-10). Jesus healed all that He touched, so don't you think that it would be worth our effort to reach out to Him, make the first move, cry out to Him, or whatever it takes for Him to touch you. A man named Zaccheus not only climbed up into a tree but went out on a limb to get a look at this man they called Savior (Luke 19:2-8). I don't think Jesus was a tree-watcher, but maybe He saw him out of the corner of His eye. Maybe all the people were pointing and jeering at this spectacle of what Zaccheus was doing. All I know is that he did climb the tree and Jesus looked up at him. What is important in this is not that he climbed the tree, but how Zaccheus touched Jesus, and how Jesus touched Zaccheus. Zaccheus touched Jesus with his hunger, that caused him to seek and put himself in a position for the Lord to see him, and he got the touch he was looking for. So one of the greatest points of contact is your hunger after Christ! Seek the Healer, not the healing! Notice in verse 5 that Jesus called Zaccheus by his name! Wow! The Lord knows us by name! Now is that not cool?

We see that anointing oil is used in the scriptures, so it is an important point of contact (James 5:13-15). Remember always that the oil does not heal, but is used as a sign of obedience to the scripture and faith in your Lord that the prayer of faith will be answered. In the scriptures, we see people, including Jesus, laying hands on people (Luke 5:13) and praying for them or commanding their bodies to be healed or to impart healing and deliverance. Se we know that laying on of hands is a point of contact. To imitate what Jesus did cannot be bad, and will very likely result in an answered prayer! Using the blessed cloth (Acts 19:11-12) is a point of contact, but again there is no power in the cloth itself, but faith in the Word of God and the power of the Holy Spirit working through man. It is the anointing transferred to the cloth and the man's hands that God can use to touch your life and heal your loved ones. If we could only touch the hem of His garments (Mark 5:27-28)! This is as simple as touching the Word of God or staying in a continuous study of the Bible. Jesus is the Word and He will send His Word to heal you (Heb. 13:8). You can also send the Word in a postcard, by telephone, letter, or by e-mail to your loved ones who are hurting either physically or spiritually, and pray healing for them. Send a preaching tape on healing to somebody who is sick, and God can and will, without any other person in the room, touch and heal them. I have been healed in my body from reading the scriptures and then saying them out loud. That spoken word touched God, and God touched me through that word and I was healed.

Many think preaching and teaching is just for note-taking and information. We need information about God, but realize that within that information is the Hand of God and the Breath of God. His Word is alive (Isa. 55:10-11; Ps. 119:105; Eph. 5:26; Jer. 23:29; Heb. 4:13) and we all need to make contact with it in our lives. Bartimaeus (Mark 10:47-52) did something to get Jesus's attention when he heard the news that Jesus was coming down the road. Everyone was telling him to be quiet, only to make him grow a little extra noisy. Jesus had to move the crowd to find the one man who was crying out to Him. We need to cry out to God! Get His attention! We will be the better for this effort (Ps. 18:6). These are things to show us how people in the Bible got their miracles, but we have to find our own point of contact. We can't just say, *oh, well, I guess* the Lord wants me to stay this way, or *He is trying to teach me something through sickness.* No! Read His last will and testament. His will is to heal and deliver our bodies, no matter what we have. It is not the will of God for us to be sick. If you are blaming God for something, you won't be looking for answers, you will be asking questions. Turn your heart back toward God! He is not your problem! He is your answer! He can fix what is broken! He is not your enemy; He is the miracle worker! Create a point of contact and He will touch your life in the name of Jesus.

6. *Jesus Saves*

The story in Mark 10:46-52 about a blind man named Bartimaeus is not a mere calling just to catch Jesus's attention. Even though this man could not see, he recognized Jesus. He addressed the son of David, the promised Savior, so that the unbelieving community would see Jesus for who He was, and that their spiritually blind eyes might be opened (Acts 26:17-18). In the Old Testament time, God took the initiative to reveal Himself to people by experience. Frequently, when God revealed Himself to a person, the person gave God a new name or described His nature. This is why we see new names or titles for God, following an event where a Bible character (person commissioned by God) experienced His presence. Biblical names, titles, and descriptions of God identify how Bible characters personally came to know God. For example the name *David* means *the beloved of God* (Acts 13:22).

When the blind man called Jesus the son of David, he was full of confidence and trust that Jesus was the promised Savior. Thank God that salvation is not by sight, but comes by faith. The blind man was helpless, according to the standard of the world. He was even rebuked for calling Jesus and was ordered to keep quiet, but Jesus, who left the throne of heaven, noticed the pledge of the helpless man. It was because of our helpless situation that Christ came into this world. Jesus notices you and me despite the oppositions and discouragements. When we call on Him, He is near us and ready to grant our request. Mercy, healing, and eternal life are found only in Jesus, and in Him there is no failure. Isaiah tells us that a child is born and to us a Son is given, and the government will be on His shoulder. And He will be called names such as wonderful counselor, mighty God, everlasting Father, Prince of peace, meaning all of His characteristics. He will establish His kingdom and uphold it with justice and righteousness accomplished from the zeal of the Lord Almighty (Isa. 9:6-7).

It was this promise that built confidence and trust in the blind man's mind that his only hope rested in Jesus. "What do you want me to do for you?" Jesus asked. Jesus could very well see that the man was blind but wanted the man to confess with his mouth that He was Lord (Rom. 10:9). The blind man knew he wanted to see, and trusted Jesus for that sight. He got more than He asked for in Jesus's process of physical and spiritual sight. Do you know what you want when you come to Him in prayer? Do you persist even if others try to discourage you? What a promise we have in Hebrews 4:16: "Let us then approach the throne of grace with confidence, so that we may receive mercy and find grace to help us in our time of need." When we kneel before the cross of Jesus, we appear as supplicants, not for justice but for mercy. Salvation is God's plan to save all undeserving men. Do you know the plan? Are you in the program?

7. Good News

While the headlines in our papers rarely declare such, Isaiah the prophet shared glad tidings amid words of discipline and chastisement. He knew God was good and had compassion and mercy on His people. People bound by sin are not unredeemable, for Christ came to reach out and redeem them from the darkness. Those who suffer need not feel they must suffer alone, for Christ came with the Spirit's anointing to impact lives with salvation and deliverance. Believers who are feeling overwhelmed by cares and trials do not need to feel helpless, for God has given them a blessed hope for the future, to help them endure their present struggles. Grief and pain are as much a part of our lives as joy and pleasure. But only the latter are characteristics of those who will dwell eternally in the presence of the Heavenly Father. Sorrow and distress have no place in the life believers in Christ will one day gain because of His suffering and sacrifice.

"The Spirit of the Sovereign Lord is on me, because the Lord has anointed me to preach good news to the poor. He has sent me to bind up the brokenhearted, to proclaim freedom for the captives and release from darkness for the prisoners, to proclaim the year of the Lord's favor and the day of vengeance of our God, to comfort all who mourn, and provide for those who grieve in Zion, to bestow on them a crown of beauty instead of ashes, the oil of gladness instead of mourning and a garment of praise instead of a spirit of despair. They will be called oaks of righteousness, a planting of the Lord for the display of His splendor" (Isa. 61:1-3). This is a passage from the Bible worth reading on a daily basis to try to fully understand just what good news the birth, death, and resurrection of our Lord and Savior really is.

Isaiah ministered during a time when his people were oppressed. He proclaimed the good news that the Messiah would come in the power of the Spirit to set them free. More than 600 years later, in the synagogue in Nazareth, Jesus proclaimed Himself to be the One of whom Isaiah was speaking (Luke 4:16-20). The Spirit of the Lord would anoint the Messiah for several purposes, including the proclamation of good news and hope for the poor, healing for those emotionally and spiritually bound, and liberation for those held captive by sin and sorrow. What is the acceptable year of the Lord? This is most likely a reference to the Year of Jubilee (Lev. 25), a time when slaves would be released from their captivity and debts would be cancelled. Jesus Christ opened the age of God's grace, in which sinners would be released from their captivity to sin, and their debt of sin would be cancelled.

Christ would proclaim the day of the vengeance of our God. Like many prophetic passages, Isaiah 61:2 blends the near with the distant future by mentioning both Jesus's first and second comings. This day of vengeance is delayed until Jesus returns, but before the Day of Judgment. Isaiah pictured Jesus as the one who will bring comfort to all who mourn. Isaiah's message was one of hope for his people. God would work a miracle on their behalf. Instead of the ashes of mourning, God would give them a crown of beauty. The Hebrew word translated *beauty* can refer to an ornamental headdress worn on occasions of rejoicing. Instead of intense sadness, God would give them the oil of joy, the perfumed ointment poured on guests at festive occasions. Instead of desperation and discouragement, God would bless them with the garment of praise, the bright clothing worn during celebrations of joy. And the people who seemed devastated would one day come to be associated with the strength of the oak trees and the fruitfulness of the vines. What a difference Christ makes in the lives of people of all ages.

8. *Dead Ringer*

In the sixteenth century, I am told, people drank ale or whiskey from lead cups. Evidently, the combination of the spirits and the elements could knock a hardy drinker out for a couple of days. Someone walking along the road might mistake an unconscious drunk for dead, and so prepare him for burial. They would lay the body on the kitchen table for a few days for the family to gather around, eat, drink, and wait expectantly for the person to wake. Ergo, the term WAKE! People finally caught on to the fact that not all who slept were dead! Now we dig further into the story and find that the plot thickens, literally, with so many bodies in the small landscape that room was scarce. The old graves were dug up and the remains, being of less volume now, were stored in a smaller space, and the graves and coffins were reused. Upon opening the occupied coffins, scratch marks were discovered on the inside of some. Drawing the eerie conclusion that one or more had been buried alive, a new and improved burial plan was devised. A string was tied to a body part of the deceased, pulled up, and tied to a bell on a post before the dirt was tossed in to cover the coffin. A volunteer would sit in the graveyard all night to listen for the bell. From this, we get our sayings, graveyard shift, saved by the bell, and dead ringer.

Jesus is on the graveyard shift! He waits by our upright tents (2 Cor. 5:1), listening for our bell to ring out, save me! Save me! Save me! The gospel is about life, yet not all who hear it will pull on the string connected to our Lord and Savior. Many will be found on the side of the road to hell and will be counted among the dead, missing the chance to ring out.

We are related to God through death. Jesus Christ died on the Cross for our sins, and according to scripture, we died to sin when we accepted Him as our Savior. The Greek *aorist*, past tense for died, suggests a specific point when the actions occurred, as salvation. Death, whether physical or spiritual, means separation, not extinction. Death to sin is preparation from sin's power, not the extinction of sin. Being dead to sin means being set free from sin (Rom. 6:2-10)! We were baptized into Christ Jesus, buried with Him in baptism, and just as Christ was raised from the dead through the glory of the Father, we too may live a new life. We are dead to sin and alive to God in Christ Jesus! Because this is true, we believe (present tense) and we keep on believing that we will also live with Him. The sharing of the resurrection life of Jesus Christ begins at the moment of regeneration, but will continue as a believer shares eternity with the Lord. What is true in reality and experience with Jesus, believers who are identified with Him by faith are commanded to regard as true for themselves (Rom. 6:8-11). Now we are related to Christ through the Spirit of Him who raised Jesus from the dead that is living in us. Christ is in you and me with the indwelling presence of the Holy Spirit. In other words, God gives spiritual resurrection life now and physical resurrection in the future (Rom. 8:9-11; 1 Cor. 6:14; 2 Cor. 4:14).

Now we are a new creature; the old has gone and the new has come. No one was more able to reflect on this transformation than Paul, who turned from a persecutor of Christ to a proclaimer of Christ (Acts 9:5, 20:22). He was in Christ, a phrase Paul used repeatedly to speak of a believer's spiritual relationship to Christ, because he believed the message of the gospel and was identified by faith with Christ (2 Cor. 5:4-17; Rom. 6:3-4; Gal. 2:20). This new creation is brought about by the Holy Spirit, the agent of regeneration (Titus 3:5) and the giver of divine birth (John 3:3, 6:8). Death is the destiny of every man (Ecc. 7:2) and it is appointed to each man to die once (Heb. 9:7), but this is only our physical death. Our souls belong to God, and whosoever believes in Jesus Christ will never die (John 11:26). The resurrection of the new life age is present right now, because Jesus is Lord of life (John 1:4). Jesus's words about life and death are seemingly paradoxical. A believer's death issues in new life and the believer will never die spiritually (John 3:16, 5:24, 10:28; 2 Cor. 5:6, 8; Phil 1:23).

Isaiah prophesied that He will swallow up death forever (Isa. 25:8) and what was written came true when death was swallowed up in the victory of the cross (1 Cor. 15:54-57). For those who belong to Christ, death's power will be removed (1 Cor. 15:53-54). Death came through man, Adam, when sin was brought into and received in the Garden of Eden. We were created to live forever, but as the scripture states; "the wages of sin is death" (Rom. 6:23). The wages (Greek word *opsonia*) originally meant a soldier's pay, and scripturally means unbelievers will earn eternal separation from God in hell (Luke 16:24-25). This is the wages an unbeliever has earned and deserves because of his sin (Rom. 5:12, 7:13). By contrast, the gift of life, charisma, of God is eternal life (John 3:16, 36). Paul is saying that you earn death through sin, but the gift of life cannot be earned (Eph. 2:8-9; Titus 3:5).

In the Garden, the devil got his hooks into man and held us for ransom. Our Lord and Savior paid the price when He died, as a ransom to set us free from sin (Heb. 9:15). He tasted death for everyone by the grace of God (Heb. 2:9). God's love is not limited to a few or to one group of people, but His gift is to the whole world. The statement of tasting death is best understood as the purpose of the Lord's being made lower than the angels in His Incarnation. The focus on the statement, despite its reference to Jesus's present glory, is on the fact that He became a man in order to die. He laid down His life for us (1 John 3:16), died for our sins once and for all to bring us to God (1 Pet. 3:18), and now holds the keys to death and Hades (Rev. 1:18). That is, He has the sole authority over death and the place of the eternal dead (John 5:21-26; 1 Cor. 15:54-57; Heb. 2:14; Rev. 20:12-14). "Behold! I stand at the door and knock" (Rev. 3:20). This is the door to your spiritual grave that holds death eternally if you have not accepted Jesus Christ as your Savior. Pull the string! Ring the bell! Let Him snatch you from the flames (Jude 2:3). The King is coming (Rev. 22:20-21)!

9. Tools of the Trade

Lawrence of Arabia became famous for his exploits as British military liaison to the Arab revolt during the First World War. During the war, Lawrence formed close friendships with many of the sheiks of Arabia. After the war, he brought some of these sheiks back to England to show his appreciation for their support against the Turkish domination. On the last night of their visit, Lawrence offered them a choice of anything they wanted to take back to their desert homes. They chose the faucet from the bathtub, and said they wanted to take faucets with them that would provide running water in their desert homes. They did not realize the water did not come from the faucet, but from the intricate chain of power behind the faucet.

God uses faucets as His tools to do His mighty work here on earth, but there are chains of events before the power of God is revealed. The widow (2 Kings 4) had only a little oil in her house and no jars. The prophet, Elisha, sent her to neighboring houses to gather up empty jars that she might fill them with the little oil she had in her house. We aren't told the woman's thoughts on the matter, but we do see that she used trust, belief, and obedience before God used His power. "We have this treasure in jars of clay to show that this all-surpassing power is from God and not from us" (2 Cor. 4:7).

Every living being—be it animal or plant life—in existence needs a tool to exist, survive, function, and grow. Think about it! Cats use their claws as tools to scratch not only their body irritants, but each other and sometimes you and your furniture. They also use your wooden tables to sharpen their tools. We all use tools, and more importantly, we are all God's tools. Does God need us to accomplish His purpose? Not necessarily! In the beginning, God was! In the Hebrew translation of Genesis, God is the noun, *Elohim* (plural of *Eloahh*), and is an extension of the Hebrew root, *El*. This means Supreme Being in the sense of the English deity or God. Since the name *Elohim* is plural, the name implies the Trinity. The words *let us* (Gen. 1:26) also implies the Trinity. *Created*, Hebrew word *Bara*, means to bring forth completely new, not from pre-existing material. God spoke the heavens and earth into existence, and then used two of His spoken tools, dirt and breath, to create man (Gen. 2:7). The uninvited Satan crept into the perfect Garden and used God's created tree to trip up man and cause the fall. After Adam and Eve were expelled from the Garden, God used a cherub to keep guard on the entrance with a flaming sword (Gen. 3:24).

Therefore, we realize that God can create whatever He needs for His use, and that is precisely why He created us. We are created for His pleasure (Rev. 4:11)! If you are thinking that He can't use you because you are not good enough, remember the words of Jesus: "No one is good except God alone" (Mark 10:18). Scripture brings to mind Solomon, who was too rich, Abraham, who was too old. Peter was a coward with a loud mouth, Lazarus was dead, Paul was a murderer, and Noah was a drunk! Moses stuttered, David's armor didn't fit, John Mark was rejected by Paul, Timothy had ulcers, and Jacob was a liar. Now if you are thinking you are better than these guys, be careful! "Do not think of yourself more highly than you ought, but rather think of yourself with sober judgment, in accordance with the measure of faith God has given you" (Rom. 12:3). "I know that nothing good lives in me, that is, in my sinful nature" (Rom. 7:18).

Our body parts are God's tools, and He has arranged every one of them just as He wanted them to be (1 Cor. 12:18). "How beautiful are the feet that bring the good news" (Isa. 52:7). This sounds like an oxymoron to me, especially since through Bible history, we have learned that feet were always dirty and caked with mud from walking the dusty roads in sandals. But wait! Read this! "And she stood behind Him at His feet weeping. She began to wet His feet with her tears. Then she wiped them with her hair, kissed them and poured perfume on them" (Luke 7:38). Maybe we should start looking at feet in a different light. We may get a surprise or an opportunity.

Along with the unsavory people God used, there were two small fish and five loaves of home-baked bread that He used to cater to five thousand people (Mark 6:38, 41-43), water to make wine for a wedding (John 2:7-9), a fish to cough up tax money (Matt. 17:27), dirt and spit that a blind man might see (John 9:1, 6:7), earthquakes and smoke to show His anger (Ps. 18:7-8), a hand with no body (Dan. 5:5), and He inserted a thorn in Paul's side (2 Cor. 12:7-9). He used water to destroy what was bad (Gen. 6:9) and water to save what was good (Ex. 14:21-29). God uses His created angels to do His bidding (Dan. 7:10; Ps. 103:20; Heb. 1:14). There is His own scripture to teach us (2 Tim. 3:16), nature to show us (Ps. 19:1-4), conscience to guide us (Rom. 2:15), and gifts to enlighten us (1 Cor. 12:8).

God's Word is a power-packed tool like fire (Ex. 13:21) and like a hammer that breaks rocks into pieces (Jer. 23:29). His Word does not return void (Isa. 55:11) but accomplishes all He desires. It lights your way (Ps. 119:105) and stills your storms (Matt. 11:33). The Word of God is sharper than a double-edged sword (Heb. 4:12) through which we are made holy and clean (Eph. 5:26). We are born again of imperishable seed through the living Word of God (1 Pet. 1:23) and will be refined and purified through His fire (Mal. 3:2-3). With His mouth, He swallowed up death (Isa. 25:8), and with the sword of His mouth (Rev. 19:15), He will strike down the nations and rule them with an iron scepter.

In 1874, Sir James Simpson discovered that chloroform could be used as an anesthetic to render people insensible to the pain of surgery. While lecturing at the University of Edinburgh some years later, a student asked what he considered his most valuable discovery in his lifetime. His answer: "My most valuable discovery was when I discovered myself a sinner and that Jesus Christ was my Savior!" No matter what we accomplish in life, we are just a faucet, an empty vessel, a tool in God's work shed. The power is God's!

10. Why a Donkey

Prophecy: "See, your King comes to you, righteous and having salvation, gentle and riding on a donkey, on a colt, the foal of a donkey" (Zech. 9:9). Prophecy fulfilled: "See, your King comes to you, gentle and riding on a donkey, on a colt, the foal of a donkey" (Matt. 21:5, John 12:15). Christ rode a donkey because He wanted the people to identify Him as the prophesied king spoken of in Zechariah. This King does not come on a horse, which is a symbol of war and battle. He came to establish a kingdom where there will be no more war, no more bloodshed, and no more tears (Rev. 21:1-4).

The disciples who witnessed this did not understand it all. Only after Jesus was glorified (John 17:1-5), did they realize that these things had been written about Him and that they had done these things to Him (John 12:16). Others in the crowd believed because they had seen Him perform miracles (John 12:17-18), but they misunderstood the coming kingdom. They were expecting a political, earthly king like David or Solomon; a king who would free Israel from the bondage of the Roman government. They thought He would overthrow the Roman leaders in Jerusalem and declare Israel an independent nation. They were all crying,

Hosanna! Glory be to God! Our King comes! The whole crowd joyfully praised God in loud voices (Luke 19:37). Look closely at the scripture. There is one who weeps (Luke 19:41). Jesus did not weep because the people mistook Him as king, but because the people failed to see what kind of king He was. He knew why the people were jumping up and down and why they were singing. Sadly, He knew they were not praising Jesus, but their own made-up version of Jesus. De we praise Him because of what He does for us here on earth or for what He had established for us eternally?

The tradition of placing your garments on the ground for a king to walk on (Matt. 21:8) is an Old Testament custom (2 Kings 9:13), recognizing the fact that the people were in the presence of a king. This is the way the people were receiving Jesus. By riding a donkey, Christ is declaring that He will suffer. One commentary states that the donkey was the common animal used whenever a covenant was made. It was common for a donkey to be torn apart and dismembered to confirm or seal the covenant. Tearing apart the donkey said: "If I break this covenant, then let what has happened to this donkey happen to me." The dismembering of the covenant animal was showing how serious it was to break the covenant. Disobedience required the life of the one who broke the covenant. Christ never broke the covenant, and was found without sin (Heb. 4:15, 1 Pet. 1:19) but Christ rode the donkey, hung on the cross, and was torn and slain instead of you and me (Isa. 53:5, 1 Pet. 2:24). We (man) are the ones who broke the covenant but Christ paid the penalty. (Note: I have no scripture of a donkey being used as described. Genesis 15:9 does not name a donkey along with the rest of the animals used in sacrifice.)

Donkeys are peaceful, strong, and willing. Christ came gently and humbly (Matt. 21:5) and it is this gentleness that makes Him accessible. This is an example of how we are to live our lives. Not in self-righteous conceit, but in humility, with an awareness of our shortcomings. The power of the Messiah would not be shown in His daring courage, but in His humility. As followers of Christ, we must cling to humility so that we are open to follow Him. The Bible speaks of yet another triumphal entry in Revelation 1:7, 19:11-16. Instead of a donkey, Christ will be riding a white horse, and instead of words of peace, Christ carried a sword (the Word of God). You and I have been invited to join in Christ's triumphal entry (Rev. 7:9-10).

11. Psalm 82

It was only when a puzzled Christian asked me what Jesus meant in John 10:34 that I referred to Psalm 82 to try to understand the message. Psalm 82 not only showed that Jesus was Israel's Messiah; it also had a message to those who had rejected Him and were attempting to put Him to death. Psalm 82 has a very awesome word to those of who live in this world today. In John 9:1-7, Jesus had just healed a man who had been blind since birth, showing that He was the light of the world (John 9:5). The blind man came to faith, the eyes of others were opened both physically and spiritually, while the Jewish religious leaders willfully closed their eyes to the identity of Jesus as Israel's Messiah. The blind—now seeing—man was brought before the Pharisees for investigation by his good friends and neighbors. They did not believe his honest, simple answer, "I washed and now I see," but called in his parents to question them. They did not want to be in trouble with the leaders, so they hedged on their answer, saying that their son should be the one questioned. Wanting to be right, they questioned the man again, to which he gave a condescending answer. "I have told you already and you did not listen. Why do you want to hear it again? Do you want to become His disciples too?" Have you ever felt like using this man's answer when some just continue to question your belief in God? Even though the leaders continued to heap insults and accusations on this man, he stood his ground and kept his faith that Jesus was from God and did heal him. This infuriated the leaders and they threw him out! If this ever happens to you, then re-read this passage: "Jesus heard they had thrown him out and He went to find Him!"

In the tenth chapter of John, Jesus claimed to be the Good Shepherd, the door through which everyone must enter in order to be saved. He promised to lay down His life for the sheep. Now this did upset the leaders and caused great division among them. Some insisted that He had a demon and ought to be ignored, while others found it hard to believe that a demon-possessed man could give sight to a man born blind. Was He the Messiah or not? They asked! Jesus answered by saying that those who were His sheep heard His voice, but the rest did not, and boldly announced that, "I and the Father are one" (John 10:30). This enraged Jesus's enemies and they took up stones to put Him to death, accusing Him of blasphemy. Jesus responded by quoting from Psalms 82:6—"I said you are gods." If God could call those gods to whom the Word of God had come, why was it wrong for Jesus to claim to be God? They were not convinced and attempted to put Him to death, but He eluded their grasp (John 10:39). How convincing do you find Jesus's defense? Can you explain it to others, or do you use it just to embarrass and confuse the ones talking erratically or irrationally against your belief in Jesus?

Asaph, in Psalm 82, envisioned God presiding over an assembly of judges. The word "gods" (*elohim*) is used in this passage for the rulers of Israel who have failed to carry out their responsibilities as God's representatives. Old Testament scriptures using the term *elohim* as rulers are Exodus 3:14-16, when Moses was whining about not being able to speak well and God, burning with anger, sent Aaron to speak to the people for Moses, telling him that it would be as if Aaron was Moses's mouth, and as if Moses was God to him. He made Moses like God to Pharaoh (Ex. 7:1). Rulers are appointed by God to carry out His purpose of restraining evil and rewarding good (Rom. 13:1-4). In this sense, rulers act for God and as gods. If you are acting as judge in the name of Jesus, be very careful. The Lord our God will have no part in unrighteousness or partiality or taking a bribe (2nd Chron. 19:6-7). When sitting in judgment, acting as god and for God, leaders must speak up for those who cannot speak for themselves, for the rights of all who are destitute (Prov. 31:8-9).

The human judges roam the earth without spiritual or intellectual understanding, and in moral darkness, so that the foundations of the earth are shaken; that is, law and order are undermined. These foundations refer to the law and order of society based on the Lord's rule. God warned the wicked judges that they would perish. He had appointed them as gods and as sons of the most high, His representatives on earth. Jesus appealed to Psalms 82:6 when He was accused of blasphemy in John 10:34. Since Israel's judges were, in a sense, sons of God, Jesus said He was not blaspheming to call Himself The Son of God. Ultimately God will reign in the person of His Son, the Messiah. For now, He reigns through His sons, the gods who are appointed to reign in His stead. God is to reign, in and through His people collectively, and we who are His sons are destined to reign with Him in the future (2 Tim. 2:12; Rev. 20:6). The kings in the ancient days were often worshiped as gods and thought of themselves as a god and were punished immediately for not giving praise to the one and only God (Acts 12:21-23). Perhaps this is what the Jews were making reference to in John 10:33. If they truly believed this and truly believed in the one and only God, can't you just see their surprise when Jesus was not immediately struck down and eaten by worms (Acts 12:23)?

When Jesus referred to Psalm 82, He identified Himself as the fulfillment of the written verses. The warning of the psalm was being fulfilled in their midst. God had finally come to judge the gods. How much better the name of God suited Jesus than the title *gods* suited the scribes and the Pharisees. To have understood the message of Psalm 82 and Jesus's application of it would have been to bow the knee to Him as the Son of God, the promised Messiah. To reject this message was to reject the Messiah, which in fact many did. No one better interpreted or applied Psalm 82 than Jesus, and no one better fulfilled it than He. Today, men must make the same decisions to either bow the knee to the Christ Jesus as Savior, or we will bow to Him as Judge; "At the name of Jesus every knee will bow, in heaven and on earth and under the earth and every tongue confess that Jesus Christ is Lord, to the glory of God the Father" (Phil. 2:10-11).

Psalm 82 is directed against the Israel leaders but carries a warning to us, as Christian leaders today. Psalm 58 asks if rulers indeed speak justly and if we judge uprightly among men. Isaiah tells us that the Lord will rise to judge the people, and enters into judgment against the elders and leaders of His people. He sent Ezekiel to prophesy to the shepherds of Israel who only take care of themselves. He adds that He is against the shepherds and will hold them accountable for His flock (Ezek. 34:2-10). Luke 20:46-47 warns us to beware of such teachers, and they will be punished most severely. We may begin to be passive because we view the time immediately preceding Christ's return as days of apostasy (2 Tim. 3:1-13). Therefore we stand idly by as spectators, often delighting in what we see because we think this means that Jesus's next visit to earth is near. Let me remind you that the psalmist also believed in the coming of Christ. This did not stop him from warning the unrighteous rulers, and our knowledge that Christ's return is nearer than ever should not stop us. We are God's gods in the sense that we are speaking for Him when we turn a sinner back to Jesus and save him from death (James 5:20). Remember, it is the Lord that gave you your mouth, and He will help you to speak and will teach you what to say (Ex. 4:11-12).

12. Jesus in the Old Testament

Information about Jesus Christ is not confined to the New Testament. The Old Testament might appear to be just God's message to the Jewish people and an account of their history, but it is much more. You can read all about Jesus in the Old Testament. The Old Testament shows a greater Jesus Christ, and the New Testament explains clearer who He is. These Old Testament scriptures explain the reasons for His birth, the work He was to accomplish, and the glory in store for Him and all who come to Him. They also show the works He did in the Old Testament when He appeared to the people and the prophets as the angel of the Lord, Lord, I Am, *Yahweh, Elohim, Adonai,* Spirit, Jehovah, and Messiah. The word *Messiah* is the Hebrew word taken right out of the Old Testament, meaning *anointed*, which is Greek for *Kristos*, our English word being Christ. In the Old Testament, Messiah stood for the promised one, the coming King, and the one whose right it is (Ezek. 21:25-27). When Jesus appeared to the disciples on the road to Emmaus, He opened their minds to the Old Testament scriptures (Luke 24:44-48).

The first time we see Jesus in the Old Testament is in Genesis 1:1: "In the beginning." John explains the beginning in the first verse of his book: "In the beginning was the Word and the Word was with God and the Word was God." God and Jesus are one (John 10:30, 17:21), therefore Jesus Himself is the Word and was the beginning. Revelation 1:8, 22:13 tells us that He is the Alpha and the Omega, the beginning and the end. When the Lord spoke to someone in the Old Testament, it was Jesus speaking, and when the people saw the Lord, they were seeing Jesus. Jesus Himself tells us in John 5:37, "you have neither heard His voice nor seen His form." Then in John 8:58, Jesus revealed the identity of the one that spoke and appeared in the Old Testament: "Before Abraham was born, I Am." This is the same I Am that spoke to Moses in Exodus 3, saying, "This is what you are to say to the Israelites, 'I Am has sent me to you.'"

The angel of the Lord that appeared to Moses in the burning bush was Jesus (Ex. 2:2), the Word of the Lord that came to Abram in a vision was Jesus (Gen. 15:1). No one has ever seen the Father (John 6:46), and if we read John 1:18, we learn that no one has ever seen God, but God the one and only, who is at the Father's side, has made him known. Jesus is God revealed in the Old Testament, since He is the image of the invisible God (Col. 1:15), therefore if anyone at any time has seen God, then we should expect that they saw the image of the invisible God, the Word, Jesus. Jesus and the Father were here on earth together, as stated in John 8:29, and we need to believe that Jesus is the invisible God and believe that He is who He says He is (John 8:24). The I Am that spoke to Moses (Gen. 3:14) is the same I Am in Revelation 1:8 and John 14:6; Jesus the image of the invisible God. Isaiah said he saw the King, the

Lord Almighty (Isa. 6:5), which is the King of Matthew 27:27; "This is Jesus, the King of the Jews," and the "King of Kings and Lord of Lords" in Revelation 19:16.

Since it has been established that no one has heard God's voice nor seen His form (John 5:37), then all of the Old Testament scriptures where they saw and heard the Lord, they were seeing the image of the invisible God, Jesus. The Lord Jesus came down in a cloud and spoke to Moses (Num. 11:25), from the Father, by the Son, through the Holy Spirit which was upon Him. Exodus 33:20 tells us that no one can see God's face and live, and again in 1st Timothy 6:16, we read that we have not seen God and cannot see God. It stands to reason that the ones in the Old Testament who write that they saw the Lord face-to-face (Gen. 32:30) as Jacob did, were seeing Jesus. Manoah thought he and his wife would surely die because they saw God (Jud. 13:22), the Lord appeared to Solomon twice (1 Kings 11:9), and Isaiah saw the King (Isa. 6:5), but they all lived, proving that the one they saw was the image of the invisible God, Jesus.

The Apostle Paul stated that the Israelites were all baptized into Moses in the cloud and in the sea. They all ate the same spiritual food and drank the same spiritual drink; for they drank from the spiritual rock that accompanied them, and that rock was Christ (1 Cor. 10:2-4). This same spiritual rock was recorded in Deuteronomy 32 as the Lord, faithful God, and the Rock. God is the Lord of Lords in Deuteronomy and Jesus is the same Lord of Lords in Revelation and in 1st Timothy, where He is again called God, whom no one has seen or can see. God spoke to Zechariah, using the word *me* in conjunction with the one being pierced (Zech. 12:10), yet the Apostle John referred to the same scripture and says that it was fulfilled when Jesus was pierced (John 19:34). The psalmist writes that God will remain the same and His years will never end, just as the author of Hebrews writes the same about the Son (Ps. 102:24-27; Heb. 8:10-12). In Isaiah 45, God, a righteous God, is the Savior and in Acts 4 and John 4, we find that Jesus the Son is the Savior of the world.

Angels are God's messengers, but where it says that the angel of the Lord did or said something, we need to read carefully to decide if this messenger was an angel or Jesus Christ. In Genesis 16, the angel of the Lord told Hagar that he would increase her descendants; however, angels do not have the power to increase, so this must have been Jesus. When John fell at the angel's feet, the angel told him not to do this, since he was a fellow servant. Worship God, he said (Rev. 19:10)! If the angel did not identify himself this way, then the angel of the Lord appearing to man was Jesus. This is shown in Joshua 51, when the commander of the army of the Lord came to Joshua. Joshua fell face-down to the ground in reverence, but was not told not to do this, but rather the commander said, "Take off your sandals, for the place where you are standing is holy." The angel that Jacob struggled with was Jesus (Hosea 12:4; Gen. 32:29-30) and Jacob said that he saw God face-to-face, and yet his life was spared. Now we have already learned that no one can see God's face and live, and that God and Jesus Christ are the only ones who can give blessings, so it was Jesus that Jacob saw and Jesus that gave the blessing. The part of God that Moses spoke to face-to-face as a friend was Jesus (Ex. 33:17-20), because there is too much glory around God for us as mere men to take in and live. If you want to get to know God, then learn about Jesus. Jesus revealed God in Himself throughout the Old and the New Testament.

Isaiah saw the Lord sitting on His throne in the temple, and His glory was all around (Isa. 6:3), yet John said that Isaiah said this because he saw Jesus's glory and spoke about Him (John 12:41). In Judges 13:3, Jesus is called the angel of the Lord, 13:6 He is the man of God, 13:9 the angel of God, and in 13:17 again He is called the angel of the Lord. Why did they not die? Because it was the Son and not the Father they saw and spoke to. John 5:22 tells us that the Father judges no one, but trust judgment to the Son. On that great judgment day, we will meet Jesus as Judge, and He has always been the Judge. Jesus brought judgment on the world through Noah's flood and rained down judgment on Sodom and Gomorrah. The

New Testament word for Lord is *Jesus,* and it was He that brought His people out of Egypt (Jude 5), He that brought us out of sin (John 3:16), and it will be He that leads us home (John 3:5).

Abraham, Jacob, Moses, Isaiah, Hagar, Joshua, Gideon, and Job all saw the invisible God revealed in Jesus Christ. They saw the great I Am, the King of Kings, the Lord of Lords. The Lord told Habakkuk to "write down the revelation and make it plain on tablets so that a herald might run with it. For the revelation awaits an appointed time; it speaks of the end and will not prove false. Though it linger, wait for it; it will certainly come and not delay" (Hab. 2:2-3). This revelation is written down for us from Genesis to Revelation, and our appointed time is around the corner. He who testifies to the book of Revelation says, "Yes, I am coming soon" (Rev. 22:20). Man is destined to die once, and after that to face judgment (Heb. 9:27), and that Judge will be Christ (1 Pet. 4:5). He is preparing a place (John 14:3) for all who accept Him to live with eternally, but it is usually a normality that we get acquainted with someone before we move into their house. Jesus asked Philip why he did not know Him, even though he had been around Him a long time (John 14:9). Will He have to ask you the same question?

13. *Questions and Answers*

Q: Why did Jesus say "peace be still"? Why did He use *peace* and *still* together?

A: Jesus is the Prince of Peace (Isa. 9:6). Jesus was not only speaking to the storm in Mark 4:39, but also to the disciples and to all who would follow Christ in the future. Even in the midst of outward turbulence, Jesus placed emphasis on peace. The elements obeyed His command, and the elements in our lives which rule our storms have within their center the presence of God. When Jesus spoke the word *peace* followed by *be still,* He caused the attention of the disciples to be directed toward the inner peace of God, rather than the outer storm. The moment they were reminded of the peace of God within them, they became still with reverence, and the storm ceased. Jesus promised an inner peace (John 14:27). Psalms 46:10 tells us to be still and know that He is God. Therefore, the words *peace* and *still* are used together to remind the storm on the sea and we who have storms in our lives that He is in control and will give us peace if we just be still (Job 37:11-12).

Q: What did Jesus mean about His statement in Matthew 10:24-25, 32-33?

A: Matthew 10:24-25 holds the meaning that since Jesus had been denied, rejected, and persecuted many ways, including being called Beelzebub (Satan), His disciples would suffer as He did. He was warning His disciples they would face the same persecution because a student is not above his teacher, but becomes like his teacher. He is saying since people were calling Him Beelzebub, then the disciples, who were taught by Him, must be demons (Matt. 12:22-28).

Matthew 10:32-33 is pretty plain in the fact that if you are not a born-again, believing Christian, you will not go to heaven. A person must confess what he believes about Jesus (John 9:38, 11:27, Rom. 10:9). Then you may have eternal life, to which you were called when you made your confession (1 Tim. 6:12-13). If you do not confess Christ as your Savior, then upon death, He will say, "Depart from me I never knew you" (Matt. 7:23). "Then they [the unsaved] will go away to eternal punishment" (Matt. 25:46).

Q: Why does Jesus Christ ask whether Peter loves him more than anyone else (John 21)?

A: The scripture does not explain why, but my theory is that Peter denied Jesus three times; therefore, in order to reinstate him, Jesus forgave him three times by asking the threefold question in John 21:15-19. Peter's three denials are listed in Matthew 26:69-75.

Q: In Luke 17:11-19, why did the nine out of ten lepers not return to thank Jesus after He healed them?

A: Only one of the men, a foreigner, that is, a Samaritan, came back to thank Jesus. This one understood the significance of what had been done for him. He apparently understood that Jesus was God, for he placed his faith in Him. Whether or not he understood that Jesus was the Messiah is not mentioned by Luke. The lack of gratitude by the other nine was typical of the rejection of His ministry by the Jewish nation. The nation did not respond properly to Jesus, accepting the things Jesus could do but not wanting to accept Him as Messiah. Those outside the nation, such as the Samaritan leper who was doubly repulsive to the Jews, were responsive.

Q: Did Jesus withdraw regularly for a quiet time with His Father or was it only on a few occasions?

A: The Bible only lists a few occasions, such as Matthew 14:23, Mark 1:35, and Luke 6:12. However, as it is written, "Jesus did many things as well. If every one of them were written down, I suppose that even the whole world would not have room for the books that would be written" (John 21:25).

Q: What does Jesus want us (Christians) to actually do? Does He want us to copy Him in everything we do? As we are human and sin however hard we try not to, how can we do this?

A: Yes, we have all sinned and fall short (Rom. 3:23) but we have been justified through faith and have peace with God and through repentance daily, we receive forgiveness. When we sin, we do not stumble so as to fall beyond recovery (Rom. 11:11). God wants you to not let sin reign in your mortal body, and do not obey its evil desires. Do not let your bodies be instruments of wickedness. Do not let sin be the master of your life (Rom. 6:11-14). He wants you to set your mind on Him and not earthly things (Col. 3:2) and whatever you do, work at it as if working for the Lord and not for man (Col. 3:23-25).

Part III. Good and Evil

1. Order of Angels

Cherubim are guardians, such as the Cherub placed at the east end of the Garden of Eden to prevent Adam and Eve from coming to the tree of life after they were expelled from the Garden (Gen. 3:22). A Seraph stands before God, crying holy, holy, holy. They execute God's purpose of holiness in the world. It is believed that Gabriel was the Seraph that came to Daniel to explain to him what would happen in the future to the people (Dan. 10:14).

There are at least five divisions of angels. The Seraphim are connected to the worship of God (Isa. 6:1); the Cherubim are connected to worship, moved by the Holy Spirit. Seraphim and Cherubim are connected with heaven, protecting the Throne of Heaven. Zoa is a living creature or beast and could be the creatures in Revelation 4 surrounding the throne. The Archangel Gabriel announced the coming of the Christ Child (Luke 1:19, 1 Thess. 4:16) and the second coming of Christ. Michael was the war angel and protector and the Archangel that came to Daniel (Dan. 10:13). Lucifer was also an

Archangel in charge of one-third of the angels in heaven before being cast out and becoming known as Satan (Isa. 14:12-15). Common angels look like men and are connected to the church, appearing on earth to bring God's messages and to protect mankind (Acts 1:10, Heb. 1:14).

Some truths about angels are that they are wise (2 Sam. 14:20), powerful (Rev. 18:1), obedient (Ps. 103:20), and have their own will (Isa. 14:12-14). They also need no rest (Rev. 4:8), can eat (Gen. 18:8), can appear and disappear (Heb. 13:2), and can speak (1 Cor. 13:1). They strengthen us (Luke 22:43), protect the saints (Ps. 34:7), bring answers to prayers (Acts 10), must not be worshiped or prayed to (Col. 2:18), and are without number (Dan. 7:9). Angels impart the will of God, help you to plan, clarify God's Word, and assist in fulfilling God's will (Acts 5:19). These angels must not be mistaken for butterflies or fairies, and should never be called up to do your bidding, as only God can send them as messengers and to minister to us.

2. More about Angels

There are different types of angels depicted in the Bible that have varying degrees of divine missions, names, and descriptions. They are said to be with God (Luke 1:19). There are more than 250 references to angels in the Bible, and 59 of the 66 books mention something about them. The Old Testament Hebrew word for *angel* means *messenger*, as does the New Testament Greek word. *Sons of God* is a term used in the sense that angels were created by God: "when the morning stars sang together and all the Sons of God shouted for joy" (Job 38:7). Angels are referred to as God's host and are spiritual beings created by God (Gen. 3:1-2; Gen 1:1; Col. 1:16-17; Neh. 9:6). Origen, one of the earliest biblical scholars living in the first century, recognized the notion of guardian angels. The Bible is not explicit on a personal guardian angel, but most believe they are under their protection.

They base their belief on "take heed that you do not despise one of these little ones, for I say to you that in heaven their angels always see the face of my Father who is in heaven" (Matt. 18:10).

Angels guard the righteous (Ps. 91:11), bring deliverance (Dan. 6:22), get you out of jail (Acts 5:19), execute His judgment (Ps. 78:49), and will be used to find everything that causes sin and all who do evil (Matt. 13:41). They will throw people into the fiery furnace on Judgment Day (Matt. 13:49-50); Jesus will come with the angels (Matt. 16:27), they will gather the righteous at the point of the rapture (Matt. 24:31; Mark 13:27), and they will carry the righteous to their home in the afterlife (Luke 16:22). God is just and He will pay back trouble to those who gave us trouble, and give relief to we who are troubled. This will happen when the Lord Jesus is revealed from heaven in blazing fire with His powerful angels (2 Thess. 1:6-7). Angels are powerful but do not have authority over their strength, but do God's commandments (Ps. 103:20). Bold, arrogant men are not afraid to slander celestial beings, "yet even angels, although they are stronger and more powerful, do not bring slanderous accusations against such beings in the presence of the Lord" (2 Pet. 2:10-11). The power of one angel is shown in 2 Kings 19:35, when the angel of the Lord went out and put to death 185,000 men in the Assyrian camp. Not bad for a night's work!

Angels are created beings who never die, grow older, or reproduce (Matt. 22:30; Luke 20:36). We are not only an example to the whole universe but to angels as well (1 Cor. 4:9). "Do you not know that we will judge angels?" (1 Cor. 6:3). Do you think we should be more careful in setting our examples, since we may be judging the actions that result from them? Since we are born of man and born again of Christ, and the angels are created beings, there is no way we will become angels when we die. The statement that "God needed another angel in heaven, so that is why so-and-so died" needs to cease. Jesus is not and never has been an angel, since in the beginning He was the Word and was with God. He and the Father are one, and through Him, all things were created (John 1:12, 10:30). Angels care for and encourage the outcast (Gen. 21:17), ministered to Jesus (Matt. 4:11; Luke 22:43), and explained the empty tomb (Matt. 28:56). They were on hand to instruct the disciples at the ascension of Jesus (Acts 1:10-11), and again to instruct Philip (Acts 8:26). They shut the mouth of the lions (Dan. 6:22), drove the chariots of God (Ps. 68:17, 2 Kings 6:17), freed Peter from prison (Acts 12:7), and gave encouragement to Paul (Acts 27:23-24).

"Immediately, because Herod did not give praise to God, an angel of the Lord struck him down and he was eaten by worms and died" (Acts 12:23). "So shall it be at the end of the world; the angels shall come forth and sever the wicked from among the just. And shall cast them into the furnace of fire; there shall be wailing and gnashing of teeth" (Matt. 13:49-50). The angels fight the dragon in end time (Rev. 12:7) and will announce the end of time Satan is doing a number on the saints this very day. Satan is an adversary! The dictionary defines *adversary* as one that contends with, opposes, or resists; an enemy! The Greek word, *diabolos, meaning devil according to the internet dictionary,* is an opponent/archenemy. The Hebrew word, *tsar,* is enemy/foe/tribulation. Webster's definition of Tsar is a former ruler of Russia; an autocrat which is a domineering ruler with absolute power. Jesus called Satan "the ruler of this world" (John 12:3, 16:11, 14:30). Paul called him "the god of this age" (2 Cor. 4:4). Paul emphasized this point: "In which you used to live when you followed the ways of this world and the ruler of the kingdom of the air" (Eph. 2:2). Satan influences what we hear from the air, such as what is projected over the radio and TV and movies, whether spoken, sung or suggested (Dan. 10:13-20, Matt. 9:34, 12:24).

Satan's fall from heaven is described in Isaiah 14:12-14 and Ezekiel 28:12-18. He fell because he tried to put himself above God. Scripture does not give an exact time for his fall, but we do know the angels, Satan then Lucifer being one of the most important angels, were created before the earth was (Job 38:4-7). Satan fell before he tempted Adam and Eve in the Garden of Eden (Gen. 3:1-14). Notice how many "I will" statements are in Isaiah 14:12-15. Don't imitate the devil and fall into the "I will" trap! "Why, you do not even know what will happen tomorrow"

(James 4:14). "Do not boast about tomorrow for you do not know what a day may bring forth" (Prov. 27:1). "Do not worry about tomorrow" (Matt. 6:34).

Satan is not omnipresent! He cannot be in more than one place at a time, however he has numerous helpers. He was persuasive enough to convince one-third of the angels to join in his rebellion (Rev. 12:4). He is very powerful, and evidently feared, since not even Michael, the archangel, dared to confront him without the Lord's permission (Jude 9). It is my opinion that Satan cannot read our minds, but he and his demons have been watching and tempting man for thousands of years. They can figure out our plans and use it to their advantage. There, we are commanded to "submit yourselves, then, to God" (James 4:7), before we are told to "resist the devil" (James 4:7).

The devil and his angels do not know all things, as God does (Matt. 24:36), but they seem to have a great knowledge of humans. They were created before the foundation of the earth, and shouted for joy as they watched (Job 38:4-7). They do not have to study the past, since they were part of it. Although not believers, they believe in God (James 12:19, Matt. 8:29). They are cunning and creative (2 Cor. 11:3, 14-15). Good angels, Satan, and demons are curious about the gospel (1 Pet. 1:12), show emotions (Rev. 12:17, Luke 8:28), and have wills (Jude 6; 2 Tim. 2:26). Satan stays close to God. "One day the angels came to present themselves before the Lord, and Satan also came with them" (Job 1:6-7, 2:1-2). He stands alongside of God, ready to accuse you (Ps. 109:6; Zech. 3:1). He can and will enter the body of an unbeliever (Luke 22:3; John 13:27). However, he needs the Lord's permission to test you (Luke 22:31), and be assured when this happens, God will pray for you (Luke 22:32). The devil lies and fills your thoughts (Acts 5:3), stops your spiritual progress (1 Thess. 2:18), and tricks the whole world (Rev. 12:9).

Don't look for a red ugly creature with a fork in his hand to be the devil. I hope you find time to read Ezekiel 28:11-19 and find out what Satan looks like. God said he was perfect, full of wisdom, and beautiful!

Even Satan changes himself to look like an angel of light, a messenger from God. So it does not surprise us if Satan's servants, false prophets, apostles, also make themselves look like servants who work for what is right (2 Cor. 11:14-15). "But in the end they will be punished for what they do" (Matt. 25:41; 2 Pet. 2:4; Rev. 19:20). He is only a created being, and his power does not compare with God's. When the right time comes, God will command an angel to tie up the devil and throw him into the lake of fire (Rev. 20:1, 10). The one who was born of God, Jesus, keeps the believer safe, and the evil one, Satan, cannot harm him (1 John 5:13). "Keep yourselves in God's love as you wait for the mercy of our Lord Jesus Christ to bring you to eternal life" (Jude 21). "Therefore, stand firm, let nothing move you, always give yourselves fully to the work of the Lord, because you know that your labor in the Lord is not in vain" (1 Cor. 15:58). "I pray that the God who gives hope will fill you with much joy and peace while you trust in Him" (Rom. 15:13).

3. Satan's Abode

It has come to my attention that some believe that Satan lives in hell and has no access to the earth we live in. Nor do they think that he has access to heaven, since the scripture says that he was kicked out. It has also been asked why God even created the devil. We can't learn too much about Satan and the evil demons that do his bidding. In the last days, he will wear out the saints (Dan. 7:25). God never created the devil as we know him, but a pure spirit being of great wisdom and glory. "You were an example of what was perfect, full of wisdom and perfect in beauty. You had a wonderful life, as if you were in Eden, the Garden of God. Every valuable gem was on you; ruby, topaz and emerald, yellow quartz, onyx and jasper; sapphire, turquoise and chrysolite. Your jewelry was made of gold. It was prepared on the day you were created. I appointed a living creature to guard you. I put you on the holy mountain of God. You walked among the gems that shined like fire. Your life was right and good from the day you were created until evil was found in you" (Ezek. 28:12-15).

These verses refer to the angel Lucifer, who had a special position at the throne of God. When he tried to put himself above God, he was cast out of heaven and down to the earth (Isa. 14:12). When God created mankind, Satan was on hand to ruin the perfect being (Gen. 3:1-4, 22-23). He is so vain and prideful, he even tried to spoil Jesus Christ (Matt. 4:9). Satan and his angels are not in hell. They are free and have tremendous powers if you allow them into your life. This is why Ephesians 6:11-12 tells us to put on the whole armor of God, that you will be able to stand up against the devil's schemes. He is the prince of the power of the air, such as things coming through the radio, TV, etc. (Eph. 2:2) and the god of this world (2 Cor. 4:4).

The Bible speaks of three heavens. (l). The heaven of earth's atmosphere; "God gave us rain from heaven" (Acts 14:17), "and fowls that may fly above the earth in the open firmament of heaven" (Gen. 1:20). (2). The heaven of the stars. Here are high or heavenly places where the principalities and powers of evil have their abode (Eph. 6:12). (3). The heaven where God dwells. This was the third heaven where Apostle Paul was caught up (2 Cor. 12:1-4). Satan is able to enter God's presence. When the sons of God came to present themselves before the Lord, Satan came with them (Job 1:6, 2:1). He told God he had come from roaming through the earth (Job 1:7, 2:2). He still has access to heaven, and is the accuser of our brethren (Rev. 12:10). Isaiah refers to the king of Babylon as Day Star, a son of Dawn which the King James Version translates, *Lucifer* (Isa. 14:12). The word means light-bearer, and signified the planet Venus, which preceded or accompanied the rising of the sun. Jesus may have had reference to the Isaiah passage when He spoke of Satan falling from heaven (Luke 10:8).

The devil is not very interested in leading men and women into gross sin, but is satisfied just to get man's heart away from God. He is an imitator and works in the realm of religion. Through the influence of Satan, the authority of God's Word is being questioned everywhere. We are told that all the miracles of Jesus can be explained naturally, that the Virgin Birth is incredible, that the second coming of Christ is not true and has no literal acceptance. These lies are not taught in bars and crack houses, but in some of our new age churches today. Satan told Eve in the Garden of Eden that if she ate of the fruit, she would not die as God said, but she would be as smart and all-knowing as God (Gen 3:5). This is the same false promise Satan dangles before the eyes of our high school and university students. They are taught that to be learners of truth they must accept the authority of modern scholarship over and above the authority of the Bible.

The Bible teaches that the devil quotes scripture (Matt. 4:6), but be careful that you listen carefully. He twists it and leaves out words to confuse you. He transforms himself into an angel of light, afflicts the body, causes weakness that paralyses, sows harmful tares, brings impure thoughts, tempts us through pride, uses outward circumstances to hinder, causes evil men to pervert the gospel of Christ, seduces some from Christ by pleasure. We are warned that he is a roaring lion, and we are commanded to resist him. We are forbidden to hold any discussion with him as the provoker to wrath, and instructed to fight with truth (Matt. 4:6, 13:38-39; 2 Cor. 11:14, 12:7; 1 Cor. 5:5, 7:5; Mark 4:15; 1 Tim. 3:6, 5:11, 15; 1 Thess. 2:18; Acts 13:10; 1 Pet. 5:8; James 4:7; Eph. 4:27, 6:14).

Learn all you can about Satan from the Word of God, so you will know where he is coming from and how to fight him. We can overcome the enemy and enter into the victory which Christ won on the cross by yielding our lives as living sacrifices unto our Savior (Rom 12:1). Our sophisticated, materialistic world does not want to be disturbed by the idea of a personal devil. It would upset one's freedom to sin if he does exist and has come to kill, steal, and destroy (John 10:10). "He is filled with anger because he knows he does not have much time" (Rev. 12:12). Let us praise God that there will be a final victory over Satan. God promised such a victory at the beginning of time. "I will make you and the woman enemies to each other. Your descendants and her descendants will be enemies. One of their descendants will crush your head, and you will bite his heel" (Gen. 3:15). We have the same promise in Romans

16:20. There is a second time recorded that Satan is kicked out of heaven (Rev. 12:7-9). This is the second boot, and he does not return. During the millennium, the devil is bound. Following this 1,000-year reign of Christ, he will be loosed for a time (Rev. 7), but will meet his final doom in Revelation 20:10. "And the devil that deceived them was cast into the lake of fire and brimstone, where the beast and the false prophet are, and shall be tormented day and night for ever and ever!"

4. Sin Creator

In the Bible, the sin creator is called the devil (Matt. 13:39), Satan, dragon, and snake (Rev. 20:10), the prince of the world (John 12:31), the deceiver (Rev. 12:9), and the serpent (Rev. 12:9). Where did the devil come from and why hasn't God destroyed him? The Word of God tells the truth about Satan. The devil has been sinning from the beginning (1 John 3:8). When Adam and Eve sinned, it was the beginning of our trouble. However, the real beginning in 1 John took place in heaven. Lucifer was his name in heaven, and he was a guardian cherub, ordained and blameless in his ways (Ezek. 28:14-15). The cherub that covered is a description of the angel that stood next to the throne of God in heaven (Ps. 80:1) and was one of the most honored of all created beings. Lucifer rebelled against God and decided he would be king of heaven. Although all his glory was from God, this mighty angel began to give himself credit for it. Not content with his position, probably one of the most high in heaven except for God, he soon found himself coveting homage due the Creator, and trying to make himself greater than God (Isa. 14:12-15, Exe. 28:17).

This was not to be! He was cast out of heaven along with the angels that followed after him (Rev. 12:7-9). All peace and harmony were gone and there was war in heaven. Had God permitted Satan and the angels with him to continue their rebellion, peace could never again have been possible, not only in heaven, but also throughout the entire universe.

God could have easily eliminated Satan and all his rebellious angels in one blinding flash. Had He done so, the other angels along with all the inhabitants of the world would have served and obeyed Him out of fear, rather than love. Only if they obeyed would they not be destroyed. God wants us to obey because we love Him, so He allowed sin to run its course, to demonstrate to the whole universe the consequences of rebellion and disobedience, and to prove beyond a shadow of a doubt God's unchanging character and the nature of His love.

No longer free to stir up rebellion in heaven, Satan's hatred against God found a new area to cause havoc. He found Adam and Eve in the Garden of Eden and sowed weeds among the wheat and planted seeds of doubt (Matt. 13:24-30, 37-40). Note that the devil knows the scripture better than you and I. He will use it against you, changing just one word or perhaps leaving out one word. He will also lie about himself! He will assure you that if you are a child of God, you can do as you please and nothing can harm you. He did this to Jesus in the wilderness (Luke 4:9-10). God appointed Adam the governor of this world, its king and ruler (Gen. 1:28). As soon as Adam was overcome, the dominion of this planet was claimed by the deceiver (Job 1:6-8). He will claim whatever you allow him, and when you let him have rule over something in your life, it is hard to reclaim. Refuse to give in to him, and stand strong in your faith. He still goes around like a roaring lion, looking for someone to devour, and we are not to let our guard down (1 Pet. 5:8-9).

Do not look for the sin creator to be a little red creature when you feel the devil tormenting you. Remember, he was the brightest of the angels (Isa. 14:12) and even now can change to an enticing angel (2 Cor. 11:14). Sin and temptation come in beautiful forms! He is the ruler of the evil powers that are above the earth (Eph. 2:2), which most likely includes the airways that in turn include our computers, so be careful what you bring into your home by way of modern technology. The devil is working viciously to gather all to him that will come, because he has little time left to deceive this world (Rev. 12:12). He knows the warning that God gives that He will destroy and expel him (Ezek. 28:16-19), and he will be no more. We are dealing with an intelligent being that once lived in heaven and knows the final chapter of God's book. This great imposter, who swayed the angels of heaven by his false logic and cunning sophistry, is certainly more than a match for us. We are safe only as we trust in God's power, and in all Satan's ranks, there is not enough power to overcome one soul who casts himself in trust at the feet of Jesus (Isa. 40:29).

During His ministry on this earth, Christ was constantly harassed by the devil. He dogged His footsteps, continually trying to destroy the Savior before He accomplished His mission. Satan, through Herod, had all the male children under the age of two put to death in a frantic effort to rid the world of the Savior as a baby. After His baptism, Christ was led into the wilderness for a time, to be tempted by Satan, but countered with scripture, and Satan fled (Luke 4:12-13). Notice that the scripture says that the devil left to wait until a better time! Be on your guard, lest he comes in the back door while you are watching the front. On several occasions, Satan tried to kill Christ by inciting a riot on the part of the Jewish rulers, but each time Jesus was protected (John 10:31-39). Satan must have been elated when Christ drew His final breath on the cross, and hurried to place a guard at the tomb and have it sealed in an attempt to keep the Savior in the tomb forever. But Roman guards and Roman seals were powerless to confine the Lord of life within the tomb.

When Satan saw that the Lord had taken up His life again, he knew that his doom was sealed. Furious with defeat, he has zeroed in on Christ's followers in an all-out effort to keep Christ from the rightful fruits of His victory. This is the only way he can now bring pain to the heart of God. The only defense for man against the devil's deceptions is the full armor of God (Eph. 6:11-17). Remember the 1040 window? There is a triangle from South Africa, across the Indian Ocean, including India and China, on to Japan and across and including Russia, Iran, and Saudi Arabia, down to Turkey, Lebanon, and back to South Africa. This is the hardest place to get Christianity into. This is Satan's seat! But do not be deceived into thinking that we are not in his sights!

What a God we have to provide such abundant means for successful warfare against the evil one. The Bible is an armory where we may equip ourselves for the struggle. Don't leave home without it!

5. *Signs of Time*

We have learned that Satan got into the Garden of Eden illegally (Gen. 3). He slithered in, disguised as a serpent. Although he was created by God and an angel (Ps. 148:2, 5), he has no soul or spirit. He cannot be saved! He was not born of the flesh, and therefore cannot be saved by the Spirit of God. When he caused Adam and Eve to eat of the forbidden tree and sin, he then told them that they could live forever in the Garden. God had other plans! He cast them out of the Garden, just as He cast Satan out of heaven! God then put an angel at the gate of the Garden, so they could not get back in and partake of the fruit of the Tree of Life (Gen. 3:22-24). And the Lord said, "The man has now become like one of us, knowing good and evil. He must not be allowed to reach out his hand and take also from the Tree of Life and eat and live forever." What Satan wanted them to do after they had fallen into sin was to get the fruit from the tree and live forever in their sinful state, and he would have partners in his crimes.

So the Lord God banished Adam from the Garden of Eden to work the ground from which he had been taken. After Adam was out of the Garden, God put an angel there on the east side with a flaming sword to keep intruders out. Ever since this time, the devil has been trying to find a way back into the Garden without God and without going through the angel with the flaming sword. One way of trying to do this is the cloning of a baby girl in Israel named Eve. The name *Eve* means "the mother of all living things" and the cloning is man's attempt to live forever without God. In 1980, a cult leader said he encountered aliens, and the aliens brought life to earth. The leader of the cult said, "We are trying to create a sect of people, through cloning, who will have eternal life and they will never die if cloned." Cloning is life on this planet that God did not bring about. Why is this prophetic? If that child has been cloned, and they say that it has, that messes up the human race as God created it. "If you want to know what it will be like when I come back, go to the days of Lot and Noah. As it was in the days of Lot and Noah, so also will it be in the days of the Son of Man. You will see the same things going on then as you will see when I am about to come again" (Luke 17:26).

Do you remember what the days of Noah were like? We read in Genesis 6 about the sons of God (fallen angels) coming to earth and having relationships with the daughters of men. They produced a new race of people on the earth that God did not create. Then God decided He would kill the entire race. As it was then, we are seeing a new race of people through cloning. We are living in the days that the prophets told of. God wiped out the people, except for Noah and his family. He said in Noah, He found perfection in the bloodline. Not intermingled with demonic power. Do not be passive, saying that none of this cloning stuff and alien sightings affects you! Everything around you affects you in some way, and we have to stand up for the rights God gave us and proclaim our inheritance of eternal life.

6. *The Devil's Lies and The Christian's Solutions*

The Bible tells us about Lucifer, the most important angelical creature, who decided he would go up and sit on God's throne. As a result, the Lord cast him out of His presences, and division was caused among the angels (Isa. 14:12-15). Since that time, Satan's main purpose has been to cause division wherever he appears. He divides families and churches alike (1 Pet. 5:8). Just a few of the devil's lies include: If you were a Christian, you would not continue to sin, which scripture will counteract with 1 John 1:8-10. You must not love the Lord or you wouldn't have sinned, to which Romans 3:23 states all have sinned but we are justified by the grace of God. Satan tells you that this Christian idea is just not working for you, so give it up. But Galatians 6:9 says we will be rewarded for our good deeds in time if we do not lose heart and give up. The evil one will say that all around you are lost and going to hell but you are doing nothing about it. You just continue to follow Jude 23 and snatch them from the fire. The greatest lie that Satan will tell you is that you have committed the unpardonable sin, which is to deny that Jesus is the Son of God and your Savior. Prove the devil a liar by reading out loud John 3:16 and Romans 8:1-7. "The weapons we fight with are not the weapons of the world. On the contrary, they have divine power to demolish strongholds" (2 Cor. 10:4-5). Fight the devil with the armor of God, and be obedient to the Lord, even to your thoughts, and fight against the devil's schemes (Eph. 4:27, 2 Tim. 2:26).

There is safety in numbers. Jesus prayed for our unity: "I will remain in the world no longer but they are still in the world and I am coming to you. Holy Father, protect them by the power of your name, the name you gave me, so that they may be one as we are one" (John 17:11). Don't forget to put on the whole armor of God (Eph. 6:11), have your feet shod with the preparation of peace, walk in peace wherever you go and in whatever you do, and have peace through our Prince of Peace (Isa. 9:6). Put on the belt of truth (Isa. 11:5) and speak the truth in love, being a doer of the Word and not a hearer or reader only (James 1:22). The ancient soldier's belt girded up or tied up all the loose clothing hanging down from his waist so he could move freely, unencumbered to fight the enemy. Truth is what girds up the loins of our mind! Put on the breastplate of righteousness (Isa. 59:17), for we are the righteousness of God in Christ (2 Cor. 5:17). Righteousness is right standing with God. Our hearts are free from guilt and condemnation. This defends our hearts from the enemy's corruption.

Put on the helmet of salvation and ask Christ to guard your mind, your will, and your emotions (Isa. 59:17). "Think only on those things that are good and pure and just and right and of a good report (Phil. 4:8). The work of salvation in our life is a helmet that covers the nerve center of our lives. Hold out the shield of faith to put out all the fiery darts that Satan can throw at you. God said that no weapon formed against you will prosper (Isa. 54:17). All those who rise up against you, including the devil, will fall. Every tongue that speaks against you, including the devil's lies, will cease immediately (2 Cor. 10:4-5), and you will not fear, for the Greater One is living inside you. Satan has indeed come to steal our peace, destroy our faith, and kill our trust in God (John 10:10), but Jesus came to give us life. We have been redeemed from the curse of the Law, and now we are living under the protection of the Most High God (Ps. 91:1-2).

Finally, take out the sword of the Spirit, which is the Word of God, and use these powerful words against the devil. Every time Jesus was tempted, He responded offensively with God's Word. We must know God's Word in order to use it to conquer the assaults of the devil.

In the third century, one man tells another about a quiet and holy people. It seemed to him to be a cheerful world when he view it from a fair garden under the shadow of hanging vines. But if one climbed some great mountain and looked out over the wide lands, they would see Brigands on the high road, pirates on the seas, in the amphitheaters men murdered to please the applauding crowds, under all roofs misery and selfishness. It seemed to be bad world, an incredibly bad world. Yet, in the midst of it, he reported that he had found a quiet and holy people. They have discovered a joy which was a thousand times better than any pleasure of this sinful life. They were despised and persecuted, but they did not care because they have overcome the world! These people were Christians, and he one of them.

Do you deserve this compliment? If so, God bless you! If you feel you do not measure up, God bless you and may you study God's Word daily to become "one of them"! I, for one, am still working on the "quiet" part (Ps. 141:3).

7. Demons

We are never specifically told where demons come from. The Bible does seem to indicate, however, that the demons are fallen angels—angels who, along with Lucifer, rebelled against God and fell from heaven. Jude 6 mentions angels who sinned, so it is likely that demons are the angels that followed Lucifer in sin. Satan and his demons now look to destroy and deceive all those who follow and worship God. The Word of God declares that demons do indeed exist (1 Kings 22:21-23; 2 Chr. 18:20-22; Matt. 25:41; Luke 8:26-40; Rev. 12:4). Even though they are spirit beings, demons have a will, mentality, self-consciousness, emotions, a conscience, and an old sin nature (Luke 11:24-26). As angels, demons speak to each other in angelic languages (1 Cor. 13:1). Those demons who are not in jail waiting for the Great White Throne Judgment, Satan has organized into a spiritual army (Eph. 6:12, 2 Pet. 2:4, Jude 6, Rev. 20:13).

The rulers in Satan's spiritual army are called principalities and powers (Eph. 6:12). A principality is a Greek term meaning the highest-ranking rulers in Satan's army. Powers refers to those demonic rulers who supervise the five divisions in this army of darkness: (1). Kosmokrator demons: Their assignment is to attack government leaders and believers. They are called rulers of darkness of this world (Eph. 6:12) and prince of the kingdom of Persia (Dan. 10:13). Their main objective, as with all demons, is to get man to follow Satan's policy of evil. His plan is to destroy the divine institutions of freedom, marriage, the family, and divine established government (2 Sam. 24:1-25; 1 Chr. 2:11; 2 Cor. 2:11). (2). Nosos demons: These spirits indwell unbelievers and cause various physical and mental abnormalities, such as dumbness (Matt. 9:32, 33; Luke 11:14), insanity (Matt. 17:14-18), and physical ailments (Luke 13:10-17). (3). Engastrimuthos (ventriloquist): These spirits are responsible for séances and fortune-telling (Lev. 19:31; Deut. 18:9-14). (4). Anomos (lawless): These demons concentrate on counterfeit religious and political false doctrine (1 Kings 22:20-23; 2 Chr. 18:22; 1 Tim. 4:1). (5). Magos (magician): These spirits indwell unbelievers and perform miracles (Ex. 7:10-13; Matt. 7:22).

The Bible also does not specifically tell us if a Christian can be demon-possessed. However, since a Christian is indwelt by the Holy Spirit (Rom. 8:9-11; 1 Cor. 3:16, 6:19) it seems unlikely that the Holy Spirit would allow a demon to dwell in the same person in which He is living. "You dear children, are from God and have overcome them, because the one who is in you is greater that the one who is in the world" (1 John 4:4). God is the one in us and the devil is the one in the world, along with his demons. We are never given a reason to believe that a true believer can be demon-possessed, but many reasons to believe that a believer can be oppressed, harassed, and literally harmed by these demons. Now, believing that a Christian cannot be possessed by demons, remember that a Christian can indeed be influenced by them (Acts 5:3; 2 Cor. 11:3; 2 Tim. 2:25-26). They can and will suggest evil but cannot coerce the will of another creature. They are limited in their power and can do nothing without the urging of Satan, and Satan can do nothing without the permission of God (Job 1:8-12).

It is possible for a person to be saved who was previously demon-possessed (Mark 16:9). One way that demons prevent unbelievers from being saved is to cause them to forget the gospel before they respond to it. This is done through influencing them to be occupied with other things (Luke 8:12). When you are witnessing to someone and they change the subject, they probably are under the attack of the devil. Pray and never give up on witnessing! There will be more demonic activity in the tribulation than at any other time in history of the world (Rev. 9:20-21, 12:7-9, 16:14, 18:2). We as believers will be the judge over the demons at the throne (1 Cor. 6:3; Rev. 20:11-15). Don't let them get the best of you before we get our chance to get the best of them. As with Satan, don't look for demons to be ugly and mean, for as also with Satan, they appear as beautiful, showing the grass to be greener on the other side. Actually, I have not written this for you to begin looking in all the corners for demons. Do not invite them into your life and do not fear that they are in every nook and cranny in your house. No believer should ever be afraid of demons, but be aware that they do indeed exist, and resist them if you feel their presence in your territory (James 4:7).

8. *Questions and Answers*

Q: Are all strongholds sin?

A: Sin is Satan's stronghold! There are many scriptures to guide you to safety and deliverance from Satan's strongholds under God's care. A godly stronghold would be a place of refuge or defense, such as a mountain fortress, guard tower, or hideout (Jud. 6:2; 1 Chr. 12:8; Isa. 33:16) or a strategic point on the walls of a city (Isa. 25:12; Ps. 89:40; Lam 2:2). Stronghold is a frequent metaphor for God as the one who gives judgment on behalf of the oppressed (Ps. 9:9; Jer. 16:19) or the one who guards the lives of those who trust Him (Ps. 27:1; Nah. 1:7). The Lord is our stronghold over Satan through Jesus who appeared (was born) to destroy the works of the devil (1 John 3:8). As long as we have a relationship with Jesus as our Savior, Deliverer, Lord, and King, then He is our stronghold (Ps. 18:2, 46:4). The Holy Spirit is our stronghold (Rom. 8:24-26) and the Blood of Jesus is our stronghold (John 1:7).

Q: If, at one time, a person in your life was a devil, will they always be a devil?

A: The first thing is that no human was or ever will be a devil. The devil is Satan, who was Lucifer, a God-created creature (Ps. 148:1-5) and is a spirit (Heb. 1:14) and will never be a human being. God can do all things, and an evil person can be changed through repentance and salvation (John 3:16; Rom. 10:9; Acts 2:21). God desires all to be saved (1 Tim. 2:4) and draws people to Himself (John 6:44), and the Holy Spirit teaches them the truth of the gospel (John 14:17, 26).

Q: How in Matthew 7:21-23, can people cast out demons in Jesus's name and do miracles in His name without knowing the Lord and being saved?

A: These doing miracles that Jesus denied are false prophets. They are all throughout the Bible, starting with Satan, that old serpent in the Garden of Eden. Moses's miracles were duplicated by Pharaoh's magicians (Ex. 7:11-12, 22, 8:7). Paul tells us of some non-believing Jews who were driving out evil spirits with the name of Jesus, but even the evil spirits said they did not know them, and Jesus warned not to believe them (Acts 19:13; Matt 7:21-23; Matt. 24:23-26). Paul calls them deceitful workmen (2 Cor. 11:13-14), and John tells to test every spirit to see if it is from God (1 John 4:1-6).

Q: Why does the Bible talk about the heart being evil? I thought sin originated in our minds and thoughts.

A: We are born with deceitful hearts (Jer. 17:9-10); evil hearts are the hearts of unsaved people (Luke 6:45; Gen. 8:21; Ps. 14:1). Now that we are saved, God has circumcised our hearts, cutting away the evil, sinful part (Deut. 30:6), putting in a heart of flesh (Ezek. 37:26-27). This is the only new body part God offers, and even after this, we do things we do not want to do because of our sinful human nature (Rom. 7:15), because there is evil working on the mind (Rom. 7:23, 7:14). Your heart is new when saved but your mind must be continuously renewed (Rom. 12:2; Eph. 4:22-23).

Q: Is it wrong for a Christian to carry a gun when the devil is trying to "take you out"?

A: The weapons we fight with are not the weapons of the world, and worldly weapons would do no good against the devil and his schemes (John 10:10; 2 Cor. 10:3-5). God will save you from the hands of the wicked (Jer. 15:21), the Lord will rebuke the devil (Zech. 3:2), Jesus will give you anything you ask in His name (John 14:14), and you have been given the armor of God to fight the devil (Eph. 6:10-17).

Q: Does the Bible say anything about drug dealing, and is it a sin that can be forgiven?

A: Anything that causes one to lose his senses or turn away from God is a sin. Drug dealing is not listed in the Bible under detestable practices, but comes under the heading of witchcraft, sorcery, casting spells, etc. Anyone using these practices, including dealing drugs, can cause another to come under their control and sin against God (Deut. 18:10-12; John 8:44; Rev. 22:15; Gal. 6:7-8). God has already forgiven all people of all sin (Isa. 43:25; Ps. 85:2; Heb. 8:12; 1 John 2:12), but all must repent and ask for this forgiveness in their life (1 John 1:9; Acts 2:38; John 3:16).

Part IV Prayer

1. Learning to Pray and Why We Should

The weather was strange that day. The sun was shining but an unusual fog-like condition in the air over Texas brought consternation to many a pilot zeroing in on Dallas. They could see the city itself, but not the airport. It was a big airport where giant 747s land and take off, but they could not spot it through the cloudy atmosphere. "We ought to get a glimpse of it any minute," the pilot said. He picked up his radio and called the tower, and the answer came sharp and clear: "Proceed on course!" As they continued flying on course, there were more exchanges between the pilot and the tower. At last, they saw the airport, and the tower told them which runway to use. The plane banked sharply, leveled off, and landed safely. A man in the tower, completely unseen by the pilot and the passengers, had guided their landing. God's mighty cable of prayer, like the radio beams by which the pilot and the tower communicated, provides a two-way system of communication between heaven and earth.

"Well, I don't know," some say. "I'm not sure prayer is that good. I prayed once and didn't get any results; no one answered." Many are asking, "Is prayer real or just an exercise of the mind? If prayer isn't any good for holding off disaster, what is it good for?" Is there a certain formula that some people use? Let's look at a few secrets of successful prayer. It is my prayer that your own prayer life will be extended as we study God's Word on the subject.

The disciples once requested Jesus to teach them to pray, and it would be good for all of us to be very familiar with what He taught them—commonly known as the Lord's Prayer, found in Matthew 6:9-13. And if you allow God to pour down on you all the words contained in this prayer, you have to get results. Prayer is not just asking for things. God is not connected to a slot machine, nor is He to be compared to Santa Claus, who brings stuff in secret and you never really know who he is. Prayer is opening your heart to God, as your would to a friend. At times, it may be communion in utter silence with a sacred sense of God's presence (Ps. 46:10). While on earth, Christ missed the face-to-face communion with God that He had enjoyed in heaven. He spent much time in prayer, talking to His Father. Jesus came not only to save us and heal us but to set examples for us to follow. Prayer is one of His best examples.

We cannot earn God's favor through prayer, because "He sends rain to those who do right and to those who do wrong" (Matt. 5:45). Praying to show how religious you are does not impress God. Jesus called the ones who prayed to be noticed hypocrites (Matt. 6:5). David said, "Lord, you have examined me and know all about me" (Ps. 139:1), so why then do we need to tell God our needs? He never tires of our coming to Him in sincere prayer. We may unburden our hearts to Him whenever we need, and we can take our time in prayer. He will never rush you and He is never too busy to listen and give peace. He is willing to give the Holy Spirit to those who ask (Luke 11:13). We pray because we need God (Luke 18:13), and apart from God, we can do nothing (John 15:5).

We have promises from God for those who pray. "Enjoy serving the Lord and He will give you what you want" (Ps. 37:4). "If you remain in me and follow my teachings you can ask anything you want and it will be given to you" (John 15:7). "Then you will call my name. You will come to me and pray to me and I will listen to you" (Jer. 29:12). And my personal favorite, "I will provide for their needs before they ask and I will help them while they are still asking for help" (Isa. 65:24).

There are requirements of prayer. Believe, trust (Mark 11:14), pray in faith (James 1:5-7), if we have sin in our heart, the Lord will not hear (Ps. 66:18), so we pray and ask God to remove the sin (Prov. 28:13). There are requirements for answered prayer also. Believe that you are going to get what you ask for, and it will happen (1 John 3:22), believe He hears us (1 John 5:14-15), and pray according to His will. Our Savior was facing the greatest trial of His life in the Garden of Gethsemane. Sweating large drops of blood, He prayed three times for the cup of suffering to pass from Him. Jesus was tempted to go back to His Father and leave the human race to the results of their own sins. However, His prayer went on: "But do what you want not what I want" (Matt. 26:39). Remember this scripture the next time you are tempted to pray a purely selfish prayer.

Additional scriptures on prayer include Luke 11:2 stating that we are to pray to the Father, in the name of Jesus (John 14:14). The Holy Spirit joins you in prayer (Rom. 8:26), and always mingle your prayers with thanksgiving (Phil. 4:6). We are to be in a spirit of prayer all the time (1 Thess. 5:17), while we work, while we talk, while we drive, especially the way some of us drive. There must also be earnest, secret prayer (Matt. 6:6). The devil will do all he can to stop this communion, for he knows he is no match for the one who connects himself to heaven by the holy habit of prayer.

Jesus prayed early in the morning, in the evening, and at times, all night. He prayed in public, in private, for the disciples, for His enemies and for all who would ever believe, and that includes you and me (John 17:20). And now He is in heaven, making intercession for us (Heb. 7:25). Shall we, who are only weak mortals, neglect to pray when we have available, through Christ, all power in heaven and earth (Matt. 28:18)? In addition to prayer, we should "stand like a guard to watch and place myself at the tower. I will wait to see what He will say to me; I will wait to learn how God will answer my complaint" (Hab. 2:1). Don't just pray and jump up, going about your business. Wait on the Lord! He may have something to say to you!

2. Prayer

I love to pray, and schedule time into every day for prayer. I pray online, on the phone, on my porch, and to myself if there is no one else around who wants me to pray for them. I don't mean to sound weird here, but I pray a lot for my computer. That old serpent, the devil, gets into it once in a while and causes havoc. After having it worked on a couple of times and reprogramming everything, I have learned to pray over it before I go to work. The devil hates these computers that are used for the Lord's work, and especially writings that might have brought someone out of the darkness into the light because of receiving them (John 1:1-5, 8:12; 1 Pet. 2:9).

Is prayer really necessary, or is this something you do as you grow older because of lack of anything else to do? If God is sovereign, doesn't that mean that He will accomplish what He wants when He wants (Rom. 9:14)? Then why the need for prayer? Is God's will for a Christian automatically guaranteed or is it linked to prayer? Why does it often take so long to get an answer to your prayer? Why is persistence required? Jacob wrestled with God all night until he received the blessing he wanted (Gen. 32:24-28). Have you ever wrestled with God in prayer all night long? Try it! It works! What about prayer for the lost? How many ways can you pray for the lost and watch them continue to go their own way? Have you ever walked up to one and said, "Hey! I am praying for you and you are causing my prayers to go unanswered?" Try that on also if God gives you the courage, but be prepared for any comment that comes back to you. Before you go out to try this, put on the full armor of God (Eph. 6:11-18). Notice in verse 18, it says never give up. How many ways can you ask God to save someone and wonder why He has not done so? It is as though we try too hard! We try very hard to save people, forgetting that saving people is not within our capacity. God wants everyone to be saved (2 Pet. 3:9), so why do we have the feeling we have to talk Him into saving the one we are praying for? Do you give God their excuses for them? Have you asked any of these questions? Are you getting tired of asking and not getting answers? Many people have stopped asking these questions, and when they did, they probably stopped praying. "Let us not become weary in doing good, for at the proper time, we will reap a harvest if we do not give up" (Gal. 6:9). That harvest, of course, is the lost being brought to Christ.

If Satan is defeated and Christ has all authority, then why must we persevere in prayer to save their souls from the devil and his hell? Intercessory prayer is standing in the gap (Ezek. 22:30) to build up a wall of prayer before the Lord on behalf of someone so that He will not destroy them. It is your duty to pray for the wicked (Ezek. 3:18-19), and if you do not, then God just might hold you responsible for their spiritual death. The Lord asked who He might send, and Isaiah (6:8) answered: "Here am I! Send me!" Do you set yourself up to be sent to bring the unsaved to Christ, to heal the sick and to witness? Ask and He will prepare you to go, where to go, and what to say after you get there (Matt. 10:16). He will speak through you, and it is a privilege and a honor to be sent by God.

When we are praying, we must bear one another's burdens (Gal. 6:2). How do we bear another's burden? The word *bear* in the scriptures means to carry away. We can bear each other's burdens and go boldly to the throne of grace with confidence and receive mercy and find grace for ourselves and the one you carry with you in prayer (Heb. 4:16). Jesus set us an example of praying for our own needs. "During the days of Jesus's life on earth, He offered up prayers and petitions with loud cries and tears to the one who could save Him from death, and He was heard because of His reverent submission" (Heb 5:7). Jesus prayed for everyone, including you and me, and because He did, we should (John 17:1-26).

No one is born a prayer warrior. They are shaped and refined, and put in a lot of practice. There are few born singers, painters, or anything else, but all take practice and dedication. Now, of course, the potential is there for artists, but so do we have potential to become a prayer warrior. The instructions are in the Bible, and we must schedule our time to get in practice sessions. Paul says to be joyful when you pray and pray continually, giving thanks in all circumstances (1 Thess. 5:16-18). Don't be anxious, but ask God for what you need (Phil. 4:6), devote yourself and your time to prayer (Col. 4:2), and pray and make intercession for everyone (1 Tim. 2:1).

God is not offended by sincere questions. He will not satisfy the skeptic, and is displeased with unbelief, but He loves an honest seeker. If you look for God with all your heart and soul, He will let you find Him (Deut. 4:29). Do you need to pray for one thing more than once? Elijah prayed seven times for the sky to open up and drop out rain, and not only did he pray, he continued to send his servant to check on the cloud condition. Only after the seventh time did the servant come back to say there was a tiny cloud in the sky (1 Kings 18:44-45). This was enough to stir up Elijah's faith, and he warned Ahab to ride fast to beat the rain, and rain it did. Daniel prayed for twenty-one days without ceasing and without eating choice food until his prayer was answered (Dan. 9:22-23, 10:12-14). Now God heard his prayer from the first day he prayed, but Daniel had no way of knowing that, so he continued to pray until the angel came to tell him it was answered. Were these answered prayers the work of Elijah and Daniel? No! It was the obedience of Elijah and Daniel! God chose to shut up the heavens for three years and six months, and then He chose Elijah to be his servant of prayer to open the sky again.

Daniel was reading the prophecy of Jeremiah, that Israel would be taken captive and would find release in seventy years. Realizing that the seventy years was at an end, Daniel did not sit back and rest on his heels, rejoicing in his coming freedom, but began to pray. When we realize that our prayer has been answered for revival, healing, salvation, restoration, etc., we tend to sit back passively and wait for God to act. This is not what Daniel did. Something told him that God desired his involvement, because he said that he turned to the Lord and pleaded with him in prayer and petition, in fasting and in sackcloth and ashes (Dan. 9:4-19). No verse in Daniel tells specifically when and how Israel was restored because of Daniel's prayer, but the insinuation is there. We know the Angel Gabriel was dispatched immediately after Daniel started praying, but we do not know if Daniel was aware of the spiritual warfare going on the heavens before Gabriel got through to him. I don't think he knew Gabriel was just within arm's reach, and even if he did, he continued to pray until the prayer was answered. I wonder how many answers are halted because we give up and quit praying.

When I asked God to make me a prayer warrior and bring people to my mind and presence to intercede for, it did not turn out like I expected. I expected God not only to give me easy prayers, but to honor my prayers quickly and painlessly. I didn't expect to invest three to four hours of my life every day, and I didn't expect to be sent to some of the people and places He sent me. I didn't expect humiliation and insults and gossip on the prayer subjects. I didn't expect to cry so much or to feel others' pain so deeply. I didn't expect to be so bold at times or so intimidated at other times. I didn't expect for it to take so long to get some answers or to be thrown into an extensive Bible study to know what to pray for and how. You must go to the Word of God to intercede at the Throne of Grace for someone who has come to you brokenhearted. I have been accused of being stubborn and have "stubborned" myself into a lot of trouble at times. However, stubbornness can be channeled into a righteous force for persistence and endurance. Charles Spurgeon said that by perseverance, the snail reached the Ark. Lack of endurance is one of the greatest causes of defeat, especially in prayer.

How do we pray the will of God? "So is my Word that goes out from my mouth, it will not return to me empty, but will accomplish what I desire" (Isa. 55:11). Pray the Word of God to God. Remind Him of His promises. He has not forgotten what is written, but He does not want you to forget either. Learn to recognize the answer God gives you and accept it. Moses asked to see God's face, but God revealed His glory. Moses asked to cross the Jordan into the Promised Land, but only got a view of it from the mountaintop. However, God took him straight to glory and the real Promised Land. A far, far better place. Mary and Martha asked for Lazarus to be healed, but instead Jesus raised him from the dead. Don't have such a mindset on your answer that you miss God's answer.

3. Pray for the Lost

"In our churches, we spend more time praying to keep the saints out of heaven than we do praying lost people into heaven" (Minette Drumwright).

God desires for people to be saved. Jesus said He had come to find the lost and save them and did not come to be served but to serve (Luke 19:10; Mark 10:45). We are to ask what others need and then pray for them (1 Tim. 2:1), and therefore please the Lord by bringing lost ones to the truth (1 Tim. 2:3-4). God is always patient with us and He is not slow when it comes to fulfilling His promises, but He does expect us to ask in prayer for the things both we and He desire (2 Pet. 3:9). What does it mean to be lost? Those who are lost have been judged guilty of not accepting Jesus as their Lord and Savior, and will not enter the Kingdom of Heaven but perish in hell forever and ever (John 3:16-18, 16:9). Lost people are unbelievers and have separated themselves from God, refusing to believe in God or Jesus as the Son and Savior of the world. Lost people are spiritually blind (2 Cor. 4:3-4). Blind combines two words, one meaning to burn, and refers to the dulling of the intellect, and the other meaning a covering with a callus or a thick skin, and means a darkening of understanding (Rom. 11:25; Eph. 4:18). The lost do not understand spiritual truth (Rom. 3:11; 1 Cor. 2:14), are deceived by Satan (Gen. 3:13; 2 Tim 3:13), and are in bondage to their master, the devil (John 8:44). Enslavement is the result of deception, and lost people are enslaved not only mentally, but materially and morally as well (1 John 2:15-17; Matt. 4:3-11; Rom. 1:18). They have the potential for a wide range of expression of depravity and evil (Rom. 1:18), they are spiritually dead (Rom. 6:23; Eph. 2:1), and are alienated from God (Luke 15:4; Eph. 2:12). Evangelist Billy Graham stated that he had observed four factors that were characteristic of lost people worldwide. They are: a sense of emptiness, loneliness, guilt, and fear of defeat.

Jesus is the only one who can save anyone. His name is the only power in the world that has been given to save anyone. We must be saved through Him (Acts 4:12). So then if God does all the work and He is the only one that can save and promises to do this, what good does it do to pray for the lost? How do we pray? He does require us to pray to Him and ask in faith for this salvation to come to everyone, especially the ones He puts you in contact with. Pray that the person's heart be prepared so that it will be good soil for the seed (Mark 4:8), that Satan not be able to steal the seeds of truth that you plant (Mark 4:15), and that nothing else will be able to destroy the seeds (Mark 4:16-19). Pray that the Word becomes revelation through the lifting of the veil (2 Cor. 4:3-4). An excellent verse to use in prayer is Ephesians 1:17: "That the God of our Lord Jesus Christ, the Father of glory, may give to you a spirit of wisdom and of revelation in the knowledge of Him." Pray that the root of pride in them be broken (2 Cor. 10:3-5), the person comes to true repentance (2 Pet. 3:9), and "that God grant them repentance, leading to the knowledge of truth and they will come to their senses and escape the snare of the devil, having been held captive by him to do his will" (2 Tim. 2:25-26).

Never give up on a lost one you are praying for, even it your prayers seem to go unanswered. God will hear your prayers, what you ask will be done, and those who humble themselves will be saved. Some will be delivered through the cleanliness of your hands (Job 22:27-30). He will rescue the children of the godly (Prov. 11:21), your tears will not be wasted (Ps. 56:8), but you will shout with joy, bringing in sheaves with you (Ps. 126:5-6). Jesus said, "But I tell you, open your eyes and look at the fields ready for harvest now" (John 4:35). These are the lost people who need your prayers (Matt. 13:38-39). Don't let them down (Matt. 13:42).

4. Prayer Chains

There are thousands of prayer chains active across the Internet, e-mail, and the phone lines. Are they necessary? Do they help situations? Are they right or wrong? These are questions I have been asked, and I will give you my take on prayer chains, according to how I read and understand the scripture.

We may think there was no need for the prayer chain in the Old Testament, since God was in their presence when He wanted to speak to the people. Enoch walked with God (Gen. 5:24), Noah was blameless among the people of his time and walked with God (Gen. 6:9), God spoke to Abram (Gen. 12:1), struggled with Jacob (Gen. 32:28), and came to Moses in a burning bush (Ex. 3:2). The Lord stood before Moses by the rock at Horeb (Ex. 7:6) and called to him from Mount Sinai (Ex. 19:3), and the voice of God answered Moses. The Lord descended to the top of Mount Sinai and called Moses to the top and dictated to him the Ten Commandments. Later, in those days, the Word of the Lord was rare, however, He called Samuel when he was only a child (1 Sam. 3:1-11). The Lord spoke directly to Elijah (1 Kings 19:11) and then took him up to heaven in a whirlwind.

God can build a prayer chain out of anything, including a donkey. Remember the story of Balaam and the conversation he had with God about going with Balak's men (Num. 22:1-19). God came to him in the night and told him to go with the men, but to do only what He told him to do. Well, I am not sure what Balaam did wrong, and it was more likely what he said wrong. You know how we gripe and complain when doing something God tells us that we do not want to do? Anyway, he was not pleasing the Lord, and God sent an angel to block the reckless path, but Balaam was so into himself that he did not see or sense the angel. So God sent word down through the angel and of all things, a donkey. The donkey saw the angel with his sword drawn and turned away three times to save his master's life, only to be beaten three times. So we find for the first time in scripture, a talking donkey (Num. 22:28-29). Does three make a chain?

Now let's talk about one of my favorite guys. Daniel got down on his knees three times a day and prayed, giving thanks to God (Dan. 6:10). Some of the troublemakers and men with influence over the king came and helped the king make the decision to throw Daniel into the lions' den. The king, greatly distressed, tried to rescue Daniel, and made every effort until sundown to save him, thus connecting him to the prayer chain, whether he was aware of it or not. The chain of angels came down and shut the mouths of the lions and Daniel was spared. No wound was found on him, because he had trusted in God. Not only was Daniel saved physically, the king was saved spiritually. Daniel was a member of a very elite prayer chain, with angels forever coming to his rescue. Two members of this chain that come to mind are Michael and Gabriel (Dan. 9:21-23, 10:12-13).

Then God sent His Son to earth to be present in people's lives, to touch them and pray not only for the people but for Himself. He prayed that heartbreaking plea on the cross: *"Eloi, Eloi, Lama sabachthani?"* (Matt. 27:46). But since our sins were upon Him, and the Holy Spirit had left Jesus temporarily, the prayer chain had been broken and God did not hear. This break was only temporary, and restored after He paid the full price of our redemption and admission to eternal life. While Jesus walked the earth before the Crucifixion, the prayer chain was alive and active. Jesus healed the deaf and mute with a touch and a prayer; "He looked up to heaven and with a deep sigh said to him, Ephphatha which means, be opened" (Mark 7:33). I don't think Jesus was speaking to the deaf ears and silent mouth of the man, but to the Father in heaven in prayer.

The beggar prayed for Jesus to have mercy on him, calling Him the Son of David (Mark 10:47) and the demons prayed (Matt. 8:29-31). The disciples usually just watched as Jesus prayed, but at long last, they asked and He taught them how to pray (Luke 11:1-4). How in the world do you get a prayer chain out of these scriptures? I get the idea from Matthew 18:19, where Jesus tells us that where two or three come together in His name, He is there also, and if we agree on something, it will be done by the Father in heaven. When these people in the Bible asked Jesus for something, there was always a crowd there watching, and probably hoping for healing of a loved one. Three may be a short chain, and two even shorter, but if it is connected to Jesus Christ, it will stretch to the Throne of God.

A prayer chain is a way of sharing a prayer request with other prayer warriors. Prayer chains are very powerful if the list includes people who have agreed to respond to prayer requests by asking God to help the needy person. A large number of brothers and sisters in Christ can be reached with a chain-reaction prayer chain, where each one contacted contacts another and another and another. Prayer chains tug at our hearts, whether we personally know the prayer need or the one in need. As your prayer request goes out through the chain, the Holy Spirit may prompt each individual to pray differently. Prayer chains are a response to people in need, and will lift up a person or persons to God our Father for immediate attention. Some call this storming the gates of heaven with prayers. God opens up the gates and hears every whisper.

Paul loved prayer chains. "I urge you brothers, by our Lord Jesus Christ and by the love of the Spirit, to join me in my struggle by praying to God for me" (Rom. 15:30). He told his congregation to devote themselves to prayer, praying that God would open doors for the good news, and asked that they also pray for him (1 Thess. 5:25). He starts most of his letters with a prayer for the churches, because he had heard of their faith (Col. 1:3-4; 1 Cor. 1:4; Eph. 1:3; 1 Thess. 1:2).

I in no way mean to indicate that God does not hear your prayer if you have no one to pray for or with you. If this were true, then Jesus would not have mentioned the closet prayer in Matthew 6:6. This is just an encouragement for you that in fact others are willing and able to pray with you when you ask. There is safety in numbers, so the old saying goes, and there is comfort in numbers when we pray together. Remember when Moses was praying with his hands extended toward heaven? "When he grew weary and could no longer hold his hands up, Aaron and Hur stepped in and held his up, one on one side and one on the other, so that his hands remained steady until sunset" (Ex. 17:12). The purpose of a prayer chain is to hold your hands up when you grow weary. Prayer warriors will hold your hands up until sunset or until you have peace about the prayer request or until you have your answer. They are not illegal and do no harm when done in the will of God and with discretion. Just a word of caution: No prayer chain should be a gossip line!

5. *This Prayer's for You*

It is the middle of November, and here in West Texas, the weather is beginning to show signs of a fast-approaching winter. We are on Daylight Saving Time, and the sun has set early, leaving an eerie air of anticipation around the house. It is quiet and warm inside, with only the light from this computer piercing the darkness. I settled here with intentions of writing you a little story from the Bible, but found myself with a heavy heart. I have a strong feeling that God is trying to tell me that one of you or perhaps several are in need of prayer tonight. Therefore, with the guidance of the Holy Spirit, who helps us with the right words when we do not know what to pray, I pray first that He also be with you as you read this and open your hearts to accept the words as yours from God. I pray that each of you will be blessed so that you can be a greater blessing to others. Combine these two dynamic sources with the power of the Holy Spirit, and spiritual energy is unleashed in the believer's life, resulting in answered prayer.

The prophet Jeremiah wrote about God's words where He tells us to call to Him and He will answer and tell us great and unsearchable things that we do not know. It is reaffirmed by the New Testament writer James, who wrote to draw close to God, and He will draw close to you. There is no greater truth in the entire universe than the fact that God loves you! Prayer is our safe place, our place of refuge in difficult times. President Abraham Lincoln wrote; "I am oftimes driven to my knees by the overwhelming conviction that I have nowhere else to go!" My prayer is that none wait until the last resort to call on the name of Jesus, but each will let the Word of Christ dwell in you richly in all wisdom.

Father, for those who feel they have fallen short of your glory and sinned against you, I pray that you forgive them. By their repentance they will understand that they are changed and can, through your strength, change the course of their life. I pray that now, today, they turn in the opposite direction from the way of sin and determine in their heart to follow you, no matter what the cost. For the ones, Father, who are childish in their spirit and tossed to and fro, be guided to the truth and grounded in the faith that granted them salvation. Forgive them, Father, for the times they have been so easily influenced by others, and bring them back into the body of Christ. Give them an exciting realization that you are the goal in their life. Please forgive the ones who have rebelled against you, urging them to repent of all the acts of disobedience. Help them to see that obeying you leads to so many good things. Lord, fill them with the promised Holy Spirit and with the joy that comes whenever they do your will. Let them wait before you to receive this promise, and help them to see what it really means.

Father, for the ones who are oppressed by the devil, the accuser of the brethren, show them once again the victory you have over Satan. Guide them on the right path, that they might walk in this same victory, because they are believers and not doubters. For the ones living in the past who cannot fully live for you while there, I pray that you assure them you have erased the past with the blood of Jesus. Let them not be preoccupied with either the past or the future, but to live fully in the present moments of their life. Father, you have come to heal the brokenhearted and the bruised, and it is my prayer that you do this now for anyone who will reach out and receive this healing. Rejection, bitterness, resentment, and lack of esteem and love for oneself can become an addiction and hold a person captive. I ask you to come in power and deliver all who are brokenhearted and set the captives free. Lord, there is no fear in your love, and because of this, I ask that all fear be renounced and the love of Christ replace fear in the hearts of the insecure.

Lord, thank you for the gift of speech. One needs help to use it responsibly. Put a watch before their lips that they might always honor you with their words. Keep them from sowing strife, Lord, knowing that a whisperer (gossiping person) separates close friends and causes a separation from God. Guilt no longer has any dominion in the lives of these people since you have set them free. There is one who is lonely. Thank you, Lord, for the promise that you will be there always and have sent the Holy Spirit for comfort, and He dwells within each person. Just as Jesus turned to the throne of grace in His loneliness in the Garden, teach this one, Father, that he too will find mercy, comfort, and grace there in his time of need. The lust of the eye and the lust of the flesh are creating great problems for someone's loved one. You will not permit a person to be tempted above their ability to resist. Make a way for them, Lord, to escape so that they will be able to bear it.

For the one who lacks self-confidence and cannot escape the negative attitude that seems to control their life, remind them that they are fearfully and wonderfully made and you have changed them and are perfecting them in your own image. Now, Lord, I ask that you show them that your strength is made perfect in their weakness, that you have begun a good work in them and will perform it until the day of Jesus Christ. You, Lord Jesus, were despised and carried the sorrows of the one who is feeling the pain of rejection. It is not your will for them to have hurt, so I ask of you, Father, to give them courage and not fear what men may do to them. Forgive the ones who worry, for they do not have to. I pray that they cast their burdens on your strong and willing shoulders and that you will give them rest.

Father, for the ones here who have lost loved ones in death, through accidents, sickness, military fatalities, miscarriages, or aging, I ask that you grant them a peace that surpasses human understanding. Assure them, Lord, that even in death, they will live again in your presence and that you have wiped all the tears from their eyes and erased all of their aches and pains. Lord Jesus, you are the Great Physician, and all healing comes from you. Thank you for caring so much about those who are ill. I pray that the sick receive your healing now, Lord, in their area of physical need, and believe you are restoring them to health and vitality. I pray for the ones who are confused about tithing, Father, that you assure them if they obey you with tithes and offerings, that you will open the windows of heaven and pour your blessings forth abundantly to them. Your Word says that you have given everyone a spirit of sound mind, and this I pray for the mentally disabled in the entire world, that they do not have to live with imperfection any longer.

Those who are in need of jobs to provide for themselves and their families, Father, lead them to the place that you have prepared for them, for it is your desire that they walk in success. I pray for broken families that they be united in the love of Jesus Christ. For the unborn child that is a precious gift from God, I ask that you cover the womb with your love. Bless this child with a supernatural awareness of your presence that she or he may be sensitive to your Spirit. Help husbands and wives to submit their lives to you and each other in reverential fear of you. Thank you for your promise, Father, that whosoever will call upon your name shall be saved. I ask that you send the Holy Spirit to woo the lost, that they will feel conviction and turn to the Father, who will gladly and faithfully grant them eternal life. Help everyone to know the will of God, to walk in God's Word and holiness, and to grow spiritually daily.

I bow my knee to you, God, the Father of my Lord Jesus Christ, of whom the whole family in heaven and earth is named, that you would grant, according to the riches of your glory and strength, with might by your Spirit in the inner man, that Christ may dwell in these hearts by faith. That they, being rooted and grounded in love, may be able to comprehend with all saints what is the breadth and length and depth and height of God's love. Now to Him who is able to do immeasurably more than all we ask or imagine, according to His power that is at work within us, to Him be glory in the church and in Christ Jesus throughout all generations, for ever and ever! This I pray in the name of Jesus. Amen!

6. *Questions and Answers*

Q: Why is it necessary to pray for Jerusalem?

A: We pray for Jerusalem because the scriptures direct us to do so. Zion (Jerusalem, Israel): "Whoever touches you touches the apple of His eye" (Zech. 2:7-9). "The Lord will have compassion on Jacob; once again He will choose Israel" (Isa. 14:1). Israel is God's people (Isa. 45:3); He will cleanse them and pardon them (Jer. 33:8); He will redeem Israel out of their troubles (Ps. 25:22); He will bring health and healing to their land (Jer. 33:9) and restore everything that has been removed from them (Joel 2:25). He will make their enemies be at peace with them (Prov. 16:7); seek them out where they were scattered and bring them to their own land (Ezek. 34:12-13). Pray for peace of Jerusalem (Ps. 122:6).

Q: My husband says he is a believer in God but hates to show or speak of it, even to me. Is this just my husband's concern or should I be involved in his relationship with God? Or should I just pray and leave it between him and God?

A: Yes, this is between your husband and God. Yes, it is your business to pray. It is truly difficult for some to voice their faith and should not be judged improper, but you should pray for a spirit of power rather than timidity (2 Tim. 1:7). Vocal praise fills the Bible (Ps. 100, 108, 150; 1 Pet. 3:15; Prov. 18:20; Rom. 12:11; Heb. 13:15; 1 Pet. 1:8; Luke 6:23). The scripture states that a believer should walk after the Spirit, minding the things of the Spirit (Rom. 8:4-5), because of the indwelling of the Spirit (Rom. 8:9).

Q: Are there positions to be taken when praying?

A: Nowhere in scripture does it command one position over another for you to pray, but to pray without ceasing (1 Thess. 5:17). Daniel got down on his knees and prayed (Dan. 6:10), David spent the nights face down on the floor praying (2 Sam. 12:16-20), and Ezra threw himself down before the house of God while he wept and prayed (Ezra 10:1). Hezekiah turned his face to the wall while lying on his bed dying (Isa. 38:1-3), Peter got down on his knees (Acts 9:40-41), and Jesus fell to the ground and prayed in the Garden of Gethsemane (Matt. 26:39). There are no instructions on the position to pray, and we should not assume a position of someone else that makes you uncomfortable, but find your own spot with God.

Q: Do you think that if we pray to God and ask Him to tell someone in heaven we are okay that Jesus will do that?

A: I do not know of any scripture that tells us Jesus will deliver messages to loved ones in heaven. Scripture tells us that Jesus is a mediator between God and man in prayer (1 Tim. 2:5-6), not a messenger between earth-man and heaven-man. Revelation 5:8-9 says the saints in heaven offer the prayers of the holy ones (saints on earth) before God. Revelation 6:9-11 reads that souls seem to be aware of what is taking place on earth. Revelation 18:20 shows an angel addressing saints, apostles, and prophets living in heaven, telling them to rejoice over God's judgment of the earth. Moses and Elijah seemed aware of what was happening on earth (Luke 9:3) and God has put apostles on display for the angels to see (1 Cor. 4:9).

I do not believe you can get a message to your loved one in heaven, but since there is no pain or tears there, perhaps they know. This remains one of the mysteries of God.

Q: Is it ok to pray for financial success for a family member who is not a Christian?

A: Philippians 4:7 tells us to present our request to God by prayer and petition, and 1 Timothy 2:1 urges us that request and intercessions be made for everyone. Now, for the person who is not saved, we must gently instruct him, in the hope that God will grant him repentance, leading him to a knowledge of the truth (2 Tim. 2:25-26). Pray for your family member to seek first the Kingdom of God (Matt. 6:33), for it is God who gives the power for success (Deut. 8:17).

Q: Why can some pray for every occasion without a problem and others are unable to do so, such as myself? What is wrong with me?

A: There is nothing wrong with you. Read all of Matthew 6:5-14, and Jesus Himself will teach you how to pray. There are different kinds of gifts, different kinds of service, and different kinds of working for God, all given by His Spirit. God arranged you where and how He wants you (1 Cor. 12:18, 25). Jesus teaches that we not pray to get attention or just to be seen (Matt. 6:5-8). This is not to suggest that your friends pray for this reason, but that each must find his own mode of praying to the Father.

Part V Food for Thought

1. Thoughts

Proverbs 4:23: "Be careful how you think; your life is shaped by your thoughts."

Behind everything you do, there is a thought! So if you want to change your life, you have to change your thinking. Imagine riding in a speedboat with an automatic pilot set to go east. If you suddenly decide to head west, you have two possible options. One is to grab the wheel and force it to head in the opposite direction from where it is programmed to go. By sheer willpower, you could overcome the autopilot, but you would feel constant resistance. Your arms would eventually tire, you would let go of the wheel, and guess what? The boat would instantly head back east, the way it is internally programmed to go. This is what happens when you try to change your life through your willpower. I will force myself to eat less, exercise more, quit being disorganized, etc. Willpower can produce short-term change, but it crates constant stress, because you have not dealt with the root cause. The change does not feel natural, so eventually you give up, go off your diet, quit exercising, and revert to your old pattern of life.

Thank God there is another way! Change your autopilot, which is the way you think. God can and will transform you into a new person by changing the way you think (Rom. 12:2). Change always starts in your mind, since the way you think determines the way you feel, and the way you feel determines the way you act. Paul told Timothy to reflect on what he was telling him, because the Lord will give insight into all of it (2 Tim. 2:7). Man must look intently into the perfect law that gives freedom, and never forget what he has read or heard, but rather puts it into practice. Then he will be blessed in what he does (James 1:25). Your life is worth taking the time to think about where you are going and why.

There is a mental condition that is essential to the life God wants you to live. It is the fuel your heart runs on. It is the single biggest difference between those who persevere and those who give up. It is called hope! It is a powerful force that arouses your mind to explore every possibility and overcome every obstacle. Your courage to change your life comes from this hope (Job 11:18), and God has been this hope and confidence since youth (Ps. 71:5). Don't lose hope! You can survive many losses by keeping your thoughts on God.

Reasoning is a product of your head and opens the door to fear and impossible "I can't" thinking. Discernment is a product of the Spirit, and it opens the door to faith and great accomplishments. Your head does not understand spiritual things, so when your spirit brings forth discernment from the Holy Spirit, and your head starts arguing about it, you never make any progress. Why? Paul says that the natural does not receive the things of the Spirit (1 Cor. 2:14) and that your spirit knows things that your head does not know. Some things you have dismissed as a hunch or an intuition were actually God's Spirit trying to convey the answers to you, but you kept rejecting it because it did not sound reasonable. "What I have planned that will I do" (Isa. 46:11). God does not argue with us. He leads us by a persistent desire, an impression, a still, small voice within, and a scripture that is illuminated to us.

Get rid of all this thinking on your own and let God transform you into a new person by changing the way you think to the way He thinks (Rom. 12:2). Ever notice how some people on a roller coaster close their eyes, clench their teeth, and wait for the ride to end, while up front, the wide-eyed thrill-seekers relish every peak and plunge? They are all on the same trip, but their attitudes are entirely different. You cannot always control what happens to you, but you can decide how you will respond to it (Heb. 12:3). Consider thinking like God, and let God do your thinking, lest you be wearied and faint in your minds.

Sometimes we think too much or too long before we act or react. "Trust in the Lord with all your heart and lean not on your own understanding" (Prov. 3:5). God will not tell you what you do not need to know. Furthermore, He will not do for you what He has already told you to do with His strength. Stop trying to figure out things that should be left in His hands. When you put something on the shelf that is bothering you and say you are going to trust God with it, do not take it back because you do not like the way He is handling it, or the length of time He is taking to deal with it. "He that believes shall not make haste" (Isa. 28:16). Your mind likes to slot things and put them in the order that you want them to happen. If you are one of God's obsessive-compulsive children who has to put everything in a neat little package with no loose ends, remember Proverbs 3:5.

There is a story told about Charlton Heston that illustrates our need to let God do the thinking. During the making of *Ben-Hur*, Heston worked long hours with stunt trainers, learning to drive a chariot for the movie's crucial chariot race. He improved greatly in his mastery over the horses and rig, but finally became convinced that the task was more of a challenge than he had initially anticipated. So he approached the legendary movie director, Cecil B. DeMille about the scene. "Mr. DeMille, I have worked very hard at mastering this rig. I think I can drive it convincingly in the scene, but I don't think I can win the race." DeMille looked at Heston and said, "You just drive, I will direct and see that you win the race." The chariot race became one of the most memorable highlights of the entire movie. He won the race!

You do not need to know all the answers! Let God do the thinking and directing, and you will win the race. "Along unfamiliar paths I will guide them. I will turn the darkness into light before them and make the rough places smooth. These are the things I will do. I will not forsake them" (Isa. 42:16).

2. *Thoughts about Food*

What food did the Bible's people eat and how did they come by their food? Let us start with the milk products, which seemed to be plentiful. A plentiful supply of milk typified the prosperity of ancient Canaan, the Land of Promise for God's people (Ex. 3:8). The shepherd out on the hills depended largely on the milk of his flock for his daily food. "Who tends a flock and does not drink of the milk of the flock?" (1 Cor. 9:7). He used the milk of the sheep as well as that of the goats (Deut. 32:14; Isa. 7:21:22). Village families who could not have large flocks might still raise a few goats in order to have their own milk supply. People on the ranches of the East-Jordan Gilead and Bashan country practically lived on the milk of their herds of cattle, as nomadic people always have.

Families in the settled areas might have a cow or several sheep to provide milk (1 Sam. 6:7) and milk products for themselves and their neighbors. The cow might also do some of the heavy work. However, milk must have been scarce among city dwellers, particularly the poor. Fresh raw milk furnished an important item in the diet of the village family. It served as a beverage at meals (Gen. 18:8), especially for young children (Heb. 5:12-13) and the sick. It was kept in jars immersed in cool springs of water or in the depths of limestone caves. Soured and thickened to the consistency of custard, it became a delicacy and still is among people of the Near East. Commentators have suggested that Jael brought milk to Sisera (Jud. 5:25).

Soured milk can be made into cheese, and the Israelites seemed to have had many varieties. Palatable and delicious cottage cheese was most easily prepared. Dehydrated in the form of tough curds, it found its way into the shepherd's lunch along with dried fruits and nuts. Cottage cheese might also be pressed into lumps the size of a large ball, dropped into boiling water, and allowed to age. Such may have been the ten cheeses that Jesse sent with David when he went to see his brothers (1 Sam. 17:18). Many other varieties of homemade cheese quickly made out of sour milk or aged through a number of processes are still used in the Near East and in southeastern Europe, no doubt in much the same form as they were used in the biblical times.

Butter is mentioned in Genesis 18:8, where Abraham entertained God and two of His companions. It was made of cream, skimmed off the top of soured milk. The fat cells were broken down by rocking it back and forth on the knees in a jug or other containers, until the butter formed little lumps floating in the buttermilk. I am revealing my age here, but I actually remember churning butter with a jar when I was very small. "The churning of the milk becomes butter" (Prov. 30:33). A device used by modern Arabs may be the same as that used nearly 4,000 years ago by Abraham. A goatskin bottle is made out of goatskin, sewn together where it had been cut to remove it from the carcass. This formed a sack that could be tied at the neck and hung up. Half-filled with sour cream, it was then inflated with air to make it comparatively rigid. It was suspended by the legs of the goatskin so that it could swing freely from a tripod support made of sticks. The housewife jerked it back and forth with a rope attached to the neck of the bottle until the agitation produced butter. This method of preparing butter is still used by Bedouins today.

Butter, boiled down to remove the water and impurities, was stored in jars and used in the preparation of baked goods, in frying, and for various other cooking purposes. We find no evidence that it was used on bread as we use it today. Buttermilk, the by-product of butter-making, furnished a refreshing and nourishing drink. In a country as hot as Palestine, particularly on the fringe of the wilderness, milk and milk products were vital to the life and health of the inhabitants, as their chief supply of protein, calcium, and fat. Fresh milk, sour milk, and buttermilk provided a pleasant variety of refreshing beverages. Butter and the many varieties of cheese helped greatly in balancing and diversifying an otherwise bland diet. "A Land flowing with milk" says Exodus 3:8.

3. Marriage Dos and Don'ts

Social standing and government laws and culture changes and moral degeneration and personal views and, and, and! The list goes on and on as to why nearly no one stands on the Word of God concerning marriage. Here are the rules according to the Bible.

God intended for one man to marry one woman for life, as set down in Matthew 10:4-6. Notice not more than one spouse and until death do them part as set forth in 1 Corinthians 7:39. Christians should not date non-Christians, because this could lead to marriage as the couple becomes emotionally soul-tied during a courtship period (2 Cor. 6:14-15). Therefore, by not dating non-Christian, one would not have the opportunity to marry a non-Christian. Christians should only date and marry Christians, and thus avoid a lifetime of problems, such as the spiritual welfare of their children. Sex before marriage, fornication, is strictly forbidden for Christians (1 Cor. 6:9-10). As a practical matter, people who fornicate will have a tendency to have affairs when they marry, due to the ungodly habits formed before marriage, which are difficult to break. In addition, when husband and wife perform their conjugal duties, they will be comparing their spouse to former sex partners, which would be unhealthy for any marriage (1 Cor. 6:16, 7:1-16).

A wife should submit to her own husband as unto the Lord (Eph. 5:22-24). By submitting to her husband, the wife is respecting, honoring, and obeying him, which shows the love of Christ in a practical way. This does not mean that the wife is a doormat, or to be subjected to a husband with ungodly demands. A Christian wife should be excited about submitting to her husband, especially as he follows Ephesians 5:25-29, which explains his duties to his wife. The husband loves, protects, provides, comforts, and is affectionate toward his wife, and is able to show Christ in a practical way. When both husband and wife love each other in this manner, there is less opportunity for Satan to interfere with this godly union (Prov. 18:22; Heb. 13:4; 1 Cor. 7:5).

There are only two biblical reasons that a Christian can divorce. A Christian may divorce only if your spouse has committed adultery according to Matthew 19:9, or if your spouse is an unbeliever and leaves according to 1 Corinthians 7:15. In the case of adultery, God would have us forgive our spouse for the healing of the marriage to occur. God, through His mercy and grace, has forgiven us of our sins through Jesus Christ, so how much more should we forgive each other their wrongs? A Christian should use every means possible to heal the marriage, including much prayer. We might try fasting, reading the Word of God, counseling, spiritual counseling, teaching, and keeping company with godly friends. I cannot overemphasize that adultery by one spouse is not an excuse or an out clause to divorce. God intended for marriage to be until death do them part, but because of the hardness of heart, Moses permitted divorce (Matt. 19:8). Christians desiring to please God should use every means possible and available to forgive adultery and to restore the marriage (Eph. 5:25-31; Mal. 2:13-16; Matt. 5:31-32; Rom. 7:1-3).

Divorced Christians can remarry, provided the divorce was due to adultery (Deut. 24:1-4; Matt. 19:19). In addition, widows can remarry, provided they marry in the Lord (1 Cor. 7:39), otherwise to remarry is considered adultery to the Lord. Divorce is common and the easy way out for many, but it is not of the Lord. The grass is seldom greener on the other side. This is not to say that you must put up with abuse or be a doormat for each other. Pray together, trust each other; be honest at all times and get as much out of life as out of married life as you can with God in the center.

4. Anger

Family trait, attitude, reaction, temper, disgust! Use whatever name you will, but the Bible calls it anger, and God says it is a sin! Check the following scriptures scattered throughout this message, with an open heart and honest mind to see if they apply to your lifestyle. If none apply, then you are truly blessed. If some or all apply, then repent (along with me) and let us ask God to forgive us and renew our minds (Zeph. 3:17; Ezek. 36:26).

We are commanded not to make friends with anyone who is given to anger, or his anger will rub off on us and we will find ourselves caught in the trap of always being angry (Prov. 22:24-25). Think back to the last time you witnessed an argument between two friends or members of your family. Did you get angry at one of them? Did you want to take sides? Did you try to stop the argument? If you cannot help the situation, then walk away like Jesus did (Matt. 10:14; Mark 6:11; Luke 9:5). Oh, and another thing you must do is forgive the ones with whom you are angry. "But I say to you that everyone who continues to be angry with his brother or harbors malice against him shall be liable to and unable to escape the punishment imposed by the court, and whoever speaks contemptuously and insultingly to his brother shall be liable to and unable to escape the punishment imposed by the Sanhedrin, and whoever says, you cursed fool shall be liable to and unable to escape the fire of hell" (Matt. 5:22). Now that is harsh and very clear that fussing and fighting is just not a good thing to be doing, especially if you cannot come to an agreement and be brothers and sisters in Christ once more.

Anger causes you to miss the message from God. Stephen was trying to preach the Word, but the people did not understand, so they became angry. After they heard all the things Stephen said, they were cut to the heart and infuriated, and ground their teeth at him. They shouted to drown out his speaking and put their hands over their ears and ran to attack him (Acts 7:54, 57). They did not want to listen to Peter either when he told them he must obey God, and continued to preach. They were again cut to the heart and wanted to kill him (Acts 5:33). James says that everyone should be quick to hear, or ready to listen, slow to speak, slow to take offense, and slow to anger. We are to get rid of everything including uncleanness and wickedness, and welcome the Word with a gentle, humble, and modest spirit, so God can promote righteousness. Let the Word which is taught take root in your heart, and receive the power to save your souls (James 1:19-21). "Do not be quick in spirit to be angry or vexed, for anger and vexation lodge in the bosom of fools" (Ecc. 7:9).

Anger will distort your memory, just as it did King Xerxes, along with being drunk, and he made a fatal mistake of listening to his also-drunk and angry friends, and dismissed Queen Vashti. Later, when he was not so angry and with a hangover, he remembered he had no queen for his kingdom (Est. 1:19-21, 2:1). Anger takes you out of the presence of the Lord. "Why does your heart carry you away? Why allow yourself to be controlled by feeling? Why do your eyes flash in anger or contempt? That you turn your spirit against God and let such words as you have spoken go out of your mouth?" (Job 15:12-13). Now, if anyone had a right to be angry, it would be Job, but he held his faith and was blessed twofold when the Lord ceased his testing from the devil.

If you hold your anger inside instead of confessing it to God or to the person with whom you are angry, it can cause all kinds of damage. You may say that you are not mad anymore, but your stomach and mind tell you differently. I read somewhere that if you hold in your anger, it is like starting a fire in a wastebasket, putting it in the closet and closing the door. It may burn itself out or it may burn down the house. Do not hide the anger but instead ask God to put out the fire. Analyze the source of your anger before you confront someone. The psalmist writes to tell us to commune with your own heart upon your beds and be silent, meaning to be sorry for the things in your heart. This Psalm closes with the word *Selah*, meaning "to pause and calmly think" (Ps. 4:4). The New Testament teaching comes from Ephesians 4:26, saying not to let the sun go down on your anger, not to cover it up and do not get so angry that it causes you to sin.

Now that we all know and admitted that we have had anger in our lives, I will give you the good news. God promises He will show us the way if we will seek Him, and that He will counsel us and keep an eye on us (Ps. 32:8). Do not go and ask your best friend what to do about your anger or just be angry because the entire world around you seems to be. Instead, we must ask God to transform us and change us by the renewal of our minds, new ideals, and new attitudes, so we may prove for ourselves what is good and perfect in His sight (Rom. 12:2). If you turn loose of your anger, you will be able to forgive, and if you forgive them, our Father in heaven will forgive you. Read the Lord's Prayer and find this promise (Matt. 6:9-15). This message is really much too short, according to all the passages in the Bible on the subject, but I did not want to continue and make someone angry.

5. Pro-Life

In 1973, the United States Supreme Court legalized the abortion of unborn babies. Since then, more than 25 million have been legally aborted in this country. The fact that an act is legal according to civil law, however, does not make it moral. "We must obey God rather than men" (Acts 5:29). Is there life in the womb? God created only three basic classes of life, each of which reproduced after its own kind: plants, animals, and people (Gen. 1:11, 12, 20-25, 26-30, 5:1-4). Is the life in the womb just a part of the mother's body, like an appendix or gallbladder that can be removed, or is it a separate and distinct individual from the mother? The Bible refers to a human person by calling it a man, woman, child, son, daughter, baby, or infant. The unborn baby is also referred to as a child or children, such as when Rebekah conceived twins; "the children struggled together within her" (Gen. 25:21-22). The scripture also says that she conceived and bore a child (Gen. 4:1, 17, 21:2, 29:32) and does specify that there is a time period before the conception becomes human.

Babies that die before birth are called infants that never saw light. The King James Version of the Bible uses the word *infant* always to refer to human individuals (Hos. 13:16). When Miriam became leprous, she was described as one dead, of whom the flesh is half-consumed when he comes out of his mother's womb (Num. 12:12). If the baby dies before it is born, the woman who conceived it is still a mother. Elizabeth addressed Mary as the mother of her Lord before Jesus was born (Luke 1:43). The word *mother* in contexts refers to physical human reproduction and to one who has procreated or formed another human individual, a separate and distinct individual from the mother herself (Num 6:7; Gen 3:20; Luke 1:60). A woman who has conceived even if the child is not yet born and even if it dies before birth is a mother.

Elizabeth conceived (Luke 1:24) and the life in her womb is called a babe or baby. This is the second most common New Testament word for a baby. It is always used for that which is human individual separate and distinct from its mother (Luke 2:12, 16; Acts 7:19). The life conceived in Elizabeth's womb before it was born is called a son. The word *son* refers to the physical offspring and distinct individual from a parent. A baby conceived and living in the mother's womb is referred to by God as child, son, infant, baby, or man-child. God makes no distinction between born and unborn life with the names He calls them. He uses exactly the same term for both. The life in the mother's womb is human life, connected to the mother for life support but separate in identification. Children are blessings from God and a source of happiness and joy to their parents (Ps. 127:3-5, 128:3-5). It has been proven that when you talk to an unborn baby, it will respond. This lifeline between the baby and mother is there before conception, so God must surely have planned this baby to be life from the beginning.

God has made us stewards of our kids (Prov. 22:6; Eph. 6:4) and has entrusted us with something that belongs to Him. We will be condemned and punished by the owner and Master if we dare to abuse or mistreat or misuse that which He has entrusted to us (Luke 12:42-46; Matt. 25:14-30; 1 Cor. 4:2). Many passages teach us not to deliberately kill innocent human beings (Ex. 23:7; Rev. 21:8, 22:15; Matt. 15:19-20; Rom. 13:8-20). Herod is considered wicked because he killed all the male children in Bethlehem. Abortion clinics could be referred to in the Bible in Deuteronomy 27:25; "Cursed is the man that accepts a bribe to kill an innocent person." If indeed an unborn baby is a person, then who could be considered more innocent? If given the choice, choose life. Mary did!

6. Does a Christian Have Two Natures?

If we are born again, saved by the Blood of Christ, a believing Christian, do we still have a righteous nature and a sinful nature? Sanctification, to provide the simplistic definition, is the process in which God makes the Christian holy and enables the Christian to grow into more holiness through time. In order to discover how this is done, the Christian must become a student of the scriptures and decide how the old nature, or old man, or sin nature relates to the new nature, new man, or righteous nature. Notice that sanctification is an ongoing process, and not done in one swift stroke of the pen when we are saved.

What is the actual definition of nature is the question that needs to be answered, and the word defined to determine how some see the distinction between the old man and the new man and its relevant working in the life of the Christian. One way to understand nature is the capacity within the Christian. The old man is consumed and his capacity is filled with sinful nature before salvation while living his worldly life. At the moment of conversion, the Christian receives a new nature, but all of his sin, although forgiven, might tend to control his life at times. In this sense, the Christian has two competing natures within him, but through salvation and sanctification, the old sinful nature is being crucified, resulting in the Christian no longer being a slave to sin (Rom. 6:6).

The old man, sinful nature is dead according to Romans 6, but the Christian still has a natural tendency to sin. I suppose in this light, the man actually has three natures: the sinful, the righteous, and the human nature. This is why believers are encouraged to put to death the deeds of the body (Rom. 8:13), to put to death that which makes a Christian sin (Col. 3:5), and to put to aside other sins such as anger, wrath, and malice (Col. 3:8). All this to say that the Christian has but one nature, but that nature needs continual renewing (Col. 3:10). This renewing is a lifetime process for the Christian, and even the Apostle had trouble understanding and controlling this seemingly double nature. "I do not understand what I do. For what I want to do I do not do, but what I hate I do" (Rom. 7:15-25). He goes on to explain that it is the sin living in him that makes him do these things which he hates.

Nature is a desire and the Christian has a war going on inside (Gal. 5:16-17). Even though the battle against sin is constant and sometimes a battle the Christian will lose, we do not stumble beyond recovery (Rom. 11:11). Strive toward perfection, but do not be down on yourself unnecessarily when you are tempted. Asking forgiveness, repentance, and starting over is a continuous process for the Christian, but when you fall one step back, God will bring you two steps forward.

7. *Paul and the Woman*

Paul starts his message in 1st Timothy 2:9-15 to women with the word *also* or *in like manner*, meaning that he wills or commands what follows as he had commanded before. He told the women to "dress themselves modestly, with decency and propriety, not with braided hair or gold or pearls or expensive clothes, but with good deeds, appropriate for women who profess to worship God." The Apostle seems to refer here to different parts of the Grecian and Roman style of dress. The *stola* was originally very simple. It was a long piece of cloth, doubled in the middle and sewn up on both sides, leaving room only for the arms, reminding us women of today of the caftan. At the top, a piece was cut out or a slit made so the head could go through. It hung down to the feet and was belted with the *zona* or sash tied around the body. It was sometimes made with, sometimes without, sleeves, and was gathered on each shoulder with a scarf, belt, or buckle of some kind so as to fit better. Some of the women wore them open on the side or both sides to above the knee, so that a part of the thigh was exposed. This was generally the dress code for young girls. However, if an older woman wore her dresses this way, she was considered immodest.

Although the dress in itself was simple, the ornaments worn with them were gold and precious stones. The hair was often crisped and curled in a complex way with braids and more ornaments. To the Apostle Paul, this was an imitation of the extravagant costume those with impurity of mind would wear to attract the eye of admirers and cause the tongue to resort to lying flattery. He was telling the women to be decent but be moderate and modest. He added that what was most becoming to a woman was good works which the women professing Christianity adorned themselves with. There was a Jewish custom where the matrons at a wedding cried out to the bride, "There is no need of paint, jewelry, or braided hair for she herself is beautiful." Perhaps Paul too, thought this way about the women.

He said the women were to learn in silence, not to teach or have authority over men. A woman should attempt nothing, either in public or private, that belonged to a man in his peculiar function. This was prohibited by the Roman laws. It was lawful for men to speak in public assemblies and to ask questions or even interrupt the speaker when there was a statement they did not understand. This was not a liberty for the women, for one or two reasons. First, it was the law, and second, the women usually stood at the back and could not hear very well what was being said at the front of the assembly. They might yell out to ask a question, and the speaker suggested that they wait until they got home and ask their husbands, who were close enough to hear, and therefore not interrupt or delay the messages (Acts 22:2; 2 Thess. 3:12) meaning to settle down and not be unruly.

In emphasizing godly conduct for women, Paul stressed, with Peter, the unfading beauty of a gentle and quiet spirit, which is of great worth in God's sight (1 Pet. 3:4). Why is such a quiet and submissive spirit of great worth to God? Because it manifests an understanding and acceptance of His design for the human race. As elsewhere (1 Cor. 11:8-10), Paul here based his view of male/female relationships in the church on the account of Creation recorded in Genesis 2. He made no reference whatever to the so-called curse of Genesis 3:16; rather, the roles Paul spelled out here are a product of God's fundamental design, wherein Adam was formed first and then Eve. More is involved here than mere chronological priority. Paul saw the priority in time as indicative of the leadership given to the male, to which the woman, the helper suitable for him, should respond (Gen. 2:18). Without getting all bent out of shape with Paul and searching your heart and mirror, test yourself to see if you are pleasing to God and of great worth with a gentle and quiet spirit. I, for one, must work on this daily and have found that the better I get, the more respect I receive both from men and women. Respect covers over resentment of being submissive, and submission comes more easily without resentment, therefore gaining respect and around and around we go.

8. Renewal

Only the idea of Adam was conceived. He, in his entirety was created from the dust of the earth by God. Eve was then created from the rib of Adam. The rest of human life is conceived inside the womb of the woman until upon reaching maturity, we witness the miracle of physical birth. This in itself would be a miracle, but the miraculous process continues throughout our life here on earth. Are you aware that body cells replace themselves at a rate of 2½ million cells per minute normally, so our physical bodies can keep renewing themselves? The liver replaces itself with new cells every seven months, the heart in five years, and the stomach lining every four minutes. This continuous replacement of cells is vital to our existence.

When this tiny body begins to grow, his little skin must stretch in order to continue covering the flesh, muscles, tendons, etc. that are all progressing in perfect proportion to the expanding bone structure. Scientists have a handle on all of the facts here and you can check out hundreds of Web sites for further information from your favorite scientist. Much like the majority of you, I take this all for granted and do not dig too deeply into the medical aspects of body growth. I do, however, take a special interest in spiritual growth and the renewing of our spirit cells. Don't let anyone or anything put you in a fleshy mind because of their human way of thinking. "They do not hold tightly to Christ the Head. It is from Him that all parts of the body are cared for and held together so it grows in the way God wants it to grow" (Col. 2:10).

The number-one cell that will need to be renewed is the mind, and according to Romans 12:2, we stop conforming to the patterns of this world. 1 Peter 1:13 tells us to prepare our minds for action. We realize that the mind is probably the most active part of our being, and left uncontrolled, it can wander into dangerous territory. We start by setting our minds on things about and not earthly things (Col. 3:2), which will help you to rid yourselves of all malice and all deceit, hypocrisy, envy, and slander of every kind, using the wisdom that comes from heaven (James 3:17), which God gives generously to all who ask (James 1:5). Understand what the Lord's will is, and be made new in the attitude of your minds (Eph. 5:17, 4:23). Paul teaches that keeping the mind where it is should be is a pressing goal that we have to continuously strain toward, and none have been made perfect yet! He cautions Christians to live up to what God has already taught us, not letting our minds drift back into earthly things, where our destiny is destruction (Phil 3:12-21). Those controlled by sinful nature have their minds set on what nature desires and cannot please God (Rom. 8:5-8). We then become enemies of God in our minds (Col. 1:21). God has put His laws in our minds (Heb. 8:10) and we will rely on this mind with wisdom to understand the last days (Rev. 17:9, 17).

The Lord has been grieved over the thoughts of man since creation, and He saw how great man's wickedness on earth had become. "Every inclination of the thoughts of his heart was only evil all the time" (Gen 6:5-6). The Lord always knows all the thoughts of man, not just the holy, righteous ones (Ps. 94:11). "He detests the thoughts of the wicked, but those of the pure are pleasing to Him" (Prov. 15:26). Nothing is hidden from God; "the Word is sharp and judges the thoughts and attitude of the heart" (Heb. 4:12-13). Notice we are not the ones to judge lest we discriminate through evil thoughts (James 1:3-4). We are urged to change and be transformed by the renewing of our minds (Rom. 12:2), to meditate on His Word and Law day and night (Ps. 1:2), and whatever we do we are to work at it with all our hearts as if we were working for God and not men (Col. 3:23).

Now comes the part that you all have been waiting for! The mouth that harbors the tongue! We, the entire Christian church body with one heart and mouth, glorify the God and Father of our Lord Jesus Christ (Rom. 15:6). Are we doing this? Dies the same message come out of all Christian mouths? Would you want everyone to hear what you say? Things that come out of our mouth should come from a godly heart, but are our heart and words always godly? Or do we have evil thoughts that include murder, adultery, sexual immorality, theft, and slander (Matt. 15:17-20)? Paul teaches to lead a quiet life and mind our own business (1 Thess. 4:11). For the majority of us, this would mean keeping our mouth shut, opening it only when it is helpful for building others up according to their needs (Eph. 4:29). James speaks of a double-minded man (1:7-8) and suggests we be slow to speak and slow to become angry (1:19-21). Let the tongue loose and we deceive ourselves and our religion is worthless (1:26). My term for this is Christian Snob, since the tongue makes great boasts (3:5), and corrupts the whole person. These people praise God and curse men with the same tongue, often in the same sentence, and do not speak as one speaking the words they have read in the Bible (1 Pet. 4:11). We should teach in accord with sound doctrine and set examples and show integrity in our lives so our speech cannot be condemned (Titus 2:7-8).

I borrowed a couple of prayers from Paul for all of you: "Make it your ambition to lead a quiet life, to mind your own business and to work with your hands, just as we told you, so that your daily life may win the respect of outsiders and so that your will not be dependent on anybody" (1 Thess. 4:11-12). "Do your best to present yourself to God as one approved, a workman who does not need to be ashamed and who correctly handles the Word of Truth" (2 Tim. 2:15-17). And if you will, "pray also for me, that whenever I open my mouth, words may be given so that I will fearlessly make known the mystery of the gospel" (Eph. 6:19).

9. *Knowing Our Own Faults*

Do you know the truth about yourself? The Word of God tells us the only way to know the truth about ourselves is to know the truth about God. Is this true knowledge only to be found in the actual presence of God? Scripture tells us that we may find the true knowledge of God, and therefore the true knowledge of ourselves, in the Word of God as we find God himself revealed to us.

Isaiah found this when he entered the temple of God and he saw the thrice-holy God exalted in majesty and glory. "Woe is me! For I am undone, because I am a man of unclean lips" (Isa. 6:5). Peter said, "depart from me, for I am a sinful man" (Luke 5:8). Paul found true knowledge of himself: "Oh wretched man that I am! Who shall deliver me from the body of death?" (Rom. 7:24). David too, found this knowledge; "Who can understand his errors?" David cried out not so much in despair but in painful knowledge of himself.

We must say to ourselves that we are creatures of the day and life is very short. We must recognize we have an immortal soul. One book reveals the truth about God to me, and that is the ministry of the Word in the psalm telling us that the Law of the Lord is perfect, converting the soul (Ps. 19:7). We must beware of regarding sin in our hearts and beware of sinning against light, knowing what the Law of God says. We must beware of hypocrisy, secretly enjoying sin, seeking to take grace for it. The tempter (Satan) says why not go ahead and enjoy yourselves and the things of this world, God will forgive you anything. Satan is a liar and has come to steal our peace, kill our faith, and destroy our trust in God (John 10:10). There is no such thing as a small sin. If you have and keep and cherish small sins, you must find for yourself a small god, for God is too great, holy, and infinite to overlook or sweep these sins under the carpet. David cried out that only against God had he sinned, and did evil in God's sight. Surely God has seen it, even though we conceal it from everyone else.

We read in the epistle to the Hebrews 12:15, that the root of bitterness begins with the root of sin. We are so embarrassed and ashamed when our sins come to our conscious mind because we often do not see them in their roots. Sometimes we only want the embarrassment, shame, and troublesome nature of our sins removed. In other words, we want our conscience saved but not our soul. Salvation is too much commitment for some. Often, there are the sins we do not even notice because they have become a habit. Sow a thought, reap an action; sow an action, reap a habit; sow a habit, reap a character; sow a character, reap a destiny. How easy we find it to excuse ourselves or justify our actions. We must watch our hearts and watch sin in its first rising. "Above all else, guard your heart, for it is the wellspring of life" (Prov. 4:23).

If we left it here with, *who can understand our errors*, as David asked, we might be left thinking that we could not understand our errors or would not be able to deal with them and that is ok with God. We have a brighter side to this text that says *cleanse me, Lord, from secret faults.* There are two texts in the New Testament that we need to keep together. "Having therefore these promises, dearly beloved, let us cleanse ourselves from all filthiness of the flesh and spirit, perfecting holiness in the fear of God" (2 Cor. 7:1) and "but if we walk in the light, as He is the light, we have fellowship one with another, and the blood of Jesus Christ His Son cleanses us from all sin" (1 John 1:7). We are to cleanse ourselves from every type of sin, but we have the encouragement and assurance that the blood of Jesus Christ His Son is sufficient to cleanse us from all sin.

The Greek language tells us the word *cleansed* may be translated in a continuous sense, in that the Blood of Jesus goes on cleansing us in a continual work and is continually available to us. The contamination of sin is the guilt that we carry with us. When you confess your sin to God, leave the guilt with Him also. He has boundless sympathy for us. "He is full of grace" (John 1:14) and "If we confess our sins, He is faithful and just to forgive us our sins, and to cleanse us from all unrighteousness" (1 John 2:1).

To know our own faults is great, if you want Jesus Christ to change you. Knowing your own faults and saying "that is just the way I am and I cannot change" is denying yourself the blessings of God. "I praise you because I am fearfully and wonderfully made. Your works are wonderful and I know that full well" (Ps. 139:14). This means you and me! God loves each and every one of us just the way we are, but He also desires to make us into His image. I choose to be a person who walks in the Spirit and is covered with the Blood of Jesus. Will you join me?

10. Attitude Adjustments

To work together in the body of Christ, most of us need an attitude adjustment. All the hard work and talent in the world cannot make up for wrong attitudes. To have unity in a church body, we first must develop the right attitude toward God (Matt. 22:37-38) with a faithful outlook (Heb. 11:1-6; Rom. 10:17). It is required that we have a truthful attitude and not stir up God's wrath by suppressing the truth (Rom. 1:18-21), ultimately forgetting to glorify Him. If our relationship with God is right, then most likely, our relationships with others will go well (Prov. 16:7). Servant attitude is a must, and it has been suggested that instead of changing others that we humbly look to ourselves (Rom. 12:3) and be willing to do even the lowest tasks (John 13:16-17) in order to receive the blessings in store for us (Matt. 25:21).

Here is the really big adjustment: changing your attitude toward learning! This means you have to be teachable, and to be teachable is to be wise (Prov. 15:31-21). To be teachable, one must have an eagerness to learn (Titus 2) and grow (2 Cor. 13:11) and be open to correction, advice, and criticism (Prov. 1:5, 9:9, 16:21). This includes a willingness to admit our mistakes (James 5:16). Guidelines toward loving our brothers in Christ is a must-read (John 13:34-35; 1 Pet. 1:22-23; Phil. 1:27, 2:2-7). This will bring about a willingness to work together (1 Cor. 12:21) and an appreciation for others (1 Cor. 1:14; 1 Thess. 5:12-13). We are to submit to others (Eph. 5:21), and submit to those in positions of leadership (Heb. 13:17). Too many bosses and not enough workers is a common problem.

Mental attitude when confronted with an unexpected situation has the potential to overcome many challenges, beat incredible odds, and come out a survivor, provided the mental attitude is godly. A wilderness emergency could possibly happen to anyone, anywhere, but remember that survival is a state of mind (Matt. 19:26; Mark 9:23). Your brain is your best survival tool, and you most likely will not use your physical skills if you do not have a positive mental attitude (Luke 18:27). The mind is a powerful force that has control of the body, its actions, and its reasoning (Col. 3:1; 1 Cor. 2:16). Pressure attitude deals with the setting of goals that will give motivation and allow you to survive pressures in life (Luke 12:22-31; Rom. 12:2). Your brain will be your best asset or your most dangerous enemy; therefore, you will have to defeat negative thoughts and imaginations, control and master your fears (2 Tim. 1:7).

The attitude of peace, hospitality, friendliness, gentleness, and meekness is a necessity, and guidelines can be found in scriptures throughout, so I have limited the list here (Rom. 14:19; Eph. 4:1-3; Matt. 5:9; James 3:17-18; Rom. 12:13; Heb. 13:2; 1 Pet. 4:9; 3 John 5:8; Acts 2:44-47). And don't forget forgiveness, patience, and all those things that are so, so hard for most (Eph. 4:2-32). Our attitude toward work should be a privilege and enthusiastic (1 Tim. 1:12; 1 Cor. 15:9-10; 2 Cor. 9:7). Like those in the days of Nehemiah, we need a mind to work (Neh. 4:6) and to serve heartily (Col. 3:23) because the slothful person is just as harmful as the destructive person (Prov. 18:9).

Initiative has been defined as the willingness to do what is right and needed without having to be prodded. We should not have to be reminded of our responsibilities or have them pointed out to us (1 Tim. 4:14). No murmuring and grumbling is allowed while working for Jesus (Phil 2:14), and remember to finish what you start (John 4:34; Heb. 6:12) not leaving a mess for someone else to clean up. A cheerful attitude is probably the hardest to obtain but can be had (Jud. 5:3; Ps. 30:4; Eph. 5:19) and we most certainly should be cheerful knowing all the blessings God has stored up for us that we cannot even imagine or envision the worth (1 Cor. 2:9). "So my dear brothers and sisters, stand strong. Do not let anything change you. Always give yourselves fully to the work of the Lord, because you know that your work in the Lord is never wasted" (1 Cor. 15:58).

11. Clean Up Your Act

Have you ever heard that cleanliness is next to godliness? Do not spend too much time searching the Bible for scripture on this, because it is not there, that I can find. Benjamin Franklin actually coined this phrase; however, there is a strong inclination of the phrase throughout the Bible. It seems that God created man out of dirt and spends our lifetime cleaning it out of us. The Law of Moses commanded bathing both for physical cleanliness and as a religious ceremony. Already at the time of Jacob, pure bodies symbolized purity from sin (Gen. 35:2). Special purifications were ordered on special occasions throughout Israel's history (Jos. 3:5). Even Pilate washed his hands before the Jews to claim innocence of the crime of killing Jesus (Matt. 27:24). Years earlier, David spoke of clean hands as a sign of innocence (Ps. 73:13).

People may have bathed in a river, either for ordinary cleaning (Ex. 2:5) or to achieve Levitical purity. Well-equipped homes of the wealthy had bathing facilities in the courtyards (2 Sam. 11:2) or in special rooms. A stone bathtub has been found in the remains of a Greek civilization from the time of Exodus. This tub had running water and a drain for waste. In the time of Jesus, the Greeks and Romans built extensive and luxurious public baths. This arrangement still exists in the larger Roman cities of Palestine.

The ancient bathtubs were made of clay mixed with finely chopped straw, resembling the bricks the Israelites were forced to make for the Egyptians. Copper was introduced to the builders around 2500 BC, and a bathroom of the well-to-do could measure about fifteen feet square. The lower part of the wall and the floor were lined with baked brick. The floor sloped to the center of the room to allow the water to run off into a small brook through baked and glazed earthenware tiles. The septic tanks were covered with layers of brick. King Nebuchadnezzar's bath actually was a shower. Slaves poured water over him as he washed with soap made of ashes of certain plants and fats. Any of you remember lye soap made from hog fat boiled outside in a large pot over an open fire?

The book of Leviticus deals with the issues of cleanliness and impurity. The Children of Israel needed to be clean as a sign of separation from the surrounding nations. The priests were washed with water to consecrate them before entering the Tent of Meeting (Ex. 29:4). A bronze basin on a bronze stand was placed between the Tent of Meeting and the altar. "Whenever they enter the Tent of Meeting, they shall wash with water so that they will not die" (Ex. 30:17, 21). The basin, the last piece of Tabernacle furniture, is described here because of the emphasis on its use, rather than on its construction. It was to be of bronze, not silver or gold, because it belonged in the sanctuary courtyard between the bronze altar of burnt offering and the entrance to the tent (Ex. 40:30). When officiating in the tent or before the altar, the priests were required to wash their hands and feet. If they failed to do so, they would die. This was to be a lasting ordinance (Ex. 12:17). The laver (basin) symbolized the need for purity through cleansing from defilement. The altar speaks of salvation through a sin offering. The laver speaks of sanctification which is progressive and continual.

Spiritual cleaning runs throughout the Old and New Testament. The prophet Isaiah wrote that Zion would be cleaned by a spirit of judgment and a spirit of fire, as the judging would be like fire that would burn away the nation's undesirable filth (Isa. 4:3-4). People who think they are pure or morally clean before God, but still are not cleansed of their moral filth of sin, are hypocrites (Prov. 30:12). Israel's restoration would be more physical. God promised that He would sprinkle clean water on them and they would be clean. He would cleanse them from all impurities and from all their idols (Ezek. 36:24-25). In Old Testament times, sprinkling, or washing with water, pictured cleansing from ceremonial defilement (Lev. 15:21-22; Num. 19:17-19). The cleansing was to be followed by the impartation of new life, which God promised to give them through an undivided heart and a new spirit (Ezek. 11:19). Joshua's filthy clothes, representing his sins and guilt and that of the nations and those which Satan accused him of wearing, were removed. He was then clothed with rich garments, representing purity and forgiveness (Zech. 3:3-5).

Contact with the dead was an especially contaminating experience, because of the association of physical death with spiritual death (Gen. 2:17; Deut. 30:15; Rom. 6:23). Some means of purification had to be done for those coming in contact with the dead, otherwise he would remain unclean, and if he approached the tabernacle, he would be killed (Num. 19:9-13). The Israelites became unclean by killing the Midianites, and had to be cleansed along with prisoners, animals, clothing, and weapons (Num. 31:19-24). Read Judges chapter 7 in your spare time to see what empty hands can do if they are clean. The Eastern peoples were as thick as locusts (Jud. 7:12), but the Lord delivered them into Gideon and the 100 men that were with him because their hands were clean and empty (Jud. 7:19-22).

New Testament cleanliness is in relationship to cleaning of the believer's life (1 John 1:9; John 15:3; James 4:8; Eph. 5:26). Peter clearly taught that baptism was not merely a ceremonial act of physical purification but the pledge of a good conscience toward God (1 Pet. 3:21). Obedience to God requires purification, which here implies separation from everything that contaminates body and spirit and from every person who pollutes the truth (2 Cor. 7:1). It is essential to put away or remove all moral filth and all the abundance of evil, and humbly receive the implanted Word (James 1:21). You must rid yourself of all such things—anger, rage, malice, slander, and filthy language (Col. 3:7-9). The word *rid* means to put off like a suit of clothes. Here, it means throw it off like a dirty shirt.

To draw near to God demands His cleansing. "Wash your hands you sinners and purify your hearts you double minded" (James 4:18). When Jesus washed the disciple's feet, and Peter, thinking he understood but continued to miss the spiritual lesson, asked Jesus to was his hands and head as well (John 13:9-10), Jesus answered him saying that a person who has had a bath (salvation), then all one needs is confession of sin (the continual application of Jesus's death to cleanse one's daily sins (1 John 1:7, 2:1-2). The disciples had been cleaned by Jesus and His message but one, Judas, was not cleansed (John 13:10-11). Christian's failures are under the cleansing power of the shed blood of Christ (1 John 1:7).

When someone clean touched something unclean, the clean became unclean. Luke, in describing Jesus's actions by touching and healing the leper, showed that Jesus was the source of ceremonial cleansing (Luke 5:12-16). If He was the source of cleansing for the leper, He is the source of cleansing for us and our nation, for God is the same yesterday, today, and forever (Heb. 13:8). How miserably we feel with unclean bodies. How much more miserable are we with unclean spirits, minds, worship, and offerings to the purest of the pure, Lord. There is no virtue in having a clean Bible. Natural body oils from your hands, highlighted passages and notes in the column make for a worn, dirty Bible. These are signs of a well-read and loved book. "Blessed are those who wash their robes that they may have the right to the Tree of Life and may go through the gates into the City" (Rev. 22:14).

12. Temptations

Only those who try to resist temptation know how strong it is. A person who gives in to temptation after five minutes does not know what it would have been like an hour later. Until you fight temptation, you cannot realize the strength it has. The first temptation was in the Garden (Gen. 3:1-10), when Satan told the big lie that Eve would not die if she ate what God told her was forbidden. He planted both doubt and confusion in her mind and has been doing this to man every since. During temptation, you have promises from God and refuge in Him. He assures us that no harm will come on us and that angels will guard us (Ps. 91:9-16). You know that misery loves company and people try to pull you into sin, but do not give in to them (Prov. 1:10-19).

Jesus overcame temptation when tempted by the devil right after He was baptized (Matt. 4:1-11). You will also be tempted by the devil right after you make a commitment to the Lord in any way. Jesus answered the devil with scripture (Matt. 4:4, 7, 10) and we too can overcome temptation with the written Word. The seventy-two men (Luke 10:1) Jesus sent out ahead of Him came back and joyfully reported that even the demons submitted to them in Jesus's name (Luke 10:17). However, Jesus was not impressed and told them He saw Satan fall from heaven and reminded them that He gave them the power and authority to overcome Satan (Luke 10:19). "Do not rejoice that the spirits submit to you but rejoice that your name is written in heaven" (Luke 10:20).

The scriptures remind us of the Israelites in the desert, in saying lean not to sin. "These things occurred as an example to keep us from setting our hearts on evil things as they did (1 Cor. 10:6). All of the sinful happenings in the Old Testament were written as warnings for us, so we need to stand firm and not just think we are, or we might just fall (1 Cor 10:11-12). Although the devil is still our there in this old world, tempting man with every trick he can come up with, the Bible tells us that this is common and we all will face Satan's tempting schemes (1 Cor. 10:13). We are to consider it joy whenever we face trials, because we know we are being tested and God is teaching us perseverance (James 1:2-3). Never do we think or say that God is tempting us, because He cannot be tempted and does not tempt anyone with evil (James 1:13-14). He is faithful to His Word and to believers, and will not let this temptation get the best of us, but will provide a way out of it (1 Cor. 10:13).

God helps us to avoid sin in many ways, if only we would search the scriptures for his directions. Wisdom lets us see the world as it really is, giving us awareness, discernment, and keeps us from falling into traps. It opens our eyes to the consequences of sin (Job 28:28; Ps. 111:10; Prov. 2:1-6). Solomon did not choose wealth or power, but rather wisdom (1 Kings 3:2-15), and God answered his prayer and made him one of the wisest men in the world with the benefits of wealth galore. The Spirit that God causes to live within us envies intensely, since God is a jealous God and therefore, He says for us to submit ourselves to Him, resist the devil, and the devil will flee (James 4:7). God's jealous nature was revealed in the second of the Ten Commandments. It can be hard to follow God for all times, but He will help and uphold us. He can change minds so they can accept the truth and escape the traps of the devil (2 Tim. 2:26). Hebrews 4:16 tells us that we can approach the throne of God boldly, but do not confuse the word *bold* with *bossy, arrogant,* or *demanding.* The word *boldly* here means with confidence that God hears and answers sincere prayers.

"Blessed is the man who perseveres under trial because when he has stood the test, he will receive the crown of life that God has promised to those who love Him" (James 1:12). We cannot exist in continuous sunlight. There has to be a period of darkness in our lives or we would roast. We cannot always live in a protected environment. Satan wanted Job, who was upright in the sight of the Lord, and challenged God to take down the hedge and allow him to strike everything he had. The Lord, having great faith and trust in Job, agreed (Job 1:12). Job's world got very dark! Satan asked God if he could sift Peter as wheat and the Lord, having great faith and trust in Peter, agreed (Luke 22:31). Peter's world got very dark! God protected Job from death and restored all he lost twofold. He prayed for Peter and had faith that he would not fail, and Peter passed the test.

Jesus prayed for us living here on earth also (John 17:20-26) who believed in Him, that they might live in Him and allow Him to live in them. He knew we would face temptations and trials and wanted us to know, just as with Peter and Job, that He would bring us through. The word *tried* or *tested* was used to refer to the refining of metals. During this process, the impurities are heated out. When God tests us or allows the devil to put us through trials, we are being refined (Job 23:10). Do you feel the heat?

13. Questions and Answers

Q: As a child of God, can one fall out of His favor?

A: There is bad news and good news here. Men are without excuse to know that God exists but neither glorify Him nor give thanks (Rom. 1:20-21). In this case, God gives these over to their sinful desires to do as they please (Rom. 1:24-32). If men have a stubborn and unrepentant heart, they are storing up wrath against themselves from God (Rom. 2:5-11). Some allow sin to become their master, and a child of God should be dead to sin (Rom. 6:6-14). Isaiah 59:2 assures us that we can be separated from God through sin in our lives. The wonderful good news is, "Again, I ask; did they stumble so as to fall beyond recovery? Not at all!" (Rom 11:11). "It does not, therefore, depend on man's desire or effort, but on God's mercy" (Rom. 8:16), this referring to God's saving grace. A child of God can be convinced that nothing will be able to separate them from the love of God, for God's gifts and His call are irrevocable (Rom. 8:38-39, 11:29).

Q: What does the Bible say about pastors who use scripture to make people feel like he is telling them to do like he says and not ask questions?

A: The scriptures are filled with wayward, selfish shepherds. James 1:22 tells us not to just read the Word, but to do what it says. This includes pastors! Matthew 23 speaks against pastors who do not do like they preach, saying that everything they do is for man to see. Jesus calls them blind guides and blind fools. Isaiah 56:10-11 tells us that shepherds who lack understanding turn to their own way and seek their own personal gain. They do not inquire of the Lord and have not given care to the sheep. They have led the sheep astray and take care of themselves. The Lord's anger burned against them (Jer. 10:21, 23:1-3, 50:6; Ezek. 34:1-10; Zech. 10:2-3).

Q: What does the Bible say about people being negative all the time?

A: Negativity comes from your thoughts, which become actions, and these actions become habits. "Take every thought captive to make it obedient to Christ" (2 Cor. 10:5). Jesus came that we might have life abundantly, and that leaves no room for negative thoughts (John 10:10), and God's Spirit will give you the power to live like God wants you to live (John 14:26). The fruits of the Spirit include love, joy, peace, patience, kindness, goodness, faithfulness, gentleness, and self-control (Gal. 5:16, 22-23), again leaving no room for negativity. Think right and change your negative attitude (Phil. 4:4-13) and others should warn the negative person (Titus 3:10-11).

Q: What does the Bible say about pride?

A: The Bible is filled with scripture about pride, arrogance, and the proud. The point of them all is that God hates all of them (Prov. 8:13), because with pride comes disgrace (Prov. 11:2). Pride causes disagreement and fights (Prov. 13:10) and God tears down the house of the proud (Prov. 15:25). The most famous and often-quoted proverb is: "Pride goes before destruction and a haughty spirit before a fall" (Prov. 16:18). The New Testament speaks against pride and warns that the people will turn to pride in the last days (2 Tim. 3:1-5) and God still opposes the proud (James 4:6; 1 Pet. 5:5).

Q: What does the Bible mean when it speaks of renewing of your mind?

A: Quite simply, renewing of your mind means putting your thoughts back on God and not on yourself, others, or things of the world. We are not automatically mature in Christ when we are saved, but we must let God's Spirit go to work within our spirit and develop godly character. This is a lifetime process and we must watch our thoughts, "for as he thinks within himself, so he is" (Prov. 23:6-7). To renew our minds, we must discipline it by setting thoughts on things above and not the things in this world (Col. 3:1; 2 Cor. 10:5; Phil. 2:5).

Q: Where in scripture does it talk about thinking too highly of ourselves?

A: The exact wording you ask for is found in Romans 12:3, and Romans 12:16 goes on to say not to be proud and not to be conceited. 1st Timothy 6:3-4 calls a person conceited when he teaches false doctrine and says he understands nothing. His wisdom is only foolishness (1 Cor. 3:18-23) and our thinking becomes futile and our foolish hearts darken (Rom. 1:21-23).

Part VI Power

1. Power

"This is the Word of the Lord to Zerubbabel, 'not by might nor by power, but by my Spirit,' says the Lord Almighty" (Zech. 4:6). God is still speaking to His people today the same Words He spoke to Zerubbabel. His Word, spoken through His Spirit, is living and active. It is still sharp and still penetrates even to dividing soul and spirit, joints and marrow. It still judges the thoughts and attitudes of the heart (Heb. 4:12). The Greek word *zao*, meaning live and quick, is used throughout the scripture. This Word has penetrating power to reach the innermost being of a person to judge the thoughts and attitudes of the heart. In doing this, it is able to discriminate successfully between what is spiritual in man and what is merely natural. The Word can separate these inner elements, even when they are interwoven as closely as joints and marrow. The inner life of a Christian is often both genuinely spiritual and completely human. It takes a supernaturally discerning agent, such as the Word of God, to sort them out.

Moses was in the desert, with the angel who spoke to him on Mt. Sinai, and he received living words to pass on to us (Acts 7:38). When we receive the Word of God, then it is at work in us (1 Thess. 2:13). The Word of God is the Sword of the Spirit (Eph. 6:17). The Lord declares that His Word is like fire, and like a hammer that breaks a rock to pieces. The fire refines and the hammer convicts. Notice the prophet Isaiah was in anguish because he was a man with unclean lips, and the seraph flew to him with a live coal, touched his mouth, and told him the guilt was taken away and his sin atoned for (Isa. 6:6). This was not only atonement, refining by fire, but a conviction, God hammering His point, since in the next verse, God asked who would go for Him, and Isaiah was convicted to answer: "Here am I. Send me!" Gold perishes even though refined by fire, but we are refined by the Word of God and are shielded through faith by the power of God (1 Pet. 1:3-9). The Holy Spirit is the one who convicts the world of guilt (John 16:8), and we remember that He came with tongues of fire (Acts 2:2-4).

The Word of God is a seed to which Christians have been born imperishable through the living and enduring Word of God (1 Pet. 1:23). The farmer (God) sows the seed (the Word), and in turn, we scatter seeds all on the ground (into others' minds and hearts). The seeds sprout and grow without our understanding, and by itself, the soil produces grain. As soon as the grain is ripe, the harvest has come (Mark 4:14-29). When it is time for Christ to come again, this harvest will be gathered, because the time to reap will be upon us (Rev. 14:15). Newly planted seed needs water to grow. Jesus planted a seed and watered it all in a matter of minutes with the woman at the well (John 7:15). The water in the Bethesda Pool was healing only when the angels came to stir and the cripple could not get there to be healed. Jesus, with water the man knew nothing of, told the man to pick up his mat and walk (John 5:3-9). These streams of living water that flow from within all who believe in Jesus will give a continual source of satisfaction, which will provide life continually (John 7:38; Rev. 22:1). John explained that the living water was the coming of the gift of the Holy Spirit that would provide the believer with power (Acts 1:8).

The Word of God has cleansing power, as mentioned by Paul for the husbands to love their wives and to make them holy by cleansing them by the washing with water through the Word (Eph. 5:25-26). "As we enter the Most Holy Place and draw near to God, we have a sincere heart in full assurance of faith, having our hearts sprinkled to cleanse us from a guilty conscience and having our bodies washed with pure water" (Heb. 10:21-22). This water is life and it is free to everyone who is thirsty for it (Rev. 21:6). "The Spirit and the Bride say, 'come'! And let him who hear say, 'come'! Whoever is thirsty, let him come, and whoever wishes let him take the free gift of the water of life" (Rev. 22:17). God will gather His people in that day and they will rejoice and shout for joy and they will be like a well-watered garden, referring to the original Garden of Eden, and they will sorrow no more (Jer. 31:12).

God has given us this living water and eternal life and this life is in His Son. 1 John 5:7 explains that the Spirit, the water, and the blood are in agreement and testify to this. The term *water* here refers to the baptism of Jesus, by John the Baptist, by which His public ministry was initiated (Matt. 3:13:17). *Blood* would then refer to His death on the cross by which His earthly work was terminated (Luke 23:44-46). John insisted that Jesus did not come by water alone but by water and blood, because of the false teachings going around. These people taught that the divine Christ descended on the man Jesus at His baptism, and left Him before His crucifixion, denying that one person, Jesus Christ, came by both water and blood. The Spirit's witness may be thought of as coming through the prophets. The Spirit's witness, then, was made stronger and further confirmed by the historical realities involved in the water and the blood. Both the baptism and the crucifixion of Jesus are strongly attested historical facts (John 1:32-34, 19:33-37).

The Lord came to the prophet Zechariah and He was angry because the forefathers had not listened or paid attention. They turned away from God and stayed with the idol worship and their evil ways. God had declared that if the people would come back to Him, that He would return to them, but to no avail (Zech. 1:1-6). Then God asked a question we should think hard about! "Where are your forefathers now? And the prophets? Do they live forever?" Malachi 3:6-7 tells us the Lord does not change and urges again that His people return to Him (Heb. 13:8). Zechariah is a short book with only fourteen chapters, and in my Bible, only fourteen pages, but it is power-packed. God gave Zechariah eight visions, one right after the other. This first vision intrigued me, and when I started researching it, I found it intrigued many others. This is the vision of the man riding a red horse. This red horse does not seem to have the same significance as the red horse in Revelation, although some think they are the same. The four horses mentioned in Zechariah are called the four spirits of heaven and are sent out into the world to report on the condition of the world. This brings some to believe that they are speaking of the 1,000-year reign, since they report that all is at rest and peace. Perhaps they were God's eyes and represented the four corners of the earth. Perhaps the color of the red horse here does represent the condition of the 1,000-year reign, and then the reverse condition in the tribulation, when the release of the horses brings disaster to the earth. Maybe what the rider reported was passiveness, thinking the Lord had not yet come, as some had hoped (Hag. 2:21). As for me, I believe that there "was a man riding a red horse" and that "they are the ones the Lord has sent to go throughout the earth" (Zech. 1:8-10), just as written.

Take time to read Zechariah chapter three, where we find Satan standing, as always, accusing, degrading anyone and everyone who is in the presence of God of being filthy (Dan. 7:25; Zech. 3:1). Here again we see the power of God when He said to Satan, "The Lord rebuke you Satan" (3:2). Then He said to Joshua, "See, I have taken away your sin" (3:4). Joshua and his priestly companions were symbolic of things to come. In their official priestly cleansing from sin, they prefigured the future cleansing of the nation of Israel. This future cleansing was linked with the coming of the Sin-Remover, who was given three Messianic titles in this vision: My Servant, The Branch, and The Stone. Christ would be the Branch of David who would rise to power and glory out of the humiliation into which the line of David had fallen. This is the power of the Word of God, and as we well know, if it is not God's Word, it will fail (Acts 5:38). We serve a just and patient God, however, His Spirit will not strive with us forever (Gen. 6:3). We are warned, commanded, and expected to watch in hope for the Lord and wait (Mic. 7:7).

While writing this, I got the feeling I was searching! Perhaps I am! Perhaps we all should! There is a mighty power in the Word of God that many have hardly touched. Jesus sent the Holy Spirit to empower Christians that we might do the things He did and more (John 14:12-14; Acts 1:8) when we ask in faith. I am going to search this power and strive to use it to its fullest. Will you join me?

2. Understanding The Holy Spirit

Jesus told His disciples or followers to baptize people in the name of the Father, Son, and Holy Spirit. This biblical figure is your best friend, and you can learn about Him in God's book, the Bible. "Now the Lord is the Spirit" (2 Cor. 3:17), so we know that the Holy Spirit is God. Also, a husband and wife sold their land and brought part of the money to Peter, but lied about holding back some of it. Peter told them that Satan had made them lie to the Holy Spirit, and therefore, they had lied to God (Acts 5:3-4). The Spirit has qualities only God has such as being eternal as stated in Hebrews 9:14, and He is omnipresent, as told by David when he admitted that he could not escape or get away from God's Spirit. He is equal with God (Matt. 28:19), as He is one of the three persons of the One God (Matt. 3:16-17). He was involved in the creation, hovering over the waters (Gen. 1:2), and He helps the people of this creation to be born into God's Kingdom (John 3:5). He came from heaven because Jesus saw the Spirit coming down like a dove after He was baptized (Matt. 3:16).

The Holy Spirit feels, thinks, and acts like a person. The Bible calls him "he," never "it," and tells us that He will guide us into all truth (John 16:13). He knows things and understands all things (1 Cor. 2:10), gives and makes decisions as all of the gifts are produced and given by the

Spirit, just as He decides (1 Cor. 12:11). Jesus says He will be our friend after He goes back to the Father and sends the Holy Spirit back to earth (John 14:16-17). He can be lied to and he feels grief (Eph. 4:30). He is a person, kind of like us, and He is God and not like us at all. What an awesome friend! When you read the Bible, ask the Holy Spirit to help you to understand Him, and He will guide you to the scripture to explain Him and His works.

Imagine that you only had a picture of someone who you have not met personally. What do you really know about this person? Not much! Now, you meet the person and watch as he or she does his or her work in and out of the home. You watch them play sports, volunteer for charities, and interact with Christian friends. Now you know a lot more about them, right? People's actions show who they are. A great way to know the Holy Spirit is to see what He does. The Holy Spirit came on Mary so she would have God's Son, Jesus (Luke 1:35), He came upon Jesus like a dove when He was baptized (Luke 3:21-22) and He anointed Jesus and filled Him with everything He needed, in order to do what God wanted. Jesus said that the Spirit of the Lord was on Him and had anointed Him to tell the good news to poor people, announce freedom to prisoners, make the blind see again, free those who are beaten down, and announce the year when He will set His people free (Luke 4:18-19). Later, before Jesus was crucified, He told His disciples to wait for the Holy Spirit (Acts 1:4-5).

A few weeks later, at the Feast of Pentecost, there was a big, exciting commotion with wind and tongues of fire that separated and settled on each of the disciples, and they were all filled with the Holy Spirit (Acts 2:2-4). They were filled with courage and told everyone about Jesus and what had happened. God had promised this would happen hundreds of years before when He said through Joel that He would pour out His Spirit on all people (Joel 2:28-29). That was the beginning! The Holy Spirit had come to help all Jesus's followers obey God and spread the good news. He enabled them to perform miracles, including healing and raising people from the dead! He guided and changed them which are His main jobs, to make Jesus's followers more like Jesus. His job has not changed and He will do for you what He did for the disciples.

The Holy Spirit did not start His work with Jesus, but has been around since the beginning. In the Old Testament, He came on people and helped them to obey God. For example, God chose Bezalel to make a meeting place for Him, and the Holy Spirit filled him with skill, ability, and knowledge in all kinds of crafts (Ex. 31:3). He came on leaders and helped them to defeat Israel's enemies, came on King David with power, spoke to prophets, gave Daniel wisdom, and helped Zerubbabel rebuild the temple. The Holy Spirit does all this work with a smile and a song! This I know because He is God and like God, and God is love. This means that the Spirit's attitude to everything He does comes from love. He is gentle (Matt. 11:28-29) and will never force His way into our lives. He wants to work with us, but we can stop His work if we resist Him (1 Thess. 5:19; Acts 7:51). He has feelings, and His heart is open to us, because He loves us, and like the God that He is associated in Triune with, He pours love into us (Rom. 5:5) and gives us joy (1 Thess. 1:6). Because of His emotions (Eph. 4:30), we know that He understands ours.

God poured out the Spirit freely on us and gave us new life because of what Jesus our Savior has done (Titus 3:5-6). When we pray for God to save us and make the decision to accept Christ as our Savior, the Holy Spirit comes into our lives and we are never alone again. This salvation is the beginning of a lifelong adventure. Philip had such an adventure when he met an Ethiopian reading the Bible. The Holy Spirit was drawing the Ethiopian to God, and He told Philip to talk to him and explain the Bible to him. The man believed and was baptized (Acts 8:26-40). As Cornelius, a Roman commander, was praying, an angel told him to send for Peter, and in turn, the Holy Spirit told Peter to go with Cornelius's messengers to tell Cornelius's family about Jesus. The Holy Spirit came on all of them and they were saved and baptized (Acts 10). There is no more exciting adventure than leading someone to Jesus Christ. I will attest to this, as I am sure will Philip and Peter.

We are not born full-grown Christians. We have to grow up, since sin had us separated from God, and try as we might, we cannot grow without the new spirit that will move us to follow God's rules (Ezek. 36:26-27). When we believed, He marked us with the seal of the Holy Spirit (Eph. 1:13), and put His Spirit in our hearts (2 Cor. 1:22). God wants us to live great lives so He planned for us to become like His Son (Rom. 8:29). The Spirit's job is to guide us to become loving and obedient, allowing God to work in us to become more like Jesus (Phil. 2:13). If we say that we will never be what God wants, then we are trying to do it ourselves and need to back off and allow the Holy Spirit to do His work. He will give us strength and help us make right choices, and if God is on our side, who can be against us (Rom. 8:31)? We find comfort through the Holy Spirit, and then God's peace will watch over our hearts and minds, because we belong to Christ (Phil. 4:6-7). We will learn all things (John 14:26) and be guided to the truth (John 16:13).

Don't you love gifts that are free, bought especially for you, and suit you just as you are? The better a person knows you, the better the gift matches you. God, through the Holy Spirit, gives each and every one of us gifts that perfectly match who God made us to be. God planned for each of us to have a special place in the Body of Christ, in order to use these gifts (Rom. 12:4-8). Do not keep your talents (gifts) to yourself, and do not always expect to do it right the first time. Doctors have to start out as students, and may take years to become excellent at what God called them to do. Remember that these gifts are not for showing off, but to build up the body and must be used in love. Churches have different ideas about how they work, because of tradition, and this is of no spiritual consequence. The main thing is to listen to God and follow the Spirit. Following the Holy Spirit is like an amazing roller coaster ride. We know something exciting is around the corner, but we are not sure what to expect. God knows! His Spirit prepares us and if we believe and trust them, we should go for it!

3. *The Holy Spirit and His Works*

Have you ever wondered why some believers are spiritually vibrant, while others act unexcited about their salvation, or even despondent about life? Some churches are on fire but others seem asleep. Their worship services are cold and no one is preaching the truth of the Gospel. What accounts for the difference is our relationship with the Holy Spirit.

God's Spirit is essential to the life of faith, but tragically, many believers do not understand who He is, why He came, or how He works in our lives. First of all, the Holy Spirit's ministry is crucial to salvation, even though the person is unaware of His work while being attracted to Jesus and investigating Christianity. The Father uses the Spirit to draw us toward the Savior. Before we are saved, we are spiritually dead and unable, on our own, to understand things of God. The Holy Spirit enlightens our mind, so that we are able to understand what the Word says. In addition, He convicts unbelievers of their sin and convinces them about the Savior's righteousness, as well as the coming judgment for sin. Through the Spirit, we receive new life in Christ upon our salvation. Another aspect of the Spirit's ministry is our sanctification. Though we will never be perfect in this life, the Spirit is at work building godly character in us so that we increasingly resemble Christ. A brand-new revelation about a familiar verse, or a peaceful reaction to a trial can be evidence of this progressive transformation (Gal. 522). A third characteristic is that the Spirit's ministry is vital to our service. Every believer is called to serve the Lord for the greater good of the entire Body, and the Spirit of God endows each Christian with a spiritual gift for that purpose (1 Cor. 12:7). Jesus assigned His disciples a humanly impossible mission, but then sent the empowering Spirit, who enabled them to succeed in leading the lost to Christ (Matt. 28:19-20, Luke 24:49). God has a purpose for each of us, but in our own strength, we are doomed to failure and must rely on the strength Jesus gave the disciples (Phil. 4:13).

The Holy Spirit is not a vague, ethereal shadow, nor an impersonal force. He is a person equal in every way with God the Father and God the Son. God is Father, Son, and Holy Spirit, and all the divine attributes ascribed to the Father and the Son are ascribed to the Spirit. When a person becomes born again by believing and receiving Jesus, God resides in that person through the Spirit. Primary roles of the Spirit are that He bears witness of Jesus and tells people's hearts the truth of Christ. He is the Christian's teacher, therefore, revealing God's will and truth to the believer. He will build into our lives joy, peace, patience, kindness, goodness, faithfulness, gentleness, and self-control (Gal. 5:22-23). We are to walk in the Spirit, be filled with the Spirit, and allow spiritual growth in our Christian lives.

The Spirit performs functions for the non-Christian as well. He convicts persons of the truth, concerning how sinful the unsaved is and how much they need God's forgiveness. He tugs at hearts and minds, asking, never pushing, for repentance, and urging the unsaved to turn to God and a new life. We do not pray to the Holy Spirit to confess our sins, nor do we plead to the Spirit for forgiveness. As Jesus taught in the Lord's Prayer, prayers go to the Father so that the Son may step in for us now as He did when on earth. The different persons of the Trinity do different things, but all for the glory of God the Father. The Spirit prays with you, and when you reach the point where your prayers get stopped by human limits, the Spirit picks it up and keeps it pointed toward the Father (Rom. 8:26-27). The devil will do anything to get our minds off of our praying by telling us that someone else can do it better and that God only listens to preachers, teachers, or by telling us that we need to learn to pray before we speak to the Lord. The devil is a liar and the father of lies, so put him out of your mind and pray your needs and praises.

Throughout Christian history, there have been stories of people whose prayers have astonishing effects. In the book of Kings, Elijah prays and God makes incredible things happen. Today, there are some leaders whom many people look to as prayer warriors, and this is a great name for the ones who seem to have perseverance in their prayer life.

Although, James writes (5:16-17) in praise of Elijah's powerful prayers but then says that Elijah was a man just like us. This meant that God's Holy Spirit had entered him and he was operating in the gift of faith. Anyone who believes that God hears and answers is a prayer warrior. The gift of faith is a special gift which is given supernaturally by the Spirit as He wills (1 Cor. 12:9, 11). Those who operate in the gift can believe God in such a way that God honors their words as His own and miraculously brings to pass the desired result. You can be a mighty prayer warrior. It takes hard work and a dedication to read the Bible regularly, with the faith that the Spirit that resides within you can teach you all things, including how to pray. In prayer, we go from thinking about or talking about God to talking with God and listening when God calls. It is by grace through faith that we were saved, and it is by faith that we can approach the throne of grace that we may receive mercy (Heb. 4:16). "Let us draw near to God with a sincere heart in full assurance of faith" (Heb. 10:22).

One of the great spiritual problems with man is that God keeps doing things in us, with us, and for us, but we still believe it is our own choices and by our own strength. We are so blessed to have a God that will continue to work within our pitiful minds to steady us and be our strength, even in times that we do not recognize where the strength comes from. Our opening up to Christ is something that is done solely in the Spirit. He starts to recreate you to have the character of Christ. The new you powered with new gifts from the Spirit, willingly works with the Spirit on this remaking. The old you is still within you, fighting these changes, and the devil will help you all you will allow. A person spends his entire life in this struggle, but we are encouraged by Paul's words: "Not that I have already obtained all this, or have already been made perfect, but I press on to take hold of that for which Christ took hold of me" (Phil. 3:12-20). Know this: After entering you upon salvation, the Spirit will not leave you as you were, but take you from glory to glory (2 Cor. 3:18). How quickly the Spirit works in changing you will depend on how quickly you submit to His will.

There are greater gifts and lesser gifts! The greater gifts are listed in 1ˢᵗ Corinthians 12:1-10, and the lesser gifts are special gifts given also by the Spirit in order to administer or use the greater gifts. These little gifts can be recognized by the things you do that you cannot explain how you knew to do them. Such as comforting someone when you do not know the circumstances, an uncanny sense of timing, and the sudden disappearance of fear that may have held you back from something you needed to say or do. These little gifts include: Missionary, to minister whatever other spiritual gifts you have in a second culture or community (2 Cor. 2:7); Intercession, enables Christians to pray for extended periods of time with great positive effect for the building of the Kingdom (Eph. 6:19); Craftsmanship, ability to use your hands and minds through artistic or creative means (Ex. 28:3-4); Hospitality, opening up your homes willingly and offering food, bed, and fellowship (2 Kings 4:8-10); Mercy, exceptional empathy and compassion for those suffering (Luke 10:33-34); Giving, material blessings offered to the church willingly (2 Cor. 8:1-7); Administration, keeping the church on course (2 Cor. 8:17-21); Help, bearing the burdens of others (Gal. 6:2); Serving, identifying unmet needs and making plans to meet those needs (Isa. 58:6-7); Exhortation, standing by fellow Christians in need and bringing comfort, counsel and encouragement (Acts 11:23-24, 14:21-22); Music, praising through various forms of music (1 Cor. 14:26, Mark 14:26).

What the Holy Spirit gives us is not an unspecified magical power or method or tool which gives each of us ability to be like Jesus. Instead, the Spirit gives us Jesus Christ Himself. It is no longer you who lives but Jesus in you (Gal. 2:20), and this is the greatest gift of all. Ask God for a renewing of the Spirit, accept His power in your life, live like you are a child of the King, and the peace of God will live within you and guard your heart and mind (Phil. 4:7).

4. *Spiritual Guidance*

If you were preparing to go on a road trip, would you take along your cookbook to guide you? Would it be just as foolish to start out on your first safari or river rafting trip without an experienced guide? I know! Some of you are thinking you could handle these situations with no help, but the majority would not even consider such dangerous ventures alone. Why then do we try incessantly to live life without the spiritual guidance of God and His inspired Word, the Bible? All people everywhere, at some time in their lives, realize they have spiritual needs. Sadly, many look outside the Word of God for answers.

Today, just as in biblical times, many turn to the unreliable word of mediums, fortune tellers, and seers. You might almost say that witchcraft is respectable today, with people openly identifying themselves as witches, unashamedly dabbling in the occult. We jump from religious belief to ritual cults, to find our inner peace that only God can offer (Phil. 4:7; 2 Thess. 3:16). We typically use the word *peace* to mean simply *no war*. The Bible's words, *shalom* in Hebrew, *eirene* in Greek, are richer than that, carrying the idea of well-being, wholeness; people existing in harmony and not vexing each other. This peace is pretty elusive in this fallen world, but the Bible holds out the possibility that anyone can have peace inwardly if not outwardly. These witchcraft practices were forbidden in the Bible, as were mediums or fortune tellers (Lev. 19:31). Purity, even purity of the heart, is the main objective in life. In some ways, the world has not changed any since biblical times. We still see white as the color of purity and innocence. In the Bible, white was also the color of holiness, so in a sense it is God's color, as well as the color of holy people.

We are made clean through the Holy Word; for it is written: "Be holy, because I am holy" (1 Pet. 1:16). It is also written that God will be against anyone who goes to mediums or fortune tellers for advice, because that person is being unfaithful to God (Lev. 20:6). God says that people should ask Him for help, since the fortune tellers and mediums are supposedly speaking to the dead, and the living should not expect anything from them (Isa. 8:19). Isaiah speaks of spiritual blindness, calling it a darkness that covers the earth and the people (Isa. 60:2). Ezekiel says that their eyes do not see, their ears do not hear, and they refuse to obey the Lord. Therefore, they are spiritually blind (Ezek. 12:2). Since we know from scripture that God is the same yesterday, today, and forever (Heb. 13:8), why do we ignore the fact that these outside-of-the-Bible helps are surely just as forbidden today?

We do not have to continue to live in the darkness of the unknown world, because God has chosen us and called us into His world of light (1 Pet. 2:9). This spiritual light is required of believers so that we might be a light for others and bring praise and glory to our Father in heaven (Matt. 5:14-16). Light in the Bible more often refers to something spiritual than physical, and God is light to those who walk with Him, whereas Satan and the wicked are on the side of darkness. Physical light is a mysterious thing. Physicists still are not sure whether to describe it as waves or particles, and even more mysterious is spiritual light, which is a powerful force in the universe.

We are expected to be without fault while we are being surrounded with false teachers and/or fortune tellers who criticize the Christian beliefs. Peter said that these people blaspheme in matters they do not understand (2 Pet. 2:12). Christians offer teachings that give life, shining like stars in a dark world, according to Philippians 2:12-16. While making a stand for the truth, we will be put upon, perplexed, and in despair, but not destroyed (1 Cor. 4:8-9). The Proverbs instructs us to cry out to God and to hunt His wisdom like hidden treasure (Prov. 1:1-8) so that we might know immediately when a false witness is in our midst.

Mankind has tried and failed to provide spiritual answers on their own (Jer. 10:23), therefore, we need to find and study a source of spiritual direction and guidance from someone who really knows the answers. The psalmist calls the Word a lamp unto our feet (Ps. 119:105), and to put these in understandable terms, we need to know what this meant to the ancient world. The lamps were tied to the ankles of those who dared to travel the snake-infested roads at night. Your road may very well be infested with that ancient serpent called the devil (Rev. 12:9), so take God's lamp on your next trip. The Bible is true, and all else is guesswork affirmed by belief in the gospel giving the guidance and spiritual direction we need to show us the meaning and purpose of life (John 17:17; 2 Tim. 3:16-17).

There are other words that lead us astray besides those of fortune tellers, etc. The theories that we all came into existence with a big boom or that we came through evolution are acceptable to many. Rather than believe the impossible-to-believe God story, some just accept the could-have-happened theory. No one has ever seen this God, but we have seen the lower case animals, such as monkeys or reptiles, that we supposedly evolved from. We as believers are positive that different kinds of life exist because God created them with the power to reproduce after their own kind (Ex. 20:11). Critics of the Bible generally believe that the Bible's stories are just like the myths of Greek and Roman mythology, false stories, not history. The Greek word *mythos* meant nothing more than story, with no judgment as to whether the story was fact or fiction. The few times it is used in the New Testament, it is clear the Christian authors did not put much stock in the factuality of myths (1 Tim. 1:4; Acts 14:12-13).

We have a weapon that apparently is a secret to unbelievers, and has been pushed from the mind of skeptics and simply laid aside by the majority of believers. This powerful weapon is the Holy Spirit of God. He is the Spirit of truth (John 16:13) and the most important truth that He teaches is that "if God is with us, who then can be against us?" (Rom. 8:31). The Bible is God's Word! Don't leave home without it!

5. *Power Surge*

There are people living their lives as though they are the pilot who announced to his passengers that he had good news and bad news. The bad news was that the communication systems had gone out and he had no idea where they were. The good news was that they were making good time! Some only live their lives pursuing what they feel, making good time, but looking back years later and not realizing exactly where they came from or where they are. Like the baseball player who made it to the Baseball Hall of Fame and was quoted as saying: "I wish that someone would have told me that when you reach the top, there is nothing there!" Throughout centuries, people have testified that while they achieved wealth and power, there was still a void inside.

Things were not too different in the days of the prophets and ancient kings. Solomon had wealth beyond measure, wisdom beyond any man, women by the hundreds, palaces and gardens that were the envy of the kingdom, and yet he summed up his life in a few words: "Everything was meaningless, a chasing after the wind, nothing was gained under the sun" (Ecc. 2:11). Why this void? God has given us a heart and mind set for eternity (Ecc. 3:11), and nothing on this earth will satisfy us, because this is not our home. The more we get, the more we are left wanting, and that desire for more can only be satisfied through a relationship with our Father in heaven. The power we gain will always be overshadowed by the mighty power of God. People on earth are not truly important! God does what He wants with the power of heaven and the people on earth. "No one can stop His powerful hand or question what He does" (Dan. 4:35). This is a quote from King Nebuchadnezzar. The powerful king of Babylon learned of God's power the old-fashioned way! God showed up and brought the earthly king under the heavenly King's control.

Nebuchadnezzar was born in 630 BC and became king of Babylon at the age of twenty-five and ruled forty-three years. This reign was longer than any monarch of the Chaldean dynasty. He succeeded his father, Naboplossar, who founded the dynasty. Nebuchadnezzar played a prominent role in the history of the Israelite people and is mentioned numerous times in nine different Old Testament books. This monarch's defeat of Pharaoh Neco at Carchemish, about sixty miles west of Haran (Gen. 11:31-32), in 605 BC, established Chaldean supremacy in Syria and Palestine, and the southern kingdom of

Judah became subject to the new ruler. At this time, many of the Hebrew upper class were taken captive into Babylon. Daniel and Ezekiel were among these prisoners. During another invasion in 579, thousands more captives were taken to Babylon, including King Jehoiachin (2 Kings 24:14-15). In London's British Museum, there is a baked clay tablet inscribed in cuneiform writing, which records the activities of King Nebuchadnezzar between 605 and 594 BC. Included in the inscription is: "On the second day of the month of Addaru, he captured Jerusalem and its king." This is in keeping with the scripture (2 Kings 24:15). The story of the Ark of the Covenant ends with Solomon. Scholars presume it remained in the temple for almost four hundred years until the destruction of Jerusalem by the Babylonians in 586 BC, yet it is not listed among the spoils the Babylonians took from the temple (2 Kings 25:13-17).

Nebuchadnezzar was the pagan king of the Chaldean Empire. He was the most powerful monarch of his dynasty, and is best known for the magnificence of his capital, Babylon, his vast military conquest, and his role in biblical history and prophecy. He had considerable prior military experience, having campaigned against the Egyptian armies just south of Carchemish, and won an important victory. Shortly thereafter, he received word of his father's death and hastened to Babylon to claim the throne. For the next three years, he waged war in Syria and demanded forced payment for protection from a number of cities, including Damascus. He then campaigned against the forces of Neco II of Egypt and in Arabia, where he appears to have had success. By 597, he was in Palestine, where he overtook Jerusalem with armed forces and placed a certain Zedekiah, the uncle of the former ruler of Judah, Jehoiachim, on the throne. According to Josephus's *Antiquities*, Nebuchadnezzar returned to Jerusalem a second time, in 586. The book of Jeremiah states that this campaign resulted in the taking of the city, the destruction of Solomon's temple, and the deportation of the Hebrews into captivity. Unfortunately, no contemporary cuneiform account of this event is known to exist, since the Babylonian Chronicle is incomplete after 594. Josephus referred also to the accounts of campaigns against Tyre and Egypt, but records are not in existence, but it is likely they did occur.

When Nebuchadnezzar gained the throne in Babylon, he faced several challenges. Although Babylon had been rebuilt by the Assyrian king, it was not suitable to be the headquarters of an imperial administrative bureaucracy. All the towers had to be restored and fortified, and Nebuchadnezzar had to build a royal residence of his own. He repaired temple sanctuaries, restored divine images, and oversaw construction work in twelve or more cities throughout the realm. It is believed that he created the Hanging Gardens, which later Greek writers regarded as one of the Seven Wonders of the Ancient World. The Hanging Gardens were built to please his homesick wife, Amyitis, who was from Media. She longed for the meadows and mountains of her homeland. Although the gardens no longer exist, they portrayed a magnificent feat of engineering.

King Nebuchadnezzar ordered that some of the young Israelite men from the royal family and nobility, without any physical defect, handsome, showing aptitude for every kind of learning, be brought to serve in the palace. Among these young men was Daniel, whom God had caused the official to show favor and sympathy (Dan. 1:3-9). Daniel had three friends named Shadrach, Meshach, and Abednego, and they ate their veggies and drank distilled water and remained healthier than all the others; therefore, they were chosen to enter the king's service. Along with youth and good looks, they were healthy and wise, especially Daniel, who understood visions and dreams of all kinds. In the second year of his reign, Nebuchadnezzar had dreams, his mind was troubled, and he could not sleep. He called on the magicians and enchanters to tell what he had dreamed and why, but they could not do as he asked, which sent the king into a rage. He ordered them executed, cut to pieces, and their houses turned into rubble. Talk about flexing your power!

Daniel spoke with wisdom and tact, and asked that the men be spared, putting himself up to interpret the king's dreams. During the night, the mystery was revealed to him in a vision from the true God, which Daniel followed. He interpreted the king's dream, and the king acknowledged that Daniel's God was the God of gods and the Lord of kings and a revealer of mysteries (Dan. 2:47). He missed the point entirely, and although he promoted Daniel and his friends, he continued to build golden idols and gain power throughout the kingdom without turning to God.

Now, Daniel's friends refused to bow down to the idols, so the king— furious with rage as he often was—ordered them into the fiery furnace. The three declared their allegiance to the true God of heaven, causing more rage and a hotter oven. Protected by the angel of the Lord, they came out of the fire untouched, causing the king to once again praise God but again acknowledging Him only as the God of Shadrach, Meshach, and Abednego. Talk about a thick skull!

With the king's next dream, he acknowledged that the spirit of the holy gods were in Daniel after the interpretation. He is still missing the point but getting closer to the truth of the True God. Daniel told the king that his kingdom would be taken away and he would live with the animals among the plants of the earth. Daniel begged the king to take his advice: "Renounce your sins by doing what is right and your wickedness by being kind to the oppressed. It may be that then our prosperity will continue" (Dan. 4:27). One year later, the king was boasting of his accomplishments rather than praising the God of heaven as Daniel advised, and disaster struck. A voice came down from heaven, royal authority was taken from him, he was driven away from his people, and ate grass like a cow. His hair grew like the feathers of an eagle and his nails like the claws of a bird. Finally the message comes through loud and clear and the great and powerful king raised his eyes toward heaven, and his sanity was restored. He praised the Most High and honored and glorified the One who lives forever, and in turn God returned him to honor and splendor; his throne was returned to him and became greater than before.

God not only converted Nebuchadnezzar into a believer and worshiper of the only True God, but Nebuchadnezzar's testimony became part of the Holy scriptures (Dan. 4:1-3). His conversion did not come easily or quickly. After being warned by the prophet Daniel, the king was struck down with bestial madness and then restored after the Lord's supreme power was made wholly evident to him. He went from arrogant to humble, and praised, honored, and extolled the King of heaven. There are many messages in this short book of Daniel, but the main theme is that all power on earth and in heaven belongs to God. The comforting message is that He will walk though any fire that you may be in if you remain faithful to Him. And of course, don't miss the fact that the dreams, interpretations, and prophecies of the book of Daniel all point to the end of time, when our Lord and Savior comes again. The Lord came with fire (Ex. 24:17) and He will come again with fire (Heb. 10:27; Ps. 50:3; Isa. 66:15; Dan. 7:9; 2 Thess. 1:6-7).

6. *Dynamic Duo*

It is not good to have zeal without knowledge, nor to be hasty and miss the way. Zeal is an emotion or passion of the mind. Solomon says it burns like blazing fire, like a mighty flame (Song of Songs 8:6). It is sometimes used for the strong affection God has for His people expressed in His care for them and indignation against their enemies, and is called the zeal of the Lord of hosts, and His great jealousy (Isa. 9:6; Zech. 1:14). Paul had zeal without knowledge when he breathed out murderous threats against the Lord's disciples (Acts 9:1-2). Then Jesus blinded him with a knowledgeable light and he then became zealous for God and at once began to preach that Jesus was the Son of God (Acts. 9:20). Sometimes zeal is only a temporary passion, such as the Galatians who once would have plucked out their eyes for Paul (Gal. 4:15) but then turned back to weak and miserable principles (Gal. 4:8). Sometimes there is misplaced zeal, as when Peter drew his sword and cut off the ear of the high priest's servant, and when the disciples called fire from heaven upon those who showed disrespect to Christ. Both were rebuked by Jesus (Luke 9:55; Matt. 26:51).

Zeal, nepes, normally translated, soul, in Proverbs 19:2 means inner drive or vitality. It refers not so much to ecstatic exuberance as to ambitious drive, which without adequate knowledge may lead to hasty blunders. Such haste may lead to a person missing the way; that is, making mistakes. As the modern-day proverb puts it, "haste makes waste." And you thought your old great-great-aunt made that saying up! Proverbs 21:5-6 refers to wealth, warning that a person who diligently and carefully plans his work and works his plan contrasts with a careless one who makes hasty decisions and actions without thinking them through. The one results in profit and the other in poverty. Without knowledge that comes from patiently examining the situation through observation, reason, or prayer, one becomes so urgent in obtaining their desire, they actually become counterproductive to themselves. They become hasty and miss the way. Zealous desire can become energy that misleads us into unsound reasoning. Zeal needs a curb, or often it will lessen charity, burn like a wildfire, and do more harm than good when uncontrolled. "Brothers, my heart's desire and prayer to God for the Israelites is that they may be saved. For I can testify about them that they are zealous for God, but their zeal is not based on knowledge" (Rom. 10:1-2).

Zeal, by some, may be referred to as obsession, perseverance, and even an addiction. What is often called our drive is a distant kin to obsession. This obsession, drive, or zeal can destroy lives but can in fact, with knowledge, obtain the highest goals in life, both personal and spiritual. Achieving such success requires discipline (Job 36:10; Rev. 3:19; Heb. 12:6), gifts (Rom l:1; James 1:17), practice or pray continually (1 Thess. 5:17), gather together (Heb. 10:24-25), and drive or perseverance (Phil. 4:1; Eph. 6:14-18).

Thomas Edison had tried hundreds of different materials, all failing, to use as a filament in the creation of the common light bulb. Time after time, every material he used heated up and burned away in seconds when current was passed through. But he was determined to accomplish his goal, and eventually realized it was not so much the wrong type of thin wire, but the necessity to vacuum out the air. That was the missing element to his success. Knowledge added to zeal became success and brought artificial light into the world.

It is reasonable and admirable even, that someone has zeal for great athletic achievement, but do it for the sake of the gospel (1 Cor. 9:23). All runners in a race compete for the same prize, but only one can receive it. We should run our spiritual race in such a way as to receive the prize. Everyone who competes goes into strict training but does not get a crown that will last; but our training will result in an eternal crown. Therefore, we must be like Paul and run, not aimlessly or beating the air, but with knowledge and purpose (1 Cor. 9:24-27).

When zeal becomes obsession and turns up to full gear, haste is the order of the day. "It is not good to have zeal without knowledge, nor to be hasty and miss the way" (Prov. 19:2). The commandment "do not envy," if applied, will help guard us from our overzealous selves. It warns us against entering into situations hastily with total abandonment to reason or consequence. If put in more perspectives than just the most thought of don't envy, covet, want, or wish you had something of someone else's, it will bring to light many envious situations where disaster could have been prevented if knowledge with zeal would have been used. For instance, unplanned pregnancies, prison sentences, health issues, lost finances, marrying too young, and changing jobs without forethought could be considered zeal without knowledge. This can cause a person to abandon all sense of reason, and focus only on immediate desires, and the aftermath and consequences of obsessive zeal that goes unrestrained, without knowledge, are sometimes brutal.

The object of zeal is God, and we worship Him in spirit and in truth. The Word of God is an object of zeal, and we must preserve it pure and incorrupt, and above all, we need to have zeal for the cause of Christ. The Lord's Supper fits into this category, but we are warned to examine ourselves before we eat of the bread and drink of the cup. Scripture says that Epaphras was always fervently in prayer for the church of Closse, and it is the effectual fervent prayer of the righteous man that avails much.

The churches at one time all had zeal and knowledge, but some put aside the knowledge and lost their zeal for the Lord. God speaks to these churches through John in the book of Revelation. To the church in Ephesus, He says they have lost their first love; to the church in Pergamum, they hold to the teachings of the idols and are told to repent; to the church in Thyatira, they tolerated Jezebel, and the scariest of all are the easiest to do and overlook and those are the ones who have become lukewarm. God said that He was about to spit them out of His mouth! (Rev. 2:4, 14-16, 20, 3:15-16). Hold on to your knowledge by staying in the Word of God, and keep your zeal by acting on the Word of God and doing what it says.

7. Feasting on the Manna

One evening, an old Cherokee told his grandson about a battle that goes on inside people. He said, "My son, the battle is between two wolves inside all of us. One is evil! It is anger, envy, jealousy, sorrow, regret, greed, arrogance, self-pity, guilt, resentment, inferiority, lies, false pride, superiority, and ego. The other is good! It is joy, peace, love, hope, serenity, humility, kindness, benevolence, empathy, generosity, truth, compassion, and faith." The grandson thought abut this for a minute and then asked his grandfather, "Which wolf wins?" The wise old Cherokee replied simply, "The one you feed!"

You know that we all have read about the disobedient, whiny, poor pitiful me Israelites in the Old Testament, and sometimes we really do not understand why they did not trust God to take care of them and accept all the blessings He bestowed on them. Well, look around you and perhaps within you. The Israelites still exist today. We are given the same promises that they were because our God is the same yesterday, today, and forever (Heb. 13:8) but do we always accept His blessings? Do we still want what is not good for us? Do we trust Him totally to provide our daily bread? Do we sharpen up our knife and cut into the Word or do we sit with folded hands and wait for someone to feed us? The scripture tells us to go (Matt. 28:19), to study (2 Tim. 2:15), and divide the Word to truth (2 Tim. 2:15). It is hard to divide something unless you first have the whole of it. Paul was feeding the infants in Christ but seemed to be a bit frustrated that they had not grown out of the milk stage and started eating solid food (1 Cor. 3:1-2). If you are feeding the worldly wolf within you, maybe you need to go back to the fridge and choose another diet.

The spiritual famine is caused by evil (Ps. 37:9)! The entrance to the kingdom of self-pity is right by the meadows of joy and peace that God provides for us. The second we allow self-pity to come into our lives, we are stuck in miry clay, and it is really hard to get out. "This day I call heaven and earth as witnesses against you that I have set before you life and death, because you are being tested by God (James 1:2-8). Scripture also tells us that our worldly desires cause greed (James 4:1-3), arrogance (Prov. 6:18),

a list of earthly desires in Colossians 3:5-9 which tells us will bring on the wrath of God, and the old Cherokee understood most of them.

In truth, famine is normal on the journey of faith. Sometimes where you think blessings should be, there is famine. God used famine to further His plan in the Old Testament, New Testament, and today. The biblical story of Abraham describes his divine selection as the ancestor of Israel and sets in motion the long process by which his descendants eventually become a populous nation in a land of their own. Yahweh commanded him to leave his ancestral home and move to a new land, where his descendants would be divinely blessed and grow into a great nation (Gen. 12:1-3). This promise could be fulfilled within Abraham's own lifetime, but its realization if foreshadowed in the ensuing events, as Abraham and Sarah take up residence in the land promised to them and Isaac, the son from whom the nation will descend is born. Abraham went to a land he knew nothing about, waited ten years until he was one hundred to have the promised son, and then was told to sacrifice this only son. Now that is famine! But notice how Abraham expected the blessings God had promised! He told his servants to stay at the bottom of the mountain, saying that he and his son would go and worship, and then WE will come back to you (Gen. 22:5). That is faith and trust in the midst of famine (Heb. 11:1). Believe, in spite of the fact that you cannot see the promised blessings, and wait for the feast.

Now, there was another famine in the land, but the Lord told Isaac to live where He told him for a while and He would bless him (Gen 26:1-6). Joseph endured several chapters of famine before God's blessings manifested in being put in charge of the whole land of Egypt (Gen. 41:41). This wilderness with blessings to follow carries over into the New Testament with Jesus in the wilderness, and now He sits on the right hand of the Father (Matt. 4:1-10; Mark 16:19). Sometimes I think I cannot write anything concerning the Bible without mentioning David's name, but God was even good enough to let David choose between famine and being handed over to his enemies. David chose famine, and the Lord sent a plague upon Israel until God told the angel, "Enough! Withdraw your hand" (2 Sam. 24:13-17), causing David to confess his sins and repent. That is all God wanted then, and all He wants now from you and me: repentance! Read the first chapter of Isaiah, where He is weary of the sins of His people and asked them to come and reason with Him and He would wash them white as snow. Oh, what a Savior that invites to talk things over and gives us every opportunity to come clean. The people in Jeremiah were experiencing a famine and they knew why! They said they had sinned and their backsliding was great; still, they were asking the Lord not to forsake them. However, instead of accepting God's grace, they turned to false prophets which God did not send. Still He gives us this promise: "Who shall separate us from the love of Christ? Shall trouble or hardship or persecution or famine or nakedness or danger or sword?" (Rom. 8:35-39). He will deliver us from death and keep us alive if we happen to be in a famine only if we fear Him and hope in His unfailing love (Ps. 33:18-19).

Now we will read a little about feasting! The most beautiful promise in the Bible comes from Isaiah 11:1: "A shoot will come from the stump of Jesse, from his roots a Branch will bear fruit." Continue to read the rest of the story from Isaiah and find what our Lord and Savior will do for you. Isaiah chapter 12 continues with telling us that God is our salvation and with joy we will draw water from the wells of salvation. Now that is a glorious feast! The Beatitudes will explain how we will be blessed and we are to rejoice (Matt. 5:1-12) in these blessings. We are to feast on the love of God because it is kind, not proud or rude, nor self-seeking or easily angered (1 Cor. 13:4-7). The fruits that we feast on come from the Spirit and include a steady diet of love, joy, peace, patience, kindness, goodness, and self-control. The old Cherokee Indian got most of these right too. We are all given a measure of faith, but must make every effort to add to this faith and rejoice in God through our Lord Jesus Christ, through whom we have now received reconciliation (Gal. 5:22-24; 2 Pet. 1:5-7; Rom. 5:1-5). Stay away from evil and stay within the bounds that God has set for us, including righteousness and godliness. We are born-again Christians, saved by the blood of the Lamb, and we should live like it. Since we are so blessed, we should bless others with compassion, humility, and patience, bearing each other's burdens and forgiving (Col. 3:12-15).

Before we were saved, we were disobedient, deceived, and enslaved by all kinds of passions and pleasures. God saved us not because of anything good we have done, but because He loved us. Now we must be careful to devote ourselves in doing what is good (Titus 3:3-11). In order to feast on God's blessings continually, we must first put our minds on heavenly manna that is alone praiseworthy. The feasts in the Bible are a shadow of things to come, and the manna that God provided in the Old Testament wilderness was an example to keep us from setting our hearts on evil things like they did. God was not pleased with most of them, even though they drank and ate the spiritual food. They just never got the point of the food. Have we gotten the point yet? Am I suggesting that we have a festival today to celebrate the blessings of God? Yes! We should praise Him each and every time we feel His healing touch, each time a soul is saved, every time we come to a sudden realization that Jesus is indeed coming, then we should rejoice. We should be a witness to our salvation, and testify on any occasion given us to all that will listen. Tell the world that we are going to a place where there will be no more hunger, tears, pain, or death, for He will make everything new. Get excited! Have a feast! Celebrate that we will see His face! Feast on God's manna! It's free! Feed the good wolf!

8. *How Did They Know?*

There are happenings in the Bible that make me wonder why and how! One that stands out in my mind more than the rest is in Luke 23:32-47. Two criminals were led away and nailed to crosses along with Jesus, one on His right and one on His left. The crowd grew quieter after the crosses were erected, so the priests and leaders started a disturbance among the crowd by sneering and mocking Jesus. Do you suppose the leaders somehow knew that the crowd, if allowed to think things through, would decide Jesus was innocent and turn on them, insisting that Jesus be set free? The soldiers mocked Him, and even the two criminals that hung on either side of our Savior hurled insults at Him. Then a change took place in the heart and mind of one thief. He rebuked his insulting cellmate, saying, "Don't you fear God?" The fear of God is the beginning of wisdom, and this fear suddenly took hold of this criminal. Where did this fear and knowledge come from? Sticking up for Jesus was not going to get him any favors from the soldiers or the priests. The criminal continues to rebuke his fellow thief, saying, "This man has done nothing wrong." Surely he did not learn this in prison. Jesus was never in prison, right? He could not possibly have heard it on the way to the place of the skull, since there were large numbers of people following, and it was most likely extremely riotous. True, the women mourned and wailed for Jesus, but could this have been distinguished from the curses hurled at Jesus in this mob?

This crook, after turning from his sinful thoughts, asked Jesus to remember him when He came into His Kingdom. Everyone else, including the disciples, expected the Messiah to establish His Kingdom here on earth, so how did the criminal realize that the Son was going to the Father? Could this be encouragement from the Father to the Son? By giving Jesus a convert, God gave Him proof and a reminder of why He was going through all of this. The dying convicted man recognized the righteousness of Jesus and His power and authority. Jesus told the repented sinner that "today, you will be with me in Paradise," proving that if you call on the name of Jesus, you will be saved (Rom. 10:13)! This is also proof that it is possible and within God's will that a last-breath person be saved on his deathbed. However, it is not wise to wait until that last breath to make the most important decision of your life. "Today, if you hear His voice, do not harden your hearts" (Heb. 3:15, 4:7). "He who is coming will come and not delay" (Heb. 10:37).

The devil took Jesus out to tempt Him to jump off the highest point of the temple. Satan used scripture from Psalms to make his point (Matt. 4:6; Ps. 91:11-12). How did he know the scripture? He was there with God when the earth and heavens were created (Neh. 9:6). He was one of the angels created before earth. He is an eavesdropper (Job 1:6) and an imitator (2 Cor. 11:14). He knows the scripture better than you and I, and will not hesitate to use it to tempt us. Do as Jesus did and answer the devil with scripture, for even the powerful angel Michael did not accuse Satan but instead said, "The Lord rebuke you" (Jude 9).

When the first two disciples were called, they left their nets, their lifelong trade, their livelihood, and followed Jesus. How did they know this man was the Christ? The same thing happened with the next two fishermen He came upon (Matt. 4:18-22). They followed immediately, leaving their nets and families behind. Isaiah 53:2 tells us that Jesus had no beauty or majesty or anything to attract us to him and nothing about Him would make us desire to be around Him. He was a carpenter and probably looked and dressed much like the working men He called. (Although later, during the Crucifixion, He was wearing the one-piece robe of a priest.) Matthew (Levi) obviously knew more about this man than just the way He dressed and looked. Jesus said just two words: "follow me" and Matthew got up and followed (Matt. 9:9). The scripture does not say that Jesus promised this wealthy tax collector substantial monetary increase; in fact, it does not say Jesus offered him anything at this time.

Here is another favorite of mine. "Two demon-possessed men coming from the tombs met Him. What do you want with us, Son of God? Have you come here to torture us before the appointed time?" (Matt. 9:28-29). How did these demons know Jesus? How did they know about His appointed time? Could it be they were among the angels when this plan was made, and followed Satan when he was kicked out of heaven as Lucifer? In Mark 1:23-25, another man in the synagogue was possessed by an evil spirit and cried out, "What do you want with us, Jesus of Nazareth? Have you come to destroy us? I know who you are, the Holy one of God!" The demons not only knew who Jesus was, and where He was from, they knew where they were going! When the evil spirits saw Him, they fell down before Him. This is the accepted posture of worship, and also, they called Him the Son of God. But He gave them strict orders not to tell who He was (Mark 3:11-12). Like the demons said, His time had not yet come, and they were commanded not to speak or tell who He was.

Now we know how the Pharisees knew everything. They were always peeking through windows (Matt. 9:11), lurking in the crowd (Matt. 10:34), ducking behind the stalks of grain (Matt. 12:1-2), and they even arranged to catch a woman in adultery to test Jesus (John 8:3-6). They followed Jesus into the synagogue, not to worship, but looking for a reason to accuse Him, and even followed the disciples into the washroom and reported, "They do not wash their hands before they eat" (Matt. 15:2). Can't you just see them pointing and yelling like a tattletale three-year-old? Actually, the disciples were nearly as bad when they tattled to Jesus, "Do you know that the Pharisees were offended when they heard this?" (Matt. 15:11-12).

We know how Simon Peter knew that Jesus was the Christ, because Jesus told Peter and others that this information was not revealed by man but by God. I am sure Peter was as surprised as he was proud when this bit of knowledge fell out of his mouth. Seems it made him a little zealous, though, since he rebuked Jesus (Matt. 16:13-22). Jesus transfigured Himself on a high mountain in the presence of Peter, James, and John. Then the scripture says that Moses and Elijah appeared, talking to Jesus. This particular passage was not spoken by Jesus, but recounted by Matthew. How did the three know Moses and Elijah? The Bible does not say that Jesus introduced them or revealed who they were. He simply told the disciples not to tell anyone what they had seen (Matt. 17:1-9).

You would think this far into the scripture that we would have lost the Pharisees, but we have not. They have been in the courthouse, looking up divorce records to accuse not only Jesus but also Moses (Matt. 19:3, 7). Later, in Matthew 21:45-46, the Pharisees finally caught on to the fact that most of Jesus's comments were directed at them, but instead of repenting and believing, they looked for a way to arrest Him. They continued to try to trap Him with tax evasion, who would be married to whom after the Resurrection, and which was the greatest commandment in the Law. Jesus told the crowd that they had to obey the ones who sat in Moses's seat, the Pharisees, but not to do what they did, since they did not practice what they preached! Sound familiar?

The king's wife tried to persuade him not to judge Jesus, indeed, not even have anything to do with Him. How did she know this would bring judgment? She had a dream about Jesus, which leads us to believe that God used an Old Testament method to reach her. "In a dream, in a vision of the night, when deep sleep falls on men as they slumber in their beds, He may speak in their ears and terrify them with warnings" (Job 33:15-16). God still spoke through dreams in the New Testament, such as the angel appearing to Joseph in a dream, telling him to escape to Egypt with the baby Jesus and His mother. If He wants, God can still speak through dreams but be sure and test the spirits to see if your dream is from God or just a late-night supper. Remember too that the devil is a copycat and can also cause you to dream.

Last, but certainly not least, I wonder about John 19:25-27. "When Jesus saw His mother there, and the disciple whom He loved standing nearby, He said to His mother, 'dear woman, here is your son', and to the disciple, 'here is your mother.'" I think I know this answer. There are two meanings, just as there were in many of the parables that Jesus taught. The first is that He found a home for His mother, and the second appears to be an introduction or a confirmation that He is His mother's son. Isaiah 52:14 speaks of His suffering, saying that His appearance was disfigured beyond that of any man, and His form marred beyond human likeness. How did Mary know for sure this was her son? Was she in the court when they beat Him beyond recognition? How could she be sure this was not just another criminal hauled to the cross? I think this is one of the reasons that Jesus spoke to her. You may mar a person beyond human recognition, but a mother always knows the voice of her son.

9. Questions and Answers

Q: How do you know when God or the Holy Spirit is convicting you and when Satan is making you feel guilty?

A: One sure way is that Satan does NOT make you feel guilty. He builds you up and tells you what you are doing is right. Remember Eve? The serpent (Satan) said that she would not die but her eyes would be opened and she would be as smart as God (Gen. 3:4). Satan even encouraged Jesus, telling Him that he would give Him all the kingdoms of the world (Matt. 4:8-9). As long as you are living in sin, whether it is for a minute or a life time, the devil is happy to leave you alone. It is always the Holy Spirit that convicts you of guilt in regard to sin (John 16:8).

Q: What verses specifically address the power of the spoken Word besides the obvious when God spoke the creation into existence?

A: The next "big powerful spoken words" would be the entire Bible (2 Tim. 3:16; 1 Pet. 1:10-11; John 1:1-14). We speak according to the Word (Isa. 8:10-20), He spoke through prophets and later through His Son (Heb. 1:1-2). God gives life to the dead and speaks things that are not, as though they were (Rom. 4:17). A group was praying the Word, and the place was shaken (Acts 4:24-31); Jesus spoke it in the wilderness to ward off Satan (Luke 4:4-8); and Paul and Barnabas answered questions with the Word (Acts 13:46-48). Paul and Silas sang the Word of God and an earthquake opened the jail (Acts 16:25-34).

Q: Tell me something about self-control as one of the gifts of the Holy Spirit.

A: The gifts of the Spirit are listed in 1 Corinthians 12:1, 7-11, and they include Word of Wisdom, Word of Knowledge, Faith, Healing, Working of Miracles, Prophecy, Discerning of Spirits, Tongues, and Interpretation of Tongues. The fruits of the Spirit included self-control, and are found in Galatians 5:22-23.

Q: If we are born into sin, is there any good in us without God's grace?

A: There is no good in us at all. "Not one is good except God alone" (Mark 10:18). Justification means that Christ defended the sinner and made him righteous by grace, received through faith given by God because of His birth, death, and resurrection (John 3:16-18). Redemption means the act of delivering from sin or saving from evil. Jesus paid this debt for us on the cross. We were redeemed from the power of sin (Gal. 3:13) through Jesus (Rom. 3:24) and bought with a price (1 Cor. 6:20, 7:23).

Q: What happens when we do things God's way?

A: A good start comes from Romans 10:9 that if we confess Jesus as our Lord and Savior, we will be saved. What could be better than that? When we continue to do things God's way, we are safe (Isa. 54:17), our name is written in heaven, and we have eternal life (Luke 10:19-20), and we are given strength to do everything (Phil. 4:13). He forgave us our sins (Col. 2:13-15), we will live in the New City (Rev. 3:11), and sit on His throne (Rev. 3:21).

Q: Where are verses that speak of faith, believing in God, and trusting God while in prison?

A: Most of the disciples at one time or the other were put in prison for preaching the gospel of Christ. Paul was in prison and still exalted Christ (Phil. 1:20, 27). Paul, while in chains, served to advance the gospel (Phil. 1:12-14). Paul and Silas, while in prison, sang praise (Acts 16:25). Peter was in prison and people prayed for him and the angel of the Lord rescued him (Acts 12:1-19). John the Baptist was thrown in prison (Luke 3:19-20, continued to preach and defy the king until his head was cut off (Matt. 14:10). Joseph was in prison and the Lord was with him (Gen. 39:20-23). Don't forget Daniel in the lions' den (Dan. 6:16, 21-23). None of these men ever lost faith, stopped believing, or ceased to worship God.

Part VII
Why, Where, and How

1. Statement of Faith

I believe totally that the Bible was inspired by God, both the Old and the New Testament (Matt. 5:18; 2 Tim. 3:16-17). I believe that it is infallible, God-breathed, and the complete and final authority for faith and practice (2 Tim. 3:16-17). The Holy Spirit was the divine author of scripture (2 Pet. 1:21) by supernaturally using the talents and personalities of the human authors to write without error or omission. I believe in God and that He is one of three and Creator of all (Deut. 6:4), eternally existing in three distinct persons, the Father, the Son, and the Holy Spirit (2 Cor. 13:14), yet one in being, essence, power and glory, having the same attributes and perfections (John 10:30). He is sovereign (Ps. 93:1), unexplainable (Rom. 11:33-34), omniscient (Ps. 139:1-6), omnipresent (Ps. 139:7-13), omnipotent (Rev. 19:6), and unchanging (Mal. 3:6). God is holy (Isa. 6:3), just (Deut. 32:4), and righteous (Ex. 9:27). God is loveing (1 John 4:8), gracious (Eph. 2:8), merciful (1 Pet. 1:3), and good (Rom. 8:28). I believe that Jesus Christ is the Son of God, but fully God the expressed image of the Father who, without ceasing to be God, became man that He might reveal God and redeem sinful man (Matt. 1:21). God the Son became incarnate in the person of Jesus. He was conceived of the Holy Spirit and born of the Virgin Mary. He lived a perfect and sinless life and all His teachings are true and from the Father (Isa. 14; Matt. 1:23). He died for you and me (1 John 2:2) and his death is effective for all who believe (John 1:12; Acts 16:31). He rose on the third day (Matt. 28:6), ascended to heaven in His glorified body (Acts 1:9-10), and now sits on the right hand of God as our High Priest and Advocate (Rom. 8:34).

The deity and personality of the Holy Spirit (Acts 5:3-4) is that of God, and He convicts the world of sin, righteousness, and judgment (John 16:8-11). He regenerates sinners (Titus 3:5) and indwells believers (Rom. 8:9). He is the agent by whom Christ baptizes all believers into His body (1 Cor. 12:12-14) and is the seal by whom the Father seals believers unto the day of redemption (Eph. 1:13-14). He is the Divine Teacher who enlightens believers' hearts and minds as they study the Word of God (1 Cor. 2:9-12), and is ultimately sovereign in the distribution of spiritual gifts (1 Cor. 12:11). Angles and demons are real, and God created an innumerable company of spiritual beings who were to be His servants and messengers (Neh. 9:6; Ps. 148:2). I believe in the existence of Satan and demons, and that they are fallen angels who rebelled against God (Isa. 14:12-17). He is the great enemy of God and man, and the demons are his agents in his unholy purposes, and will be eternally punished in the lake of fire (Matt. 25:41; Rev. 20:10).

Man came into being by direct creation of God and is made of the image and likeness of God (Gen. 1:26-27). The human race sinned in Adam (Rom. 5:12) and is universal in man (Rom. 3:23). Sin is exceedingly offensive to God, but man inherited a sinful nature and became alienated from God. He is utterly unable to remedy his lost estate (Eph. 2:1-5), is guilty and in a lost condition apart from Christ (Rom. 2:1) until receiving salvation, the gift from God. Through faith and by grace, we receive this salvation, because Christ shed His blood for our sins (Eph. 2:8-9; Rom.

5:8-9; 1 Pet. 2:24). I believe that all those who have truly placed their faith in Jesus are eternally secure in their salvation, kept by God's power, secure and sealed in Christ forever (John 6:37:40, 10:27-30; Rom. 8:1, 38-39; Eph. 1:13-14; Jude 24).

I believe the church is the body of Christ and is a spiritual organism made up of all born-again believers of the present age (1 Cor. 12:12-14). We follow Jesus in baptism (Acts 1:5), the Lord's Supper in remembrance of Christ's death and shed blood (1 Cor. 11:24-25), and the Great Commission as the primary mission of the church. It is the obligation of believers to witness by word and live to the truths of God's Word. The gospel of the grace of God is to be preached to the entire world (Matt. 28:19-20). There is blessed hope (Titus 2:13), a second coming of the Lord (1 Thess. 4:13-18), and a physical resurrection of all men, the saints to everlasting joy and the wicked to conscious and eternal torment (Matt. 25:46; John 5:28; Rev. 20:5; Luke 23:43; Mark 9:43) just to name a few scriptures on the subject.

2. Acts

It is agreed by most that Luke is the author of the book of Acts, however, there are several suggestions as to the purpose of the writing. One believes that Acts gives a historical account of what happened to the original apostles whom Jesus called and trained. After listing the eleven apostles and the new one elected in place of Judas, Luke never mentioned nine of them anymore. He gave one sentence about James and only a slight mention of John. After Acts 12, Peter moved off the stage and even the story of Paul was not complete, leaving us to doubt that this is actually the Acts of the Apostles. Another suggests that the book should be called the Acts of the Holy Spirit, since this is the first account for the coming of the Spirit. Luke specifically referred to the Spirit fifty times, but eleven chapters do not mention the Spirit at all. Others have said the book was written to reveal the geographic expansion of Christianity, using Acts 1:8 as an outline. Christianity was evidently already in Rome before Paul got there, so Luke missed a major part of the story, if the geographic expansion of Christianity was his intent. What then was he trying to do with this book? His purpose was to proclaim the expansion of Christianity to all the men known world without hindrance (28:31). God was doing something in the world in Christ that could not be stopped by anyone or anything. Luke wrote and God guaranteed that no barriers cold prevent the spread of the gospel across the world.

In every century, God's people have asked, who are we? Why are we here? These answers are found in the book of Acts when the church was empowered by the Holy Spirit for the ministry to which God had called it. Luke epitomized the ministry of the church and stressed that it was to take the resources available and apply them to the needs of those around us. The mission was to move out in obedience to the command of Christ and to be His witnesses in the world, no matter the cost. The book of Acts reminds us that our purpose as God's people is to be on mission for Him today. The mission outreach started with the Jews, gradually expanded to include the Samaritans, and then to the Gentiles. The book is about God and His presence in the life of every believer through the power of the Holy Spirit. The disciples relied on that power in their bold proclamation of the gospel, and that same power is ours today. The picture Luke gave us of God is completed with a statement from Peter concerning God's love and an opportunity to respond to His love and grace, so that they may be redeemed. "I now realize how true it is that God does not show favoritism but accepts men from every nation who fear Him and do what is right" (Acts 10:34). Luke reminds us of the roots of our faith, the reason for our existence as the church and the resources by which we can carry out our work.

The New Testament is clear about these two things. All Christians receive the Spirit, and only Christians receive the Spirit. The Spirit is a gift of grace fulfilling God's promise that cannot be gained through human effort or achievement, but through repentance and salvation. Luke prayed, "Now Lord, consider their threats and enable you servants to speak your Word with great boldness. After they prayed the place where they were meeting was shaken and they were all filled with the Holy Spirit and spoke the Word of God boldly" (Acts 4:29-31). This is a prayer that should start each and every meeting of Christians at whatever function they are attending. We need to acquire this boldness in our prayers and our witness for Jesus. Perhaps we will be ignored, made fun of, or even scorned, but our answer should be the same as the apostles': "we must obey God rather than men" (5:29). If we are bold enough to do this, God will send a Gamaliel to our defense. "Therefore, in the present case I advise you; leave these men alone! Let them go! For if their purpose or activity is off human origin it will fail. But if it if from God you will not be able to stop these men. You will only find yourselves fighting against God" (Acts 5:38-39). God controls the growth of His church. If the church resulted from human plans, energies, and manipulations, it would have died long ago.

In this book, we find the first deacons. The seven men chosen to assist the Twelve are not identified as deacons, but the verb "to wait on," *diakonein*, comes from the same root as the noun, *diakonos*, translated into English as deacon. The selection of the seven grew out of the needs of the apostles in ministering to the congregation, and the special responsibilities of the seven involved practical service. Those chosen for this assignment had already demonstrated evidence of the working of the Spirit in their lives and ministry. Following the example of these seven deacons of today will see their responsibilities as serving with the pastor in ministering to the needs of the church, the congregation, and the community. One of these practical duties is prayer, which when done consistently, will bring on effective ministry. They chose Stephen, a man full of God's grace and power, and amid opposition from the Synagogue of the Freedmen, other leaders, he stood and boldly proclaimed the gospel of Jesus. He minced no words but called them stiff-necked people with uncircumcised hearts and ears that resist the Spirit. This made the men furious, but Stephen, still full of the Spirit, looked up to heaven and saw the Right Hand of God standing! And while they were stoning him, he prayed for Jesus to receive his spirit. This proves two other points in the scriptures: that "to be away from the body is to be with Christ in heaven" (2 Cor. 5:8; Phil. 1:23) and that Jesus Himself will come to bring you home (1 Thess. 4:16). What a joy to know that if we live close enough to our Lord and Savior that Christ Himself will stand to greet us as He did Stephen.

In chapter 10, we find where God tries to do away with prejudice when he sends a vision to Peter. Peter, being Peter, argued with God about the vision and about what was clean and unclean, three times; the same number of times that he denied Jesus (Luke 22:54-62). While he was still wondering what God was trying to teach him, three men came for him on request of Cornelius, who got his instructions from a holy angel. Peter went with them but was sure to remind them that it was against his law for a Jew to associate with a Gentile or even visit one. However, he did not go against God's will in this matter, and became a witness for God when he told them that God had shown him that he should not call any man impure or unclean. Peter saw what we all should see and that is that God does not see you as you are but as what you can be through Jesus. God gives believers His Spirit, regardless of human barriers. Our opinions and thoughts about others pale into insignificance alongside the will of God. Peter was criticized severely for going into the Gentile's house, but explained that he could not oppose God, since it was He that gave the gift of salvation to one and all. The great Gentile church at Antioch was born! A point to remember through the apostles, Peter, Paul, Barnabas, and others, is to be sure you are filled with the Spirit, and not full of yourself, such as the Pharisees and teachers of the Law (Matt. 5:20).

Evangelism continued as God started the worldwide mission of the gospel by leading the church to dedicate two experienced evangelists. This was the final significant breakthrough in the New Testament for the spread of the gospel. Paul and Barnabas led the church's active evangelistic efforts among Gentiles to the ends of the earth. These men were set apart by and for the Lord to do the work to which He called them. No one spoke more boldly than Paul, and considering that the Lord dropped him on the road and blinded him with a bright light and spoke to him in a voice like thunder from heaven, this is most understandable. We should all be dropped and spoken to loudly so that we can see, hear, and understand that our mission is the same as Paul's. Paul and Barnabas had a sharp disagreement over where they would go and whom they would take with them. They parted ways, Barnabas choosing Mark and sailing to Cyprus, and Paul choosing Silas, going through Syria and Cilicia. Notice that even in the disagreement, he was commended by the others to the grace of the Lord, giving us an example to agree to disagree but continue to teach the gospel of Christ (Acts 15:36-41).

Still another great lesson comes from Acts, when Paul and Silas were tossed in jail, after being severely flogged, for preaching the Word of God. The site of the prison was probably an underground dungeon, with their feet and hands bound to hooks anchored in the mortar between the stones. Although they were in a desperate situation, their prayers were not prayers of despair. They sang and prayed at midnight, and God honored that spirit and attitude, sent deliverance and conversion as a result. God used an earthquake to shake the entire jail area and provide opportunities for witness, revealing to the nonbelievers the power of God. He can use the same shaking today, and the scripture calls to: "rise at midnight to God thanks for His righteous laws" (Ps. 119:62). Paul and Silas found a group of people who tested everything, and they were called the Bereans and were of more noble character than the Thessalonians, for they received the message with great eagerness (Acts 17:10-11).

God is not served by human hands, since He needs nothing and all we are comes from Him. He does, however, want man to seek Him and reach out for Him and find Him, just as the apostles did, following in their footsteps in spreading the gospel. The book of Acts lets us hear the Lord as He tells us not to be afraid, keep on speaking, and be silent. Keep your courage, have faith in God that it will happen just as He told the apostles and still tells us through His Work. I like to think of the book of Acts in yet another light. As I study to show myself approved, I can imagine a physical ax which I use to rightly divide the Word of truth (2 Tim. 2:15).

3. *Praise the Lord Anyway*

The book of Habakkuk was written when Judah was making alliances with other nations. The king of Judah led the people back into idolatry and away from the Lord. Jehoiakim was evil, ungodly, and rebellious (2 Kings 23:36-24:7). Shortly after Jehoiakim ascended to power, Habakkuk wrote his lament over the decay, violence, greed, fighting, and perverted justice that surrounded him. God was bringing judgment on Judah through Babylon. Habakkuk had trouble understanding why God would use a heathen nation like Babylon to punish His people. He, like Job, cried out to God, wondering why God did not just purge Judah's sins and draw them back to righteousness. In the second verse, he asked God why He was ignoring his cry for help. Notice carefully that Habakkuk was not complaining on behalf of the people, but because he was having to witness evil. He sounded fearfully resentful that God had called on him to prophesy. I love God's answer: "Look! Watch! And be amazed and shocked! I will do something in your lifetime that you won't believe even when you are told about it" (Hab. 1:5). God uses verses 6-11, telling just how He was going to do things, but I don't think Habakkuk was listening, since he continued to complain.

Look and watch, which in Hebrew included the plural *you*, meant that God addressed both the prophet and the people. Habakkuk had complained about being made to look at injustice, but both he and the people suffered from myopia. They were too nearsighted to see the broad picture that God had painted. God instructed them to get their eyes off the immediate havoc, themselves, and look out on the international horizons. They would have to develop a world view that included the nations and then they would be utterly amazed, astounded, bewildered, and dumbfounded. Habakkuk still questioned why would the absolutely Holy One tolerate wrong and let His pure eyes look on evil. The beginning of chapter 2, verse 1: "I will stand like a guard to watch and place myself at the tower. I will wait to see what He will say to me. I will wait to learn how God will answer my complaint." This may at first glance seem arrogant, defiant, and perhaps pouting a little bit. I see him as being a spokesman for God's revelation. He waited for God's message, not simply for his own satisfaction, but standing ready to carry God's message to His people. "Be still and know that I am God" (Ps. 46:10) is what I see Habakkuk doing.

God was not ready for the message to be delivered, but told His prophet to write the revelation down. He was to put it plainly on tablets and wait for an appointed time, because the message spoke of the end time. For the rest of chapter 2, Habakkuk writes down the woes that will come upon the rebellious people. God did not mumble! Although He would use the Babylonians to punish His people, reference to the end seems to signify the coming destruction of evil Babylonia. It also carried the broader fulfillment of the Messianic judgment in the fall of Babylon the Great at the close of the Tribulation (Rev. 17-18). Those in Judah were about to experience the awesome Babylonian invasion and captivity, but had great comfort and assurance of this prophecy. Their barbaric captors would themselves suffer divine judgment in God's due time. Now, just to bring the title of this story into play, I refer you to Habakkuk 3:16-19 What Habakkuk heard and wrote made his heart pound, his lips quiver, and his legs tremble. Then he lists the entire calamity to come on them through the invading nation, thus bringing us to the words spoken against all hope: "yet I will rejoice in the Lord. I will be joyful in God my Savior!" If your troubles are just a portion of Habakkuk's and Judah's, will you praise the Lord anyway?

I am willing to step out and say that I do not have enough numbers in my head or words in my vocabulary to thank God for all the past blessings, to praise Him for my present daily supplies, or to honor His Word for the promises for my future. Today I am going to try! Will you join me?

The praise at the top of my list is salvation. Paul wrote the letter to the Romans to teach the Christian faith to the first believers in Rome. Sin paints an ugly picture in people and in cultures. Without God's intervention, we have no way to deal with sin. Paul said that he was proud of the Good News because is the power God uses to save everyone. The psalmist wrote that God gave him the breath to praise Him, and His love was so great that He saved him from spiritual death and delivered his soul from hell (Ps. 86:23, 150:6). Jesus was born into this world to take our sins away, and not only provided salvation but also great confidence for Christians. If you are a child of God, claim you victory over sin. Be confident that no matter what happens, you are always His because your name is written in heaven. You have been made right with God through your faith and have peace through Jesus, right beginning with belief. It sounds so simple, but yet many times, we disbelieve God and think, is that all there is to be saved? Yes! According to the Bible, it is as simple as God can make it and as quick as you can say *I accept it* (John 3:16; Eph. 2:8).

We may not always know what God is doing, but we can always trust Him to do what is right. We may not always understand His plan, but we can praise Him anyway and trust that He has made the best plan for you and me. No matter how things may appear, God is still in control, therefore always be joyful. Pray continually and give thanks to God. Circumstances may change, but God never does, and He will always be God the Father, and you will always be His child. Things may get bad here, but this world is not our home, and that is enough to praise Him here and now that we have an eternal home waiting for us. God has been good to me, but the best is yet to come (1 Pet. 1:3-4; 1 Cor. 2:9).

How many times in the past week have you praised God because of the inheritance He has promised you? We might also take time to praise Him for allowing us to bear fruits, that we are predestined, that we have a safe place with Him, and just because we are called to praise Him anyway. Praise Him that He hears and answers prayers, that He is with us always, that He has prepared a city for us in eternity, and that He has and will heal us. We who are enjoying good health have extra reasons to praise Him, and we who are not should praise Him for the fact that Satan has no power over us; we are strong in the Lord and are redeemed. We do not have to worry, for our Lord is faithful and will do what He promised.

"The Lord is my strength, and He makes my feet like the feet of deer and enables me to go on the heights" (Hab. 3:19). Deer feet speaks of grace, agility, and swiftness. High places speaks of the mountaintops where the deer are free from the dangers found below. Habakkuk is telling us that God enables him and us to rise above our circumstances and that God gives the strength to stand above the battle and to enjoy precious freedom in the Lord. In other words, he is saying that God turned his doubts to shouts! He gave him peace in the middle of his problems, just as He did for Job, and just as He will do for you and me. Be a prisoner of hope (Zech. 9:12) and although your heart pounds and your lips quiver at the sound of trouble, rejoice and praise the Lord anyway (Hab. 3:16-18)!

4. *The Anointed*

"Touch not my anointed" (Ps. 105:15). The Hebrew word for anointing is *mashach*, meaning to daub or smear. Anointing is used for painting a ceiling (Jer. 22:14), anointing a shield (Isa. 21:5), applied to sacred furniture (Ex. 29:36), and to the sacred pillar (Gen. 31:13). The most significant uses of anointing are its application to sacred persons, such as a sacred ceremony of pouring oil on the head of the appointed king (Jud. 9:8; 1 Sam. 9:16). Actually, throughout the books of 1st and 2nd Kings and 1st and 2nd Samuel, the anointing appears to be reserved for the king, which accounts for the fact that the Lord's anointed became a synonym for king. Among the Hebrews, it was believed the anointing brought holiness and virtue of God and a special endowment of the Spirit of Yahweh (Isa. 61:1).

God protected His anointed (Israel) from physical harm. The word *touch* actually means physical harm, but it does not cover them from publicly telling whether their teachings or leadership is right or wrong. Remember, David did not raise a hand to bring physical harm to King Saul, God's anointed. Saul was anointed as king over Israel, but his reign would soon be over. David knew he was the next in line for the throne, but refused to touch God's present anointed king to remove him from his position. It was God, not David, who would remove Saul (1 Sam. 26:19-23, 8-10). However, this anointing did not stop David from rebuking Saul before all the troops, asking why he was trying to kill him, since he was innocent.

The importance of this story is that Saul was hunting David and trying to kill him. Why? Because David was challenging Saul's position and was exposing Saul for wrongdoing and neglect of the nation's leadership. The same thing is going on in the leadership today, but we are trained to listen and believe the ones in the ministry, because we are not to touch God's anointed. It is not easy, nor easily accepted, to confront a pastor, deacon, or teacher, when your spirit quickens to a misquote of the scripture or an explanation that does not line up with the Word of God.

It was Paul who called the Bereans nobler than others because they looked to the scripture to see if what he was teaching was accurate. Today, when a Berean steps up, there is always someone to back them down with the words *do not touch God's anointed*. Paul did not say this to the Bereans, nor in fact did any of the apostles. This protective phrase is not found in the New Testament.

John tells us to test every spirit and see whether they are from God (1 John 4:1), and it is too sad that many are kept from learning the truth and are in fear of questioning the higher-ups because of the misuse of scripture. "Woe to the experts in the Law, because you have taken away the key to knowledge. You yourselves have not entered and you have hindered those who were entering" (Luke 11:52). Even David, later in his ministry as king, accepted rebuke and correction from Nathan. He did not hide behind his anointing, and neither should the leaders today. Unless someone is speaking the truth of the Word of God correctly (John 17:17) it does not matter if they call themselves anointed or how big or successful a ministry they have, they are wrong.

We, the body of Christ, are all anointed! God anointed us and set His seal of ownership on us and put His Spirit in all of our hearts (2 Cor.

1:21). All who have received Jesus in their hearts and have been baptized into the body of Christ are anointed (1 Cor. 12:13). It is not a certain church group who are supposed leaders over the church, like the kings in the Old Testament; whole body is anointed. Men and women who are anointed "hold firmly to the trustworthy message as it has been taught so that he can encourage others by sound doctrine and refute those who oppose it" (Titus 1:9). All Christians have the same anointing from the same Spirit (1 John 2:20-27).

We are not to protect one another by using the term, *do not touch God's anointed,* when we hear a contradiction or correction of what was said by a leader, pastor, or teacher. God does the protecting of His anointed, and this means you and me (Ps. 105:14-15, 20:6-7, 28:8; Isa. 26:3). This revelation that we are all anointed does not give us a free rein to judge or condemn everything we hear, just to exercise our spiritual muscles. We are not to use it to chase down a certain person we dislike. Mature believers are those who, by reason of use, have their senses exercised to discern both good and evil (Heb. 5:14). It takes time to learn and grow in discernment.

Use this knowledge to put away the idea that you only need to come to church and be fed the Word of God through an anointed minister. "In fact though by this time you ought to be teachers, you need someone to teach you the elementary truths of God's Word all over again" (Heb. 5:12). It is understood that we as believers are anointed, now begin to use the material and resources God has given you. We have a menu, the Bible, and this Bible contains God and His Word. We have a teacher, the Holy Spirit, and the Counselor whom the Father sent will teach us all things and remind us of all that is written (John 14:26).

Remember, that which is touched or anointed by God is no longer common. Anything and anyone that is touched by God is considered sacred, since we are to be holy as He is holy. Our body is the temple of God, and He did not tolerate His temple to be defiled in the Old Testament; Jesus did not tolerate it in the New Testament, and those who touch His children today will give account to God for their actions (1 Cor. 3:16-17). Under the Old Testament covenant, God protected His anointed, and under the present covenant, that protection is extended to the entire body of Christ. A failure to understand the Lord's command to not touch His anointed has bound the hands of many, and made them prey for the devil. Our silence has caused us to forsake the ministry of watchmen (Ezek. 3:17-21). Knowing that we have the authority to act and should act raises the question of how to act when we see someone not doing right according to the Word of God. It is our responsibility to state the facts only and nothing more. It is for God to deal with them, for it is His to avenge, and He will repay any wrong they bring onto His church (Rom. 12:19).

5. *Worship*

Lately, I received a page of questions all concerning worship. What exactly is worship? Where do we worship? Are there required postures or positions for worship? When do we worship? How does God receive our worship? Thinking I had snap answers for all these easy questions, I sat with pen in hand, excited about writing some simple facts on the subject that "I knew so well," only to find myself at a loss for words! You who know me doubt this! However, it is not always an easy transference from your heart to inquiring minds. I know that my Redeemer lives, and I am persuaded that He is able, and for that I worship Him, yet to rejoice in this knowledge only to see confusion on another's face is heartbreaking. If only we could bring them with us into the presence of God, to join in our worship, that they might share our joy.

In the Old Testament, the people built worship altars, usually at each stop (Gen 12:8). One of my favorite stories is where the Lord Himself built an altar of worship in Jacob's dream. This altar was a stairway, resting on the earth, with its top reaching to heaven. And there above it stood God! When Jacob awoke he said, "Surely the

Lord is in this place" (Gen 28:10-16). Do not miss the next line, "and I was not aware of it"! God calls us to worship anywhere we are, even in our sleep, since that is the only time He can get a Word in for some of us. But do not be caught wide awake and unaware that the Lord is standing next to you. God called the nations into worship so that He might show them His ways (Mic. 4:2) and He will call the nations into worship in the hour of judgment (Rev. 14:6-7). Here also, the angel commanded John to worship God (Rev. 19:10)! Don't you think it would be wise to do a bit of worshiping in between now and judgment? We should not forsake gathering together in worship, to thank God for the unshakable kingdom we are receiving. I take everything Jesus said as a command, since I have not read where He asks if we want to do this or that, or where He asks if we feel like it. For instance, we read in Luke 4:8 to worship the Lord and serve Him only. The comment that we have all heard is, *well, I go to church and listen to the praise and worship but I don't enter into it much.* Is this good enough? Several instances show Jesus instructing the ones He healed to go and show themselves to the priest and offer the gift Moses commanded. Notice, these healed persons were taking with them a reason to worship, not waiting to find something to worship in church. Surely one day a week we can bring something to mind, some wee miracle that God has performed in our life, and take it with us to our place of worship.

Romans chapter 12 will tell you what worship is, and has a complete list of things to do. Now we go to Hebrews chapter 9 to learn the regulations for worship in the first covenant. Starting with Hebrews 9:11, the scripture explains how Jesus Christ came and died for us to take away our sins, and by this sacrifice, we were made holy once and for all. Praise and worship are expressions that acknowledge God as the Ultimate source and giver of all good gifts. Worship is to figure out what pleases God and then doing it, since He has made it plain that He wants our love and obedience offered with gladness in our hearts. God loves for you to boast about Him by telling about His justice and righteousness, reading and meditating on His Word, and telling Him all your troubles. All these things, no matter how small they may seem, are worship of our Lord and Savior, and He loves to hear it.

The posture of worship would be the same as for prayer, and that would be wherever and however you are comfortable. Everyone does not worship the same, and there is no need to copy anyone, but just follow your heart and the lead of the Spirit, and it will come naturally. "The whole assembly bowed in worship while the singers sang and the trumpeters played" (2 Chr. 29:28). The conditions of the heart are mentioned in numerous scriptures throughout the Bible. We are commanded to love God with all our heart, soul, mind, and strength, and set our hearts on seeking the Lord. We need a broken spirit and a contrite heart, destroy what is devoted to destruction that is running around in our minds, and get our minds on the one that we have come to worship. We need an undivided heart, meaning all for Jesus and none for deceit, and to be thankful and worship God with reverence and awe (Heb. 12:28). There should not be divisions among the congregation and no sin cherished in our hearts (Ps. 66:18; 1 Cor. 11:17).

God receives our worship with delight, according to the psalmist (Ps. 147:11). He will come close to you and hear from heaven those who call on Him (James 4:8; 2 Chron. 7:14-15). He upholds you, comes near you, fulfills your desires, and saves you (Ps. 145:14-21). Your were created for God's pleasure (Rev. 4:11), and life and worship is all about letting God use you for His purpose, and not using God for your purpose. Jesus called us His friends IF we do what He commands, so you see, the form of worship is of no importance to God but worship we must to find Him and receive all the blessings He has in store for us.

God is worthy of our worship, or at least that is what the living creatures, the twenty-four elders and angels say in Revelation 7:11-12. They are all gathered at the throne, and the scripture says that they all fell down on their faces before the throne and worshiped God, saying, "Amen! Praise and glory and wisdom and thanks and honor and power and strength be to our God for ever and ever. Amen!" That is a great example of how, when, and where we are to worship our Lord and Savior. Just call out the name of Jesus and cry *holy* and God will hear from heaven and consider that you love Him enough not to get in any particular position to worship, but that you have the heart to worship.

6. *Faith*

Let's pretend that we are all in church—a stretch of the imagination for some—and we hear the preacher say that faith is being sure of the things we hope for and knowing something is real, even if we do not see it (Heb. 11:1). Now, the next people you visit with, you quote what you heard the preacher say, and you ask this person if they have faith. You may get a blank stare, and you may get a variety of questions such as, what is faith? Are you prepared to answer these questions?

To have faith, you must first have God. I do not mean to know who God is but to have God. Walk with God, commune with God and have Him living in you, then your faith will become real. To have God in you life is to accept Him as your Savior (John 3:16), since He is always the one that saves and the only one that saves. He created man for His glory and pleasure, and you were saved by His grace through believing (Eph. 2:8). Salvation is a gift, as is faith, and we are all given a measure of faith (Rom. 12:3). Most of the saved only need to exercise the faith they are given for it to become a strong part of daily life. Daily Bible reading is the best exercise to strengthen the faith muscles. "The Word is near you. It is in your mouth and in your heart. That is the teaching of faith that we are telling. If you use your mouth to say that Jesus is Lord, and if you believe in your heart that God raised Jesus from the dead, you will be saved (Rom. 19:8-11).

Faith is a decision to believe, but many are waiting for a bright light to knock them down or a spoken word from an angel or to be rescued by a zealous angel (Acts 9:1-6, 10:3-4, 12:7-11). Even some of those who saw

Lazarus raised from the dead did not believe (John 11:43-46). Thomas, one of the twelve disciples, did not believe until he touched the wounded hands and side of Jesus. Faith is a choice, not an event, and is like stepping where there is no place to put your foot. As soon as they stepped into the River Jordan, the water piled up, and not before (Jos. 3:13). Faith is not a power you possess, but rather the belief that God has the power to do what He says. Faith is not magic, and there are no words or chants to memorize before it is manifested. Faith comes from hearing the message, and the message is heard through the Word of God (Rom. 10:17) and the Word is then kept in your heart (Ps. 119:11).

If you do not have faith, you cannot please God, because anyone who comes to Him must believe by faith that He exists and that He rewards who earnestly seeks Him. Faith produces obedience, and it is a power that results in godly living and surrender. Faith enables you to understand the Bible as you read it, and doubles for an extension cord to life (2 Kings 20:1-6). It assures you that you will never have to go back to being the old you, living in the sin of the world, once you have decided to follow God (1 Kings 19:16, 21). My faith is unwavering because I know and believe that Jesus was put to death on the cross for my sins, and now lives within me. I still live in my body, but I live my faith in the Son of God who loved me and gave His life for me. He has power to do what He has promised, and that is to give me eternal life with Him in heaven after this life on earth is over. I know this and am convinced that He is able to do all things and that the one who stands and accurses me before God has been defeated (Rev. 12:10).

If you had been living when Christ was on earth, and had met the Savior kind.

What would you have asked Him to do for you, supposing you were stone blind?

The man considered and then replied, I expect that without a doubt,

I would have asked for a dog with a collar and chain to lead me daily about.

And how often thus, in our faithless prayers we acknowledge with shamed surprise,

We have only asked for a dog and chain when we might have had opened eye!

Author unknown (Mark 9:19).

7. *Where We Got the Bible*

The Bible has been banned, burned, scoffed, and ridiculed. Scholars have mocked it as foolish. Kings have branded it as illegal, but it survived. Not only has it survived, but it has thrived. It is the single most popular book in the world for years. The Bible's durability is not found on earth but rather it is found in heaven. The Bible's durability comes from the fact that it is God's Book and God's voice and God's words. The purpose of the Bible is to proclaim God's plan and passion to save His children.

The word *Bible* comes from a Latin form of the Greek word *biblia* which means "little books." The New Testament, canon, literally means cane or rod of measurement. In Christian use, it came to mean the written rule of faith, that is, the list of original and authoritative books that composed God's inspired Word. The Canonical New Testament books were those which came to be generally recognized by the churches as the genuine and authentic writings of apostolic authority. In the days of Christ, there was in the literature of the Jewish nation, a group of writings called The Scriptures, now called the Old Testament, which the people commonly regarded as having come from God (Deut 10:45, 31:26, 17:18). As the writings of the apostles appeared, they were added to these Jewish scriptures and were held in the same sacred regard.

Paul claimed for his teaching the inspiration of God (1 Cor. 17:13), as did John for the book of Revelation. Paul intended that his Epistles should be read in the churches, and Peter wrote that these things might remain in the churches after his departure. Paul quoted as scripture 1st

Timothy 5:18: "the laborer is worthy of his hire." This sentence is found nowhere in the Bible except Matthew 10:10 and Luke 10:7, evidence that Matthew or Luke was then in existence and regarded as scripture. The New Testament books, Matthew, James, and Hebrews first appeared in Palestine. John, Galatians, Ephesians, Colossians, 1st and 2nd Timothy, Philemon, 1st and 2nd Peter, 1st, 2nd, and 3rd John, Jude, and Revelation first appeared in Asia Minor; 1st and 2nd Corinthians, Philippians, 1st and 2nd Thessalonians, and Luke appeared in Greece, leaving Titus showing up in Crete, and Mark, Acts, and Romans in Rome.

Eusebius (AD 264-340) bishop of Caesarea, church historian, lived through and was imprisoned during Diocletian's persecution of Christians, which was Rome's final effort to blot our the Christian name. One of its special objectives was the destruction of all Christian scripture. For ten years, Bibles were hunted by the agents of Rome, and burned in public marketplaces. To Christians, the question of just what books composed their scripture was no idle matter. Constantine became in charge and one of his first acts after ascending the throne was to order, for the churches of Constantinople, fifty Bibles, to be prepared by skillful copyists on the finest of vellum, and to be delivered by royal carriages from Caesarea to Constantinople. The books that made up the New Testament of Eusebius are the same books that now constitute the New Testament as we know it. The original manuscripts of all the New Testament books, as far as is known, have been lost. Copies of these precious writings began to be made from the very first, for other churches, and copies of copies, generation after generation, as the older ones wore out. The writing material in common use was papyrus, made of slices of the water plant that grew in Egypt. Two slices, one vertical and the other horizontal, were pressed together and polished. Ink was made of charcoal, gum, and water. Single sheets were used for short compositions, and longer sheets were fastened side-by-side to form rolls. A roll was usually about thirty feet long and ten inches high. The Codex or modern book form with numbered pages came about in the second century AD. The invention of printing from movable type made

Bibles cheap and abundant, and greatly promoted the circulation and influence of the Bible among the people. In 1454, John Gutenberg's first printed book was the Bible. One of them is in the Library of Congress in Washington, for which $350,000 was paid.

The Old Testament was written in Hebrew, and the New Testament in Greek. The first English Bible was translated from vulgate in manuscript only, in 1382. The pope was against this, so he excommunicated the author, and after his death, his bones were burned and cast into the river. The King James Version was ordered by King James, for the sake of uniform service in Presbyterian Scotland and Episcopal England in 1611.

There are thousands of pages of history on the translations of the Bible and how it was handed down through the years. The important fact to remember is that no man has been able to destroy this book of God's, and this should convince the world that it was inspired and will stand (Matt. 5:18, 24:35). This is the best book you will ever read, full of hope, peace, joy, and instructions. Open it and let the words pour into you hearts and minds. And do not forget to share (Matt. 28:20).

8. *The Wheat and the Weed*

While driving down a Texas country road one Sunday afternoon, we rode past a milo crop. The entire field of feed was uniform in size and height except for a "scattering" of single stalks that were two feet taller and the grain heads were a bit skinny. Biologists call this a "gene flow." It is how plants swap genetic material through cross-pollination. The scripture calls the unwelcome plant a tare or weed and Jesus tells about it in His first parable. The word *parable* comes from two Greek words, *para* and *ballo*, which together mean "to throw alongside." A parable makes a comparison between a known truth and an unknown truth and throws them alongside each other. Jesus tells about a farmer who sowed seed in his field; however, the emphasis in this story is on the results of the sowing. The seed fell on four kinds of soil: along the path (Matt. 13:4), on rocky places (13:5), among thorns (13:7), and on good soil (13:8).

In Jesus's interpretation of the parable of the sower, He compared the four results of sowing to four responses to the Kingdom message. This was the message preached by John, Jesus, and the apostles. First, when one hears the message but does not understand it, the devil or the evil one snatches away the Word that was sown. This is seed sown on the path. The next two results, the seed on rocky places that had no root and seed among the thorns, meaning worries that choke it out, speaks of hearers' initial interest but with no genuine heartfelt response. The seed on rocky soil speaks of a person who hears the Word but falls away, meaning is offended, when he faces trouble for having expressed interest in the Word (Matt. 13:57, 15:12). Only the seed that fell on good soil had an abiding result and the production of a crop that increased. The one who believes in Jesus's Word, the man who hears the Word and understands, will then receive and understand more (Matt. 13:12).

The difference in these results was not in the seed, but in the soil on which the seed fell. As the gospel of the Kingdom was presented, the good news was the same. The difference was in the individuals who heard that Word. The Lord was not saying that an exact 25 percent of those who heard the message would believe, but He was saying that a majority would not respond positively to the good news. In this parable, Jesus demonstrated why the Pharisees and religious leaders rejected His message. They were not prepared soil for the Word.

The second parable tells of the sower who sowed his wheat seed, and the enemy came at night and sowed weeds on the same soil, resulting in cross-pollination. As a result, the wheat and the weeds grew together and would continue to do so until the time of harvest. The sower of the good seed is the Son of Man, the Lord Himself. The field is the world into which the good news is spread or planted. The good seed represents the sons of the Kingdom, Christians who produce fruitful crops. The weeds are the sons of the evil one or the devil that has been sown among the wheat by the enemy. Do not be deceived, for just as there is no tag on the seeds that cross- pollinate the feed crops, these evil ones do not wear signs on their chests saying they are of the devil so you should beware (2 Cor. 11:14-15; Matt. 17:15-20).

The harvest is the end of the age, and the harvesters are angels. At Jesus's second coming, the angels will gather the wicked and throw them into judgment (Rev. 19:15). Farmers are finding widespread contamination from the hybrid seeds mixing into their good seed. Tons of money and many hours of research are put into solving this problem. Christians should put in this kind of research on what is being brought into our churches and youth activities. The bad seeds are being planted without opposition in most cases. Everyone, kids and adults alike, needs to search, pry, get nosey, talk, pray, beg, and whatever else it takes to sow the good seed into our generation now before the reaper comes and gathers the weeds and ties them together to be burned.

9. Truth

Do you always tell the truth in all things, or do you tell a white lie, justify, and try to get by? The most common term for truth in the Old Testament is Hebrew, *emet,* meaning a reality which is firm or certain. It contains the idea of solidity, validity, faithfulness, and steadfastness. As a legal term, *emet* denotes authentic facts which can be verified. What is the truth? Jesus says that He is the Truth (John 14:6). David asked and answered this question, saying that anyone who wanted to live on God's holy hill speaks the truth from his heart and has no slander on his tongue, does no wrong, and casts no slur on his fellowman (Ps. 15:2-4). He adds that one keeps his oath even if it hurts! God's love is before us, allowing us to walk continually in His truth. The entire book of Psalms is filled with truths, and God would love for each and every one of us to read it daily, memorizing the parts that we are able, so that we can pull out a verse of truth when we feel a lie seeping out of our minds and onto our lips.

Truth proceeds from the nature of God, as seen in the words of the prophet Elijah. He raised the widow's son from the dead and was proof to her that the Word of the Lord was in his mouth and was true (1 Kings 17:24). Zechariah sets forth the essence of prophetic moral teachings as rendering true judgments along with showing kindness and mercy (Zech. 7:9). The judicial aspect of *emet* is also present in Zechariah's instruction to speak the truth to one another, render in your gates judgments that are true. God desires truth in the inward being (Ps. 51:16). One who speaks the truth from the heart has the moral qualification for a position in the congregation, because he has his mind fixed on the truth and walks blamelessly, doing what is right (Ps. 15:2).

The world rests on three things: righteousness, truth, and peace. The Apostle Paul uses truth in the sense of that which has certainty and force, in contrast to the pagan ways and of the truth that was in Jesus. For Paul, truth means a legitimate standard, that which is proper, which could be used to measure the claims of his opponents against him, and also in a sense of uprightness (Gal. 2:5). Paul calls the gospel the truth and speaks of preaching the gospel as the word of truth (Col. 1:5). The Holy Spirit promised by Jesus is the Spirit of Truth, functioning as part of revelation and as a witness sin the community. Truth can also indicate the real state of affairs in the Greek philosophical sense, as when Paul speaks of people giving up the truth about God for a lie, serving the creature rather than the Creator (Rom. 1:25). This is reflected in 1 John 3:18, which exhorts the reader to love not in word or speech, but in truth and action.

However, truth received only as information can never save. It is not enough to enjoy reading the Bible and listening to sermons, or even to believe the truth. It takes courage to say that we should obey God rather than man, or even though they kill me, I will trust in the

Lord. My personal favorite is, "if I perish, I perish" when Esther took the chance of losing her head by telling the truth (Est. 4:16). Truth must be acted upon, and even though you have studied the Bible and have been informed, you have learned and you have been inspired, God wants you to do something about it. Who, me? Yes, you and I! The Bible was written for you and me, and we should act upon the instructions it offers. Jesus says, "those who listen and do not obey are like the man who built a house without a foundation and when the floods swept down against the house it crumbled into a heap of ruins" (Luke 6:46-49). Here is another truth: The floods will come! Physically, mentally, financially, and spiritually! Be ready with the Word of God; that is where our hope lies.

Jesus says to build a foundation and He will show you, everyone, how to do this, if they will only come to Him and obey His Words. He explains this in yet another parable, telling us to build our house on rock and put the foundation in deep. Then, when the floods come, the water cannot wash away our house or shake the foundation because it has been well built (Luke 6:48-49). This Rock that we must build our spiritual foundation on is Christ Jesus (1 Cor. 10:4). Action in truth is studying the Word of God, prayer, witnessing, and obedience. Resisting the devil, faith, and trusting Jesus fully is also action. If you have Jesus, you have the truth, because Jesus says that He is the truth and we simply cannot separate the two. How serious is it to fail to obey the truth? Very serious indeed, since Jesus Himself will render the punishment with burning fire from heaven and powerful angels and then the sad, terrible, final words from His lips will be, "I never knew you" (Matt. 7:21-23).

You are not reading this by accident! It is by divine appointment that the truth has found its way into your life. What will you do with it? Shut out the world and see nothing but the Cross of Calvary and the Savior who says, "If you love me, keep my commandments" (John 14:15). The truth is there for all to accept! What will your decision be?

10. Questions and Answers

Q: How can I adore God? What should I do or say?

A: Figure out what pleases God and them do it (Eph. 5:10), follow God (Gen. 6:9), love Him (Hos. 6:6). He takes pleasure in those who honor Him (Ps. 147:11), do everything in faith (Heb. 11:6), and obey Him gladly (Ps. 100:2, James 2:24). He loves you to boast about Him (Jer. 9:24), read and meditate on His Word (Job 23:12), be honest (Job 42:7), and tell Him all your cares and troubles (Ps. 142:2-3).

Q: Since there is only one verse in the Bible about lifting holy hands, how would you teach a lesson on the subject? (1 Tim. 2:8)

A: Some are gifted enough to teach an entire lesson from one word. However, 1 Timothy 2:8 is not just about lifting hands. This is a lesson on instructions on worship. Notice that in verse 1, Paul is saying that first we pray and then give thanks for everyone. He also includes to pray for those in authority, that we may live holy lives. The scripture says that we are made holy because God is holy and we belong to God (1 Pet. 1:16), so therefore if we are holy, then our hands are made holy and can be raised in worship. Paul's main focus to the lifting of hands refers back to when Jesus ascended into heaven: "When He had led them out to the vicinity of Bethany, He lifted up His hands and blessed them and was taken up into heaven" (Luke 24:50-51). Those in the Old Testament raised hands to the Lord (Gen. 14:22), God lifted His hands to heaven (Deut. 32:40), Moses held up his hands and finally needed help to continue (Ex. 17:11-12). David prayed with uplifted hands (Ps. 28:2), and Lamentations 2:19 and 3:4 tells to lift our hands to Him and also our hearts. Ezra praised the Lord and all the people lifted their hands (Neh. 8:6), and even the angels lifted their hands to heaven (Rev. 10:5).

Q: What is worship and how do we go about it?

A: Romans chapter 12 will tell you what worship is, and has a complete list of things to do. The posture is not important, however in 2 Chronicles, the whole assembly bowed in worship while the singers sang and the trumpeters played. The conditions of the heart means to love God with all of your heart (Deut 6:5), have a broken spirit and contrite heart (Ps. 51:17), and worship with reverence and awe (Heb. 12:28). God receives your worship with delight (Ps. 147:11) and will meet you there (James 4:8).

Q: What type of man was Job and why didn't he curse God to His face?

A: These questions are answered in the book of Job. "This man was blameless and upright. He feared God and shunned evil" (Job 1:1). Job's wife asked him the same question about cursing God, or rather she told him to do so, but Job answered, "Shall we accept good from God and not trouble?" (Job 2:9-10). Job understood that he was unworthy and admitted to God that he spoke out of turn with his questions during times of trouble (Job 40:4-5). These who deny God, curse God, and do not accept God will be thrown into the lake of burning sulfur with the devil that deceived them (Rev. 20:9-10). Job knew that only God is worthy of praise and worship, and although he whined a lot, he never denied God (Rev. 5:9-14).

Q: Does the Bible say what happens to God when we sing/worship?

A: I find no actual scripture to tell you how God reacts (smiles, laughs, cries) to our worship, but the Bible is filled with ways to worship which gives God pleasure. When we read the Psalms, we are gripped by the celebratory aspect of worship. God is a God who wants us to praise Him and is pleased with those who worship Him, praise Him and trust His love (Ps. 147:11, 81:1, 98, 149, 150, 33:1-3, 47:1, 66:1-2). He rejoices in His works, which is us (Ps. 104:31), has emotions (Ps. 18:19), and we are made from His image, therefore I believe God expresses all the emotions that we feel when we worship (John 5:2-3, 15:9-13).

Q: How does one offer praise as a sacrifice?

A: Praise is an expression of worship which recognizes and acknowledges God as the ultimate source and giver of all good gifts. The call to praise can be expressed in a variety of ways, including thanks, honor, love, and any emotion coming from the heart. The form of praise spoken of most in scripture is song (Jud. 5:3; 2 Chr. 23:13; Ps. 9:2). The word *sacrifice* does not mean to give up something that you cannot live without, but rather give up something that causes you to live life more fully.

Part VIII
God Uses People

1. What Happened to the Apostles?

Some have commented on how wonderful it would have been to have been chosen as one of the apostles, or to have been among the earliest Christians who actually saw and heard Jesus in person. What a great honor and joy. However, with this honor of being chosen came responsibility. They were expected to go out into the world and be active witnesses to what they saw and heard (Matt. 28:18-20). The God-defying hatred that got Jesus killed also cost many of the disciples their lives. The Bible does not record what happened to all of them, however, there are other references to their activities that have led scholars to figure out mostly how the disciples lived and died.

Peter was reportedly crucified, upside-down, during the reign of Emperor Nero. Remember Nero? He was an insane emperor who was accused of fiddling while Rome burned. His behavior was excessive and cruel. It was the custom to line the lanes and passages around the palace with stakes with torches on them to light the way. The stories are that Nero preferred to hang Christians on the stakes and set fire to them to light his driveway. Then he would drive his chariot in the nude at top speed through the burning, tormented Christians. He also used Christians as live torches to illuminate races at the Vatican Circus. It was rumored that Nero caused the burning of Rome, although he blamed it on the Christians. Whether or not he was responsible for Peter's crucifixion is unknown. Peter would have most likely been in his mid sixties at the time of his death.

Peter was one of the twelve apostles, the brother of Andrew, and also called Simon (Luke 6:14) and Cephas (John 1:42). Although Jesus predicted that Peter would deny Him, and though he did deny Jesus three times (Mark 14:27-72), after His Resurrection, Jesus commissioned Peter to shepherd His flock (John 21:15-23). At Pentecost, he became bold and preached a power-packed sermon (Acts 2) and continued to heal and preach, even though challenged by the Sanhedrin (Acts 3:1-10, 3:11-26, 4:1-22). Later God spoke to him in a vision, and Peter went to the Gentile Cornelius to tell him about Jesus, even though at that time, the Jews and Gentiles did not associate with one another. The name *Peter* means "stone" or "rock," and was given to him by Jesus (Matt. 16:18). He was a fisherman with James and John, his partners, and was or had been married (Acts 4:1-22) and owned a house he shared with Andrew. Peter appears in every Scriptural list as one of the twelve apostles, and then on the inner core of three (Mark 5:37). All four gospels place Peter at the Resurrection appearances, and Jesus appeared to him separately after the Resurrection (John 21:1-4; 1 Cor. 15:5).

Mark 1:16-17, Luke 5:1-11, and John 1:35-42 each introduce Peter a different way. John states that Peter was first a disciple of John the Baptist, and was introduced to Jesus by his brother Andrew. 1st Peter was written to the Christians who lived in the northern provinces of Asia Minor. These Christians were being persecuted because of their faith, so Peter wrote to encourage them. Peter told them to remember how much Jesus had suffered for them and to follow His example by being brave and trusting God. He said that because God chose them to be His people and because Jesus suffered and died for them, they should live the way God wanted them to.

2nd Peter was written to the same group of Christians, who were now in danger of being led astray by false teachers. Peter reminded them that the best way to resist false teachers was to grow in the knowledge of the Lord and practice of the Christian faith. The same method should be taught and used today, since it proved to work. He warned them that God would destroy the false teachers, and they were to live holy and godly lives, because Jesus would keep His promise to come again. Peter's life was not without controversy. The gospels report that Jesus had to correct him on occasion (Mark 32:33). The book of Acts pictures him as the center of controversy over his acceptance of table fellowship from the Gentiles (Acts 11:2-3), and Paul censured his behavior in public (Gal. 2:11-14). Jesus reinstated Peter, however, and by the power of God, he healed people simply when his shadow passed over them (John 21:15-19; Acts 5:15-16). What a guy! What a God!

2. Elijah's Brook

Chad Walsh wrote that it was safer, from the devil's point of view, to vaccinate a man with a mild case of Christianity, so as to protect him from the real disease. Nothing is more disastrous or more of a turnoff than a phony Christian. The Hebrew prophet Elijah was no phony! He was convinced God was alive, and he became God's personal representative to proclaim a message to King Ahab. This was short, simple, and to the point message with a power-packed preface: "I serve the Lord, the God of Israel. As surely as the Lord lives no rain or dew will fall during the next few years unless I command it!" (1 Kings 17:1). James states that Elijah was a man just like us, but he prayed earnestly that it might not rain, and it did not rain for three years and six months. Elijah was convinced of the reality of God. Ahab and all of his cohorts thought they had completely stopped all Jehovah worship, but they made one serious miscalculation. They forgot about a man with a nature just like ours, a man of God named Elijah. All it takes in any generation is one man who is totally overwhelmed by the living God, believing that only God can bring about miracles through a mere human, and the world is changed.

The next step God takes we may think is strange. After He shuts down the heavenly water power plant, He sends Elijah to sit by the brook. Put yourself in Elijah's position for just one moment. Here he sits on the bank of a brook that is slowly but surely drying up. It becomes a trickle, a few muddy puddles, and then evaporates completely. How would you respond? Did you misunderstand God? Did you say your prayer backwards? Did God really intend you to pray for no rain for three and one half years? I am not sure I could have just sat there without some doubt about my interpretation of God's intentions. I truly think I would have started looking for another brook with a little water left in it. But first I would have cried! When in doubt, pity parties always come into the picture. Imagine Elijah's thoughts. Since God sent him to this particular brook, surely it was the only brook left with water. God would not let His faithful servant thirst, right? He was not to be punished and die with all those sinners, was he? What had he done that God did not command? Finally it dawned on him! His prayer had been answered! Are you sitting by a drying brook wondering why? An emotional dryness, needing more? A financial drought that has you buried in debt? A physical dehydration that you may not live through? Are you asking the Lord what happened? His answer may very well be, "Nothing! I am just answering your prayer!"

Have you asked God to make you like Jesus? He took you at your word and began the process and you cried out, "Lord, what happened? Why did you allow this incident or this person to come into my life?" God's answer can be found in Hebrews 5:8. "Even though Jesus was the Son of God, He learned obedience by what He suffered!" Have you prayed for God to teach you to pray, and found yourself dissolved in tears, unable to speak? Again, your answer is in Hebrews. "He [Jesus] prayed with loud cries and tears to the one who could save Him from death, and His prayers were heard because He trusted God" (5:7). Maybe your needs are not met because you never ask! Many passages in the Bible tell us to ask and we will receive, but as you read them, do not overlook the fact that the promises come with conditions. If you believe you will receive, if you have faith, you may ask in my name, if you have faith, you may ask, and if the request brings glory to the Father. We do not have because we do not ask, says James 4:2-3, but adds that we must not ask with wrong motives. Jesus tells us that the reason the Father answers is that our joy be complete, but again we are told to ask in the name of Jesus. The disciples were afraid of the storm and woke Jesus, asking if He did not care if they drowned. Jesus nearly always answered the disciples with a question of His own, and asked them why they were so afraid and where was their faith (Mark 4:38-40). God does not give us a spirit of fear but of power (2 Tim. 1:7); still we fail to use this power and I wonder if God is wondering the same about us as He did the disciples: "Do you still have no faith?"

There were times in the Bile when God answered prayers for the good of the people, and other times the answers were not so beneficial. However, God always gets His way and the glory. This is not to say that God is self-centered, selfish, or vindictive, but men will not alter His overall plan. A prime example can be found in 1st Samuel 8:4-22. When Samuel retired, Israel rejected his sons as judges and asked for a king in spite of God's warning against this. Their request for a king was based on their desire to be like other nations. The Lord answered the plea from the prophet and said that he should listen to them and give them a king. Israel demonstrated that our desire to imitate the world may seem righteous at first, but the final result will be destruction. "So I gave you a king, but only in anger, and I took him away in my great anger. The sins of Israel are on record, stored away, waiting for punishment" (Hos. 13:11-12). The Israelites were disobedient one day and singing praises to God the next while in the wilderness, escaping Egypt. They forgot what God had done for them, and did not want His advice. They were hungry and became greedy for food in the desert, and they tested God. So, as with the desired king, He gave them what they wanted, but He also sent a terrible disease among them (Ps. 106:1-5). When we place our trust in God and relinquish control of our lives to Him, He provides for our needs and takes care of us. Do not ever presume to tell Him what is best for you or He may just allow you to have it.

It was neither convenient nor comfortable for Elijah to take a stand for the Lord in his generation. It never is in any generation! What is the secret of a Christian communicating with a generation of chaos? The most convincing thing about Christianity is its power to change people. The world is not impressed by your success story, but by how you live within the success. You convince the world that God is alive by giving Him the glory for your success. What is there in your action that is proof positive of the reality of God in your life? In the midst of a generation where the world is screaming for proof of a living God, Christians are timid. Shame on all of us! Ezekiel was a hard-fisted prophet who spoke the Word of the Lord loud and clear. The Lord spoke His Word through Ezekiel, reminding the people of Elijah's time, "You are a land that has not had rain or showers when God is angry" (Ezek. 22:24). It was a sad message God spoke in Ezekiel 22 when He looked for someone to build up the walls and to stand in the gap to defend the people, so that He would not have to destroy them. But God found no one to do this, so He let His anger loose and it seemed like fire because of all the things they had done.

If Jesus were to speak to you personally or to your church congregation, what would He say? God has commanded! God has promised! He has searched for someone to stand in the gap! You ask yourself what resources are available to stand in the midst of this apostasy? Elijah did not have one thing that is not available to everyone today. He had the Word of God! He had the power of prayer! "How is it you have no faith?" (Mark 4:40). Privilege creates responsibility! Revelation demands response! God has done all He has ever promised and all He is going to do, and now the next step is yours and mine. It is the step of obedience, and you will be tested. You may find yourself sitting alone beside a drying brook! We can look at it this way. You need not know how to swim but to stand (Eph. 6:13) and God will do the rest. Oh, what a God!

3. *Amasiah, a Willing Volunteer*

"For the eyes of the Lord range throughout the earth to strengthen those whose hearts are fully committed to Him" (2 Chr. 16:9). The Lord found someone fully committed to Him in Jehoshaphat's army. Amasiah—the name means *whom God bears*—was a secular career soldier in the king's army, but his priority was not to serve King Jehoshaphat but to serve the Lord. The navy coined a phrase: "better one volunteer than three pressed men" and this is what the volunteer Amasiah was. He needed no pushing, and brought with him 200,000 men for the service of the Lord. Our priority should be service to the Lord, with reasonable service meaning we owe it all to Him, and honorable service meaning that you feel good when you serve the Top Man. Are you a ready volunteer or do you need a push? Do you ask first what is in it for you? Do not be too picky about the job God calls you to do or where He sends you to do it, or He might decide you are not worth fooling with and find someone else to carry out His plan. Then you will wish that you had been the one to bring honor and glory to the one that saved your soul from hell.

Romans 11:29 says that God never changes His mind about the people He calls, but He may very well do some changing within the person He calls. God's servant never works for nothing, but you may not be able to spend what He gives you for your labor. You are earning His love, receiving His power, gaining His pardon, living in His peace, and you have a retirement plan that assures you will live forever with Him in heaven. You must understand when you sign on to work for God that He is the boss. He is in charge and He does not accept ultimatums about what you will do for Him if He does this or that for you. "Not many of you should presume to be teachers, because you know that we who teach will be judged more strictly" (James 3:1). We are all part of the body of Christ, and God has arranged us just as He wants us (1 Cor. 12:18). We cannot all preach from a pulpit, but remember that you may be the only Bible some read, so preach daily wherever you may be. Give of yourself and do not be content to grease the collection plate on Sunday morning or sing the special or paint and decorate the fellowship hall. God wants all of you all the time.

One Sunday morning, the ushers were passing the plate to collect money for missions. When the plate came to a little boy, he asked the usher to put the plate on the floor beside him. With a sigh, the usher did as asked and surprisingly watched the little boy step into the plate, and with a satisfied smile said, "Now I have given all of myself to the service of God." Each man should give what he had decided in his heart to give, but maybe the decisions of the heart should be rethought. Maybe we should step into the plate and give our all. If you follow God's plan and remain obedient, you will see results, not because of your ability, dynamic personality, or intelligence, but because you are a willing volunteer. God will use obedient willingness to cause His church to grow. Paul speaks about jealousy and quarreling among the church members causing division. He was assuring all of us that preachers, teachers, leaders, and laymen are only willing servants to whom the Lord has assigned to each their task. Paul considered himself and Apollos field hands, explaining that he planted the gospel seed and Apollos watered, but God made it grow (1 Cor. 3:1-9). In the same way, Jehoshaphat, king of Judah, planted the seed of the fear of the Lord in the minds and hearts of Israel. It was his willing volunteer Amasiah, along with experienced fighting men, that watered this seed. However, notice "The Lord established the kingdom under His control, because his heart was devoted to the ways of the Lord" (2 Chr. 17:5-6).

Not all of the people in the Bible that God called were volunteers, and most of them were far from willing. Moses gave every excuse known to man when God came to him to deliver His people out of Egypt. The first of the whining begins in Exodus 3. Then Moses asked God who he was and why he should have to go to Pharaoh and bring the Israelites out of Egypt. When God assured Moses that He would be with him, then Moses asked what he was to tell them when asked who sent him. He continued to question God with more excuses that maybe the people would not believe that God sent him. The Lord showed Moses how to perform miracles to prove himself, but Moses was not out of excuses. He complained that he was slow of speech and tongue, but for a man with this problem, he was doing a good job of talking back to God. Another unwilling agent was Saul, when told by Samuel that God had chosen him to be king of Israel. He was stunned and began to explain that he was from the smallest tribe of Benjamin, and his clan was the least of all clans (1 Sam. 9:21). And who can forget Jonah? He ran so fast from the calling of the Lord that he ended up in the belly of a great fish, spit out upon dry ground and given a second chance. Rather than go through this entire trauma again, Jonah went where God told him. However, he tried to get in the last word by getting angry with God and furthermore telling God that he had every right to be angry enough to die (Jonah 1:3, 17, 3:9). Now that is not what I call a willing volunteer!

Not all were so rebellious and hard to convince that they should follow God's calling willingly. Judges 5 records the Song of Deborah, which includes the people willingly offering themselves, praising the Lord. Isaiah 1 states that those who are willing and obedient will eat the best from the land. Isaiah was a willing servant when he heard the voice of the Lord, answering, "Here am I. Send me!" Elisha was not only a willing servant but a sticky companion. Elijah tried to make him go his own way when he knew that the Lord was about to take him away. Elisha would not turn loose, telling Elijah that he would never leave him. This willing obedience gained him the double portion of his master's anointing. Ruth did not realize that she would become a servant of God when she desperately clung to her mother-in-law, declaring that her God would be Ruth's God. She was rewarded by being added to the lineage of Christ.

How do we become a willing volunteer? First we stop (Ps. 46:10), second we look (Deut. 4:29), third we listen (1 Sam. 3:9), and fourth we go (Matt. 28:19-20.

4. *Nahum*

The name Nahum means "comfort or consolation." The only thing we know about Nahum is that he was from Elkos, but we do not know exactly where that was, because it is not mentioned elsewhere in the Bible. Some think it is the town of Capernaum near Galilee because Capernaum in Hebrew is Whn~rp K', which means village of Nahum. If you remember, Jonah prophesied to Nineveh about 150 years earlier. This resulted in a national repentance; however, this change of heart was short-lived. Nineveh repented of its repentance! The people of Nineveh had quickly reverted to their cruel and heathen practices. They had not transmitted their knowledge of the true God to their children. God, through Nahum, foretold the complete destruction of this kingdom. He had spared them once during the time of Jonah, and He would not do so again.

Unlike Jonah, Nahum did not actually go to the city of Nineveh; rather he declared his oracle from afar. There was no hope of any repentance taking place, so no reason to go into the city. With Jonah, God was a God of mercy, emphasis on the prophet, only one prophet in the entire book of Jonah, disobedient prophet and obedient nation, deliverance from water and repentance of Nineveh. In comparison, Nahum's message was the Judgment of God, emphasis on the prophecy, obedient prophet, disobedient nation, destruction by water and rebellion of Nineveh. In only 150 years, the nation became so bad that it had to be destroyed.

Nahum spoke of the fall of the city of Thebes, which was in Upper Egypt. Thebes fell to the Assyrians in 661 BC. Ten years after its fall, Thebes had begun to rise from its ruins, to rebuild and to regain its former glory. If Nahum had waited too long after the fall of Thebes to use its destruction as a warning to Nineveh, the force of this warning would have been lost. Nineveh might assume that if Thebes could recover, then so could they. Nineveh was founded by Nimrod (Gen 10:8-12), and was destroyed by the Babylonians, Medes, and Scythians in 612 BC. The Khosr River, which ran through the city, flooded, broke down the floodgates, and part of the wall which allowed the enemy to come in, fulfilling part of Nahum's prophecies. "With an overflowing flood, He will make a complete end of its site" (Nah. 1:8, 2:6, 3:13). The Tigris River had overflowed its banks and eaten away at the walls. The walls of Nineveh were almost eight miles around. They were one hundred feet high and wide enough that three chariots could ride on them side-by-side. Around the walls were towers that stretched an additional one hundred fifty feet above the top of the wall. In addition, there was a moat around the city one hundred feet wide and sixty feet deep. There were fifteen main gates with huge stone bulls standing guard at each. Nineveh had enough provisions within the city to withstand a twenty year siege.

Nahum's prophecy of the overthrow of this city seemed unlikely to the inhabitants. Nineveh was never rebuilt, and this confirms Nahum's prediction that distress will not rise up twice (Nah. 1:9). It was not until 1850 that Nineveh was discovered by archaeologists. Today, the site is covered by fields, a water tower from a nearby village, a cemetery, and a local dump. Before 1850, there were problems believing the books of Jonah and Nahum because there was no record of Nineveh.

Nahum alternates between the destruction of Nineveh and the restoration of Judah to show contrast (Nah. 1:11-15). The one who was on top would be brought down, and the one on the bottom would be restored. The last will be first and the first will be last (Matt. 19:30). God humbles those who exalt themselves and exalts those who humble themselves. Nahum assumed the role of watchman in the tower, and he announced the coming of Nineveh's enemies and the reason why. The reason was to restore Jacob. The enemy army approached with their red (copper) shields and red uniforms (2:3-5). This was the image of bloodshed that was coming. The references to the torches and lightning flashes probably refer to the light flashing off the enemy chariots, the soldiers' armor, and their swords. Some suggest that the stumbling in verse five was over the dead bodies.

The Assyrians had a fascination with lions. It was important that the king demonstrate his prowess as a hunter, then he would be a better ruler over the people. Assyria is compared to a lion, because this lion fetish and because of her fierce conquests. Because Nineveh was the capital of Assyria, it is called the lion's den (2:11-13). The destruction is mapped out, and when you shake a ripe fig tree, the fruit falls off easily. Nineveh's fortifications would fall easily. The troops being like women and being easily defeated by an army of men is not politically correct today, but it was the truth pertaining to Nineveh. The Assyrians fled like locusts when the attackers came through the walls. They could not depend on other nations for help, because every other nation hated them for their cruelty, and would rejoice at their destruction (3:19).

This book reveals quite a lot about the character of God. He is sovereign and He is in control of both nature and the nations. He used the Babylonians to bring His judgment on the Assyrians and the flood to help the Babylonians. God is just, and although God used Assyrians to destroy Israel, it went to their heads and gave God no credit or honor, so the same atrocities they committed on others were put on them. God protects His people and would remember Israel. This is a message of condemnation for those who disobey God, and a message of consolation for those who trust and obey Him. Nineveh exalted herself, but she was humbled by God. In the parable of the Pharisee and the tax collector, the Pharisee compared himself to the tax collector and exalted himself before God. The tax collector was humble and asked for mercy, and Jesus said it was the tax collector who went away justified (Luke 5). If your exalt yourself, God will humble you. When proud sinners are brought down, others should learn not to lift themselves up. The fall of this great city should be a lesson to you and me. When we seek our fortune by fraud and oppression we are making enemies, and if the Lord sees fit to punish us on this earth, there will be no one to pity us. This is not to say that you are not to seek prosperity, safety, and peace, but act upright, honorably, and with kindness to all involved (Nah. 1:1-7).

This book provides strong testimony to God's ultimate power and justice. He calls all people to live under His rule: nations, cities, parents, neighborhoods, and you! Regardless of how things may seem, God does not forget His people. The book of Revelation is a perfect example of this message. God Himself is the ultimate ruler. "I warn everyone who hears the words of the prophecy of this book; if anyone adds anything to these words, God will add to that person the disasters written about in this book. And if anyone takes away from the words of this book of prophecy, God will take away that one's share of the tree of life and of the holy city, which are written about in this book" (Rev. 22:18-20). He is coming soon and He will have the final word!

5. Ezekiel

For the average reader of the Bible, the book of Ezekiel is mostly a perplexing maze of incoherent visions, a kaleidoscope of whirling wheels and dry bones that defy interpretation. This impression often causes readers to shy away from studying the book and to miss one to the great literary and spiritual portions of the Old Testament. The name *Ezekiel* means "God will strengthen" or "God will harden." Read Ezekiel and draw strength from God.

Ezekiel was ministering in Babylon, predicting the coming collapse of Jerusalem. His message fell on deaf ears until word of the city's destruction was received in Babylon. Have you ever warned someone as disaster coming into their life only to have your words fall on deaf ears? Where you giving glory and honor to God with your message? Ezekiel emphasized the glory and character of God. God's character determines His conduct throughout the book. Fifteen times, God declared that He had acted for the sake of His name to keep it from being profaned (Ezek. 20:9, 14, 22, 39, 44). More than sixty times, God said He had acted so that the people would know that He was Lord.

Ezekiel was prepared for his ministry by receiving a vision of the glory and majesty of God before he was called to serve God. The record of God's commissioning of Ezekiel is the longest such prophetic call in the Bible (Ezek. 1). "I saw visions of God" was Ezekiel's summary of the visions, which he then described in detail. As God spoke, He provided power for Ezekiel, told Ezekiel of his assignment, and challenged him to be faithful. When God told Ezekiel to stand, He also enabled him by the Holy Spirit to stand. In Old Testament times, the Holy Spirit did not indwell all believers, but indwelt selected persons temporarily for divine services. Ezekiel's assignment was difficult. His message was to be directed to a rebellious nation with people who were obstinate and stubborn. Ezekiel's talk was to declare God's Word; whether they responded was the people's own responsibility. But in the end, when the events did transpire, they would know that a prophet had been in their midst. God said to listen when a prophet of the Lord was among them, for He revealed Himself in visions and spoke to him in dreams.

Three times, God told Ezekiel not to be afraid. He needed this encouragement, because the task was difficult; briars and thorns are all around you, and even dangers, you live among scorpions. Ezekiel learned his lesson well. Nowhere does the book hint that he cowered in fear or hesitated to proclaim God's message. Every book in the Bible tells us in some way not to fear, and God did not give us a spirit of fear; Ezekiel took Him at His Word. Now God told Ezekiel to eat the scroll that the instructions were on. The purpose was so he could then go and speak to the house of Israel and deliver the Word of God. As Ezekiel ate the scroll, it tasted as sweet as honey. Though his message was one of judgment, it was still God's Word, and the sweetness came from the source of the words (Ps. 119:103), rather than the content of the words (judgment).

Ezekiel was not being sent to a people of obscure speech and difficult language, but to his own people. His message was not for some distant land with an exotic language. Had Ezekiel gone to another nation, they would have listened to him (Luke 4:24). Amazingly, those who knew nothing of the true God of the universe would have been more responsive than those who claiming His name. Sound familiar? The people were not willing to listen to Ezekiel because they were not willing to listen to God. Sound more familiar? God also told Ezekiel he would make his forehead like the hardest stone and even harder than flint. Flint was the hardest stone in Palestine and was used for knives and other implements. This God-given strength would withstand any opposition.

After the vision, Ezekiel was returned by the Holy Spirit and went in bitterness and in the anger of his spirit. He was not angry *at* God, but angry *with* God. As he associated himself with God, he felt the same emotions toward sin as God did. Oh, that we would live so close to God that sin angered us! He sat among the exiles for seven days, overwhelmed. The vision was awesome and the prophet was stunned at what God had asked—commanded—him to do. He needed time to collect his thoughts and prepare for his ministry. After the seven days, his silence was shattered by God's Word appointing him a watchman or the house of Israel. Watchmen were stationed on city walls, hilltops, or specially designed watchtowers to be on the alert for approaching enemies and warn the city's people of any impending attack. Similarly, as God's watchman, Ezekiel was responsible for sounding the warning of impending judgment. A wicked person was to be warned to turn from his evil ways in order to save his live. The righteous person was warned to prevent his turning from his righteousness and doing evil. If Ezekiel failed to warn of approaching danger, God would hold him accountable for the blood of the people. The principle of blood accountability is expressed in Genesis 9:5-6. If Ezekiel did not warn the people, he would be held as responsible for their murder as if he had killed them himself. If he fulfilled his responsibility, then he would have saved himself. By giving warning, Ezekiel would have delivered himself from any responsibility for the coming calamity, and people who refused to heed his warning had only themselves to blame.

God told him that his tongue would stick to the roof of his mouth until told to speak. "But when I speak to you, I will open your mouth" (Ezek. 3:26-27). If only we could keep our mouth shut until God tells us to speak!

6. Jabez

There is a prayer in 1st Chronicles 4:10 that I refer to on a regular basis. It reads like this: "Jabez cried out to the God of Israel, 'Oh, that you would bless me indeed and enlarge my territory! Let your hand be with me, and keep me from harm so that I will be free from pain'! And God granted His request!" There have been many times that we have called on God, and by faith, we have requested of and received from Him, but still there are those prayers that have seemingly gone unanswered. I pray with all of you today that you come to the place where God will grant what you have requested and that He will bless you indeed!

Sometimes while reading the Old Testament, we get confused, lost, and even bored. When reading the book of Deuteronomy with all the begets—she begot, he begot, and they begot and they all forgot who begot whom, and most of us cannot even pronounce the names of the begets, we may get a little weary. Then we come across a name that God honored and blessed, like Jabez. "Jabez was more honorable than his brothers" (verse 9). When a name like this comes up, it piques my curiosity as to why God would bless this man. However, there is little known about Jabez. This name comes up only one other time, and it is the name of a city (1 Chr. 2:55). This city is where the clans of scribes lived who sat and rewrote the books of the Bible known as the Pentateuch, the first five books of the Old Testament. Jabez was apparently a name honorable enough that a city was named after him, although all we know is that he was honorable because of his prayer.

When he prayed, God answered his prayer on the spot. Have you ever known someone like this? When they pray, you can see God answering on the spot, and if not, you can feel that the answer is on the way. You know God promised that before we call, He will answer and will hear while we are still speaking (Isa. 65:24). These answered prayers come from praying in faith (James 5:15). May I suggest that the man, Jabez, did not old the honor but that the prayer of faith received the honor from God? "He was more honorable than his brothers" may indicate this was because God answered His prayer, and not that he was higher in position from his actual brothers. Prayer is not just a word, but a deeply expressed need or desire that comes from the heart. Pray with faith, knowing that we serve a God that can do all things, and believe that faith can move mountains (Matt. 17:20) and prayer will truly make a difference in your life.

Jabez prayed to the Lord of Israel to bless him indeed. The word *indeed* did not mean to bless him right now or in abundance, according to worldly standards. He was asking God to bless him *in deed*; bless him in the things that he did; in the deeds of his life. This includes walk, talk, strength, conversation, work, play, and each and every action in our lives. God saved us not because to the righteous things we have done, but because of His mercy (Titus 3:5). We are not His heirs with the hope of eternal life, but the Bible adds: "those who have trusted in God may be careful to devote themselves to doing what is good" (Titus 3:8). These were the in-deeds Jabez asked to be blessed. God watches our life and our character, and when He sees us doing what His Word commands and instructs, then He begins to bless our deeds, and prayers are answered. There is a great big example in Malachi 3:10-12: "Bring the whole tithe into the storehouse that there may be food in my house. Test me in this and see if I will not throw open the floodgates of heaven and pour out so many blessings that you will not have room enough for it." God will not give you abundance of wealth to waste and then bless you. You have to give also and give back to God the portion He asks for. The measure you use will be measured back to you, says Luke 6:38, but this not only applies to money deeds but to deeds of forgiveness and love (Luke 6:35, 38). The prayer of Jabez was that God bless him in his deeds that he might bless others.

Paul said that he would not be a burden to the church because he did not want their possessions, but they themselves. The Macedonian churches gave as much as they were able, and even beyond their ability. They excelled in faith, speech, knowledge, in complete earnestness, love, and the grace of giving, all deeds. Paul goes on to say it was the willingness that caused the gift to be acceptable, according to what one has and not according to what he does not have (2 Cor. 8:12, 12:14).

"Enlarge my territory!" Jabez was not praying for more land or property. In the history of Jabez he was a scholar, a teacher, and a doctor of the law. He did not own a vineyard or a farm, as far as the Bible teaches. All he wanted to do was teach about the goodness and the glory of the God of Israel. What he was saying was "increase my boundaries so that I can understand more of God's Word and enlarge my vision that I might see even farther than I know." I believe he wanted God to show him how to reach more people, and God answered his prayer. God wants to do this for you! He wants to expand, enrich, and enlarge your spiritual mind, that you might further the Kingdom of God (Matt. 28:19-20). The book of Proverbs is full of scriptures telling us to seek wisdom, get wisdom, and understanding and that wisdom is the principal thing in a Christian life. It is better than rubies and gold, and those who love wisdom rejoice. We are saved and bound for heaven, but God has more stored up for us that we have not yet tapped into (1 Cor. 2:9).

There was a toy sold some years ago called Stretch Armstrong, and you could pull its limbs in every direction as far as it would go. However, in a couple of hours, it would be back to the original form. Christians are this way when they are faced with a crisis. They cry out to God, and God answers. However, when the crisis is over, we go right back to our original form of passiveness. We should desire the minds of the Bereans. The minds of the Bereans were not narrowed by prejudice. They were willing to investigate the truthfulness of the doctrines preached by the apostles. They studied the Bible not from curiosity, but in order that they might learn what had been written concerning the promised Messiah. Daily, they searched the inspired records, and as they compared scripture, heavenly angels were beside them (Acts 17:11). There is no way that a pastor or Sunday school teacher can fill you with all God has prepared for you. "Study to show yourself approved to God, a workman that needs not be ashamed, rightly dividing the Word of Truth" (2 Tim. 2:15).

Then Jabez prayed that God's hand be on him. You cannot step into the next spiritual level without God's help. "Let us then approach the throne of grace with confidence, so that we may receive mercy and find grace to help us in our time of need" (Heb. 4:16). Grace is getting what we do not deserve, mercy is not getting what we do deserve, and help is what we get from God when we do not let pride intervene. 1st Peter says that God opposes the proud and can spot them a mile away (1 Peter 4:5, Ps. 138:6). If God's hand is on you, nothing can snatch you away from Him (John 10:28), and who is going to go against you with success if God is with you (Rom. 8:31), giving you strength and upholding you with His righteous hand (Isa. 41:10)?

Jabez then prayed to be free from the evil one, so that he would cause no pain. This is acknowledging that the devil is at work, and none are safe without the protection of God. When we sin, we are hurting more than ourselves but those around us whether we are aware of it or not. Jabez wanted to be so filled with the Word of God that the devil could not gain a foothold (Eph. 4:27). You cannot keep the consequences of sin bound inside of you, because it always creeps into every being around you. Jesus, knowing the purpose of Satan and our weaknesses, prayed that we not be taken out of this world, but that God protect us from the evil one. New Testament scriptures are filled with promises of protection. This is what the honorable prayer of Jabez is asking: that we may be kept from the evil one. This should be our prayer every day, and let the devil know that we serve a God that will protect us and answer an honorable prayer.

The last part of the prayer of Jabez is that he not be the cause of pain. Although the name *Jabez* meant "pain," he prayed that he not inflict pain on others. Lack of wisdom of the Word of God may cause pain in someone else's life. When you see someone who needs the Word of God, salvation, encouragement, or love, and you do not know that is in the Bible, you cause pain. Jabez's mother had named him, saying that she gave birth to him in pain (1 Chr. 4:9), and I am sure he suffered teasing from this, which inflicted pain on him, and he did not want others to feel this pain. He was also asking God to keep him from the pain the evil one is trained so well at bringing into our lives.

God wants to bless you indeed and in-deed! He longs for you to cry out to Him! He has so much more territory for you to explore and He wants to stretch you in your spiritual walk. God wants you to prosper in material things, but not to measure your spiritual life and your blessings by these things acquired on earth. When we pray for prosperity, we also pray that money does not take our hearts. We pray to use our money to entertain strangers (Heb. 13:2) and to help the needy (Gal. 2:10). We pray that we look beyond our blessings and bless others. Lord, make me more effective in increasing your Kingdom!

"Behold, I am coming soon! My reward is with me, and I will give to everyone according to what he has done" (Rev. 22:12).

7. Ezra

Philipp Melanchthon (1497-1560) was called the "Teacher of Germany." He guided the development of the educational system in Germany and was active in the establishment and reform of schools. He wrote the constitutions, composed the ordinances, and advised academic administrators throughout Europe. He was a professor of arts, along with writing many textbooks and handbooks of education. He embraced the doctrine of justification by faith, and always believed that salvation comes only by the Cross of Jesus. Education was to serve all believers in developing their callings in God's Kingdom. One function of the school was to teach understanding of what was read, and the other was to preserve and pass on the true teachings of the Bible. This view of education was summed up for him in 2nd Corinthians 10:5-6: "we destroy arguments and every proud obstacle to the knowledge of God and take every thought captive to obey Christ." He was only eleven when his father died, and only twelve when his grandfather presented him with a Bible and a Greek grammar textbook. He was small of frame and frail of health, but keen of mind and purpose. Melanchthon's one great love was to teach the Word of God, so that those who listened would understand what was being read. Paul, too, prayed that he might proclaim the gospel clearly as he should (Col. 4:4).

The prophet Ezra was the Philipp of his day. Ezra was the second of three key leaders to leave Babylon for the reconstruction of Jerusalem. Zerubbabel reconstructed the temple, Nehemiah rebuilt the walls, and Ezra restored the worship—a scribe and a priest sent with religious and political powers by the Persian king, Artaxerxes, to lead a group of Jewish exiles from Babylonia to Jerusalem (Ezra 7:8). Ezra condemned mixed marriages, encouraging Jews to divorce and banish their foreign wives. The most dramatic part of the book is the crisis over marriages by Jewish leaders with women from the peoples of the lands (Ezra 9:2). Ezra interprets such marriages as a violation of the Torah, and a repetition of the sins that caused exile in the first place. The book concludes with a third-person report describing steps undertaken to solve the crisis and separate from foreign wives. For you who are asking, this scripture does not hold the foreign meaning we think of today. This in not a warning for people not to marry out of their nationality or race, but headed more toward the scripture about not being unevenly yoked with unbelievers (2 Cor. 6:14). They and we were to be a separate, distinctive people for God, and yet avoid racism, isolationism, and separation.

Ezra renewed the celebration of festivals and supported the rededication of the temple and the rebuilding of the Jerusalem wall. Ezra 7-10 describes a shaping of the community in accordance with the book of the Torah. Ezra's goal was to implement the Torah, and his impeccable priestly and scribal credentials allowed him to remain the model leader. In Christian Bibles, the book of Ezra appears with the historical books, between Chronicles and Nehemiah. In modern Jewish Bibles, the book of Nehemiah, it is placed among the Writings, immediately preceding Chronicles, the last in the canon. It is the only biblical historiography that explicitly describes the transformation during the pivotal post-exile period. Ezra and Nehemiah are usually treated as one, since they were one in the ancient Hebrew and Greek Old Testament. Also, each is necessary to complete the other. Ezra's story is climaxed in Nehemiah, and part of Nehemiah's story is in Ezra (4:6-23).

The book of Ezra continues from the exact place where 2nd Chronicles ends with Cyrus, king of Persia, issuing a decree which permits the Jews of his kingdom to return to Jerusalem after seventy years of captivity. God is universally sovereign. He is not limited. He could use a Cyrus, polytheistic king of Persia, to make possible His people's release from captivity and return to their fatherland. He could use an Artaxerxes, another Persian king, to authorize and finance the trip to an Ezra to teach God's people God's law. This same king also helped Nehemiah restore some measure of respectability to God's holy city.

After Cyrus's edict, Zerubbabel led the first return of God's people to rebuild the ruins of Jerusalem and the temple that had been destroyed by Nebuchadnezzar. The work was repeatedly hampered by shortages of resources and external opposition. God's people faced threats from two directions. Temptations to empty formalism and meaningless legalism threatened their worship life. Just plain lack of interest and indifference nagged them constantly. The world's moral, or immoral, values threatened to replace God's standards. Racially and religiously mixed marriages were commonplace, described as unfaithfulness to God. Both threats ate at the faith of the returning Jews. Their relationship to God became as weak as water. These discouragements brought all work to a halt until God sent the prophets Haggai and Zechariah to encourage the people, who then enthusiastically rebuilt the altar and the temple of God. Some years later, Ezra led a return of priests from captivity to Jerusalem. Ezra's effective ministry included teaching the Word of God, initiating reforms, restoring worship, and leading spiritual revival in Jerusalem. Ezra and Nehemiah were written to counteract the threats and to strengthen the faith of a hopeless people. These reforms magnified the need for a genuine concern for reputation and for public image. What must the world think of God's people with dilapidated city walls? What would distinguish God's people who were guilty of intermarriage with those not in proper covenant relationship with the one true God? Nehemiah's drastic actions reminded the people and us that it does matter what others think of us and our faith. Ezra and Nehemiah are an encouragement to God's people to magnify worship as top priority, to emphasize the need for and use of God's Word as the only authoritative rule for living, and to be concerned about the image God's people show the world.

Ezra the priest came back from captivity in Babylon, expecting to find the people serving the Lord with gladness, but upon his return to Jerusalem, he found the opposite. He was frustrated and had sorrow in his heart. His heart ached, but he still trusted the Lord. He wanted the Lord to change the situation, and blamed himself for not being able to change the people's hearts. He wanted the people to know how important and essential the Word of God was. Scripture is to be trusted! Ezra and Nehemiah were written to fulfill the Word of the Lord. God's Words spoken by Jeremiah were literally fulfilled, as recorded in these two books. Worship of God is absolutely necessary and the worship center had to be rebuilt. Nothing must supersede worship of God by His people. Obedience to God is not optional, hard work is necessary for obedience, and opposition to the worship is real. It must be expected and prepared for, and encouragement should always be just within reach. The Sovereign God looks over and protects His children, always keeping His promises, and when the enemy causes a delay, He steps in to continue His plan. God is intimately involved in our lives. Ezra did the impossible "for the hand of the Lord his God was on him" (Ezra 7:6). Nehemiah got the unexpected "because the gracious hand of my God was upon me" (Neh. 2:8). No problem is too big to stop God's plan.

Every believer is a living temple, building up himself stone by stone. Satan is ever opposing our efforts, causing stops and pauses. Prayer was and is the most important part of carrying out God's plan. Both Ezra and Nehemiah books of the New Testament by focusing on the Messiah, who is our salvation.

The Lord summoned heaven and earth to be witnesses of His accusations against His people. Both the nation and the country were in a shocking condition. Vivid pictures of sinfulness are shown in 2:4-9. These people were religious, but God does not want sacrifices of animals. He hated incense, holy meetings, feasts, and He would not hear their prayers (1:10-15). He was asking them to lead clean, holy lives and stop doing wrong. From your own experience, why is it much harder to fulfill the moral requirements than just to go through the ritual activities mentioned in Isaiah 1:10-15? Does following rituals put together by someone before you seem easier than being obedient to God and maybe going against the grain? Evaluate your own religious practices in the midst of your own society, with all its needs. What reorientation does your life require if your religion is not to be just a burden to you and to God?

Standing outside the Old City of Jerusalem is one of the most sharply painful memorials in Israel to the Six Day War in 1967. It is a sculpture made of wrecked military equipment, with these words from Isaiah on it. "They will beat their swords into plowshares and their spears into pruning hooks. Nation will not take up sword against nation, nor will they train for war anymore" (Isa. 2:4). These words still seem far from fulfillment. Globally, defense spending exceeds the income of the poorest half of the world's population. As President Eisenhower said, "Every gun that is made, every warship launched, every rocket fired signifies in the final sense, a theft from those who hunger and are not fed, those who are cold and not clothed."

"Be sure your sins will find you out." Do you think of this as just a quaint saying, used warningly by mothers to their children? For Isaiah, this fact was a grave reality which applied to nations as well as individuals. Have you ever been in a situation in which you needed to confront a friend with inconsistencies in his or her lifestyle? Choosing carefully the occasion and form, a love song, Isaiah introduced the subject of a dear friend's vineyard. Read about the care that was put into the vineyard and the owner's dismay when the final product was only evil-smelling, bitter, wild grapes (Isa. 5:1-7). The vineyard was then totally destroyed in Isaiah 5:5-6. God has lavished His care upon us, answered prayers, rained when needed, healed when sick, mended when broken-hearted, given us healthy babies, jobs, safety, friends, etc. only to be rewarded or thanked with a bitter harvest of disobedience, backsliding, vanity, pride, greed, and gossip.

Judah had turned away from the light into the dark, to mediums and ghosts that whisper and mutter. King Ahaz had turned away from the sign God offered him, but a greater King was coming to put things right. This King was a child, rather than a mighty conqueror, yet He would have shoulders adequate for the task. He would share God's character as a wonderful counselor. He was described as Mighty God. Although a son, He was described as the Everlasting Father. He was described as Prince of Peace and His kingdom would share His character. He was a descendant of David and would rule His kingdom with justice and righteousness forever. The light dawned, and as Isaiah predicted, the nations grew, people were happy, and heavy loads were lifted.

The reaction to dramatic change always brings disbelief from some. Look forward to what is said about Christ: "Can anything good come from Nazareth?" (John 1:46). Has the Lord brought light into your dark corner of the world? It is always helpful when going through a time of trouble if you find some reason to hold on to hope for the future. What does hope mean to you? Do you see it as a strong word or a weak word? God is our eternal Comforter, Redeemer, and Savior. God will pardon us from our sins if we will forsake our past and turn to Him. The fleeting pleasure of sin in our lives will never be worth the extreme price we must pay for it. God is holy and will not tarry, while ungodliness persists in His Covenant people. Deliverance is of God and not of man. The greatest success in the world is being obedient to the Word of God.

8. *The Apostle Paul*

Also known as Saul of Tarsus, the name *Paul* means "little." This must have referred to his stature and not his mouth, since be breathed out murderous threats against the Lord's disciples. Tarsus was a free city in Cilicia where Paul, Saul, was a Pharisee making his living as a tent maker (Phil. 3:5; Acts 18:1-3). Before his conversion, he was an avid persecutor of the church (Acts 22:4). Paul wrote more books of the New Testament than any other person, including Romans, 1st and 2nd Corinthians, Galatians, Ephesians, Philippians, Colossians, and 1st and 2nd Thessalonians, 1st and 2nd Timothy, Titus, and Philemon. We are uncertain of the author of Hebrews, although some credit Paul with writing it also.

Saul was born around the same time as Christ and was given the name Saul, and later would be called Paul. Tarsus was home to a university, and young Saul received the best education possible. Saul's father was of the tribe of Benjamin; pure and unmixed was his Jewish blood, and he was molded with what one would interpret from his youth to adulthood in a staunch and upright character (Acts 23:6; Phil. 3:5-6). Paul was around thirteen when he was sent to the Jewish school of learning in Jerusalem to study law under Gamaliel. After his studies, he returned to Tarsus, but returned again to Jerusalem after the death of Christ and began persecuting the Christians. Saul was on the Damascus road with a list of suspected Christians in his coat when his life changed forever. You have heard it preached: "We cannot all have a Damascus Road Experience!" This came from the life of Saul, who had never met Jesus personally nor spiritually it seems, but attacked Jesus's followers with senseless violence and murderous threats. Remember, he was the one who held the coats of the men who stoned Stephen (Acts 7:58). Then he met Jesus! A man whom he knew to be dead! A blazing light from the sky struck him temporarily blind, and he had a vision of someone who claimed to be Jesus and who commanded Saul to stop attacking Jesus and become His ambassador (Acts 9:1-19). Paul made a total commitment to God!

Many people today are not living lives totally opposed to Jesus, but they still need to make a full commitment of themselves to God. Saul was zealous by nature, and now found his zeal harnessed to the work of a Christian missionary. As a religious scholar, he now used his knowledge of the scripture to understand the significance of Jesus. You too can turn your education into wisdom, to understand the significance of Jesus (James 1:5-6). When Saul began to preach the gospel, people grew confused, since this was the man who had raised havoc in Jerusalem against the Christians. Did some question you when you made a full commitment to God? Did they say, "Hey, I knew you when…?" Ah, that we would all be like Saul and baffle our critics by proving that Jesus is the Christ (Acts 9:21-22). "When he came to Jerusalem, he tried to join the disciples, but they were all afraid of him" (Acts 9:26). God, however, had a plan and brought forth one friend who explained the Damascus experience and won over the trust of the others (Acts 9:22-30).

Barnabas was Saul's first traveling partner, going to Tarsus to find him and bringing him to Antioch. They worked a year in the church and taught great numbers of people. The disciples were called Christians first at Antioch. On one of the trips, the Bible begins to refer to Saul as Paul. Now, for the first time, there was a planned expedition to take the gospel to people who had not heard of Jesus, and this continues to this day. They established a pattern of going to the local synagogues and telling everyone that God had sent Jesus to be the Messiah promised in the scriptures, and that God had confirmed Jesus's status by raising Him from the dead.

Paul and his companions traveled to Galatia, modern Turkey, Macedonia, south to Athens, and then to Corinth, the major city of

Greece. He used his earlier teaching to honor and glorify God, telling the people about Moses, Egypt, and Canaan. He quoted scripture from the Old Testament, such as: "I have found David, son of Jesse, a man after my own heart" (Acts 13:16-22), explaining that Jesus was the descendant of David, and His coming was prepared by John the Baptist. This former persecutor of Christ was on fire for Jesus, casting out demons, healing and preaching with faith and confidence that amazed all. He was not the same man who stood face-to-face with God! Within him was a fire not found on earth! And because he changed, his part of the world changed. Be encouraged! What God did for Paul, He longs to do for you!

Paul returned to Jerusalem to extend the gospel farther west. However, some non-Christian Jews saw in Paul the man who betrayed the essence of Judaism by his indifference to the Jewish law. They arrested him, and after he appealed to the higher court, they took him under guard to Rome. This was nothing new, as he had been arrested and beaten and thrown in prison in Philippi. It is recorded that while in prison, Paul and Silas were praying and singing hymns to God. The hour was midnight, which puts me in mind of the psalm that reminds me to "rise at midnight to praise the Lord" (Ps. 119:62). Couldn't hurt to remember this, since God sent an earthquake to open the jail cells of Paul and Silas. There are all kinds of jail cells, you know. Sing praises to God and allow Him to send an angel to break the chains of this world that hold you captive. On to the ship sailing for Rome with Paul as a prisoner, they were caught in a storm and eventually shipwrecked on the island of Malta. Paul escaped death from a snakebite, which resulted in the people believing he was God, which resulted in the healing of many on the island. Another clue here! God can use the storm you are in to do mighty things if you hang on and trust Him.

One of Paul's main missions was to put a stop to the divisions of the church. The divisions that are so prominent today first began in Paul's day in the city of Corinth. He had to rebuke the church there severely, because they were carnal and walking in the ways of the world. The saints there began to denominate themselves apart and to say they were of Paul or Apollos or Cephas. There was one group that even began to say they were of Christ, to the exclusion of other saints. Paul's idea was that our different backgrounds would seem to make it necessary to have different churches, but should not be the case. We must remember when one is saved, things happen that make our backgrounds and personalities of little importance as far as the functioning of the church is concerned. One of the purposes for the church is to take those differences and make one new man. When one accepts Jesus as Lord and Savior, old things pass away and all things become new. The believer does not lose his physical appearance or his personality, but through the grace of God and the guidance of the Holy Spirit he has a changed character.

The Holy Spirit has commanded us to speak the same things and to have no divisions among us, and to be of the same mind. Christians should be a Paul and try to keep the unity of the spirit in the bond of peace. Satan has been spreading the lie "let us do evil that good may come." Mankind is alienated from God and physically dying because Eve was convinced what God told them to do and not to do could be improved upon. Satan realized how effective division could be, so he began very early in the church's history doing this. Paul could not stop the division, and neither can we, but we must die trying! Paul did! Christian traditions attest that Paul died as a martyr at the hands of the Roman government, beheaded, or torn to pieces by wild animals in the arena during the time of that horrible Nero.

There is so much more to write about Paul, and you can read all about it in the book of Acts. Mostly, I think he would want us to remember him as having accepting Jesus as his Lord and Savior and never having a doubt about serving Him to the end of his life. Remember that he fought the good fight, finished the race and kept the faith and now has his crown of righteousness that we all look forward to (2 Tim. 4:6-8).

9. *Abigail*

In 1ˢᵗ Samuel 25, we meet Abigail and her husband Nabal. Nabal sounds like the Hebrew word for *fool*, and we will find that he lives up to his name. He is rich, according to his culture, owning three thousand sheep and one thousand goats. He is mean and surly and somewhat of an arrogant bully. Abigail is beautiful and clever, and is always ready when a challenge comes her way. Nabal knew David because of the help David had given his shepherds in the past, plus David was already well-known in the community by now. The Bible does not indicate that Nabal's shepherds had ever asked for David's assistance, or that David ever gave them anything except an offer of protection while they were herding the sheep. However, now that it was time to harvest the wool, David wanted a share. Nabal not only denied the debt of honor that he owed to David, but proclaimed that he did not even know him or Jesse, David's father. Then he foolishly referred to David's rebellion against King Saul, recalling that David was one of the servants who broke away from his master. Nabal had smarted off not only about David, but to an army of 600 battle-hardened warriors. The messengers brought David Nabal's answer, and woe be unto Nabal.

Well, to say the least, David was insulted and angry! He ordered his mighty men to strap on their swords, and David, always ready for a good fight, strapped on his as well, and they went to pay a call on Nabal. Granted, Nabal should have shown David hospitality, but David did not have the right or authority to demand or take by force anything that he wanted and was denied. Here is a twist to the story: One of Nabal's servants went to explain the kindness and protection that David's men had given them, and with that, he brought a warning of destruction against Nabal and his household. However, he went not to his ill-tempered master but to Abigail with the news of impending disaster. The servant wanted Abigail to be aware that her husband had refused David, and to be warned that David's wrath was coming down on her husband and all the men in his charge. Notice, the servant told Abigail, "notice and consider what you should do." The Bible does not explain this comment, but it may lead some to believe that events had taken place behind the king's back in the past. The servant seemed to know that Abigail would know what to do to save them all from the onslaught. Seems he was right! Abigail considers briefly and acts quickly. Without consulting her husband, she gathered together two hundred loaves of bread, two skins of wine, about ten gallons of wine to each skin, five measures of parched grain, between two and six bushels of ready-to-eat cereal, one hundred clusters of raisins, and two hundred cakes of figs. Yummy picnic! She did not send the supplies to David, but rather took them herself. Perhaps this is the inspiration for the New Testament scripture: "a brother or sister in Christ might need clothes or food. If you say to that person, God be with you! I hope you stay warm and get plenty to eat, but you do not give what that person needs, your words are worth nothing" (James. 2:15-16).

Tidbit: Sheepskins were tanned, turned inside out, sewn up except for the neck, and filled with grape juice. Then the neck was sewn shut and the juice fermented into wine. As it fermented, the wine gave off gases and the skin expanded. The skin could only be used once (Luke 5:33-39). Pressed figs and raisins were especially prized because of their sweetness and nutritive value, and they could be kept for some time without spoiling.

David was still a little cranky about the king turning down his request for supplies, or maybe his ego was bruised after the word came from the king that he had never heard of this David. Whatever the case, David still had revenge in his heart, blood in his eye, and his sword drawn. He swore not to leave so much as one male in Nabal's extended household alive. Abigail came to David riding on a donkey with her caravan of servants and peace offerings. Donkeys at that time were animals of the elite, and showed a measure of Abigail's wealth. She dismounted and fell at David's feet, taking on full responsibility of her husband's actions. She went on to criticize her husband, dubbing him a fool, telling David that he acted just like his name. This statement, if heard by the public, would cause serious threats against his standing in the community and against his reputation as a leader. Calming David with these comments, she became humble and admitted that she was in charge of these matters, but defended her position, saying, "I did not see the young men of my Lord, whom you sent!" Now, really turning on the charm, lowered voice and a slight tilt to her head, she gently reminded David that under the law, he had no right to retaliate and if he did, he—not Nabal—would be guilty before God.

Abigail laid coyness aside and brought in cleverness, demonstrating spiritual understanding by offering a prayer/prophecy that David's enemies would be like Nabal. Fools! She reminded David that if he fought for God, he would walk in the protection of the Lord while his enemies would be defeated. Before you begin to be overwhelmed by this cleverness of Abigail to keep her home from becoming David's latest battleground, do not miss the fact that she looked after her own interest. Reread 1st Samuel 25:31: "Please remember me when the Lord brings you success!" David was pleased and appeased by Abigail and her humble, generous contribution to the needs of him and his army. The scripture does not include the obvious fact that his ego had been hoisted to the highest level by Abigail's charming ways. He received that which was offered, and sent her home in peace with the assurance that she had saved her husband and all his men.

The scripture tells us that Abigail was clever and beautiful, and her husband was cruel and foolish. It says nothing at first about Nabal always being drunk. However, this night, when Abigail went to tell him of her late-night escapade, "Nabal's heart was merry within him for he was very drunk, so she told him nothing at all until the morning light." When Nabal found out how narrow an escape he had from David, the news so shocked him that he had a heart attack and died in about ten days. Probably a relief to Abigail! David saw this as a sign from God and, struck by the beauty and character of Abigail, he proposed marriage to her. She accepted and hurriedly rode to him on a donkey. David and his troops made their headquarters in Ziklag, a small town between Gaza and Beersheba, for about one year. In David's absence, Amalekite raiding parties burned the town and carried away his family, including his newly acquired wife, Abigail. David's people were tired and became so angry that they talked about stoning him, but David turned to the Lord and sought His will. Assured of the victory, David and his four hundred men, who were rugged enough to stand the twenty-mile rigorous march, found and defeated the Amalekites and rescued all the captives and wives, Abigail being among them.

10. *Zephaniah*

The name *Zephaniah* means "Yahweh hides." The prophet was of royal blood, descendant of the good king Hezekiah, making him related to the young king Josiah. This gave Zephaniah free access to the king, and he probably had a great deal of influence on him. The prophet played a major role in calling Judah and Jerusalem back to God. Artists of the Middle Ages painted Zephaniah as a man with a lamp, searching Jerusalem for sinners to being them to punishment. He delivered the word of warning and destruction during the reign of Josiah.

Josiah was the king who found the long-lost book of the law in the temple and tried to reform the people who had drifted so far into idolatry and wickedness (2 Chr. 34:29-30). We wonder how the book of the law or the then-Bible could be lost? Negligence of the people, especially the spiritual leaders, indifference to the Word of God, and turning to the easier-to-see and touch idols! Have you lost your Bible? Oh, I know it may be lying on the coffee table or by the bed in plain sight, but do you really know where it is or what it says? We see most everyone in our church services carry one in the building, and some even open it, but have we stored up the Word in our hearts (Ps. 119:11; Jer. 31:33; Heb. 8:10) or have we lost it?

The Christian and the Bible go together. We exist to proclaim and exalt the Christ of the Bible. If we neglect the study of the Bible, it becomes almost a side issue to talk about Jesus. Our modern-day facilities supply us with well-organized churches, Bible schools, seminaries, endless Christian literature, tapes, and recorded sermons, laying all the wealth of the Word of God within easy reach. Yet we seem to have indifference and no sense of loyalty to this great God-inspired book. We rush out today to buy the latest copy of the magazine that has an article of some sports figure or Hollywood hunk that we love, because if we love and admire a person, we love to read about them. Well, now! The Bible is the book that tells us about Christ and we, as Christians, do love Him, don't we? Is it possible to love Christ and at the same time be completely complacently indifferent to His story?

George Mulle (1805-1898), English evangelist and philanthropist, devoted his whole life to the object of exemplifying how much may be accomplished by prayer and faith. He accepted no salary for his ministry as pastor at Gideon Chapel, and the Lord provided in amazing ways throughout his sixty-six years of ministry. The history of Bristol orphanages, Muller, founder and overseer, is page after page of answered prayers. He attributes his success to his love for the Bible. He believed the one chief reason that he was kept in happy, useful service was that he had loved the scriptures. It was his habit to read the Bible through four times a year, in a prayerful spirit, and apply it to his heart, and then practice what he found there.

We got off the prophet and the book of Zephaniah. Or did we? The main point of the book is that we seek the Lord (2:3). How do you seek the Lord? Read His Book! "All who seek the Lord will be saved" (3:12-13). How do we get saved? Read His Book! The prophet Zephaniah spoke of warnings and promises. How do we find these prophecies fulfilled? Read His Book! The book of Revelation is a good place to start and the end in included.

The problem with the people in Jerusalem was that she listened to no voice; she accepted no correction, did not trust the Lord and did not draw near to Him. They were self-sufficient. Lucifer made this same mistake (Isa. 14:12-15). There is in every human a nature or longing to have something great, beautiful, or powerful to look up to, such as a hero. Sadly, we do not always recognize our Lord and Savior as our hero. We search out a god in our own image and make them up in our minds that will give us leeway to life and put no moral restraints on us. The day of the Lord came upon Judah and Jerusalem for such arrogant behavior, and we too will see that day. "'It is written, as surely as I live', says the Lord, 'every knee will bow before me and every tongue will confess to God'" (Rom. 14:11; Phil. 2:10)!

Zephaniah taught that the Lord's wrath was against those who loved money and put their trust in material things of this earth, rather than seeking Him, and this is carried over into Hebrews 13:5. Neither silver nor gold will be able to deliver us from God's judgment. Peter and John did not put much stock in it either (Acts 3:6) and Jesus tells us to store up treasures in heaven rather than here on earth (Matt. 6:19-21). The prophet believed in the hope of repentance and that the guilty could be spared from wrath if they turned to seek the Lord. He called for righteousness and humility. These are the very conditions laid down by God in 2nd Chronicles 7:14. "If my people, who are called by my name, will humble themselves and pray and seek my face and turn from their wicked ways, then will I hear from heaven and will forgive their sin and will heal their land." The prophet gave reasons why Jerusalem, Judah and the world today should listen and obey the summons. There is no escape from The Day of the Lord. There will be a faithful remnant who will survive. In His mercy and sovereignty, He will perform the conversion and secure the remnant (Phil. 2:12-13). These promises related most directly to the people of Israel; however, the promised blessings flow beyond these boundaries and include we, who through faith in Christ, became Abraham's Seed and heirs of the promise (Gal. 3:29). There is no condemnation for those who are in Christ Jesus (Rom. 8:1).

God is not prejudiced. He hates sin and loves obedience universally. God wants us to have pure hearts, not hypocritical, outward show of piety. In other words, continue to read and study His Word at home and work, not leaving it at the front door of the church each Sunday. The coming Day of the Lord will bring judgment for greater than anything the world has ever known or can imagine. Renewed fellowship with God is available to all who have genuinely repentant hearts. "The Lord loves all who repent and rejoices over those who do" (Zeph. 3:17). The Bible tells us that "there is rejoicing in the presence of the angels of God over one sinner who repents" (Luke 15:10). "As a bridegroom rejoices over the bride so shall your God rejoice over you" (Isa. 6:5). If God loves us enough to save us a place in His House (John 14:2-3) and rejoice over us when we just say those two little words, "I'm sorry," do you think we should muster up enough love for Him to read His Book?

11. Matthew

Whenever we enter a discussion of the Bible and the name Matthew is mentioned, everyone knows of whom we are speaking. A disciple of Christ, not as brazen as Peter, not as calculated and precise as Dr. Luke, not as bare-fisted as Paul, perhaps not as beloved as John. Nevertheless, Matthew will be remembered as the tax collector who gave up wealth instantly and without question to become a follower of this stranger called Jesus (Matt. 9:9). Matthew went from serving money to serving the Lord. Scripture implies Matthew willingly gave up everything as required by Jesus: "If anyone comes to me and does not hate his father and mother, wife and children, brothers and sisters, yea and his own life also, he cannot be my disciple, and whoever does not bear his cross and come after me cannot be my disciple" (Luke 14:26-27).

Matthew had a groomed donkey and a large house filled with servants at his beck and call. This I know because Jesus ate at his house with many and to prepare a meal for many, you have to have a lot of help. This feast provided a spiritual lesson. While eating and drinking, the Pharisees asked Jesus and His disciples, "Why do you eat and drink with tax collectors and sinners?" Jesus answered them and said, "Those who are well have no need of a physician, but those who are sick. I have not come to call the righteous but sinners to repentance" (Luke 5:29-32). Not much in common between these two guys, since Jesus was a walking, dusty, calloused-hands evangelist with no place to call home. This would be like the president of a country inviting, well, me, to dinner at his house. This little old country girl would not even know which fork to use! Yet, Jesus called and Matthew answered, spending the rest of Jesus's life in His presence, putting a new meaning to the marriage scripture, where it says what God has joined together, no man can tear apart. God truly blessed this union between Son and disciple, and in turn blessed we who read the first book in the New Testament.

Matthew was not just a tax collector but a publican or tax collector for the Romans. This meant that he collected taxes from his fellow countrymen for the Roman government. He made a good living but was despised by his fellow Jews and merely tolerated by his Roman employers. Luke 3 implies that tax collectors found ways to overtax everyone, including extorting money on false charges. Other ways were to impose taxes on axles, wheels, animals, roads, highways, and admission to markets. Some even charged pedestrian taxes. Matthew was probably fluent in Greek and Aramaic, and an educated writer and scribe. It is also believed that he knew a form of shorthand called tachygraphy, since he was able to write detailed accounts of Christ's spoken sermons including the long Sermon on the Mount. The Romans set up a customhouse in the region of Capernaum and appointed Matthew as the tax collector. Rome was the greatest power of the time and most likely supported Matthew in a manner to which we all could become accustomed. He gave up this life of luxury to become one of Jesus's disciples, and was blessed to witness the miracles that He performed.

This brings to mind another wealthy young man in the scriptures. He approached Jesus and asked what was required for eternal life. Jesus told him to keep the commandments, and the young man asked which one! Now there is a question I have heard! Jesus cited several of the Ten Commandments and the young man insisted that he had faithfully kept all of them. Jesus added to the requirements, telling him that if he wanted to be perfect, he had to sell all his possessions and give the money to the poor and then he would have treasures in heaven. It did not take this young man very long to decide between his great wealth and the chance to enter into eternal life, because he walked away. Since Matthew was brought into play, we supposed he witnessed this. Question is, do you think he wanted to step in and advise the rich young man? If you are faced with the questions of the young man, how would you answer? The sin does not lie in being rich but in not being willing to lay it all aside for Jesus.

Levi, called Matthew, was the writer of the first gospel, and published his gospel among the Hebrews in their own language. The book was called in the original form the Logia, and written primarily for disciples of Jewish birth, more particularly for residents of Palestine, and intended for Jewish readers. Jesus changed his name from Levi to Matthew, which means in Hebrew, "the gift of Yahweh." As far as we know, Matthew was an honest man, but still a tax collector and in a profession that attracted thieves. As long as the taxes came in, the government did not ask questions as to how they were raised. Overcharging was the custom, so that after the government was paid, the collector could pocket the profit. As a Jewish publican tax collector, Matthew was hated and his whole family viewed as outcasts and a disgrace. The Jews had a proverb: "Take not a wife out of the family where there is a publican, for they are all publicans." Jesus looked beyond this reputation and recognized the potential of Matthew.

Matthew is spoken of five times in the New Testament. First in Matthew 9:9, when called by Jesus to follow Him, and then four times in the list of the apostles, where he is mentioned in the seventh place (Luke 6:15; Mark 3:18), and again in the eighth place (Matt. 10:3; Acts 1:13). The account in the three synopses is identical, the vocation of Matthew (Levi) being alluded to in the same terms. No further allusion is made to Matthew in the gospels, except in the list of the apostles. He was one of the witnesses of Jesus's Resurrection,

Ascension, and afterward withdrew to an upper chamber in Jerusalem, praying in union with Mary, the Mother of Jesus, and with his brethren (Acts 1:10-14). Ancient writers are not as one, as to the countries evangelized by Matthew, but almost all of them mention Ethiopia to the south of the Caspian Sea, and some Persia and the kingdom of the Parthian, Macedonia, and Syria. There is disagreement as to the place and cause of Matthew's martyrdom, and it is not known whether he was burned, stoned, or beheaded. The most accepted is that he was slain with halberd, an axe-headed, two-handled pole weapon, in the city of Nadabah, Ethiopia in AD 60. It is believed that James, the lesser, translated Matthew's Hebrew writings into Greek.

Because Matthew wrote for a Jewish audience, he began his gospel by showing through family records that Jesus was a descendant of both King David and Abraham, also pointing out that God can and will use people of all walks of life in His plan, and furthering this notion by including Matthew. He shows the united hatred of Jesus by the religious-minded Pharisees and the politically minded Sadducees. In Matthew 7:12, he records the words spoken by Jesus that we have come to know as the Golden Rule. He walks us through the parables, the healings, the rejection of Jesus in His hometown, and I am sure was a comfort to his Savior upon hearing the news of the death of John the Baptist. He was with Jesus when He traveled toward Jerusalem for the last time. He listened intently and probably with great sadness as his friend and Savior talked of His death on the cross. He ate the Passover meal with Him and watched in wonder when Judas came to the realization that Jesus knew he was the one to betray Him. His gospel ends with the great commission: "Go and make followers of all people in the world. Baptize them in the name of the Father and the Son and the Holy Spirit. Teach them to obey everything that I have taught you, and I will be with you always, even until the end of this age" (Matt. 28:18-20). Are you usable?

12. *Zacchaeus*

"Jesus entered Jericho and was passing through. A man was there by the name of Zacchaeus. He was a chief tax collector and was wealthy. He wanted to see who Jesus was, but being a short man, he could not, because of the crowd. So he ran ahead and climbed a sycamore-fig tree to see Him, since Jesus was coming that way" (Luke 19:1-10).

A lot of questions arise when we read this passage of scripture, the first being why was Jesus just passing through Jericho? And what made Him decide to stay? Was He just passing through looking for someone to reach out to Him, and was it the faith of yet another tax collector that made Him stay awhile? The reaching out of someone who wanted to se for himself who Jesus was? Zacchaeus had heard all the stories of how Jesus healed, preached, and saved, but he wanted to see for himself just who this man was that drew everyone's attention. Do you think that Zacchaeus was thinking salvation, or was he just curious? Whatever the thinking, Zacchaeus sought Jesus and got closer to him than he had hoped. God says if we seek Him, we will find Him, and we who hungers and thirsts after righteousness will be filled (Jer. 29:13; Matt. 5:6).

Also in Luke, we find that when Jesus reached the spot where the tree stood, that He looked up and saw Zacchaeus. He told him to come down immediately, because He must stay at his house today. Three words caught my attention, and they are *immediately, must,* and *stay*! There was urgency in Jesus's tone! Perhaps this is a message for us to find and keep the urgency to meet Jesus and allow Him to stay at our house. He is passing through each and every day, and we need to do something to make Him look up and see us in the spot we are in. And we should welcome Him gladly (Luke 19:6). Take notice that it was not that Zacchaeus was short that he could not see Jesus. It was the crowd that kept him from seeing Jesus. When we go to church, there are crowds that keep us from seeing who Jesus is. Our ballgames, calendar events, meetings, etc. are all crowds that keep us from Jesus. We need to get to the point in our life where we get up and say that nothing else matters if I cannot get to Jesus today. You may be in church, but the crowd in your thoughts may be keeping you from Jesus. Jesus is coming to your place. Draw a line and say that you want to see Jesus, even if you have to miss the afternoon ballgame or the committee meeting tomorrow. Do not depend on the Bible stories that you have heard in Sunday school or the testimonies of others. Find out for yourself who Jesus is.

All the people saw Jesus tell Zacchaeus he was going to his house and began to mutter that Zacchaeus was a sinner. They said!!! Do not let what they say glimpse. We are waiting for an experience like Saul had on the Damascus journey (Acts 9:3-4) or Balaam and his donkey (Num. 22:22-23) or maybe see the burning bush that spoke to Moses (Ex. 3:1-3).

Jesus is the Almighty, the Author and the finisher of our faith, the Chief Shepherd, the Eternal Father, Faithful Witness, the Good Shepherd, the I Am, the Image of God and the Emanuel. He is the King of Kings, the Lord of Lords, the Lion of Judah, the Rose of Sharon, the Alpha and Omega, the Amen, Beloved Son of God and the Holy and Righteous One. He is Jesus Christ! He is the Word of God! Do you know who He is? Will you get out on a limb to find out who He really is to you? What obstacle or crowd stops you? Let Him in your house (Rev. 3:20).

You might remember from the song we sang as children that Zacchaeus was a very small man and had to climb up into the sycamore tree to see Jesus. Jesus, however did not miss the effort that Zacchaeus made and stopped, telling him to come down because He was going to stay at his house.

13. *Haggai*

The book of Haggai is two short chapters, and takes up just a couple of pages in most Bibles, yet it packs in four powerful messages. It had been twenty years since Zerubbabel, the governor, and Joshua, the high priest, led the first return of exiles to Jerusalem from Babylon to rebuild the temple of God. Haggai, already an old man, came with them. This small group with great aspirations had come upon hard times. They quickly forgot the lessons exile had taught them. They worked hard, but the crops failed. They earned money, but it was never enough. They allowed the negative influences of opposition and scanty resources to discourage them to the point of quitting after having completed only the temple's foundation. The Jews' neglect of the temple was made worse by their preoccupation with building elaborate homes for themselves. The Spirit of the Lord came upon Haggai and prompted him to stir up the people and take up once again the rebuilding of the temple.

The Jews did not say they would not build the temple, but not yet! Men do not say they will never repent and reform and follow Jesus, but not yet! So the business we are created and sent into the world to do is not done (Matt. 28:19-20). The Jews neglected the building of the temple so they would have more time and money for worldly affairs. (Sound familiar?) Many good works have been intended but not done because we supposed the right and proper time had not come (Heb. 3:13). Believers let opportunities slip through their fingers, and unbelievers delay coming to Jesus until it is too late (Luke 12:33-34). You are the temple of the Living God! Do not neglect it (2 Cor. 6:16)!

Haggai was sent by God to preach to the restored community of Jews after the return to Jerusalem. He encouraged them to rebuild the temple, which had been destroyed by the Babylonians in 586 BC. Haggai likened Judah's poverty and depressed state of affairs to the sinful indifference to rebuilding the temple. Haggai shared with them the vision that blessings come to those who put God first, and the vision of God's glory filling the new temple when it was completed. They could not build a fine and glorious temple such as Solomon built, so they were discouraged. God is pleased if we do as well as we can in obedience and service. But the Jews' proud hearts would not let them be pleased unless the work was done as well as someone whose ability was far above theirs. The house they were building would be filled with glory far beyond Solomon's temple.

Haggai's message of the hope of glory was laced with rebuke and judgment of the people for their sins. Haggai was ministering during the times of the Gentiles, when Israel had no king of her own; no descendent of David was sitting on the throne in Jerusalem. It was probably a holy festival day in Jerusalem, giving the prophet Haggai, whose name means "festival," a large, ready audience. The first message was primarily for the two leaders, Zerubbabel and Joshua, emphasizing their responsibilities. The message from the Lord Almighty—Haggai used this title fourteen times—was to these people rather than my people, and was a rebuke from the Lord as they were not acting like the Lord's people.

Haggai then rebuked the people for selfishly building paneled houses and neglecting the temple. The term "paneled houses" may only mean that they had a roof over their head, and could also mean actual luxurious paneling for the leaders and the well-to-do people. The Lord, through Haggai, rebuked them for what they had not done, showed them the fruitlessness of what they had done, then challenged them to do what they should do. Build the house! Remember back in Ezra 3:7, the lumber was bought for the temple; therefore, having to go into the mountains and bring down timber probably meant they used the temple timber to build their own houses.

The drought the Lord caused affected the three basic crops of Palestine: grain, new wine and olive oil. However, the Lord encouraged them by urging the two leaders and their people to take firm action. The Lord told them to be strong, brave, and work, because He was with them. David used these two expressions when encouraging Solomon to build the original temple (1 Chr. 28:10, 20). The Lord assured them He was with them, even as His Spirit was with the Israelites when they came out of Egypt (Isa. 63:11-14). Since He was with them, they could be calm and assured (Isa. 41:10). Even though Israel was exiled because of sin and unbelief, she still was not rejected by God. Since the covenant the Lord made with Abraham was unconditional (Gen.

15), his descendants need not fear. The Lord remains their God and will continue to be with them and strengthen, help, and uphold them (Isa. 40:31, 41:8-14).

The words "in a little while" (Hag. 2:6) elude human timetable, meaning this action could occur at anytime, according to God's timetable. The shaking of the earth is a symbol of God's supernatural intervention (Isa. 2:12-21) when Jesus returns to earth. The earth and sky will tremble (Joel 3:16). The shaking of the nations may refer to God's gathering the nations for the Battle of Armageddon (Zech. 14:1-4). The writer to the Hebrews quoted Haggai and then added that the Kingdom of God, which cannot be shaken, will survive all divine judgments (Heb. 12:28). "This house will be filled with glory" could refer to material splendor, but elsewhere, the only glory that is said to fill the temple is the *Shekinah* glory of God's presence (Ex. 40:34-35). The word *Shekinah* does not appear in the Bible that I could find. A Hebrew term in rabbinic literature which reverently expresses the Divine Presence, it is derived from *skn*, meaning to dwell, abide, or settle down. Background for the word may be found in Exodus 25:8, 40:34, when the Ark of the Lord is placed in the temple of Jerusalem, a cloud representing the *Shekinah* fills the temple, therefore, symbolizing its new habitation (1 Kings 8:10).

The significance of comparing Zerubbabel to signet ring (Hag. 2:23) is possibly Haggai saying that God was reversing the curse on Jehoiachin (Jer. 22:24-28). Zerubbabel, the signet ring, represented his position of the Son of David, not for personal fulfillment but for Messianic fulfillment in the Kingdom of the final Son of David (Luke 1:32-33). The sovereign covenant God brought about all He promised through Haggai. The temple was rebuilt and filled with the glory of God. The final Son of David will rule the earth in peace and righteousness. Therefore, the people are to be faithful now to the task to which He has called them. A job cannot be finished if you never state it. If you are faithfully working for our Lord and Savior, you are building more than you can see.

14. *Hezekiah Trivia*

Hezekiah was one of the good kings of Judah (2 Kings 18:3-7). This was no insignificant feat, since out of the twenty kings of Judah, only four were noted as good kings. Two were the best, two were good most of the time, two bad most of the time, five were bad all of the time, one was devilish, two were wicked, and two were the worst of kings.

Hezekiah was not one to be intimidated or pushed around; the Lord was with him and he had success in everything he did. The Judeans were obedient to their king, which was another significant feat to his credit. When the commander used almost an entire chapter of 2nd Kings to shout insults and threats and to slander the king Hezekiah and God, the people were silent. They did not answer the commander at all, because King Hezekiah had ordered them not to answer (2 Kings 18:7-36). Hezekiah went first to God, another creditable feat on his part, no middleman here and no fretting and pacing before going to God. "When Hezekiah received the letter from the messengers and read it, he went up to the temple of the Lord. He spread the letter out before the Lord and prayed to the Lord" (2 Kings 19:14). What happens when you go first to the Lord? He answers you and fights your battles for you. The prophet Isaiah came promptly with the Lord's answer, and the prophecy of Isaiah came to pass (2 Kings 19:6-37).

Sennacherib came with the intentions of making war against Jerusalem, and when Hezekiah saw this, he consulted with his officers and warriors about stopping the flow of the springs outside the city, and they supported him. A large force was assembled to stop up all the springs and the Wadi River Valley that flowed through the land, for otherwise, they thought the king of Assyria would come and find water in abundance. These events occurred in the year 701 BC, when the Assyrian king laid siege to Jerusalem. The Gihon Spring, which was outside the city, confronted King Hezekiah with a double dilemma: to ensure water for the besieged city yet deny the source of the water to the Assyrian forces. The Bible describes Hezekiah's solution: "It was Hezekiah who stopped up the spring of water of Upper Gihon, leading it downward west of the City of David" (2 Chr. 32:30). The waters of the Gihon were diverted into the Gai Wadi by means of a tunnel (2 Kings 20:20; 2 Chron. 32).

The Siloam inscription now in the Istanbul Museum was discovered in 1880 by a boy who was bathing in the waters of the Gihon Spring. It was studied by Conrad Schick, one of the first explorers of Jerusalem. Engraved in the rock, the inscription describes the meeting of the two groups of hewers who had begun digging from opposite ends of the tunnel. "The tunneling was completed while the hewers wielded the axe, each man toward his fellow, there was heard a man's voice calling to his fellow, the hewers hacked each toward the other, axe against axe, and the water flowed from the spring to the pool, a distance of 1,200 cubits."

Hezekiah was sick and dying, but even though he believed the prophet Isaiah's word from the Lord, Hezekiah did not want to die. He turned toward the wall while lying on his bed and prayed that the Lord remember him. The furniture of an eastern divan or chamber either for receiving company or for private use, consisted of carpets on the floor in the middle and sofas arranged on one or more sides of the room. People lounged on these sofas during the day and slept there at night. The corner of the room was the place of honor. The reason seems to be that if the person is in the corner, he is apart from the rest of the company and is guarded by the walls on each side. We assume that Hezekiah's couch was so situated that when he turned to either side, he faced a wall. He also withdrew from the ones attending him to speak alone to God (Isa. 38:2-3; 2 Kings 20:1-3). Hezekiah cried out loudly for the Lord to remember him. He did not speak as if God needed to be put in mind of anything by anyone, or as if by some works he was due the reward of an extended life. It is through Jesus's righteousness only that we receive mercy and grace, and it was through God only that Hezekiah would receive mercy. Hezekiah did not pray that the Lord spare him, but that the Lord remember him, whether he lived or died, he asked God to keep him. God always hears the prayers of the broken-hearted, and will give health, length of days, and temporal deliverances as much and as long as is truly good for you. Note that Isaiah doctored Hezekiah, even after God told him he would live and not die (Isa. 38:21). It is our duty, when sick, to use such means as are proper to help nature; else we do not trust God, but tempt Him. A stone with Hezekiah's name on it now is in Israel's museum, making this Old Testament character seem more real to the world. The name *Hezekiah* means "Yah is my strength!" He is a good role model for today.

15. Lazarus and the Dead in Christ

When God inspired the Bible to be written, He wrote to us from His point of view. However, when we read things, we have a tendency to look at what we read through rose-colored human glasses. If we take off those glasses and look at things through God's eyes instead, we may se things we really do not like about ourselves. God called us corpse in Ephesians 2:5 and Colossians 2:13. There are some of the many verses that address our spiritual estate before our salvation. God demands we look at the Bible as a whole in this light, and when we do, He then shows us more.

The climactic miracle of raising Lazarus from the dead was Jesus's public evidence of the truth of His great claim, "I am the Resurrection and the life" (John 11:25). Death is the great horror which sin has produced (Rom. 5:12). Physical death is the divine object lesson of what sin does in the spiritual realm. As physical death ends life and separates people, so spiritual death is the separation of people from God and the loss of life which is in God (John 1:4). Jesus has come so that all of us may live full lives; rejecting Jesus means that one will not see life, and his final destiny is the second death, the lake of fire (Rev. 20:14-15).

Jesus did not go immediately, but His delay was not from lack of love for Lazarus or fear of the Jews. He waited until the right moment in the Father's plan. Lazarus's sickness would not end in death, that is, in permanent death. Instead, Jesus would be glorified in this incident.

This statement is ironic, since Jesus's power and obedience to the Father were displayed, but this event led to His death (John 11:50-53), which was His true glory. Lazarus, in John 11, is God's spiritual explanation, a parable, of you and me before salvation, and then God's salvation comes. Lazarus was dead; he stunk! How much more descriptive does God have to make it? He could not see, he could not hear, he could walk or think or speak or move on his own. Yet, Jesus calls him by name and he simply comes forth as he was commanded to do. Some say that had Jesus not called the name "Lazarus," perhaps every grave would have opened and all the dead would have come out. I disagree. (Imagine that!) Several times, Jesus says that His time has not yet come, but when the Father's time is right, we will all hear His voice and those in the grave will come out (John 5:28-29; Isa. 26:19; 1 Thess. 4:13-18).

God then describes a little bit more about Lazarus's death. He was bound with grave clothes. In the literal account of the raising of Lazarus, this is what he was buried in, but it is the spiritual account that teaches us what God sees. He did not have on Christ's robe of righteousness, but wore his own sinful estate (Zech. 3:3-5). Once we are saved, God gives us a change of clothes, heart, and we wear Christ's robe of righteousness, not our filthy clothes, sin (Zech. 3:4).

"Loose him" is the same word *loose* used in Matthew 16:19. He was now freed from the bondage of Satan (Luke 13:16). The people were more concerned about his physical death, but Jesus spoke about his spiritual death and rebirth in this chapter and literally raised the dead, but it pointed to the spiritual. Not to be funny, but Jesus did not say, "Lazarus, open one eye and listen to what I am offering you." The parable here is one of complete death, no life within at all, so therefore, there was no response. The wicked cannot change on their own, and God chose Lazarus's physical death to show us what He sees inside us when He looks. The point is very straightforward that this was complete death and no life at all. If you are unsaved, God is telling you that there is nothing you can do on your own to save yourself or help with your salvation. While unsaved, you do not even know you are a dead man. God must

241

do everything, including choosing you for salvation (John 15:16). The gospel call goes out to all mankind to repent, yet God knew full well that everyone would not; therefore, He did all the work involved with our salvation. This is fair, for no one will be able to say that He did not call everyone to repentance. He did, but not everyone responded to the call (Ps. 19:1-3). All of us know the Word of God and it should be written in our hearts, but our hearts are now wicked (Jer. 17:9). No one will have an excuse on Judgment Day if we are not saved (Dan. 12:2; John 5:28-29; Rev. 20:11-15).

The miracle of Lazarus's resurrection is still nothing less than a miracle, even in light of what God is teaching us spiritually in this parable. But when we take off our man-made rose-colored glasses and ask God to give us sight, we will find we see things more clearly than ever before and we will see things as God sees them. Has God raised you from the spiritually dead yet?

16. Esther – Unquestionable Sacrifice

The book of Esther takes place in the Persian period (539-331 BC) after any Israelites had returned from the exile to the land of Palestine to rebuild the temple and set up the sacrificial system. Most Israelite captives, however, chose not to return to their homeland. Esther and Mordecai, her cousin, had not returned to the land and did not seem interested in complying with the prophetic command to return (Isa. 48:20).

Esther is the only book of the Bible in which the name of God is not mentioned. The New Testament does not quote from the book of Esther, nor have copies of it been found among the Dead Sea Scrolls. The law is never mentioned in the book, nor are the sacrifices or offerings referred to. This fits the view that Jewish people residing in the Persian Empire were not following God's will. They were shunning their responsibilities to return to Palestine and to become involved in temple worship. Prayer is never mentioned in the book, although fasting is. Both Esther and

Mordecai seem to have lacked spiritual awareness, except in their assurance that God would protect His people, even though the name of God is not mentioned. Xerxes (Zerk-sees) ruled over 127 provinces from India to Cush for twenty-one years. India corresponds to present-day West Pakistan, and Cush was a term for the Upper Nile region, which included present-day southern Egypt, all of Sudan, and northern Ethiopia.

King Xerxes was known for giving lavish, long-lasting banquets (Est. 1:5-8). Vashti, the present queen, gave her own banquets and refused the king's command to come and entertain his guest. Now all the men became worried that their women would follow the example of the queen and not obey them, so they talked the outraged king into sending out an edict declaring that the man was the ruler over his household! They also shamed him into dismissing Queen Vashti. Now, when the king sobered up and his anger subsided, he realized he had no queen. But the king's personal attendants were prepared with yet another great helpful suggestion. They certainly did not intend for the king to reinstate Queen Vashti, for fear that she would turn against them and in turn influence their wives. They offered him such an appealing deal that he followed after their plan to have a beauty contest among the unmarried girls in the neighborhood.

Mordecai was a Jew of the tribe of Benjamin who tried to hide the fact that he and his cousin Esther were Jews. Esther was beautiful, lovely in form and features, and was taken to the palace to begin her beauty treatments before meeting the king. By law, Esther was not to marry a pagan (Deut. 7:1-4) or have sexual relations with a man who was not her husband (Ex. 20:14), and yet this was the purpose of her being included in the harem. God had a plan! God protected and used Esther and Mordecai, in spite of the fact that they were not living according to the law commanded by God to the people of Israel.

King Xerxes was very attracted to Esther and made her queen, then held a large banquet and declared a holiday. Any excuse for a party, right? Haman was Xerxes's right-hand man, and was an arrogant sort who required everyone to bow to him. Mordecai, of course, refused, which enraged Haman, who began to plot how to get rid of all the Jews. Haman cast lots to decide when the execution should be, and the date decided gave the Jews almost a year to prepare. Haman, along with many people in the Persian Empire, was extremely superstitious. The Persian religious system stressed fate and chance. Haman was allowing fate, by the casting of the lot, to dictate his move against the Jewish Nation. Little did he know, or then realize, that the God who created all things and controls all events was in control of this situation as well (Prov. 16:33). Now in this situation, as before, King Xerxes took Haman's word for everything and allowed him to send out the order to kill the Jews. What a leader! Or… what? A leader? Mordecai found out about the plot and first went into mourning and then sent a message to Esther that she must appeal to the king to save her people.

We know that if not summoned by the king, one went into the inner court, that they would be beheaded without question. Esther sent this word to Mordecai, who returned with, "Just because you live in the king's palace, do not think that out of all the Jewish people, you alone will escape. If you keep quiet at this time someone else will help and save the Jewish people, but you and your father's family will all die. And who knows, you may have been chosen queen for just such a time as this." Mordecai was aware of the promises of Abraham, Moses, and David, and that they would not be fulfilled if the entire nation was wiped out. Therefore, he was confident that God would act on their behalf. Mordecai told Esther that Haman's power would reach the palace, and to die by his hand was no worse that to die by the king's hand for entering the inner court on the Jews' behalf. Her answer to this was, "If I perish, I perish."

No scripture states that Esther or Mordecai prayed, but Esther did request that the people fast for her for three days, and she did the same. When Esther showed up at the inner court and the king turned to look at her, do you really think he was thinking about beheading her? Remember, she was a beautiful young woman. He held out his scepter toward her and told her she could have anything she wanted, up to half of his kingdom. Later in this story, Queen Esther gives a couple of banquets with the guest of honor being none other than the right hand of the king, Haman. Esther, it seems, is not only beautiful, but smart and persuasive as well. She waits for the right timing to tell the king everything, including the fact that perhaps Haman, his trusted companion, had betrayed and tricked him to get his own revenge against the Jew Mordecai. The king went outside to gain control of his anger, and upon returning saw Haman by the couch, trying to convince the queen to spare his life. The king saw this as a move on the queen, and long story short, had Haman hung and gave Mordecai the keys to the kingdom.

The Feast of Purim is a springtime holiday in the Jewish liturgical calendar, falling on the fourteenth of Adar, that celebrates the defeat of Haman and the survival of the Jews in the book of Esther. It is not clear which came first, the book of Esther or the festival of Purim. The two have become inextricably linked, with the scroll of Esther being read in full in the evening synagogue service. Purim encourages a carnival atmosphere, with children bringing noisemakers to the synagogue and the congregation stamping their feet every time Haman's name is read from the scroll. Are you willing to be an Esther?

17. Joseph

Joseph was the eleventh son of Jacob (Israel) and the older son of Rachel. Rachel, the wife whom Jacob loved, was barren for a long time before giving birth to Joseph (Gen. 29:31). Her words upon giving birth to Joseph reflect the two possible derivations of Joseph's name. "God has taken away" (Gen. 30:23) and "May the Lord add to me another son" (Gen. 30:24). As the firstborn of Rachel and a son of his father's old age, Joseph was his father's favorite, a fact made clear in Genesis 37:31, stating that Israel loved Joseph more than any other of his children, and made him a long robe with sleeves. This robe is not the traditional "coat of many colors," although the Hebrew actually refers simply to a sleeved tunic or robe reaching to the wrists and ankles. In 2nd Samuel 13, it is the clothing of a princess! The significance of the special robe is that it set Joseph apart from his brothers and triggered hatred and jealousy in them. To make matters worse, Joseph brought back to his father a bad report of his brothers, then related two dreams in which his brothers, as well as his parents, bowed down to him.

Joseph's brothers first conspired to kill him, but came up with what they thought a better plan, to sell him into slavery. The latter suggestion was made by Reuben, who hoped to rescue Joseph and bring him back to his father. Joseph's coat was stripped from him and used as evidence of his death. Joseph himself was sold to slave traders, either Ishmaelites or Midianites—there are probably two traditions preserved here—who took him off to Egypt and sold him to Potiphar, an officer of the Pharaoh. Although Joseph was now a slave in a strange land, the narrative makes it clear throughout that the Lord was with him, and therefore everything Joseph did was successful, despite many setbacks that resulted from the actions of those in power. Joseph prospered in Potiphar's service, and soon was overseer of everything that belonged to him. But Joseph's fortunes soon fell again. Potiphar's wife desired Joseph! Joseph refused her advances, but left behind a garment that was later used as evidence against him. Once again, Joseph was cast out, this time into prison, into a state lower still than slavery. Once again, however, God was with him.

An opportunity for release came when Joseph was able to interpret the dreams of two of Pharaoh's officers, the chief baker and the chief cupbearer, but Joseph languished for two more years. Joseph's release finally came when his ability to interpret dreams was brought to the attention of the Pharaoh, whose own magicians and wise men had failed in that regard. Joseph not only foretold seven plentiful years to be followed by seven years of famine, but also advised Pharaoh to prepare for the coming leanness by gathering the surplus of the good years. As a reward, Pharaoh set Joseph over all the land of Egypt, responsible for organizing the collection and storage of grain against the coming famine.

Pharaoh bestowed on Joseph the name Zephenathpaneah, meaning God speaks and he lives, and gave him Asenath, the daughter of Potiphera, priest of On, as his wife. Two sons, Manasseh and Ephraim, were born to them before the famine.

The famine provided the occasion for the reunion of Joseph with his brothers. Jacob, having heard that there was grain in Egypt, sent his ten older sons. They had to approach Joseph to buy the grain, bowing before him in fulfillment of his dream. Although he recognized them, Joseph did not reveal himself, but instead accused them of being spies. He demanded that they bring their youngest brother as evidence of their innocence, and made them leave Simeon as hostage. Upon hearing this, Jacob at first refused to let Benjamin go along, but finally agreed when the need for more grain became acute. When the brothers returned to Joseph, he questioned them about the welfare of their father. When the got the grain and left, however, Joseph set them up with his own personal cup in their sacks, along with the money they had paid him, in order to have them brought back to Egypt. He declared that whoever had the cup—Benjamin—would stay in Egypt and become his slave. Judah, out of compassion for his father, offered himself in place of Benjamin, at which point Joseph finally revealed who he was and reconciled himself to his brothers. Jacob and his entire household where then given a home in the land of Goshen, and Jacob and his beloved son Joseph were at last reunited.

Joseph had a dream from God! He was thrown into a hole, sold into slavery by his own family, falsely accused by the master's wife, thrown into jail, but he had no walls in his mind. He never doubted the Word of God (Rom. 11:29). Joseph's dream took thirteen years to fulfill, but he stayed faithful to God. He knew that God had given him the dream, and that God would make it come to be. If God has given you a dream, a mission, a ministry, or a goal, stay faithful. There will be storms, but in the words of my favorite author, the storm is what brought Jesus walking on the water. When you feel yourself sinking, just reach up and He will rescue you. Remember that your dream was God's dream for you first, and before you thought of it, He did. If He is the author of the dream, He will be the finisher of the dream. "Surely I am with you always, to the very end of the age" (Matt. 28:20).

18. The Apostle Luke

Luke was written between AD 58 and 70. Luke is the longest and most thorough of the four gospels. Luke, a Gentile physician, wrote both this gospel and the book of Acts to aid a new Christian named Theophilus. As a missionary companion of the Apostle Paul, Luke was able to present a detailed historical account of Jesus's life. Luke presents Jesus's humanity more than any of the other gospels. Luke the apostle was born of pagan parents, possibly a slave, and one of the earliest converts. Legend has it that he was also a painter and did portraits of Jesus and Mary, but no positive proof has been found to support this. He traveled with Paul and evangelized Greece and Rome. He wrote the book of Luke based on the teachings and writings of Paul. He was born in Antioch and was the only Gentile writer in the New Testament. Luke was a physician and used medical vocabulary in his writings, such as the boy thrown down in Luke 9:38, meaning that he was having convulsions and "look upon my son" meaning the doctor seeing a patient. He used Greek words that the Gentiles could understand. Simon the Cananean or Simon the Zealot meaning Peter and Golgotha and Kranion both meaning the place of the skull and Jesus is Master equaling the Jewish term, rabbi. As stated in the beginning of Luke, the book was written to a friend named Theophilus, meaning lover of God. This leads us to think that the book was written in general to people who loved God and not just to the one man. Luke hoped that Theophilus and other readers would learn that God's love reaches the Jews, Gentiles and the entire world.

Luke's name means "bringer of light," and his book is most often called the most beautiful book ever written. Luke begins by telling us about Jesus's parents, the birth of His cousin, John the Baptist, Mary and Joseph's journey to Bethlehem, where Jesus was born in a manger, and the genealogy of Christ through Mary. Jesus's public ministry reveals His perfect compassion and forgiveness through the stories of the prodigal son, the rich man, and Lazarus, and the Good Samaritan. While many believed in this unprejudiced love that surpasses all human limits, many others challenged and opposed the claims of Jesus Christ's followers and were encouraged to count the cost of discipleship, while His enemies seek His death on the cross. Finally, Jesus was betrayed, tried, sentenced, and crucified. But the grave could not hold Him and He arose on the third day, assuring the continuation of His ministry of seeking and saving the lost. After appearing on a number of occasions to His disciples, His Holy Spirit promised Jesus ascended to the Father.

Luke was concerned with presenting the words and deeds of Jesus as guides for the conduct of Christian disciples and with presenting Jesus Himself as the model of Christian life and piety. Throughout the gospel, Luke called upon the Christian disciple to identify with the Master, Jesus, who was caring and tender toward the poor and lowly, the outcast, the sinner and the afflicted, and toward all those who recognized their dependence on God. No gospel writer was more concerned than Luke with the mercy and compassion of Jesus. No gospel writer was more concerned with the role of the Spirit in the life of Jesus and the Christian disciple. He was concerned with the importance of prayer, and with Jesus's concern for the women. To all who respond in faith and repentance to the Word Jesus preaches, He brings salvation and peace and life.

Luke was not part of the first generation of Christian disciples, but was dependent upon the traditions he received from those who were eyewitnesses and ministers of the Word. Such bond existed between Luke and this friend, Theophilus, that Luke would study everything carefully from the beginning, and wrote it out for his friend. With the skill of a surgeon, Luke probed for the truth so that his friend could know that what he had been taught was true. Can you imagine what would happen if we all did the same? Share the gospel with someone today.

Some accounts say that Luke died of old age, while another says that he was hanged in an olive tree in Greece for defending the gospel.

19. A Man after God's Own Heart

In Paul's sermon at Antioch in which he briefly recounts the history of Israel, he refers to the statement made by God concerning David. "I have found David, the son of Jesse, a man after my own heart, who will do all my will" (Acts 13:22; 1 Sam. 13:13-14). This beautiful compliment is one that should characterize every person who wears the name of Christ. How do we receive this compliment? We get an attitude! Develop a David attitude!

David loved the Lord and His laws (Ps. 119:97). In this psalm—if not written by David, it certainly expressed his sentiments—we find one who had great love for God's Word. This love for God's Word is due to the fact that it protected him from sin, revived him in affliction, and gave him peace of mind. Jesus loved the Word of God, as is evident from His frequent quotation of it, especially at the time of His temptation from the devil (Matt. 4:4, 7, 10). How is our love for the Word of God? Do we hide it in our hearts (Ps. 40:8, 119:11)? Do we find it to be a source of comfort in times of afflictions (119:49-50)? Does it give us peace of mind (Prov. 6:21-22)? If not, we should give heed to the instructions of David in Psalms 1:1-3. Learn to delight in the Word, learn to meditate upon it daily, and then we will be truly blessed.

David loved to pray, and vowed that he would call upon the Lord as long as he lived. His love for prayer was based upon the fact that God had answered him at all times, and the fact that God had greatly blessed him. Prayer brought David close to God (Ps. 145:18). Jesus was also a man of prayer, making it a point to often slip away to pray in private, and especially in His times of trial, He always resorted to prayer. How is our love for prayer? Have we found it to be a source of peace which surpasses all understanding, and do we pray without ceasing (1 Thess. 5:17)? If not, then let David instruct us to depend upon prayer for our very preservation (Ps. 32:6-7).

David loved to praise God, counting seven times a day that he praised him. He praised God because of His righteousness, His righteous judgments, and because of His greatness and loving kindness (Ps. 95:1-7). And he was determined to sing praises as long as he lived (Ps. 104:3). Jesus also loved to praise God, and praised Him in open public and even singing with the disciples (Matt. 11:25, 26, 30). Do we love to praise God? Do we delight in singing praises, praise Him in our prayers? Once again, David has words to encourage us in this activity (Ps. 147:1).

David loved unity among brethren. "Behold how good and how pleasant it is" (Ps. 133:1). David knew the value of good friendship and unity, as exemplified in the relationship he had with Jonathan. He also knew the terrible pain of division within a family (1 Sam. 18:1; 2 Sam. 13), sons Amnon and Absalom. Jesus loved unity and prayed diligently that His disciples might be one (John 17:20-23). He died on the cross that there might be unity (Eph. 2:13-16). Do we love unity enough to pay the price? By diligently displaying the proper attitudes necessary to preserve the unity Jesus has accomplished through His death, we show how important unity is to us (Eph. 4:1-3). Mark those who needlessly cause division (Rom. 16:17).

David hated every false way, and said it outright in Psalms 119:104. His hatred was based upon his understanding of God's precepts. His hatred affected his selection of activities and friends (Ps. 101:3-4, 6-7). Jesus hated error and false ways, as manifested in His driving the money changers out of the temple (Matt. 21:12-13). As manifested in His denunciation of the hypocritical Pharisees, scribes, and lawyers (Matt. 223:13-36). What is our attitude toward false ways? Are we soft or compromising? Do we realize that we are involved in a battle over the souls of men, and are not to think lightly of that which is false (2 Cor. 10:3-5)? While we are to love the sinner, we must ever hate the sin! Check your heart! Get a David attitude for the Lord!

20. Voice in the Storm

Elijah got up, ate and drank, and strengthened by the food, he traveled forty days and forty nights until he reached Horeb, the Mountain of

God. There he went into a cave, spent the night, and this is where the Word of the Lord came to him. "What are you doing here, Elijah?" Bear in mind that God always knows just exactly where you and I are, but is sometimes testing your obedience, truthfulness, and faith. Elijah answered the Lord with excuses, saying that he had been very zealous for the Lord God Almighty. Note that this was not the question that God had asked him. Elijah went on to explain that the Israelites had rejected God's covenant, broken down His altars, and put the prophets to death with the sword. Elijah says that he is the only prophet left, and they are trying to kill him too. The Lord tells him to go out and stand on the mountain in His presence, because He is about to pass by. Then a great and powerful wind tore the mountain apart and shattered the rocks before the Lord, and Elijah just knew that this was the Lord, but the Lord was not in the wind. After the wind, there was an earthquake, but Elijah discovered that the Lord was not in the earthquake either. After the earthquake, surely this was the Lord in the fire, but He was not in the fire. "And after the fire came a small still voice" (1 Kings 19:12).

Do you ever have the urge to get away to someplace where there are no phones to listen to, no traffic, no people to answer to, and no pressures? Just blessed isolation! I think it is healthy, both physically and spiritually, to have alone times, away from the routine we have built for ourselves. You begin to rediscover things that have been going on all around you as well as inside you, that you have not been paying attention to because of your busy lifestyle. We discover that our encounters with God become real and present when we are quietly alone.

This was true for Moses, alone on Mount Sinai, when God called him to write the Ten Commandments (Ex. 19:1-20:17). The prophet Elijah stood with the wind howling and the earth shaking under his feet and the lightning flashing when God came to him in his storm of life with a small, still voice. Do you think that God was showing Elijah a real storm in comparison with the physical one Elijah was having, and in contrast the peace we can have when God shows up quietly in our hearts, minds, and emotions?

False prophets had been enjoying success in selling the Israelites on a religion of self-serving and self-indulgence. Meanwhile, back at the palace, Jezebel was having all the prophets of God killed (1 Kings 18:4), except the 100 that Obadiah, a devout believer in God, had hidden in caves. Elijah preached against this idol worship, challenging the people to choose God. He taunted them and dared them to call on Baal to answer by burning the sacrifice. They lost the challenge and Elijah ordered them killed. The fire of the Lord had fallen, and the priests and prophets of Baal were put to shame and death. According to the record, everyone present at this demonstration of God's awesome power had fallen to the ground crying, "The Lord, He is God! The Lord, He is God!" (1 Kings 18:38-39)

King Ahab, Jezebel's husband, was impressed and returned to the palace and told Jezebel everything. Big mistake! Jezebel sent a messenger saying Elijah would join his fellow prophets in death by this time tomorrow. If Jezebel had really intended to kill him, she would have sent an assassin instead of a messenger. I think she just wanted him to run for his life in fear, so he would be known as a coward and therefore have no followers. And run he did! But he was one of God's special ones! He should have known there was nowhere to hide from the voice that had called him (Rom. 11:29).

The Lord's voice said, "Elijah, what are you doing here?" Have your heard this voice in your spirit asking you this question? Was your answer the same as Elijah's? Lord, I have been faithful but no one else has. I am the only one serving you in a godly way, but yet everyone is out to get me! Lord, what are you trying to tell me? If these questions are familiar to you, then check with God again. God may be taking the storm around you or over you so that He can first get your attention and then listen carefully for that still voice. Storms will come in this old life, but if you listen, you will hear the sweetest words: "I know the plans I have for you" (Jer. 29:11-14) and "peace I leave with you, my peace I give to you" (John 14:27).

This small, gentle voice was first heard in a manger when a tiny baby cried softly in His mother's arms (Luke 2:6-7). Only a few heard! This is the kind of sound we must be listening for (John 5:24). God, give us ears to hear your still, small voice.

21. *Nebuchadnezzar's Dream*

Have you ever wanted to pull back the curtain and see what is to be in the future? This happened to Nebuchadnezzar, king of Babylon. "He saw an image, mighty and of exceedingly great brightness and the appearance of it was frightening and terrible" (Dan. 2:31). He saw a statue with a head of fine gold, breast and arms of silver, thighs of bronze, legs of iron, and feet of partly iron and partly clay. The baked clay of the potter and while the king was watching, in his dream, a stone was cut out without human hands, and broke the statue to pieces.

Daniel explained to the king what the meaning of the dream was. The kingdom, represented by the head of gold, was Babylon. Any good politician would have stopped with the flattering word that the king himself was the head of gold, thus perhaps saving his own head, but Daniel went on, because he knew he must tell it as God gave it. He related that Babylon would fall and another kingdom would rise that would be inferior to Babylon. Then a third kingdom of bronze, which would bear rule over all the earth, and a fourth kingdom would be strong as iron. And like the feet and toes, part of potter's clay and part of iron, the kingdom would be divided.

Nebuchadnezzar was to be succeeded by three more world kingdoms. Daniel named them as Medo-Persia, represented by the breast and arms of silver; Greece, the thighs of brass; and Rome, the legs of iron. Then the kingdom would be divided. There would be no fifth world kingdom, but only these four. History has followed this prophecy like a blueprint, and we will take a glimpse at each of the passing empires.

The gold kingdom of Babylon was spoken of by God a hundred years before (Isa. 14:4). Through Jeremiah, God called Babylon a golden cup, and even historians refer to Babylon as the golden city of a golden age. Nebuchadnezzar could not help but be impressed and not only a little pleased with the fitness of the symbol, head of gold. By contact with the Hebrews, Babylon had opportunity to become familiar with the Word of God, and His will as revealed in it. As a nation, Babylon turned away from God. Because of this, all through succeeding scripture, the term *Babylon* is used in a symbolic way to refer to those who willfully turn away from God. In 538 BC, leading hordes of Medes and Persians, Cyrus the Great swept out of the mountains of Persia and captured Babylon (Dan. 5).

The silver kingdom was Medo-Persia, silver being a fitting symbol of Medo-Persia, since it was used by them as a medium of exchange and in decorations. Like Babylon, Medo-Persia turned aside from the worship of the true God. The wickedness of their later leaders undermined their strength and led to their defeat by Alexander the Great of Arbela in 331 BC. The reins of power then passed into the hands of the rising empire of the Greeks.

The brass kingdom of Greece was so called because the brazen armor and brass breastplates worn by the Grecian soldiers were reflected in the thighs of brass. With them came culture, learning, and the Greek language that later helped the spread of Christianity. After the death of Alexander the Great, the nation began to lose its power and unity. By 168 BC, the growing strength of the Romans became too great for the Greeks to withstand.

The iron monarchy of Rome, with its power broken in pieces, bruised and subdued kingdoms for nearly 600 years. During its rule, Christ was born and was crucified and under Rome, Christianity took root and thrived in spite of many persecutions. Hippolytus, a great theologian who died about AD 236, wrote of Rome, "Rejoice, blessed Daniel! Thou hast not been in error! The kingdom would be partly strong and partly brittle and broken (Dan. 2:42-43) showing that elements or ideologies can never harmonize, even as iron does not mingle itself with clay.

Broken up by the invasion of barbaric tribes from Europe, the Western Roman Empire was overrun at last. Out of its ruin emerged the nations of modern Europe, including English Saxons, French Franks, German Alemanni, Swiss Burgundians, Italian Lombards, Spanish Visigoths, Portuguese Suevi, Vandals, Ostrogoths, and Heruli. Many attempts to unite Europe have been made throughout the centuries. Popes tried to cement it together under the church. Before World War I, most of Europe's ruling families were related by intermarriage, but this too failed (Dan. 2:43). The prophecy said, "They shall not cleave one to another." And that is the way things have remained. Even today, hope flares for unification through the Common Market, and the Communists strive for domination of the area. But their plans also floundered on the rock of Bible prophecy.

How does God picture the final crumbling of all nations? The king of Babylon saw a stone that was cut out without human hands, which destroyed the image. It became like the chaff of the summer threshing floors, and the wind carried them away. Not a trace of them could be found. This stone represents a kingdom which will never be destroyed, and that is the Kingdom of God (Dan. 2:44). It has been told that this prophecy was once explained to Kaiser Wilhelm, King of Prussia and Emperor of Germany, at the height of his power and he said, "I can't accept it. It doesn't fit in with my plans!" Does it fit in with yours?

22. Fish Goes Jonahing

Christian liberals believe the story of Jonah was only an allegory and was never meant to be understood as actual history. Jonah was a real prophet and is mentioned in 2nd Kings 14:25. Christ accepted the account as true: "Jonah was inside the great fish for three days and three nights in the heart of the earth" (Jonah 1:17), "so shall the Son of man be three days and three nights in the heart of the earth" (Matt. 12:40). Scientists question whether a whale or shark—Greek and Hebrew word actually meaning a great aquatic animal—could actually swallow Jonah. Scripture says that the Lord provided a great fish and God is able! Some species of whales and sharks are capable of swallowing a man whole, but again the Bible does not say this great fish was either a whale or a shark. A whale can measure fifty feet long, and whole animals have been found in the stomachs of the sperm whale, the whale shark, and the white shark.

There are three theories as to whether a man could survive three days in the belly of a whale. Natural law: "Three days and three nights" in Hebrew usage simply means "three days," and two of them could have been partial days, or a period of thirty-eight hours. There is air inside the whale's stomach, and if the animal is swallowed alive, digestion would not have started in the thirty-eight hours. Miracle of God's Law: Remember, Jonah was running away from the mission God was sending him on, and boarded a ship. But as we all know from our own experiences, we cannot run away from the Lord. He sent a great storm and the sea was wrecking the ship that Jonah was on. After admitting to the seamen that the storm was his fault, Jonah told them to throw him overboard and the waters would become calm. "Then they took Jonah and threw him overboard and the raging sea grew calm. At this the men feared the Lord" (Jonah 1:15). Compare to the centurion (Mark 15:39). I see two miracles here in Jonah. God saved Jonah and revealed Himself to the seamen, who now made vows to Him. Some commentaries speculate that Jonah actually suffocated and died inside the great fish and was resurrected in three days as prophetic sign of the Christ's death and resurrection (Matt. 12:39-40). "From the depths of the grave Jonah cried out to God," and from the cross, Jesus cried out to His Father (Matt. 27:46). Jonah prayed from within the belly of the fish, and Jesus prayed in the Garden of Gethsemane. Seaweed was wrapped around Jonah's head and Jesus wore a crown of thorns. After rising out of the depths of the pit, Jonah preached, and Jesus, after being raised up from the depths of the pit, appeared and spoke to His followers.

Jonah likened his circumstances to a pit. The word *Shachath*, translated as pit, figuratively means "grave" or "destruction," and is nearly synonymous with *Sheol*, the word for the dead used in Jonah 2:2. But *Shachath* also has the nuance of a pit used to catch wild animals. David said that evil men dug a pit for him, and a pit was said to be dug for capturing the wicked. The wicked were described as falling into a pit of their own making. Here we have the image of Jonah as a wild animal captured by God in a trap of his own making. He was a prisoner! Joseph's experience in Genesis when thrown into a pit because of jealousy and Jonah's experience act as types for Christ, who also entered into a pit when He was separated from the Father and cried out, why have you forsaken me? With Jonah as a type for the Hebrews, he foreshadowed the kingdom of Judah that was pictured as an animal caught in a pit taken into captivity to Babylon.

There are accounts of many being resurrected in both the Old and the New Testament, but only one, Jesus, rose to life eternal. The widow's son (1 Kings 18:21), Shunammite's son (2 Kings 4:18-37), the Moabite man (2 Kings 13:21), Jairus's daughter (Matt. 9:18-25), and who can forget Lazarus (John 11:43-44)? All of these were temporary resurrections, and all had to die again to enter the eternal life with Jesus.

For such a little, short book in the Bible, Jonah has received more than its share of controversy, doubt, and revised stories. The scripture states that the Lord created a great fish to swallow up Jonah. The Bible also states that we are not to add or take away from what if written in this book (Rev. 22:18-10). As for me, I chose to go with the written Word of God, and believe that that big fish did indeed swallow Jonah. "Choose this day whom you will serve, but as for me and my house we will serve the Lord!" (Jos. 25:15)

23. Joshua's Successor

The first appearance of Joshua in the Bible is in Exodus 17:9, when the Israelites are attacked by the Amalekites. And Moses said to Joshua, "Choose some of our men and go out to fight the Amalekites." Joshua led the counterattack, defeated the enemy, and subsequently became Moses's assistant and protégé. It is believed that Joshua was not involved in the sin of the golden calf, but waited at the edge of the mountain, Sinai, for Moses to descend. Moses, as you recall, would not enter the Promised Land, so he asked the Lord for one to lead the people, so that they would not be like sheep without a shepherd (Num. 27:15-17). The Lord chose Joshua, son of Nun, a man in whom was the spirit and Moses laid his hands on him and commissioned him as the Lord instructed. Moses, the servant of the Lord, died there in Moab, as the Lord had said. The Lord buried him in Moab in the valley opposite Beth Peor, but no one to this day knows where the grave is. No one has ever shown the mighty power or performed the awesome deeds that Moses did in the sight of all of Israel. After the death of Moses, God talked to Joshua and told him to get all the people ready to cross over the Jordan River into the land He was about to give them. Joshua, son of Nun, was filled with the spirit of wisdom, because Moses had laid his hands on him. So the Israelites listened to him and did what the Lord had commanded Moses.

Joshua's charisma and skill as a leader were evident from the success of the Israelites during his lifetime and their rapid decline following his death. While Moses was primarily a spiritual leader who acted as an intermediary between God and the Jews, Joshua was a capable military commander as well as a religious leader. His leadership was quite different from that of Moses's, as shown by his capture of the city of Jericho and eventually the rest of the land of Canaan. We need to put emphasis on the role of God in this leader's victories. In the battle of Gibeon, the Amorites were winning and the day was fading. Joshua prayed to the Lord in the presence of Israel: "O sun, stand still over Gibeon, O moon, over the Valley of Aijaion." So as the scripture states, God stilled the sun until the nation avenged itself on its enemies (Job 10:12-14). Surely the Lord was fighting for Israel! Moses performed many more signs and wonders than Joshua, although Joshua's miracle concerning the sun and moon was without comparison. He served as administrator of the allotment of the land to the tribes, and when they had finished dividing the land into its allotted portions, the Israelites gave Joshua an inheritance among them as the Lord had commanded.

Joshua, unlike Moses, did not appoint a successor as his death approached. Seventeen years from the death of Joshua to the first judge, the elders filled the role of leader, and the Israelites served the Lord. After all the elders died, the nation abandoned God, lived together with the land's previous inhabitants, and allowed themselves to be swayed by their neighbors' pagan belief. The Israelites asked the Lord who would be the first to go up and fight for them against the Canaanites. Am I the only one to notice that these people do nothing for themselves? Makes one wonder if Paul had studied the reports of Moses and Joshua, and had the Israelites of old in mind when writing Hebrews 5:12-13, "you need someone to teach you the elementary rules of God!" After Joshua's death and the death of all the remaining elders, the Israelites were on their own. Now you would think they would have learned something after forty years of training in the wilderness. After all, some of us have lived as adults forty years, and we have learned to obey the Lord completely, right? I will give some of you a minute to take another stab at this answer, as I feel some were not exactly truthful. Not until Samuel's reign hundreds of years later did the Israelites find a compatible leader. The entire book of Judges is a cycle of the people sinning, being oppressed by neighboring countries, being saved by a leader, rededicating themselves to God, and starting the cycle over by committing the same sins. It was not until the founding of the Davidic Dynasty that the nation had a permanent leadership again.

The Lord answered the question of who would lead; "Judah is to go; I have given the land into their hands" (Jud. 1:2). So the men of Judah gathered the people and the bloody battles begin. They slaughtered, mangled, and terrorized everyone in their path. They attacked and set fire to the cities. They traded daughters for the capture of the opposing leaders. The Lord was with the men of Judah, and they took possession of the cities, the surrounding territories, and the hill country. The people they could not drive out, they made slaves of and confined some to the hill country, not allowing them to come down onto the plain. All of this is recorded in one short chapter of Judges (1:1-36). The angel of the Lord spoke to the Israelites, reminding them how they were brought out of Egypt and given the Promised Land. The Lord had not broken His covenant, but the Israelites had by not breaking down the altars of the idol worshipers. The people had served the Lord throughout the lifetime of Joshua and of the elders who outlived him and who had seen the great things the Lord had done for Israel. Now that this entire generation had died, another generation grew up who knew neither the Lord nor what He had done for Israel. They forsook the Lord, followed and worshiped various gods of the people around them, and in His anger, the Lord turned His hand against them. They were in great distress (Jud. 2:15).

Once again, as so many times before, the Lord felt compassion for the Israelites, and raised up judges who saved them out of the hands of raiders. The Lord was always with the judges He raised up to save them for as long as the judge lived. However, when the judge would die, the people immediately turned back to their corrupt ways. There are continuous repeated phases in the plights of the Israelites. They continued to sin, this angered God, they were defeated, they cried out to God, God relented and saved them, once again they did evil in the eyes of the Lord, and again God saw to their defeat. They went through judges like I go through a six-pack of Cokes. Who in their right mind would want to be a judge in this time? They did not all die of natural causes (Judges 3:21-22)! In Judges chapter 6, it appears that God had run out of patience or judges, because He sends Gideon, a prophet. Gideon argued with the Lord, saying that his clan was the weakest in Manasseh, and he the least in his family. The Lord assured Gideon He would be with him, but still Gideon requested a sign, and the Lord complied with fire from heaven, consuming the meat and bread Gideon had prepared for an offering. I do not know about you, but this would have convinced me that God was talking and in total control. Not Gideon! He asked for two more signs: the wool fleece and the other side of the wool fleece (Jud. 6:17-22, 6:37, 39). God patiently honored all of his requests, but sort of got back at Gideon by reducing his army down to 300 men, showing His power with unique strategic operations. Gideon was very brave and fearless in the face of the enemy, and the Israelites said to him, "Rule over us, you, your son, and your grandson" (Jud. 8:22). He refused, and for a while, he seemed to be on the right track when he told them that "the Lord will rule over you." Although the land enjoyed peace the forty years Gideon was in leadership, he fell victim to the golden idol he made from his share of the plunder.

When we hear the name Samson, we usually think of the folktales about a local hero with great strength, tearing apart lions with his bare hands (Jud. 14:6), harassing the Philistine men to humiliation (Jud. 14:12-14) and then in a fit of anger, killing thirty of them (14:19), and thousands more later in the story, and charming the Philistine women. However, the Bible dictionary calls Samson the last of the great judges, who led pre-monarchic Israel. Samson does not follow military rules, but acts alone in his personal vendetta. Samson is the only judge whom Yahweh is said to bless, and grants him his last request. The Philistines blind, shackle, and imprison Samson, finally forcing him to dance for them in the temple of Dagon, their god. Once again, betrayal and seeming defeat became the occasion for Samson to destroy his enemy. Samson, praying for vengeance, pulls the temple down. "Those he killed in his death were more than those he killed during his life" (Jud. 16:25-30). The book of Judges ends with these dreadful words: "In those days Israel had no king and everyone did as he saw fit" (Jud. 21:25).

To answer the original question as to who succeeded Joshua the answer would have to be a very patient, frustrated God. Why do you think the Israelites needed someone to see and touch at every moment? Why do you think we need someone to see and touch? We are told that we see Jesus in others, but do we? Do others see Jesus in me and you? God, realizing that the Israelites needed someone to touch, continued to provide leaders for them in the forms of judges, prophets, and even angels. He provided us with preachers, teachers, pastors, missionaries, and volumes upon volumes of literature. Do we act like the Israelites and fall back into sin every time something goes wrong in our lives? Do we as church members scatter when our pastor moves on to another place or retires? Do we hold each other up and encourage one another or do we fight among ourselves? I am not accusing or judging! Just wondering if there is anyone out there besides myself who needs self-examination! Anyone who needs to cowboy up and get back in the race for God! He will be the successor when our life here on earth ends. I do not want to get caught idol worshiping or being idle, do you?

24. Opposites Attract

Once, long ago in the land of Moab, lived a young girl named Ruth. The Moabite territory was located on a high plateau immediately east of the Dead Sea. The landscape was gently rolling, sparsely wooded tableland and was cut into small segments by extensive wadi systems or canyons. The Bible records regular interaction, often hostile, between Moab and the Israelites, from the time of Moses and Ruth into the Persian period. Most of these contacts were hostile, from the Hebrew migration through the reigns of Saul and David. Moabite religion was polytheistic, but the god Chemise was almost certainly viewed as a national god. According to scripture, the Moabites were known as the people of *Chemosh*. Chemosh's demand that Moab's enemies be killed in his honor is virtually identical to the Hebrews' notion of sacred warfare, which was often commanded by Yahweh. Moses detailed the somber story of the nation of Moab's origin in Genesis 19:30-38. Lot's two daughters, in faithless irresponsibility, got their father drunk and slept with him, and the fruits of their incest were Moab and Ben-Ammi. These sons became the founders of the Moabites and the Ammonites.

There lived in Judah in the town of Bethlehem a man named Elimelech and his wife Naomi. There was a famine in the land, so Elimelech moved his wife and two sons to the country of Moab. While there, the sons married Moabite women Orpah and Ruth. After about ten years, Elimelech and both of his sons died, leaving Naomi alone with her daughters-in-law. Naomi heard that the Lord had come to the aid of her country and decided to return home. She insisted her daughters-in-law stay with their families in their own land, saying she was unable to have more sons for them to marry and raise families, and Orpah agreed. Ruth clung to Naomi and vowed that where Naomi went, she would go and that Naomi's people would be her people and her God Ruth's God. Naomi insisted three times that Ruth stay in her homeland, knowing the influence of the pagan gods, but putting more importance on Ruth having a husband. Naomi did not make it easy for Ruth to come to faith in the God of Israel. When Ruth invoked God's name in her commitment to her mother-in-law, Naomi then stopped urging her to go home, and allowed her to return to Judah with her. However, there is no mention of Naomi welcoming her to the fold of those who trusted in Israel's God. Ruth had leapt by faith the barriers that had been thrown up before her.

Boaz was a wealthy relative of the family of Elimelech and Naomi, owner of fields near Bethlehem. Boaz is the son of Salmon, and his mother was almost always referred to as Rahab, a harlot. It is almost as if her last name were "harlot." However, it was Rahab who dwelt on the wall of Jericho (Jos. 2:1). She successfully negotiated a contract that would save her life as well as her family members' and the two spies that Joshua had sent into the land of Jericho. Rahab told the spies that she had heard all about them and how the true God had given them all the land. Rahab told the two spies that they had heard about the true God and what He had done, and their hearts melted; scripture tells us that if you believe with your heart and confess with your mouth, you will be saved (Rom. 10:9). Was she saved? Well, God made sure she was mentioned in the genealogy of Jesus (Matt. 1:5) and also a woman of great faith (Heb. 11:31), so I believe He not only saved her physically but her soul as well, that day in Jericho.

Rahab's son Boaz became the protector of Naomi's foreign daughter-in-law Ruth, by ordering the workers of his fields not to harass her and to leave extra grain for her (Ruth 2:15-16), by instructing her in the preservation of her reputation, by publicly persuading Naomi's next of kin to relinquish his right to purchase land belonging to Elimelech, and by acquiring Ruth as his wife. Talk about opposites attract! Here are two people born and raised in different countries that were always at war with each other, serving different God and gods, and the real God brought them together through a series of bizarre circumstances to be the father and mother of Obed. Obed was the father of Jesse, the father of King David, a man after God's own heart, and ancestor of our Lord Jesus Christ (Matt. 1:2-16).

These kinds of things happen in the Bible, which excites me and gives me hope that God might use even me in His mighty, perfect plan. It encourages me in the fact that I have inherited an eternal home, regardless of my earthly heritage.

25. *Moses, the Lighter Side*

Remember from Genesis, Joseph was sold into Egypt by his brothers and became ruler over all of Egypt. He eventually brought all of his brothers to Egypt, and now it was time for him to die, and he promised his brothers that God would come to their aid and take them up out of the land to the land He promised on oath to Abraham, Isaac, and Jacob (Gen. 50:24). Now Joseph, his brothers, and all their kin had died, but through them, the Israelites were fruitful and multiplied greatly and became exceedingly numerous so that the land was filled with them. The king became nervous and fearful that they would rise up against the Egyptians and take over the land, so he ordered extreme labor to destroy them, but to no avail.

New plan: Hebrew women were strong and had lots of babies. The Egyptian women were hoity-toity and did not want to ruin their figures. Also, do you remember the sweat you worked up during labor? And do you remember the makeup the Egyptian women wore in the movies? Can't you just see that black eye shadow running when they went into labor? Now the Bible does not say one word about makeup running or why the Egyptian women did not have as many babies as the Hebrew women. I just made that entire little story up to get your attention. Anyway, King Herod decided to kill all the Hebrew babies because the population was growing bigger than his and he was afraid they would overpower his kingdom. So death to all the babies born to the Hebrew women was ordered. The midwives feared God and did not kill the babies, and furthermore, they lied to the king, saying that the babies came so fast that they were born before they could get to the mothers. You see, they were supposed to kill them as they were coming out of the womb in the same manner as an abortion maybe?

Plan three: The king ordered that the baby girls live, but that all the baby boys must be thrown into the river. Moses was born to a Hebrew woman, and according to the law of the king, he was put into the river. With just a couple of changes made! First, the mother hid the baby boy for three months and nursed him; and second, she wrapped him in blankets and put him in a basket that would float downriver. Now, there are no accidents in God's plans! Moses did not just happen down the river at the same time that the king's daughter was taking her bath (Ex. 2:5). The Hebrew mother had picked up a daily newspaper at the local market and checked out when the princess went down to bathe. If she did not have the magazine, all she had to do was look for the paparazzi on the far banks of the Nile and she would know they were viewing some big event.

Big sister of Moses was following down the bank of the river to watch little Moses and make sure he got to his destination. When the king's daughter found the basket, she wanted to keep the baby but said aloud, "How would I feed him?" Big sister just happened to be there with a suggestion. She said she knew a Hebrew woman who could feed the baby Moses, so with the princess' permission she ran and got her and Moses's mother, and lo and behold, Mom did not have to give up her baby after all. Not only did she raise her own son in the palace in grand style, but it was Egypt's money that financed the man who would bring Egypt to their knees.

Moses killed a man and fled to the desert at age of forty, married and tended his father-in-law's sheep for forty years. Imagine living in a desert for forty years with your in-laws. Wow. We know from Psalm 23 that shepherds had to look for green pastures and lead the sheep there, and one day when Moses was checking out places for the sheep to graze, God showed up. There was a bush on fire that did not burn up (Ex. 3:1-32). Now where is the camera when you really need one?

When Moses was raised in the palace, he was very well educated and spoke very well, since he was raised a prince. Now, in the desert, when God told him what he was to do—go and talk Pharaoh into letting God's people go (Ex. 3:10)—Moses said, "But Lord, I cannot speak!" See what happens when you live in the desert without God for forty years? Well, God had a plan, and remember, there are no accidents in God's plans. Moses did bring the captives out of Egypt. Before Moses was born, God had a plan for him and He also has a plan for you and me. Aren't you glad you did not have to live eighty years before the plan was revealed? Or did you? By the way, how old are you now, and has God revealed his plan for your life yet? Are you still living in the desert? Then perhaps you need to look for the burning bush!

Moses answered the people: "Do not be afraid. Stand firm and you will see the deliverance the Lord will bring you today. The Egyptians you see today, you will never see again. The Lord will fight for you; you need only to be still" (Ex. 14:13-14).

26. Suddenly

After a long, strenuous day of doing nothing, I fell into bed and was instantly sound asleep. Around midnight, I was awakened suddenly! I waited for someone to come to mind that I should pray for or a scripture to loom before me that I could mull over in my mind, all to no avail. However, this one word, *suddenly*, was very strongly suggested and stayed with me for several days. Finally, giving attention the urgency pressing within me, I began to search the scriptures for the word *suddenly* and the relating instances of sudden actions. I was amazed at the quantity of God's sudden happenings and the results throughout the Bible.

The one we are all most familiar with is the Rapture or the catching up of the saints in the air to meet the Lord. Although the word *rapture* is not found in the Bible, it is commonly used in reference to the second coming when all will be resurrected. The word itself means to be caught up or taken away suddenly. "We who are still alive and are left will be caught up together with them in the clouds to meet the Lord in the air" (2 Thess. 4:17). "In a flash, in the twinkling of an eye, the dead will be raised imperishable, and we will all be changed" (1 Cor. 15:51-52). It has been determined that a twinkling of an eye is one-thousandth of a second, and I would call that suddenly.

Elisha, having been told repeatedly that his master, Elijah, would be taken from him (2 Kings 2:3, 5) stuck close to Elijah, not wanting to miss any of the blessings, teachings, or anointing that Elijah had to leave him. "As they were walking along and talking together, suddenly a chariot of fire and horses of fire appeared and separated the two of them, and Elijah went up to heaven in a whirlwind" (2 Kings 2:11). Judah was making alliances with other nations, and God was bringing judgment on them through the Babylonians, and He said it would be suddenly (Hab. 2:7). Any severe and prolonged pattern of sin practiced by people who claim to be devoted to God invites punishment from God. This was true in Judah, causing God to send Jeremiah the prophet. Jeremiah saw raging immorality, idolatry, hypocrisy, and priests who sold out to the highest bidder, and God brought destruction suddenly (Jer. 15:8).

The Spirit of God set Ezekiel in the middle of a valley of bones, comparing the dry bones to the house of Israel. Saying to Ezekiel, "prophesy to these bones and say to them, dry bones, hear the Word of the Lord" (Ezek. 37:4). So Ezekiel prophesied as the Lord told him and suddenly there was a noise, a rattling sound, and the bones came together and began to walk around.

David was anointed king three times before actually being accepted as king of Israel. Starting when he was a shepherd boy of about sixteen years of age to the age of thirty (1 Sam. 16:13; 2 Sam. 2:4; 1 Chr. 12:39). Does this remind you of some of your prayers that you may have prayed for five, ten, or more years? Then suddenly, you have the answer, just as suddenly David was king. "See, I will send my messenger who will prepare the way before me. Then suddenly, the Lord you are seeking will come to His temple, the messenger of the covenant who you desire will come" (Mal. 3:1).

There are numerous *suddenlys* in the New Testament. There is sudden deliverance when Jesus said to the woman that her sins were forgiven (Luke 7:48). I believe her sins were forgiven even before she said a word, before she was baptized, before she joined a church, before she asked anyone else to forgive her, before she made restitutions, and before she tried to reform. This woman who was evidently guilty of some of the worst sins came into the presence of Jesus and suddenly was convicted. He forgave her sins suddenly and instantly. The story of Philip and the eunuch holds two suddenlys. After Philip explained the scripture to him, he was forgiven suddenly on the spot, and just as suddenly, the Spirit of the Lord took Philip away (Acts 8:39).

How long id it take the thief on the cross to receive forgiveness for his sins? One minute, he was a thief on his way to hell, and the next minute, he was cleansed from sin and on his way with Jesus to Paradise (Luke 23:40-43). Some were set free of demons or evil spirits suddenly (Matt. 8:32). Blind Bartimaeus's eyes were opened suddenly (Mark 19:51-52), the deaf and mute man's ears were opened, his tongue was loosened, and he began to speak plainly (Mark 7:32-35). The woman with the issue of blood for twelve years was suddenly healed (Mark 5:34). On the day of Pentecost was the greatest *suddenly* of all history, when a sound like the blowing of a violent wind suddenly came from heaven and filled the whole house (Acts. 2:1-2). Suddenly, there was a violent earthquake, shaking loose the prison foundations, releasing Paul and Silas (Acts 16:25-26). When Saul, the prosecutor of Christians, was converted, "suddenly a light from heaven flashed around him" (Acts 9:1-19).

When baby Jesus was born, a great company of the heavenly host appeared suddenly (Luke 2:13). During the transfiguration of Jesus on the mountain, Moses and Elijah appeared suddenly and stood talking with Jesus (Matt. 17:1-3). When the disciples were in the boat, the sea suddenly stirred up a furious storm and then just as suddenly Jesus rebuked the wind and it was completely calm (Mark 4:34-39). Well, I could go on and on, but I sense that some of you have suddenly become bored with this word, so I will close with the most important sudden events that the Bible has to offer. "Behold I come quickly! And behold I come quickly and my reward is with me to give every man according as his works shall be. He who testified to these things says surely I come quickly!" (Rev. 22:7, 12, 20). Quickly, in a twinkling of an eye, suddenly He will be here!

27. Questions and Answers

Q: Shouldn't we try to make our own decisions independent of any supposed God?

A: First and most important, God is not supposed! He is very real! He was the beginning and He will be the end (John 1:1-2). Until you believe this and accept the Word of God, then nothing I say here will make a difference to you. Your most important decision here on earth is to believe that Christ is the Son of God (1 John 4:15), and call on the name of the Lord and be saved (Acts 2:21). Even this is dependent on God, since the Holy Spirit convicts you in order for you to be saved (John 16:8). There is only one independent free will in the universe, and that is the will of God. Most do not understand the intricacies that make up their decisions, and therefore convince themselves that their will is independent and the decisions are theirs alone. God can take a bad situation and make it good (Gen. 50:19-20), and man thinks he did it all on his own. God knows the end from the beginning (Isa. 46:10), therefore knowing all of your decisions and the outcome. God works in you to will and to act according to His good purpose (Phil. 2:13).

Q: What quality is of key importance in the life of a good steward?

A: Recognition of God's ownership is the very key in the understanding of good stewardship. Stewardship rest on the fundamental belief that God owns everything that exists. People are His servants, serving Him as stewards of what He chooses to let you have. All earthly wealth comes from Him. Stewardship is one test of our integrity to see if we act on our belief that God is Lord and owner of all (1 Chr. 29:11-16; Ps. 24:1; 1 Cor. 10:25-31). The second key of importance is attitude for only with the proper attitude of using your wealth will you glorify God (Prov. 28:20-22; Matt. 6:2-4; Acts 8:18-23; Rom. 13:18; 1 John 2:15).

Q: Is it ever okay to tell a child he is not allowed to come to church?

A: Never! The only reason I can think of where this statement would be made is if the child is too young to be in the congregation during the service. Most churches provide nursery care for this age group. Jesus said, "Let the little children come to me and do not hinder them for the Kingdom of Heaven belongs to such as these" (Matt. 19:14, 18:1-6, 21:16).

Q: Does God use unbelievers to bring about His will?

A: God used unbelievers continuously in the Old Testament to bring about His will. "Whatever the Lord pleases He does" (Ps. 135:6). The earth is the Lord's and He can do all things with anyone He chooses (Col. 1:16; 1 Cor. 10:26, 24:1). "Surely as I have planned so it will be" (Isa. 14:24). He works out everything according to His will (Eph 1:11). If this plan includes using unbelievers, then He will definitely use them to His glory (Rom. 8:28).

Q: I want to research people in the Bible who partnered in ministry. How many partnerships were there?

A: Elijah and Elisha (1 Kings 19:16, 19:21), Moses and Aaron (Ex. 7:1-7), David and King Saul (1 Sam. 16:19-22), Samuel and Eli (1 Sam. 3:1-21), Peter and John (Acts 4:1), Philip and the Ethiopian (Acts 8:26),

Priscilla and Aquila (Acts 18:26), Barnabas and Saul (Acts 11:25-26), Paul and Timothy (Phil. 1:1), just to name a few.

Q: Since Peter had betrayed God, why did He choose Peter to be the leader of His Church?

A: The first disciple to acknowledge that Jesus was the Christ was Peter (Matt. 16:15-16). It was obvious that Peter never intended to deny Christ (Matt. 26:35), but was spontaneous and uttered out of fear in a moment of weakness (Matt. 26:69-74). His repentance showed that the Holy Spirit was able to work in his heart and change him (Ps. 51:17). The difference in the way God treats sin in any person's life is always repentance.

Part IX Listen Up

1. Are Christians Sleeping on the Job?

The book of Jonah is more than a fascinating account of one man's futile attempt to run away from God. It is a story of God's love for even the most unlovable, despicable people we can imagine and our responsibility to tell them the Good News. The book is about the call of Jonah and his attempto manipulate God. His path was a downward one, just as all disobedience to God can only lead downward. Jonah was the only believer in the True God on board this storm-swept ship, and had a responsibility to be light for God. However, since he was fast asleep from exhaustion brought about from running from God, his light was not shining. The storm was all around, and the heathen mariners called out to their false god to no avail. Everyone on board needed the help of the one true God, yet the only one who could have made a difference was sound asleep. The conditions of this world are no different from those aboard that ship. The world is engulfed in a great storm, people are perishing and looking for answers to life's questions, but the Christians are sound asleep. Notice in Jonah 1:8, the sailors asked Jonah what his job was! If you listen carefully, you might hear the world ask you the same question. What is your job? The answer may be found in Ezekiel 3:18: "When I say to the wicked, you will surely die, you must warn them so they may live. If you do not speak out to warn the wicked to stop their evil ways, they will die in their sin. But I will hold you responsible for their death."

One of the last things that Jesus told Christians to do here on earth was to go! Now many of us go, but we do not carry anything with us. Take the Word of God with you and make followers of each and everyone you meet. Teach them to obey everything that Jesus has taught you through His Word. Do you understand where God is sending you to tell others about Him? Maybe you will not have to travel far, to a family member, next door, co-worker, or maybe just to give the Christian sleeping next to you a nudge! The world may not act like it, but they want a living, praying, serving, wide-awake church and a Christian friend. You are their light, and your life should reflect good things, so that the ones who are around you will give praise to the Father in heaven (Matt. 5:14-16). Remember the little song you learned as a child called, "This Little Light of Mine?" Jesus was born as the light that would shine on those who live in this dark, sinful world, in the shadow of death. It will guide us into the path of peace (Luke 1:79). Paul expressed a passion for the unsaved and wrote about patience and encouragement and the love we should have for our neighbors (Rom. 15:1-8). He admonished believers to wake up from their sleep, because we are living in an important time (Rom. 13:11-14). When is the last time you let your light shine? God uses us to spread His knowledge everywhere like a sweet-smelling perfume (2 Cor. 2:14); we should share with those we love (2 Thess. 2:8), and we should always be ready to answer everyone who asks about our Lord and Savior (1 Pet. 3:15-16).

The sailors asked Jonah where he came from, and with a "boy, am I ever ashamed of myself" attitude, he admitted that he was a child of God from the Promised Land of God. The scripture does not say that he was embarrassed, but it would be hard to stand up for God after you have just blown your testimony. They knew he was running away from God in total disobedience (Jonah 1:10). As Christians, we must never allow ourselves to forget who we are and what we have been called to do, which is to speak for Christ (2 Cor. 5:20), preach Christ to each person (Col. 1:28), using the gifts given by God through the Holy Spirit (Eph. 4:11-13). In the Parable of the Ten Virgins, Jesus compared the Kingdom of Heaven to the ten virgins who fell asleep while waiting for the bridegroom (Matt. 25:5). When the bridegroom comes (Rev. 19:7), we do not dare sleep, but do we dare sleep when we are supposed to be living in the light (Eph. 5:8-14)? Jesus said to occupy until I come (Luke 19:13), but this does not mean to occupy a seat or a pew in the church. The dictionary definition of the word "occupy" is to dwell in, take up space, or to employ yourself. The Biblical definition is to do business or to work, put to work your talents and gifts that God has provided you and to buy and sell, meaning to get a return or increase, as in to further the Kingdom of God.

Jonah was asked where he came from and from what people was he. Have you been asked similar questions? What church do you attend and where do you go to church? If you are running away in disobedience to God, can you truly answer that you are in the Body of Christ (1 Cor. 12:13)? Has your disobedience or uncaring attitude caused your testament to become silent, causing others to ask not what church you attend but rather if you attend? That's gotta hurt! Like Jonah, our citizenship is the Promised Land (Phil. 3:20) and we eagerly await the Savior to come and transport us home. It is by grace we were saved, by the blood of Jesus, and we ought to match up with our bloodlines. Although we cannot and were not saved by our works, we were created to do good works, which God prepared in advance for us to do (Eph. 2:10). It is hard to read the Word of God to find our purpose with our eyes closed.

Notice when God sends us to witness, He has the person prepared to receive His message. Before He sent Jonah to Nineveh, He sent two plagues of famine and floods and a total eclipse of the sun. These were considered signs of divine anger and may help explain why the Ninevites responded so readily to Jonah's message after rejecting others. The sad truth is that the world would prefer that we and God leave them alone.

There will be a day, however, when they will point an accusing finger at us and demand to know why we slept while they perished. We need not only to wake up but to get an urgency to speak to the lost, for the day is coming when we will no longer be able to work (John 9:4). Jonah did not like the Assyrians in Nineveh! He knew if he preached to them, they would have the opportunity to avoid God's wrath. Jonah actually wanted to see God punish his enemies. One of the marks of a true prophet was that his prophecies always came true (Deut. 18:20-22). Jonah had said that the Ninevites would be overthrown, and if this did not happen, then Jonah would be looked upon as a false prophet. His fellow Jews would be mad at him for preaching a message that brought salvation to their enemies. Before we judge Jonah too much, maybe we need to look at our own lives and examine how we respond to the Lord working out His will in our lives. Are we angry when God goes against our plan for reaching or not reaching someone? If you are harboring thoughts of such as these, beware! You may end up in the belly of a big fish!

Upon finding that Jonah was the one causing the storm at sea, the sailors asked him what they should do with him. Jonah gallantly said to just pick him up and throw him into the sea! I kind of stumbled over this scripture a bit, not quite understanding. If Jonah was convinced he was the cause of the storm, why then did he not just fling himself overboard? Why did he put the burden on someone else's shoulders? Then I realized that this plan of action would cause the shipmates to call on the name of God for mercy (1:14)! Even in the midst of our disobedience, running from our responsibilities and sleeping on the job. Jesus saves!

2. Bringing Down the Walls

God had promised the Children of Israel a land that flowed with milk and honey, but between them and the fulfillment of God's promise and God's plan and God's provisions for their life was mighty Jericho. Jericho was strong and powerful, with walls all around it representing possibly the problem in your life. It is said that the walls around Jericho were fifty feet high and fifty feet wide, representing the devil. It looked like a city that could not be conquered; the devil would have you believe that you cannot conquer him. He would have you stay away from the fulfillment of God's promises for your life. The devil will see to it that there is some great wall or obstacle between you and the plan God has for you (John 10:10). Your life through Jesus and by faith can be victorious (Phil. 4:13).

I do not know what walls you are facing. If it is a family problem, financial problem, an unhappy marriage, unholy life, unhealthy body, unfulfilled dream, or unrecognized potentiality, remember, "For I know the plans I have for you, declares the Lord, plans to prosper you and not to harm you" (Jer. 29:11-14).

Joshua might have been looking at Jericho and trying to figure out what his next move was going to be. He was looking at the problem instead of the protector. God told Joshua exactly what to do to capture Jericho, but Joshua was thinking about it. While he was thinking, along came God! "Now when Joshua was near Jericho, he looked up and saw a man standing in front of him with a drawn sword in his hand. Joshua went up to him and asked, are you for us or for our enemies? Neither, he replied, but as commander of the army of the Lord" (Jos. 5:13-15). Speaking in plain English, his reply was, I have come to take over! When God shows up, He does not take sides but He takes over. He takes over your problem and tears down walls. Then Joshua fell down on his face to worship God. True faith will worship God, even though there is a wall standing between you and what God has promised for your life. Your faith will be challenged and put to the test (Job 2:8-12).

Jericho was shut up so no one could get in and no one could get out. The devil's plan is to keep people locked out from God's promises and to keep others locked into Satan's bondage. There are some who believe they do not deserve God's blessings, and there are others who find the walls safe and secure. They have been hurt by someone, so they built a wall to keep people out of their lives, for fear of being hurt anew. The devil has convinced them they cannot go outside the walls and that you cannot have God's blessings. The devil is a liar (John 8:44) and the blessings of God are yours (1 Cor. 2:9). The only way to conquer the Jericho walls in our life is God's way, and that is by faith in the Lord Jesus Christ. By faith, the walls of Jericho fell down (Heb. 11:30). Do not lose heart (Gal. 6:9-9).

Do you wonder why Joshua instructed the people to not say anything until the day the command was given to shout? Why couldn't they talk to each other while walking around the wall? I think the answer is because it takes only a few negative people or complainers to discourage the whole bunch (1 Cor. 15:33; Prov. 10:14). You need to have patience to wait on the Lord; just had to remind you of this, because you get strength from patience (Heb. 10:36; Isa. 40:31).

The last part of Joshua 6:16 says, "Shout! For God has given you the city." Notice at this time, the walls are still standing, yet God said they had the city! The walls only fell after the people shouted or better yet, obeyed the Lord's command. Maybe that is why people have not had a breakthrough. They forget to shout! Some might say that they will shout when the walls fall or when they see results of their prayer. Psalm 47 tells us to clap our hands and shout unto the Lord God, and Psalm 5 tells us to ever shout for joy because we put our trust in the Lord, not just because He does what we want every time we want it.

Prayers are answered through faith (Rom. 10:8) and faith comes by hearing the Word of God (Rom. 10:17). Joshua did not just decide there was something he wanted and therefore, he would believe for it. That is not faith! Faith is not just cooking up something you wish and believing God for it. Faith is simply agreeing with the Word of God for what He has promised you. God will speak to you through His Word, so we need to be reading the Bible daily and worship God and wait upon Him, so you can hear what He is saying to you and what His plans are for your life. We all need to reach into God's Word of faith and shout the victory, even though it may seem like nothing has changed. God's timing is not like ours. Victory is His, and ours is coming!

3. Discipleship

I was born and raised in a tiny Texas town and never strayed very far from the boundaries of the Lone Star State. I gave my heart to Jesus at the age of ten, understanding this was my passage to heaven. I knew that if I confessed with my mouth that Jesus was the Lord and believed it in my heart that God raised Him from the dead that I would be saved (Rom. 10:9-10). However, at this young age, I did not understand Matthew 22:37: "love the Lord your God with your entire mind." I knew my soul had been saved but was not sure exactly what my soul was or where it was located. I did not know if it was a part of my physical body or floating along outside of my body. Now I knew what my heart was and where, and what functions it performed. I also knew this was the only part of a teenage body you gave to your boyfriend I the 1950s! As far as the mind, well, that had to be on school studies, dress code, makeup, and dealing with peer pressure, didn't it! It took years for me to realize that God looks at the heart of a man (1 Sam. 16:7), searches every heart (1 Chr. 28:9), and can create in each a pure heart (Ps. 51:10). I learned to hide His Word in my heart (Ps. 119:11), to allow God to search me and know what was in my heart (Ps. 139:23), and to seek Him in order that I might find Him (Jer. 29:13). Only then would He give me a new heart (Ezek. 36:26) and I would be blessed (Matt.5:8).

For you who are on the edge of your chair waiting for all the dirt in my life to spill out over your computer, or for you who are becoming bored with my personal testimony, set your mind at ease. My long, sad life history is not the main topic of this story. Instead, I will turn to an appeal to all Christians to become disciples. Discipleship is a major step in the new believer's life that is neglected in most groups. We are all faithful to go and witness, tell the good news, and bring people to church, Bible study, programs, revivals, and whatever it takes to get people saved. When a person is saved, we rejoice, clap our hands, pat each other on the back for a job well done, shed a few tears, and say hallelujah! Then we go our separate ways with a warm feeling that God is pleased that we have aided in the building of His Kingdom. Of course, He is pleased, but can you imagine His displeasure when we leave the new believer to work out his own answers to the million questions he must have? For some, without proper guidance, it could take a lifetime. For others, the warm glow of salvation waxes cold and they think, is that all there is? Many drift back into the world in search of the friends and fellowship they gave up to become a Christian, simply because the fellowship among their new church body is lacking. But we say, "I told them to ask me anything and I would find scripture to answer the questions!" We must understand that if one does not know the scripture, then they do not know any questions. "And how can they hear without someone preaching to them?" (Rom. 10:14)

Many new Christians have never been inside a church and probably do not own a Bible. Take them on a tour, starting with where to park not only their cars but themselves inside the building. Remember, in some churches, there are longtime members who have reserved pews marked as their territory, and do not want it invaded. How humiliating and discouraging would this be if a first-time person wandered into this forbidden zone? Those set in their ways cannot be budged; however, we can save a newcomer from the embarrassment of their inconsideration. If your church offers Sunday school or Bible study classes, bring them, do not point the way, to the class and introduce them. I strongly believe there is a pressing need for a beginners' Bible class, regardless of the beginner's age in every congregation. It may be a surprise to learn that new believers do not know where to find the index of the books of the Bible so they may find where the preacher is reading his sermon. Explain how to use the concordance, a valuable tool for any Bible study. Some are not comfortable in church and may say they will never attend. Do not push, bager or condemn! Have a get-acquainted party, ask them to your home, or ask if you may come into theirs to read and study the Bible to come to an understanding of God and His Word. Plan weekly small-group Bible studies for new members and mature ones, so that you may have a balance in the studies. Do not wait for a crowd! If there is only one who needs disciplining, then plan for this one as you would a hundred. Remember, this is not for your glory but for the glory of God. Abraham pleaded for Sodom to be spared for the sake of fifty righteous people. He had to continue to lower the figure to forty-five, forty, thirty, and twenty, and finally down to ten. Sadly, there were none righteous for which to save the city; however, Lot was spared and dragged out of the city by angels (Gen. 16:33, 19:15-16). Is God depending on you to save a city or one newborn Christian?

As mature members of the body of Christ, we are now designated teachers, servants of Jesus Christ (Jude 1). As the Lord's servants, we must be able to teach and gently instruct (2 Tim. 2:24-25). Be prepared at all times to correct, rebuke, and encourage with great patience and careful instructions (2 Tim. 4:1-5). We devote ourselves and pray that God may open a door for our message of the gospel, that we might proclaim it clearly. Be wise and make the most of every opportunity, full of grace and seasoned with salt so that we may know how to answer everyone (Col. 4:2-6). There is one body, one God, who is over all, and He has given us gifts through which we teach, to prepare God's people for the works of service, so the body of Christ may be built up. Then no one will remain infants, but grow up into Christ (Eph. 4:4-16).

Paul was relating his story to King Agrippa about a bright light and a voice stopping him on his way to Damascus. The voice said He was sending Paul to people to open their eyes and turn them from darkness (Acts 26:12-18). Granted, this message is so that people might be saved, but applies also in discipleship. We need to be continuously turned away from darkness, that we may continue to walk in the light. We should teach that all have sinned and fall short (Rom. 3:23), but there is rejoicing in the presence of the angels over one repentant sinner (Luke 15:10). Repentance is not a one-time occurrence, but an ongoing, lifetime experience, wherein we continue to work out our salvation with fear and trembling (Phil. 2:12-13). When a believer is baptized, the pastor usually says we are baptized in the name of the Father, the Son, and the Holy Spirit. We should teach a new person who the Holy Spirit is! He helps in our prayers, worship, witness, and work. He will make our sins known to us, so we may confess them. He will make us know and experience God's presence. He strengthens us in our weakness and comforts us in our troubles (Rom 6:25-27; Gal. 4:6; Eph. 6:18; John 14:15-17).

People need a role model, particularly when they find themselves in a new environment. Jesus showed us an ethic of imitations as He washed His disciples' feet (John 13:1-17). He called us to follow His example, so others will learn from our actions and experiences. Share your testimony of when you were saved and how, what, who helped you to learn and grow. Help the person ask, what does the Bible say about this matter? Together, study the scripture teaching on the subject. Be prepared! Have pamphlets, books, articles, and a good concordance to help find what you need quickly. Avoid two traps while disciplining the new member. Do not dismiss a person needing further help without referring them to another helper. Do not openly or unconsciously invite the person to become dependent on you. However, leave the door open and never make the person feel cut off or abandoned. The church should provide training to learn to use the Bible, develop a personal testimony, and guide people to commit themselves to Christ. This would be good for mature Christians also, in some cases.

It is hard to sum up Paul's writings in ten easy steps, but if I were asked to do this, I would write: 1) Balance your life, 2) Do not make holy huddles, 3) Make a trail, 4) Meet needs, 5) Serve, 6) Bring gladness, 7) Listen, 8) Care, 9) Share, 10) Stick your neck out for someone. From my own personal experience, when you decide to take on disciplining someone, do not be surprised to find that you will be the one to learn new and wondrous revelations from God's Word. Look around! There is someone waiting for your help!

4. *Dangers of Drifting*

The story is told of two young men were fishing above a low dam on a river near their hometown. As they were concentrating on catching fish, they were unaware that they had drifted, until they were not far from the water flowing over the dam. When they realized their situation, the current near the dam had become too powerful for them to keep their boat from going over. Below the dam the water was dashing with strong force over great boulders and through crevices in the rocks. Caught by the swirling waters under the rocks, they never came to the surface.

Spiritual drifting is deadlier than physical drifting, for you face the danger of losing contact with God. Would you know if you were drifting? It requires no effort, you know. Fail to pray one day, and the next day it does not seem so important to pray every day. Daily Bible study becomes weekly Bible study, and we say that is a full schedule. "So we must be more careful to follow what we were taught. Then we will not stray [drift] away from the truth" (Heb. 2:1). It is possible to drift unaware, and the dangers increase as the flow of the backsliding spiral speeds up. When we can hear the noise of the waterfall, we are in trouble. Keeping up the pace of striving forward is continuous work and study of the Bible. We must constantly be adding to our faith (2 Pet. 1:5) and continue to grow (2 Pet. 3:18).

A drifting ship is a danger to all other vessels at sea. Drifting parents are losing opportunities to teach and train up their children (Eph. 6:4). "We must become like a mature person, growing until we become like Christ and have His perfection. Then we will no longer be babies. We will not be tossed about like a ship that the waves carry one way and then another" (Eph. 4:13-14). You may never know who is watching and patterning themselves after your example. If you stay faithful, they stay faithful. If you stray then they stray. We are warned in the Word of God to be careful of the freedom we take in doing things that do not cause someone to stumble, especially those who might be weak in the faith. We must make ourselves acceptable to God in every way that we possibly can, so that we do His work right and not be ashamed of not knowing His Word to present to others (2 Tim. 2:15). God chose us to be holy, because we are His and we are to be like Him. He also chose us to tell everyone the wonderful things He has done for us and what He will do for others who call on His name (1 Pet. 2:9).

Drifting causes us to neglect the gathering together of Christians and makes us stay away from church meetings. When we are not there, we cannot encourage one another, which is another strong suggestion from Paul (Heb. 10:25). If your body drifts, then you can be sure that your mind started it. "Set your mind on things above, and not on earthly things" (Col. 3:1). We must not drift into the presence of the wicked and listen to the garbage that they speak of, for fear that we might become calloused to the Word of God, which we should be thinking of night and day (Ps. 1:1-2). When someone asks you to go to the Lord's house, go with joy, for you are standing at God's gate. Edify one another daily, draw strength from each other and make godly friendships, for the wrong kind leads to sin (Ecc. 4:9-12). Keep the desire to share the gospel, so that our desire for worldly things will not come to mind and begin to increase, resulting in becoming lovers of pleasure more than lovers of God (2 Tim. 3:4). We live in a world with people who do not believe and will tell you that what you are doing is wrong or a waste of time (1 Pet. 2:11-12). Remember that if you cannot change their minds and bring them to the light, then stay away from them. Anchor your lives to Christ and the Word of God, keep your roots deep in Him, and have your lives built on Him (Col. 2:6-7). Anchor your minds to the truth, possessing an unshakable hope, and be rooted and grounded in the love of Jesus (Eph. 3:16-18).

If in any way we confess that we are drifting, then may we encourage one another to give heed as warned by the writer of Hebrews: "Therefore we must give the more earnest heed to the things we have heard, lest we drift away. For if the word spoken through angels proved steadfast and every transgression and disobedience received a just reward, how shall we escape if we neglect so great a salvation which at the first began to be spoken by the Lord, and was confirmed to us by those who heard Him (Heb. 2:1-3)? Our Salvation in Christ is too great for us to neglect!

5. Help or Hindrance?

The definition of help is to assist, aid, or to be useful. To hinder is to keep back, stop the process, impede, or to be an obstacle. Which one are you, in your fellowship with God? Does your helping God become a hindrance to God's plan? It sounds funny that anyone would think that God needs our help, however, we think that all the time. Anytime we have a delay in our plans, we are quick to pitch in to give God a hand. We ask God to find us a mate, and then hang around sin-stained locations and disregard God's standards of purity. We reach people through pressure when God does not work fast enough to get them to church. We even help God bring justice by sabotaging someone's reputation or career.

Even when things do not seem to be working, we must never underestimate God's power or ability. God told Abram that he would have a son of his own (Gen. 15:4). Later, Abram and Sarai looked at the cold, hard facts and decided that Sarai was past childbearing age, Abram was eighty-six years old, and it had been ten years since they had arrived in what was supposed to the land of Abraham's descendants. This is when Abram and Sarai put their heads together and concluded that God needed some help to fulfill His promise. They never considered the fact that God might do something extraordinary! They did not trust God's timing. I wonder how hard it would be to comprehend God's timing, if at the age of ninety-nine, God appeared and told you that a child would be born to you and your aging wife. If, in fact, I should live to be as old as Sarai, and God tells me I am going to have a son, I fear I would have the same reaction as Sarai: "she laughed" (Gen. 18:12). Our God is a forgiving God and a God of second chances and fresh starts. He not only gave

Sarai and Abram a son in their golden years, but also dubbed the couple Abraham, father of many nations and Sarah, kings of nations will come from her (Gen. 17:5, 15-16).

Now that we have been reminded of the good news about God's gift to Sarah and Abraham, let us go back a page and check out the consequences of not trusting God and making choices on your own. Sarai sent Abram to her slave girl to conceive a child, in order to build a family through her, since Sarai was so old. Abram, also wanting to help God—or giving in to his wife's domineering personality—did as she told him (Gen. 16:2). When we wander away from the Lord and make our own choices, perhaps through the influence of others, we always get into trouble, and the trouble was just beginning for Abram. The plan that Sarai made started tumbling down around their tents. "When Hagar learned she was pregnant, she began to treat her mistress, Sarai, badly. Then Sarai said to Abram, this is your fault. I gave my slave girl to you, and when she became pregnant, she began to treat me badly. Let the Lord decide who is right, you or me. But Abram said to Sarai, you are Hagar's mistress. Do anything you want to her. Then Sarai was hard on Hagar and Hagar ran away." Now I hope you can figure who was to blame for what from these scriptures. But is that not the way with life when things go wrong?

There are consequences to every decision we make. People are hurt, reputations are stained, and lives are changed, and usually not for the better. The marriage of Abraham and Sarah was affected. Every time Abraham was with Hagar, it wounded Sarah. It may have been her idea, but the thought of her husband being with another woman was more than she could bear. And when Hagar became pregnant, Sarah was eaten up with jealousy and resentment, and made her life miserable. Then Sarah's wrath was turned on Abraham and then God. She wants to know how you could do this to me. Abraham is confused! I am sure things were very tense around the tent of Abraham and Sarah. To ease the tension, Abraham abandons his responsibility to Hagar and tells

Sarah to do with her as she pleases, and threw up his hands and walked away. Hagar feels she needs to leave, and who wouldn't, since she can no longer stand the abuse from Sarah.

Hagar leaves because she feels she has no other choice, and takes Abraham's firstborn son with her. Things have become unbearable, and I am sure Hagar thinks she is the victim of a terrible decision on the part of her mistress, Sarai. Back in the Old Testament days, slave girls had no choice in these matters. I caution you not to use "I had no choice" as an excuse for your bad decisions today. Once Hagar was gone, the others in this story thought they would not have to face the consequences. They would simply forget her! But God does not forget Hagar! "The angel of the Lord found Hagar near a spring in the desert" (Gen. 16:7). God does not forget us either. We have all made foolish choices. We all carry scars as a consequence of times when we deserted the path God laid for us. But He still sees us! He still loves us and still reaches out to rescue us!

In the story of Abraham, Sarah, and Hagar, no one was willing to take responsibility for their actions. Sarah blames Hagar and Abraham; Abraham blames Sarah; Hagar blames Sarah and Abraham, and they probably all blame God. Few people take the blame for the choices in their lives readily. We blame our parents, genetic makeup, teachers, spouses, or the person who is holding up traffic in front of us. It matters not that we started out for our destination an hour late and could have avoided this traffic jam; we just reach out for someone to blame. It usually does not matter much who, just so it is not us, and if we find no one handy to blame, we just run.

Are you running from something today? Have you made a foolish choice and now feel God has deserted you? Do you feel like an outsider or a Hagar? Are you suffering from the sinful choices of another? Any mistake you have made can be forgiven. Any crisis you face can be survived with God's strength. Any difficulty can be used by God to make you stronger and to make your witness more effective. Stop running and return to God. Trust God's Word over your feelings. God sees what we do not see, so we need not make decisions without first asking Him about it. Be forewarned, the devil will tell you that you do not have time to pray, but that this matter needs immediate attention. He will tell you that God gave you a brain to make decisions on your own, and this one needs to be made right now or you will lose out on something. Take time to get all the information! Abraham and Sarah got into trouble because they thought they had all the information.

I do not want to encourage you to ever be negative; however, we need to look at both sides of the outcome of a choice. Consider who will be affected by the choices you make. Consider the pitfalls. Be patient and remember that we cannot rush God. God is able to deliver what He promises, but it will be in His timing, so stop helping God and start trusting Him. "Be still and know that I am God" (Ps. 46:10).

6. *Murky Waters?*

I took a short out-of-town trip this morning, and while surveying the landscape—eyes on the road, of course—I noticed the trees were covered with icy snow, but only on the very tops. This was a beautiful scene, but a closer look—eyes still on the road—revealed the winter-dead branches and trunks. On ground level, the standing water was frozen on the top with snow crystals dancing all over to give a shimmering effect that was dazzling. I knew, however, that underneath the misleading beauty lay murky waters. In the Bible, the tombs were painted white, and greenery and shrubbery were planted in the area to make the burial grounds more pleasing to the eye, but inside, we know there was nothing but rot and decay. Is your Christianity whitewashed? Do you have an aura of purity on the outside, but inside decaying from unconfessed sin, smoldering hatred, jealously, resentment, unresolved broken relationships, etc.?

Are the churches whitewashed? Jesus went to Jerusalem and found some whitewashed men in the temple selling cattle, sheep, and doves, and others sitting at tables exchanging money. He drove them all out of God's house with a homemade whip of cords, and their cattle and sheep with them. He scattered the coins of the money changers, and even overturned their tables (John 2:13-15). This was the custom, to sell animals for sacrifices and to change money to that accepted in the temple. People came from miles around to the temple, and it was impossible for them to bring their sacrificial animals with them such a long way, so they bought them at the outer courts. This system and custom was not what made Jesus angry. The whitewash and the underhanded methods that the marketers used was what riled Him. They were overcharging for the change of money, since most of the people probably knew nothing of the value of their coins compared to the ones used in the temple. Also, the sheep and other animals sold were not sacrificed after someone offered them to the priest, but taken out back, driven around to the front, and resold. It was the lies and the cheating inside His temple that caused the outrage. "How dare you turn my Father's House into a market" (John 2:16).

The supply of adequate drinking water and removal of polluted water are the two most fundamental needs of towns and cities, and without these services, cities rapidly become uninhabitable. Storm water runoff has become one of the largest sources of pollution to waterways, and one of the most difficult to control. Storms of life are the largest sources of pollution in the Christian world, and the most difficult to control. Jesus said, "In the world, you shall have tribulation" (John 16:33) and storms, but we must not give in to the pressure. We must not drown in the murky waters, but construct an altar from the debris left by the storm, and bow down and worship, and in all things give thanks (Eph. 5:20).

God will allow the storms to come into your life, perhaps to stir up the murky waters of your mind and spirit. Jesus told Peter that Satan had asked to sift him like wheat (Luke 22:31), and God allowed it, but all the while, Jesus was praying for Peter. The storm on the lake (Matt. 14:24-25) was what brought Jesus walking on the water. No storm lasts forever (Mark 4:35); they work together for the good of those who love the Lord (Rom. 8:28) and they do not compare to the glory that will be revealed to us when the storms are over (Rom. 8:18). God does not want you to grow stale and passive in your Christian walk and relationship with Him. Do not lie in the murky waters of laziness (Prov. 6:9) or be a wicked lazy servant (Matt. 25:26). Never lack in zeal (Rom. 12:11), show diligence and do not become lazy (Heb. 6:12) and never tire of doing what is right (Gal. 6:9; 2 Thess. 3:13).

We were not washed whiter than snow with murky waters, but with the cleansing water of the Word (Eph. 5:26-27), and our hearts are sprinkled to cleanse us from guilt, and our bodies are washed with pure water (Heb. 10:22). Revelation says there will be no more sea (murky waters) and that we may drink without cost from the spring of the water of life (Rev. 21:1, 6). When your storm threatens to bring murk into your life, soar above it (Isa. 40:31). An eagle knows when a storm is approaching long before it breaks. The eagle will fly to some high spot and wait for the winds to come, and when the storm hits, he sets his wings so that the wind will pick him up and lift him above the storm. While the storm rages below, the eagle is soaring above it. The eagle does not escape the storm, he simply uses the storm to lift him higher, and rises on the winds that bring the storm. You can too!

7. Apathy – Apostasy

Does apathy cause apostasy? Does apostasy feed off of apathy?

Apathy means an absence of emotion or enthusiasm. Spiritually, apathy results from fear of ridicule and hurt, lack of knowledge, excessive pride, denominationalism, and laziness. We are to warn those who are idle (1 Thess. 5:14). This is not a new-age happening. People, after seeing the Red Sea part, incredibly failed to exercise faith. People who saw miracles and saw prophecies miraculously come to pass, apathetically retuned to the worship of false gods. Have we laid down our calling as Christians? Is it not our job "to fan into flames the gift of God" (2 Tim. 1:6)? Thousands of ministry leaders were asked the top ten issues facing today's church, and number six was apathy. The seeming lack of personal interest, support, and enthusiasm from the pews for the work of the church is on the increase. You lose interest and the devil perks up! Ephesians 4:27 warns us not to give the devil a foothold as he is looking for someone at all times to lose interest in the Word of God, so that he might devour them (1 Pet. 5:8-9). The scripture from John 3:18 that says that whoever believes in Jesus is not condemned, but those who do not believe are already condemned, has at least three different wordings from various versions, obeyeth not, believeth not, rejects, all from the same root word as the English word apathy, *apeitheo*. There seems to be apathy toward things of God such as diligence, striving to teach everyone with all wisdom, and loving the Lord with everything in us, and our neighbors likewise. It is as if we are safe and headed for heaven, so why should we get all worked up over the lost, if that is their choice? Paul had a concern about this when he wrote that some were running a good race. Who cut in on you and kept you from obeying the truth? That kind of persuasion does not come from God, but the one who is causing the confusion will pay the penalty (Gal. 5:7-10). Ezekiel has already warned us that we are responsible for warning the wicked (Ezek. 33:8-9). The church has become mostly occupied with what God can do for them, rather than what we can do for God.

We live in a very self-centered society, and rarely do we see churches and believers laying aside all their interests to serve the Lord's interest. "But mark this; there will be terrible times in the last days. People will be lovers of themselves, lovers of money, boastful, proud, abusive, disobedient to their parents, ungrateful, unholy, without love, unforgiving, slanderous, without self-control, brutal, not lovers of the good, treacherous, rash, conceited, lovers of pleasure rather than lovers of God, having a form of godliness but denying its power" (2 Tim. 3:1-4). This is a long and disturbing list and we need to think seriously about removing this list from our Christian lives. The scripture is clear on our duty as a Christian to help bring people to salvation (2 Cor. 5:20). Statistics show that only a tiny percentage of Christians attempt to share their faith with others. "We are to God the aroma of Christ among those who are being saved and those who are perishing" (2 Cor. 2:15). Too many Christians are weak in the knees when it comes to standing up for what they believe the Word of God teaches. Christians do not stand up and say that homosexuality is wrong (Lev. 18:22), therefore, we allow our pastors to perform same-sex weddings. When we deny that the Word of the Lord is true, we are denying Christ, and there in turn, He will deny us (Matt. 10:33). We have allowed an attitude of spectatorship to develop in our pews, letting our minds wander, leaving church without fully understanding what we have heard. In this apathetic state, can we be sure we have heard the true gospel or apostasy?

The Greek word for apostasy means "a falling away, a withdrawal." Abandonment of one's religious faith, a political party, one's principles, or a cause. From the Greek word, *pathos*, meaning absence of feeling, interest, or concern. The scriptures say that this is letting go of the commands of God and holding on to the traditions of men (Mark 7:8-9). We are to "see to it that no one takes us captive through hollow and deceptive philosophy, which depends on human tradition and the basic principles of this world, rather than on Christ" (Col. 2:8). Being warned against this, Jesus assured us that it would happen, and said that many would turn from the faith and be deceived about His coming to earth again (2 Thess. 2:1-3; Matt. 24:10-11).

Forsaking the Lord was the recurring sin of the chosen people, and we need not be smug, as there are strong signs of the same today. Apostasy, a falling away, is not only in the churches, but wedding vows, political leaders, and our family units. Because of this, our love for God has grown cold. Some of the causes of apostasy are a lack of a genuine conversion, meaning that your soul is saved and not just your conscience. Some drop out of church or fall away from the faith because they lack a genuine Christian experience of grace. These people may have reasons; however, you need a clear conscience to serve God, and this is spoken of often in the scriptures (Heb. 13:18; Titus 1:15; 1 Tim. 1:3-7, 4:1-7). Paul instructed Timothy of conscience and sincere faith when speaking of the duties of worship, deacons, overseers, and warnings against false teachings. Lack of biblical knowledge can lead to apostasy.

It could be possible that some of the leaders in our churches have no wisdom of the Word of God. That is easily fixed through asking God, who gives wisdom generously to all who ask (James 1:5). He does not withhold His truth from us, but does tell us to test all spirits to see if they are from Him (1 John 4:1-3). We cannot be just pew fillers and stop apostasy or apathy from invading our churches. We each must learn to correctly handle the Word of God (2 Tim. 2:15). Those who fall away from Christ become apathetic and they are robbed of a useful life of service for God. The thief, Satan, will kill your desire to learn, steal your joy of God, and destroy your faith in Jesus if we allow apostasy to slither into our midst through apathy. There is a cure for both apostasy and apathy, but it will take time, commitment, and complete dedication to Jesus (Rom. 12:1-12; Heb. 12:1-2). Start reading the Word and hide it in your heart (Ps. 119:30), pray (Luke 18:1), seek the Lord (1 Chr. 16:11), fellowship with God's people (Prov. 13:20), and above all we must be obedient to God (Matt. 12:50). John the apostle wrote: "They went out from us but they were not of us, for if they had been of us, they would no doubt have continued with us" (1 John 2:19).

It requires no strength of character to quit or to give up your faith, or even to renounce your allegiance to Christ and His church. Anybody can quit except Jesus. He says He will never forsake us, and He is still standing at the door knocking (Rev. 2:1-4). He is asking which of us will help him out (Ps. 94:16) and He is still asking someone to stand in the gap (Ezek. 22:30). This could well be the gap between the lost and hell that God is asking you to stand in. Are we brave enough to say, "Here am I. Send me" (Isa. 6:8)? Or do we sit in our pew of apathy and let apostasy take over? Time is short! We need to make a decision now so that we might hear from God, "Well done my good and faithful servant!"

Polly Gwinn

8. Illegal Turn

A young mother was hurrying her eleven-year-old daughter to school and turned on a red light where it was prohibited. Realizing her mistake, she muttered, "Oh, no! I just made an illegal turn!" "It's all right," the daughter assured her. "The police car behind us did the same thing!"

All roads lead somewhere! This I know because, hate to admit this to all of you, I have been down most of them. The dusty country lanes and the fast tracks. My curiosity and sense of adventure won out over obedience for most of my years. I encountered dead ends and detours, washed-out bridges and deep pits where pavement used to be. The road to happiness was long and filled with disappointments, and all the while the rainbow's end eluded my touch. Seeing the array of colors on a faraway hill, I would hasten to the site, only to find thorny bushes and prickly wildflowers, rather than that sought-after bed of roses. The grass always appeared greener on the other side, but the fence I had to cross usually caught me in a snare. The book of Job talks about snares of the wicked man. "His feet thrust him into a net and he wanders into its mesh. A trap seizes him by the heel, a snare holds him fast. A noose is hidden for him on the ground; a trap lies in his path" (Job 18:8-11). Sounds like these traps were set from the beginning for the wicked, just as the plan of salvation was set from the beginning to save you from them. No matter the snares you have been caught in, there is hope through Jesus Christ. Not only are we warned about the snares, we are told how to avoid them: "Be always on the watch, and pray that you may be able to escape all that is about to happen" (Luke 21:36) and "be self-controlled and alert. Resist the devil and stand firm in the faith" (1 Pet. 5:8-10).

I was disobedient, headstrong and free-willed, not giving much thought to the consequences of my actions. I was unaware of the roaring lion that prowled, ready to devour me. Paul warned the Galatians not to fool themselves into thinking they could do wrong at no cost! "Do not be deceived, God cannot be mocked. A man reaps what he sows" (Gal. 6:7-

10). Again the good news is offered in Deuteronomy 4:29 telling us that if we seek the Lord we will find Him, return to Him, and find that He has not abandoned us. You may find sorrow on the wrong paths, which will lead you to repentance, and you will no longer want to dwell in sin. John the Baptist baptized for repentance, Jesus preached repentance, and the angels rejoice over repentance.

It is sinful human nature to take the illegal turns. Adam started it when he reached out to make a right turn signal and took the apple instead, although I have not found the word "apple" in the Bible, so maybe this was a fig or grape. Something to think about and research here. If you are of the male gender and reading this, you could determine that Eve changed the road sign. Perhaps she painted an apple over the detour sign, causing Adam to fall over the cliff of disgrace. Abraham was promised a son, but did not trust God's timing, so he made an illegal turn to Hagar's tent. Jesus tells us to be watchful of the signs (Matt. 24:42), making sure that no one, false prophets, has changed them (Matt. 7:15).

Paul, when known as Saul, was on the road to destroying every Christian he could find. He even asked for letters from the high priest to help find men or women who belonged to the Way in Damascus so that he might take them to prison (Acts 9:1-2). Now Saul was on the right road. Granted, he was going to Damascus for the wrong reasons, but on the way, he got enlightened, to say the least. A caution light appeared from heaven, and with it a traffic guard's voice, and Paul was blinded for three days. Jesus took the scales from Saul's eyes and he became Paul, the mighty speaker and apostle of Jesus. Sometimes we must be blinded to the world in order to see the light of Christ. Two of the disciples were sadly going down the dusty road to the village of Emmaus when the Risen Christ joined them. They were on the right road but going the wrong way! After Jesus walked and talked with them a ways, He opened their minds so they would recognize Him, and they turned, repented, and returned to Jerusalem with great joy (Luke 24:13-53). When you return to God, He will return you joy, and the oil of gladness will replace mourning (Isa. 61:3).

All roads lead somewhere, but not all roads lead to Jesus. You are playing Russian roulette with your soul if you are buying into the theory that we are all trying to get to the same place but on different paths and in different ways. Jesus said that there was only one way, and that was through Him, and the road to destruction was wide and easy to travel, but we must stay on the narrow road in order to have eternal life (John 14:6; Matt. 7:13-14). The psalmist knew that the road had to be light and that Jesus was the lamp and the source of light to guide our steps (Ps. 119:105), and John assured us that Christ is the light of the world. John the Baptist was sent to make the way straight for Jesus, and Christ came to make the way straight for you and me. This life He offers us includes a highway that is called the Way of Holiness, because the unclean will not journey on it; it will be for those who walk in that Way; wicked fools will not go about on it (Isa. 35:8). Repentance is the only legal turn. Take it!

"Whether you turn to the right or to the left, your ears will hear a voice behind you, saying, this is the way, walk in it" (Isa. 30:21). "I am the Lord your God, who teaches you what is best for you, who directs you in the way you should go" (Isa. 48:17).

9. *Church or Denomination*

A Chinese exchange student registering at an American university was puzzled by the question on the entrance form: "What is your religion?" His answer, written in the little English he had learned, was: "Confusion!" There are thousands who are not followers of Confucius who could truthfully write that their religion is confusion. With close to 250 different denominations, how can anyone be sure he is in the right church? Or does it not matter, as long as you believe in Jesus Christ?

The "church" is not a building, but rather the Body of Christ, and the head of this church is Jesus Christ (Eph. 1:20-23). We as believers are all members of this Body, and there is only one Body, Church, the House of

God, and this House is where we study the Word of God and seek the truth (1 Cor. 12:27; Eph. 4:3-6; 1 Tim. 3:15). The more a person studies the Bible, the more he realizes that in God's thinking, truth takes top priority. For thousands of years, Satan, the rebellious angel, has been waging unceasing warfare against God. His weapons are insinuations, lies, and subtle doubt suggestions. It is his determination to deceive the whole world (Rev. 12:9), if possible, even the elect. God cannot use these weapons, for He cannot lie. Deception is foreign to His character. He must rely on the truth, for He is truth (John 14:6). Our salvation depends upon which side we choose to join. No wonder God says He wants everyone to come to knowledge of truth, for only by knowing the truth about God's character of love and Satan's of sin and hate can we hope to make an intelligent choice. Without the truth, we are no match for the devil (John 8:32).

Many are going to stay lost because they receive not the love of the truth so they might be saved and lost because they were not interested enough in truth to be able to detect Satan's deceptions and errors! Love of God's truth is something that we must develop. God does not make this complicated, because He is not a God of confusion. The Word was God, and Jesus is the Truth, and the Words are life (John 1:1, 14:6, 6:63). So we know the truth by reading the scriptures, and all can know all the truth and should not chance being destroyed for lack of knowledge. We must take every opportunity to find out the truth and accept it. We cannot claim to follow Jesus and walk in a different direction (Amos 3:3), nor can we hang on to the world and its evils (Rom. 6:2) or tamper with or change the true Words written (Rom. 1:25) or keep our traditions (Mark 7:7-9). It was upon the truth stated by Peter, that Christ was the Son of the living God, that the Christian Church was built, and He intended unity and organization.

God used the symbol of a pure woman to represent His church or people, and because Satan knows his days are quickly growing short, he will oppress the saints and persecute God's church. The great lesson of Revelation is that Satan, cast out of heaven for his rebellion, wages continuous warfare against Christ, the Son of God and His followers. We must hear our Shepherd's voice and follow the narrow road that leads us to eternal life (John 10:27).

Two neighbor boys were herding sheep, one on a small plateau and the other on a nearby knoll. A fierce storm forced the boys to take refuge under an overhanging rock. Their sheep crowded close to them but mingled with each other. After the storm, the lads found it impossible to separate the two flocks. At last, fearing their fathers' wrath, they started home. Halfway down the mountain, the boys parted, each taking the path to his home. As the sheep came to the fork in the trail, they too separated, each one following his own shepherd. The proof that we are His sheep is that we follow in His path. There is coming a great separation day, when the sheep will be placed on the right and the goats on the left (Matt. 25:31-33). May God help us to be on His side!

10. Many Reasons – Only One Way!

Have you ever asked anyone if they knew they were going to heaven when they die? How many reasons did they give you as to why people go to heaven? Through e-mail, I received a list of reasons given by children in primary grades that I found delightfully amusing. However, realizing that these answers also have come from the thoughts of adults, the humor was lost. Quoting bits and pieces of the Bible seems to qualify many in knowing the way to heaven. The key here is to combine all the words in the Bible to find the road to life. Prayerfully clear a path, haul in paving materials, put up road signs, and become certain of your route mapped out for you in the Word of God.

One might say that they are good people who never do anything bad, so there is a good chance they will go to heaven! This is not a good chance to take, since salvation is not based either on goodness or chance. The biblical texts portray goodness as a quality of lived experience. In the Old Testament, trees and ears of grain are described as good (Gen. 2:9, 41:5).

Aspects of the human experience referred to as good include hospitality, loyalty, prosperity, and old age (Gen. 26:29, 15:15; 1 Sam. 29:9; Hos. 10:1). Goodness describes the sensuous pleasures of sweetness and beauty. God also brings the Israelites into a good and broad land, flowing with milk and honey, a good land of brooks and water, of fountains and springs, but this is not the eternal land, heaven. The psalmist gives thanks to God's name, for it is good, and the Spirit and its fruits are good. However, the psalmist also emphasizes that there is no good apart from God, for only God is good.

The language of justification and righteousness occurs more that eight hundred times in the Old and New Testament. Both the Hebrew and Greek can denote self-justification, seeking to put oneself in the right. Job justified himself, rather than God. The lawyer in Luke wanted to justify himself by asking Jesus who his neighbor was. Money-loving Pharisees are said to try to justify themselves in the sight of other people. Jesus's death and resurrection is our only justification. Paul writes that we are justified by God's grace through faith in Jesus. Justification is not merely an initial step toward salvation in the believer's past, but also involves future vindication and living out the experience in the present (Rom. 5:1). Justification is the foundation for carrying out God's will in daily life by service to others, in church and in the world, including whatever is just. Old and New Testament understandings of justification stand often in close connection with judgment, with righteousness used in parallelism (Amos 5:24; Isa. 11:4).

The English translation separates the Hebrew and Greek words into justification and righteousness. The difference was showing whether the person was righteous in law, justified, or actually made righteous, implying moral transformation. But whose righteousness is involved here? God's or man's? Jesus saw His mission as directed to sinners, not the pious righteous in terms of His day (Mark 2:17). He was Himself and John the Baptist as messengers who justified God's wisdom. In the parable of the Pharisee and the tax collector, it is the tax collector who goes home vindicated or accounted righteous. Jesus was hard on those seeking self-justification. In plain English, self-righteousness just will not get you into heaven.

The New Testament affirms that the story of salvation, climaxed by God's act in Christ, had its beginning in the promises and election of the ancestors. Paul states that through the mystery of God's mercy, the election of Israel through the ancestors would not be revoked. Does this mean if you had Christian ancestors and live in the house with Christian parents, you are going to heaven? Places in the scripture suggest to some that this is the case. Study the words carefully! Simon Peter brought the message and the entire household would be saved (Acts 11:14). The jailer who mistakenly thought he had allowed the prison doors to be opened asked Paul and Silas how to be saved. They told him to believe, and he and his household would be saved (Acts 16:31). Crispus, the synagogue ruler, and his entire household believed in the Lord (Acts 18:8). When Jesus healed the official's son, he and his household believed (John 4:53). Please notice that the head of the household did not save all who lived in the house. Each person believed in the Lord Jesus Christ.

So you go to church every Sunday? Hallelujah! At the time of the composition of the New Testament, the word *church* was widely used to refer to a gathering of people in some kind of assembly. It refers mainly to the people of God gathered in the name of Jesus or the God of Jesus Christ. The New Testament understands church to refer to the visible expression of the gathered followers of Christ who have been grafted into a community created by God, under the banner of Christ, embodying in an advanced look into the life and values of the new creation. By the end of the first generation, the church was a substantial force in the life of Jerusalem. The Jerusalem church began under the direct guidance of the twelve disciples, who provided guidance and teaching. Later, a combination of apostles and elders became responsible for the leadership. We are led through scripture not to give up this practice of gathering together in the assembly. In ancient Israel, the assembly was a political institution used to bring trial and punish violators of the covenant, to arbitrate disputes and to reprimand its own leader. Hmmm! Now that's an idea!

If people say that they confess their sins daily to God and therefore they know He will allow them into heaven, they are fooling themselves. The definition of confession is to say the same thing or to agree to a statement, not just filling the air with empty words. Widely used in ancient legal contexts, in biblical texts, the term is used to express belief in God, acknowledged failure to keep God's laws and praise God for salvation. To confess served as an essential part of worship, functioning to identify, set apart, and reaffirm membership in the covenant. In the New Testament, confession refers to acknowledging that Jesus Christ is Lord. Confess that Jesus is Lord, then confess your sins, and then come to repentance, meaning turning away from the sin you just confessed to, and righteousness, meaning getting it right with God. This change of mind leads to changed actions in keeping with the Greek view that the mind controls the body. Jesus began His ministry with a call to repentance as the prerequisite for entering the Kingdom of God (Mark 4:17). At the conclusion of His earthly ministry, He commissioned His disciples to preach repentance and forgiveness to all nations in His name. Peter, Paul, and the rest proclaimed a gospel of repentance (Mark 6:12).

All of these activities are wonderful and necessary in a Christian's life, but cannot be obtained or even desired without the first step. The book of John will tell you over and again that you must believe in His name (John 1:12), believe in Him (3:16), believe in the Son (3:36), believe Him who sent me (5:24). The many reasons we listen to how to get to heaven should be turned aside. We must stand firm and confess our Lord and Savior to those who do not totally understand that salvation is the only way (2 Tim. 4:2). Open the instruction book and read so that the people can understand (Neh. 8:8), pave the way (Ezek. 2:7), remove the obstacles (Gal. 5:7-10), make the signs clear (Matt. 24:14). "Those who oppose him he must gently instruct, in the hope that God will grant them repentance leading them to a knowledge of the truth, and that they will come to their senses and escape from the trap of the devil who has taken them captive to do his will" (2 Tim. 2:25-26). Jesus said that His soul was overwhelmed to the point of death (Matt. 26:38). This death was for you and me, paving the way to our heavenly home. Let go of all the reasons and find the one and only way.

11. *Dehydration! Cause and Cure*

You have just completed a five-mile hike around the countryside! You are tired and thirsty! Suddenly, you come to a fountain in the middle of nowhere, and the water gushing from this fountain could save your life. Would you stop and drink? It's free!

You have just completed a five-year or a fifty-five-year walk in your Christian life! You are tired and your spirit is thirsty! Suddenly you come to a well in the midst of the scripture that offers water that can save your soul! Would you stop and drink? It's free!

Water is just as vital to our spiritual existence as it is to our physical existence. The body is two-thirds water, and when a person loses more fluid than they take in, it causes dehydration. If you ignore your thirst, dehydration can slow you down. Small decreases do not cause immediate serious problems, and in most cases go completely unnoticed. Thirst is the best and earliest indicator of the problem, and as the condition progresses, more of the body is affected. So then is the Body of Christ. "If one part suffers, every part suffers with it" (1 Cor. 12:26). To counter dehydration, you need to restore the proper balance of water in your body. God assures us that this balance works together for the good of those who love the Lord. There is a fountain in the square where the pure, clear water is free. Would you pass this fountain by if you were suffering from thirst? There is a fountain in the scripture where the pure clear water if free. Will you pass this fountain by while you die of spiritual death?

Just as we were born into physical life, we must be born again into our spiritual life. "No one can see the Kingdom of God unless he is born again. Flesh gives birth to flesh, but the Spirit gives birth to spirit.(John 3:3-7). And just as the physical body needs to be renewed, so must our spirit. Your spirit can dehydrate, and without proper restoration can cause serious problems within the individual body and the Body of Christ. We must be like the tree planted by the water that sends out its roots by the stream. Its leaves are always green, just as our knowledge of God should always be growing. It has no worries in a year of drought, time of testing, and never fails to bear fruit, be kind and generous to others among many fruits listed in the Bible. Spiritual survival depends on water as much as the physical survival does. Paul teaches that he gave the Corinthians mild and not solid food. Milk refers to the very simple message of Christ and the Cross, and is preached to the natural man that he might be drawn into salvation through faith and belief. The Corinthians had professed knowing Christ, but were still living by the worldly standards. Paul was saying that he had to start all over with the basic message before he could preach to them the meat of the gospel. This meat is the solid food, Word of God, that is for the mature Christians who by constant use, have trained themselves to distinguish good from evil (Heb. 5:12-14; 1 Tim. 4:6-8).

Jesus tells us that this meaty gospel is righteousness, getting right with God, and those who hunger and thirst for it will be filled. If you and I could only learn the simplicity of presenting the gospel as Jesus did to the woman at the well. He did not get in her face with accusations and threats, but asked one simple question: "Will you give me a drink?" When you ask for something for yourself, you have put the person to whom you wish to witness in a position to serve you. This shows that maybe you are just as human as they, and now they will at least talk to you. This woman got on the defensive and insinuated that Jews did not associate with Samaritans, so why did this Jew ask her for a drink? This allowed Jesus to tell her about the living water, which immediately got her curiosity aroused. Gently, Jesus led her into full confession of her life of sin, explaining that God is spirit and His worshipers must worship in spirit and in truth. The woman was drawing closer to the truth of the coming Messiah, and Jesus confirms the fact: "I who speak to you am He" (John 4:7-26).

Your body will tell you when you are thirsty by sending up signals. Your skin grows clammy, vital organs do not continue to function properly, your mouth gets dry, and the tongue thick. Your eyes need fluid to cry, your mouth needs moisture to swallow, your glands need sweat to keep your body cool, and your joints need to be lubricated. Your soul will tell you when you need spiritual water. Your heart and mind send out desperate messages for help. You have waves of worry, guilt, fear, and mistrust. You begin to notice sleeplessness, hopelessness, and loneliness. You may pass these things off as just life or just a down phase, or even blame it on the ones around you. Jesus said that there is a cure for all the above symptoms: Just make an appointment with the Physician (Mark 2:17). He will open your minds so that you will be able to understand the scripture and quench your spiritual thirst through the Holy Spirit whom the Father promised.

Jesus went secretly to the Feast of the Tabernacle, avoiding the hecklers, unbelievers, and even his own family, because the world hated Him (John 7:1-13). Jerusalem was filled to the brim for the annual reenactment of the rock-giving-water miracle of Moses. In honor of their ancestors, they slept in tents, ate outside, and welcomed all who dropped by—friend, family, stranger, and even foe. Each morning, a priest filled a golden pitcher with water from the Gihon spring and carried it down a people-lined path to the temple. Announced by the blare of trumpets, the priest poured the water out all around the altar. This was done once a day for seven days. Then on the last and the greatest day of the feast, the priest went around the altar seven times (Jos. 6:2-5). With each round, the priest poured out a vessel of water. "Then Jesus stood and said in a loud voice: if anyone is thirsty, let him come to me and drink. Whoever believes in me, as the scripture has said, streams of living water will flow from within him." By living water, He meant the Holy Spirit, who would be given to everyone believing in Him (John 7:37-39).

Water can go where we cannot, which is throughout the body, and it needs no instructions from us. It divides itself once swallowed and nourishes the vital organs as needed. Likewise, the Spirit can go where we cannot, which is to the throne of God to fill vessels of living water to bring back and pour into our soul, spirit, heart, and mind, supplying power so that we may remain strong in our faith. "The Spirit Himself intercedes for us with groans that words cannot express. And He who searches our hearts knows the mind of the Spirit, because the Spirit intercedes for the saints in accordance with God's will" (Rom. 8:26-27).

Neither Jesus nor the Holy Spirit need instructions from us as where to go; however, they both need our permission (Luke 11:10, 13). The world does not accept the Spirit of Truth because He cannot be seen. We know that we have Him living inside of us to help us survive with our permission which it through the obedience of the Word of God. Scripture tells us not to grieve the Spirit or cause Him to dehydrate, with whom you were sealed for the day of redemption. This is not a one-time drink that will last forever. Paul instructs us to be filled with the Spirit. The original text was written in bold letters, BE FILLED, as were the commands, FORGIVE, PRAY, AND SPEAK TRUTH. If you are one of those who lay out your eight to ten glasses of water per day, try this. With each glass of water you drink, read a passage in the Bible. Satisfy both physical and spiritual thirst at the same time. Make it a holy habit to water your soul!

12. Uprooting Sin

Today I helped my husband move a tractor about twenty miles down a winding dirt road. For you who are not farmers' wives, this means I trailed behind, driving the pickup at the speed of three to five miles an hour. Needless to say, I had plenty of time to study the countryside, such as it was. I grew quickly bored with the depressing sight of grubbed and sprayed mesquite trees. What had been missed by the chemicals and grubbing machinery had been beaten down by a recent hailstorm. Among the demolished trees lay the ruins of abandoned outbuildings, broken-down fences, and a few remaining mud puddles. I know that God created rabbits, coyotes, deer, and even a few rattlesnakes to live in West Texas, but none appeared on our lonely trek. There was not even a road kill! The only two living creatures here were my husband and I, and I was dwindling fast in the 110-degree heat. Then remembering I was created to give God pleasure and praising Him gives Him joy, I began to thank God for all I saw around me, and asked that He teach me something through the dreary scenery. Henceforth, this message!

I noticed the dead trees had new leaves coming out on some of the missed branches, and in my mind, I envisioned them as humans. God has used the same strong methods on Christians to uproot sin in our lives as farmers use to uproot unwanted trees. And like the trees, no matter how much sin God gets rid of, it still creeps back into our lives and leafs out. In order for the grass to grow, the trees have to be taken out! Remember the fig tree that Jesus told the man who took care of the vineyard to cut down. This was because it bore no fruit and Jesus asked, "Why should it use up the soil?" (Luke 13:7). In order for our spirit to grow, the sin has to be taken out! God created man from dirt, and the one who fashioned and made the earth has been grubbing the dirt from our sinful nature ever since Adam. He teaches what is best for us, puts His Words in our mouth, and covers us with the shadow of His hand. God tried to rid humans of all sickness and sin in one giant step when He sent Jesus to be pierced for our transgressions, crushed for our iniquities, punished for our peace, and allowed forty-less-one stripes to rip His back so that we might be healed, seemingly to no avail (Isa. 53:4-5).

Jesus did some spring cleaning in His temple (John 2:16). There were people in the temple selling God by the pound, and Jesus became furious. He cleaned with forceful love to restore the temple to being a place where His Father could be worshiped. Could our church of choice use a spring cleaning? Do we need to uproot the things that are displeasing to God? Sweep down the cobwebs of discontent, attitudes, and personality clashes? Grub up the deep-seated resentment, dissension, and envy so the fruit of the Spirit can bud out? Should we not be filled with grief over sexual immorality among us, and put out of our fellowship the man who does these things (1 Cor. 5:1-2)? Oh, yeah! While we have the bulldozer cranked up, why not dig up the Holy Spirit that seems to be buried so deeply under piles of gossip, sessions, egos, sin stains, and misguided good intentions that He can hardly breathe (John 20:22, Job 33:4)? God also took strong measures to weed out the rebellion from Jonah when the seaweed was wrapped around his head. Of course, that might have been the least of Jonah's problems, since he was swimming around in the belly of the fish. Only when his life was ebbing away did he call out to the Lord (Jon. 2:7)! Sound familiar?

In the Western United States, there grows the locoweed. This plant is poisonous to cattle, and when eaten has the effect of shortening their equilibrium, destroying their muscular coordination, and throwing their eyes out of focus. They may shy away from objects or misjudge distances, therefore walking right into the side of a building or over a cliff. Sin is a poisonous weed that throws the whole Christian nature out of order. Their normal judgment is distorted so that good appears evil and evil good. The Apostle Paul wrote about this in a somewhat confusing manner when he said that what he knew he should do, he did not, and what he knew he should not do he did. He did not understand why, but finally figured that it was not him but the sin living in him that made him do evil (Rom. 7:15-20). We need daily weeding of our earthly fields and our spiritual fields. Both are done on our knees! Satan spots the freshly weeded, tilled patch of ground and cannot wait to get in and mess it up. He does not pay much attention to the weed-infested crop, since it is already part of his estate. We need to be like the Shammah, who took his stand in the middle of a field full of lentils, beans, defending it, and the Lord brought about a great victory (2 Sam. 23:11-12).

Earlier we mentioned broken-down fences on your land. Let's talk about the broken fences in your life! Jesus told us to mend our spiritual fences, leaving instructions. "If a brother sins against you, go and show him his fault, just between the two of you" (Matt. 18:15). This step could save a lot of backbiting, gossip, hard feelings, and weedy minds, if we would just step out and do it. Peter asked Jesus how many times we are to forgive a person and the answer was seven times seventy. The traditional rabbinical teaching was that an offended person needed to forgive the offender only three times. Jesus's reply meant no limits should be set of forgiveness. You know all of the Ten Commandments since you were a child, I am sure. Do not murder, do not commit adultery, do not steal, do not give false testimony, do not defraud, and honor your mother and father are six of them. Any fences down here? Bless those who curse you, do not sin in your anger, pray for your enemies, do not exasperate your children. Any fences down here? Bear one another's burdens and forgive whatever grieves you or whatever someone has done to grieve you. Do not praise the Lord and turn around and curse man, since these two things should not be coming out of the same mouth (Col. 3:13; James 3:9-12). When you get all these fences mended, then search the Bible for more fencing material! God will provide you with everything you need to mend and rebuild, plus He will help you do it and keep you safe throughout the process. He will rescue you from the snares of your enemies and help you keep your cool in the shelter of his wing, deliver you from fear, and keep you in peace. The mind can only stand so much weight, just as water gaps can stand so much pressure from flooding, and something has to give way and break. Find relief in Psalms 55:22. God will move mountains, even the ones in your mind (Mark 11:23), and give you a spiritual workover, where and when you need it (2 Cor. 5:17).

It is probably a full-time job for Him to keep us trimmed so that we do not become porcupines. They travel solo, and when they encounter another creature, they attack with their deadly quills. James calls these quills the tongue (James 3:8). We porcupines withdraw possibly because of the hurt and suffering others have caused us, and protect ourselves by aiming our quills back at the ones who hurt us, and also innocent bystanders. This is why Paul wrote for us to live in harmony, do not act important, and enjoy the company of ordinary people (Rom. 12:16), and James added that it is hard work to get along, but we need to do it (James 3:18). It matters to God how you get along with your family, your neighbors, and your co-workers, and He will help you pull in your quills and build loving relationships with the other porcupines who share your space.

Now about those abandoned outbuildings! Well, do not worry, for they are just temporary abodes, just as our physical bodies are temporary tents. "Now we know that if the earthly tent we live in is destroyed, we have a building from God, an eternal house in heaven, not built by human hands" (2 Cor. 5:1). Our Father has built us a room in His heavenly abode, and His Son has gone to prepare for us a place with Him in glory (John 14:1-3).

13. Don't Be Lazy

Man's purpose is to provide spiritual service, as these carefully selected words in Genesis 2:15 indicate. "He was placed or set to rest in the Garden to work it or to serve, and to take care of it." Whatever he did was described as his service to God.

Solomon, speaking to his son, recommended the enjoyment of life, but he warned that there are serious obstacles to such enjoyment. Enjoy labor's fruits as God enables. The results of man's labor, wealth, possessions, the ability to enjoy them and to be happy in your work, are gifts from God (Ecc. 5:18). A person can become financially destitute by laziness as well as foolish dealings. Proverbs calls these people sluggards. The word pops up only in Proverbs in the Old Testament. A sluggard is so shiftless, lazy, and irresponsible, that he is told to learn from the ant. An ant does not have to be pushed into providing properly for its future welfare. Those who act only when commanded do not possess wisdom.

A person who does his work poorly or carelessly is a brother to one who destroys. There are two meanings for *one who destroys*: one who does a poor or unfinished job or a project that someone has demolished so it has no value, and of course we know that Satan comes to destroy (Prov. 6:11, 18:9; John 10:10).

Laziness brings on deep sleep, and the more sleep you get, the more sleep you want. Can you ever catch up on lost sleep? Have your ever had a lazy day? How did you feel afterward? Work is God's plan for people, and we were not created to be idle. Hard work is more than just necessary for comfort or survival, but pleasing to God. When you want a job done, take it to the busiest person you know, and it will be done well and on schedule.

Think about how idleness of one person affects another. Others have to take up the slack, and this causes resentfulness. An idle dad or mom can cause hardship for the entire family. Lazy, idle parents result in spoiled, out-of-control children. It is work to be a disciplinarian. What happens to children who receive no discipline is mentioned in Proverbs 17:21-25, 20:20, 23:22-25, and 28:7, and 12:24 will tell you that idleness shows lack of judgment. In biblical times, when a person could not meet his debts, he was sold into slavery. "The lazy man does not roast his game" could mean that he never finished what he started. How irritating is this? What if a deadline depended on this person finishing his part of a job? What if we were all too lazy to stand up and sing in church? The song leader would become a soloist. More seriously, what if God called you to lead someone to Jesus and you were too lazy? What would God think about that? "When I say to a wicked man, you will surely die and you do not warn him or speak out to dissuade him from his evil ways in order to save his life, that wicked man will die for his sin and I will hold you accountable for his blood" (Ezek. 3:17-18).

Did you know that the angels watch us to understand God and get to know Him (Eph. 3:10; 1 Cor. 4:9)? What do you want the angels to learn from you, laziness or idleness or godliness? If we do, nothing we gain nothing, and therefore have nothing to share. Paul wrote to the church, saying he was not idle, nor did he eat anyone's food without paying, and urged the church to follow his example. He said he had a right to their help, but wanted to set an example, and also gave this rule: "If a man will not work, he shall not eat" (2 Thess. 3:6-12). He urges them not to be busybodies, but busy bodies, and to settle down and earn the bread they eat, and if anyone did not obey this rule, he told the people not to associate with that person but to warn him. Laziness causes things to be neglected or overlooked.

In ancient times, a king had a boulder placed on the roadway and then hid himself and watched to see if anyone would remove the huge rock. Some of the king's wealthiest merchants and courtiers came by and simply walked around it. Many loudly blamed the king for not keeping the roads clear, but none did anything about getting the big stone out of the way. Then a peasant came along carrying a load of vegetables, and upon approaching the boulder, the peasant laid down his burden and tried to move the stone to the side of the road. After much pushing and straining, he finally succeeded. As the peasant picked up his load, he noticed a purse lying in the road where the boulder had been. The purse contained many gold coins and a note from the king, indicating that the gold was for the person who removed the boulder from the roadway. The peasant learned what many others never understood. "You will eat the fruits of your labor and be blessed and prosperous if you fear the Lord" (Ps. 128:1-4).

14. *The Unpardonable Sin*

A large chunk of ice onto which a carcass of a calf had been thrown was floating down the great Niagara River toward the falls. An eagle, circling overhead, came down and landed gracefully upon the ice floe beside the dead animal, eager for a good meal. Closer and closer the ice floe came to the treacherous falls, but the eagle had no fear. He knew the power of his mighty wings would put him in flight in a moment of time. A few seconds before the deadly drop, the great bird spread out his massive wings for the liftoff, but this time his wings were powerless. Unnoticed by the eagle, his talons had frozen into the ice and he could not escape. The helpless eagle frantically flapped his great wings to no avail, and the ice and the eagle were dashed to pieces on the rocks below. Much sadder than the tragic and unnecessary fate of the eagle is the human who has committed the unpardonable sin of denying Jesus as his Lord and Savior. The saddest verse in the Bible is found in one of Jeremiah's lamentations over the plight of Israel's sins: "The harvest is past, the summer is ended, and we are not saved" (Jer. 8:20)!

There is one thing God will never do, and that is to choose for us. Heaven has already chosen to pay the greatest price, Jesus, in order to provide the greatest power possible, the Holy Spirit, to be with us. Each person must decide to follow the leading of God's Spirit and be saved or to his own way and be lost. Because of the importance of the work and role of the Spirit, with which the unpardonable sin has to do, let us look at who the Holy Spirit is and what He does.

The Holy Spirit represents the truth of the Father (John 16:7-15). No one can be saved unless the Father draws him through the Spirit, and spiritual life comes from the Spirit. If a person denies the urging of the Spirit, he therefore denies Jesus Christ, and this is the sin that leads to death. This speaks of the second death in Revelation 2:11, and there is no pardon for the person who dies in unbelief (John 3:18, 36).

"If we refuse to accept the testimony given to us by the Holy Spirit, fight off his conviction of our sin, and never accept the truth, we will never come to In Christ, all our sins are forgiven. No Christian can commit the unpardonable sin. Only an un-regenerate person who refuses to come to Christ will die in their sin. Romans 8:1, 1 Peter 1:5, Ephesians 4:30, Philippians 1:6, and Isaiah 1:18, 55:6 will back up this quote; however, if a so-called Christian responds to the urgings of the Spirit and Christ in the way of the Pharisees, it is doubtful the person was ever saved, but only God knows for sure, and is not for us to judge but to be a witness and a testimony (Matt. 12:24, 33:37; Ezek. 3:18-19).

Hundreds of Bible verses promise the forgiveness, but only one passage refers to an unforgivable sin. Jesus had healed a demon-possessed man who was blind and could not speak. The Pharisees, who had witnessed undeniable evidence that Jesus was performing miracles in the power of the Spirit, were giving credit for the miracles to Satan. Jesus responded to their accusations by telling them that the blasphemy of the Holy Spirit would not be forgiven. The term *blasphemy* may be defined as defiant irreverence. We would apply the term to such sins as cursing God and for willfully degrading things considered holy.

The state of unbelief is gradual progression that leads to the hardening of the heart (Ex. 8:32-33), and the result is that the conviction of the Spirit is ignored. Some scripture, such as Isaiah 6:9-10, states that God hardened hearts. In essence, He is saying that He wants to hurry their hardness and then, perhaps some will listen before it is too late. If you are truly concerned that you have committed the unpardonable sin, the Holy Spirit is still convicting you that the sin has been committed. Here is a shocker! The hard hearts are usually found among the Christian bodies and in the house of God! It is a dangerous thing to come into the house of God and go through the motions of worship. "You will listen and listen but you will not understand. You will look but you will not learn because these people have become stubborn. They do not hear with their ears and they have closed their eyes" (Acts 28:26-27). How terrible that some of our Christians are acting like the experts of the law who have learned nothing and are preventing others from learning (Luke 11:52). People are ignorant and weak in faith, but still try to explain the gospel to others, and they are only destroying themselves by doing this (2 Pet. 3:16). If we do not heat up for God and get the zeal back into our Christian lives, God says that He will spit us out of His mouth (Rev. 3:16) because His Spirit will not strive with us forever (Gen. 6:3).

How can we be sure we know God's will? The term "let your conscience be your guide" is actually based on Bible passages from John 16:2, Acts 26:9, Romans 2:15, with most of these saying that if you are sound in the faith and your mind will be on the pure things of the gospel teachings. If not, then both your minds and consciences are corrupted. Some may say they have never been urged by the Spirit to be saved. Presumptuous sin is deliberately choosing our own way instead of God's way, and then presuming that it does not matter to Him. It is dangerous to assume that because God is good, He will forgive all sins under all conditions other than His own. God wants to save everyone but will not be mocked, and not all choose to follow the truth, and the blame should not be placed on God (Gal. 6:7; 1 Tim. 2:4; John 12:35).

Jesus said that the Father gave Him all the ones who are saved, and that every one of them will come to Him and He will accept them. He came from heaven just to save us, because that is what God planned and wanted. He will not lose any of the souls that God has given Him, those who believe in Him and those who believe that He can and will indeed raise them up in the last days. The person who accepts Christ as Lord and Savior, in faith, confessing his sins and fully surrendering himself to do God's will may be sure that he has not committed the unpardonable sin. If he does not, he can be equally sure that he is in grave danger of committing it.

Here is my personal conviction and commitment on the subject: "As Jesus Christ is the same yesterday, today, and forever (Heb. 13:8) so is my faith. Regretfully, I fall into the category of sinning and falling short (Rom. 3:23) but repentantly I have no desire nor intention of falling from grace (Heb. 12:15). My confidence comes from leaning not on my own understanding (Prov. 3:5), but I stand on faith and am convinced that neither death nor life, nor angels nor ruling spirits, nothing now, nothing in the future, no powers, nothing above us, nothing below us, nor anything else in the whole world will ever be able to separate us from the love of God that is in Christ Jesus our Lord" (Rom. 8:38-39). If you are saved and you know it, say amen!

15. *Conflict in the Church*

Conflict in the church has been a problem since the beginning of the church. Conflict is a problem that the church has had to deal with down through the ages. People often wonder why they cannot get along with those in the church, and why they have such heated arguments. Why do we have so much contention, strife, and division in the church? Look at what scripture has to say what causes conflict, and some of the cures.

Fights and quarrels among the church members come from their desires that they battle within themselves, wanting something that they cannot have. They will covet and even think of killing to get their way, but they do not, and since it is against the law to kill, they usually just settle for fussing and fighting, and some resort to pouting or not attending church at all. James, John, and Paul all tell us that we have not because we do not ask God, and when we decide that it is a good to ask God or ask because it is a last resort, then we have the wrong motives, such as asking for money to spend on pleasures. These sought-after pleasures are found in the world, and friendship with the world is hatred toward God. The scripture is written for a reason, and the Spirit lives in us, so therefore we are not supposed to envy or covet the things of the world, lest we become an enemy to God. Submit yourself to God, resist the devil, come near to God, wash your hands of your sin, and purify your hearts and stop being double-minded, that is trying to serve God and please man in one breath (James 4:7-8).

We must be humble before the Lord and love our brothers just as much as God does. After all, He died for them too, and not just for a few of us, so we are commanded not to speak against them, or you speak against God. We have conflict within ourselves because we take advantage of the things that God created to be used and enjoyed and start loving the things instead of the creator. We also take for granted the things He gave us and start using people for our own good and taking advantage of the fact that the Bible says they are supposed to love us. Since God made things for our enjoyment, then does this mean if it feels good, do it? When pleasure takes the place over what is needful, then it will cause conflict. Being too proud to compromise causes conflict. God promises that He will provide, but we would rather fight than pray. James says that we ask amiss, and the word *amiss* means to be sick or diseased, so to ask amiss is to ask God for something with a sick or diseased attitude or motive. The church is married to God, so when we have an affair with the world, we are being unfaithful to our Heavenly spouse and telling Him that we are not pleased with Him or satisfied with the way He does things. We have committed spiritual adultery within the church and need God's forgiveness.

Some cures for conflict in and out of the church begins with humbling yourself. There is only one way to get grace, and that is to humble yourself. The Greek word means to be down to earth, not to have an inflated opinion of yourself (Rom. 12:3). We must submit no only in obedience to God, rather than our fleshly desires but to others. Who is in charge of your life? If you are in charge, then anytime somebody comes along who does not go the way you want to go, then you get uptight. If God is in charge of your life, it does not vex you as much (Col. 3:12-17). Resist the devil and be alert to his schemes, and guard your heart. He plays on wounded pride and tells you what you want to hear. He says you do not have to take this kind of stuff from anyone, and the best way is to fight back until you get your way or get even and show them who is boss. If you have thought all of these things or even just one of these things in anger, then you have given the devil a foothold. If you wake up in the morning and do not meet the devil head to head, it might mean you are going in the same direction that he is, and that would be the wrong way. Clean up your life (Heb. 10:22), be sorry for the conflict (James 4:9), do not judge (James 4:11-12), be willing to ask and to give forgiveness (Col. 3:13), and do nothing out of selfish ambition (Phil. 2:305). He is not saying to forget about your own needs but do not be so wrapped up in yourself and your needs that you forget about the needs of others. What can you do to stop conflict?

16. Unbelief

Seeing is believing. Is this true? Is evidence always so convincing that we believe what we see? No! Seeing is not always believing, but rather believing is seeing. We see what and only what we are prepared to believe. Consider the effect of belief and unbelief on our ability to answer the question, who is Jesus? People either see Jesus or are blind to Him based on whether or not they believe in Him. What do you see when you look at Jesus? In John 9:1-7, Jesus performs a miracle and makes a blind man see. The rest of the chapter is a discussion, a debate, of the significance of that miracle, and in this debate, the seeing become blind and the blind see.

As God formed Adam out of the dust and breathed life into him, Jesus took the dust of the ground and His saliva, which at that time was understood to be living water, then put the mixture on the man's eyes and sent him to the pool of Siloam, which means *sent*. As God gave Adam life, Jesus shows that He is the light of the world, living water, the one who creates the sent one and the divine Son of God. The Pharisees tried to disqualify Jesus because He did not keep the rules, saying He should not have healed on the Sabbath. What rules have you made to determine whether or not you accept Jesus as your Savior? If the Pharisees could not disqualify Jesus, maybe they could discredit Him as a fraud. Have your ever considered the effect your unbelief has on your ability to consider the evidence? Unbelief is to have already formed an opinion and passed judgment, and is not interested in explanations. The Pharisees, unable to disqualify Jesus, simply dismissed Him. Is unbelief making you blind to who Jesus is and who you are and better yet, who created you? Do not dismiss Him, but ask Him to give you eyes that can see and look to Jesus.

If you are asking questions or if you are honestly looking for answers about Christ, this man that was made to see, is an encouragement and model for you and me. You do not have to know everything to know some things with certainty. Some questions may stump you, but that does not mean you then have to doubt everything. I can know that Jesus has changed my life, without being able to explain everything about how He did it. So is seeing really believing, or is it the other way around? You will only see what you believe, so believe and you will see!

A few consequences of unbelief:

 a. sin (John 16:9)
 b. inseparable from defilement (Titus 1:15)
 c. evil heart (Heb. 3:12)
 d. slowness of heart (Luke 24:25)
 e. judicial blindness (John 12:39-40)
 f. not being Christ's sheep (John 10:26)
 g. the devil blinds the mind (2 Cor. 4:4)

They who are guilty of unbelief:

 a. have not the Word of God in them (John 5:38)
 b. cannot please God (Heb. 11:6)
 c. persecute the ministers of God (Rom. 15:31)
 d. are condemned already (John 3:18)
 e. shall die in their sins (John 8:24)
 f. shall be destroyed (Jude 5)
 g. shall be cast into the lake of fire (Rev. 21:8)

Warnings against unbelief: Hebrews 3:12, 4:11

Pray for help against unbelief (Mark 9:24)

The portion of, awarded to all unfaithful servants (Luke 12:46)

Faith means being sure of the things we hope for and knowing that something is real even if we do not see it (Rom. 11:1).

17. A Famine for the Word

About 750 BC, an obscure farmer and shepherd was called by God to be a prophet. His name was Amos, and his mission was to warn Israel of God's coming judgment if they did not repent (Amos 8:11-14). Sadly, the nation did not heed the call to repent, and as a result, they were led into Assyrian captivity. Part of Amos's prophecy that was fulfilled concerned an unusual famine that would come upon the people: a famine for the Word of God! Today, there is also a famine for the Word of God; different in some ways and similar in other ways and producing similar results and we will look at some of the similarities.

Material luxury! In Amos's day, this became the cause of pride, which God hated. Their luxury prompted them to put far off the day of doom in their minds. They did not want to think about the future. God had warned Israel that it might cause some to forget God (Deut. 8:11-14). Likewise, Jesus warned that riches could choke those who had received the Word (Luke 8:14). Today, many in their search for wealth forget about God, and others have so filled their time enjoying their luxuries, they have no time for the Word of God.

Moral corruption! Consider how corrupt the people had become in the days of Amos. Who can deny that immorality is having its effect on the church today? The world's standards often become the standards of those in the church. When this happens, people will not want to feed upon the Word of God. If they did, it would make them uncomfortable because of its ability to reveal our true selves (Heb. 4:12-13).

Religious corruption! The people of Israel could not wait for religious days to be over. Today, many people cannot wait for services to be over so they can work, play, or eat. If they are unwilling to spend time in sincere worship, it is easy to see why they will not take time to feed daily on God's Word.

The present famine also produces similar results! Amos described a sad picture in Amos 8:13-14. Young people fainting from thirst, others falling and not rising again. Does this not describe the daily lives of many Christians today? Suffering from a lack of spiritual food, they are easily overcome by temptations. Even the common trials of life overwhelm them. This may help us to understand why some new Christians fall away and lose interest, and the behavior of some elders, preachers, teachers, and deacons.

There are two things that are necessary to resist trials and temptations: faith in God (1 Cor. 10:13) and fear of God (Prov. 16:6). The Word of God will provide both (Rom. 10:17; Deut. 17:18-19). Appreciate the power of God's Word. It has the power of creation (Heb. 11:3), regeneration (John 6:36), sanctification (Ps. 19:7-11), preservation (Ps. 119:9), and salvation and condemnation (James 1:21). A lack of knowledge has always destroyed God's people (Hos. 4:6). Feed upon the word of God like newborn babies longing for their mother's milk, so we need to long for the Word of God and meditate upon it day and night, praying for wisdom (1 Pet. 2:2; Ps. 1:1-3, 119:18, 33:37). Make it a holy habit to read the Bible daily!

18. *Blind Eyes, Deaf Ears, Hard Hearts*

In them is fulfilled the prophecy of Isaiah: "You will be ever hearing but never understanding, you will be ever seeing but never perceiving. For this people's heart has become calloused, they hardly hear with their ears and they have closed their eyes. Otherwise, they might see with their eyes, hear with their ears, understand with their hearts, and turn and I would heal them" (Matt. 13:14-15).

Those who do not hear choose not to hear, and those who do not see choose not to see. Those who do not receive choose to reject. They chose not to hear, not to see, and not to receive because those who hear, see, and receive the Word of God must believe, and all who believe must obey, and they did not want to obey God. No one who believes in Him continues to act like the Israelites, and some of us do. Your salvation does not come from works but from the grace of God, and James 2:14-26 is calling for total obedience. His emphasis is not on the true nature of faith, but on the false claim of faith. His argument was that works are evidence of faith, not the saving factor. All who believe in the Son of God are born again, not of flesh but of Spirit, water being the natural birth and the Spirit being born into Christ by grace through faith.

We then become the children of God and do not live like the devil but walk in this world as the Son of God walked. He who is in them is greater than the one that is in the world, Satan, and Christians can overcome the world through the strength given them through God. God's children imitate Him; they hear His Word and are heard by Him. They ask, and receive whatever they ask for because they keep His commandments and ask in the right spirit and manner and for the right reasons, not for selfish gain. They keep themselves free from the love of this old world, because His Word says that everything in the world comes not from God but from Satan.

They believe His Word and have ears that hear and eyes that see, and so they keep themselves unspotted by this world. Christians do not fellowship with the ungodly, lest they become like them in their actions and thoughts, because they are God's children and they do associate with children of darkness that call the devil *father*. The children of God have hearts that understand, and so they are not easily deceived by false prophets, but understand they are to test every spirit to see if it is from God. The Bible says that whatever is spoken in the name of God must come to pass, for God's Word will not return to Him void. Believers of God, knowing this, know that anyone who speaks a word of prophecy in His name that does not come true is a false prophet.

Christians believe His Word and they love Him with all their hearts; therefore, when a false prophet or false teacher comes to try to lead them astray, they will not hear their voices because they know the voice of their

Shepherd and will follow His lead. They will not follow another voice, and when Satan comes to entice the godly away from their godliness, the children of God stand upon the Word of God. Because of their love for God, they refuse to be drawn away by sin. They know that to love the world is to hate God, and so they keep themselves free from the desire of the things of this life, and are content with whatever God gives them and asks them to do.

It is for this reason that they never ask God for that which they desire from lust or want of the things of the world, because they have died to all these things, through Jesus Christ, and the world has no hold on them. Christ died for the sins of the world, and Christians were buried with Him in baptism upon salvation and are alive to God through the Son of God who lives forever within them. Through Him, believers are overcoming the world and laying hold of that for which Christ laid hold of them. Those who love God know well that when they find something in His Word that is difficult to understand, the Holy Spirit is there ready to make things clear so that their hearts may not become hard. The righteous hear and understand and see and perceive. The sons of God are led by the Spirit given by God. They know His voice and He leads them away from confusion, dissension, envy, bitterness, and fear, for where these things are, you will find the children of iniquity, for these are the fruits of sin.

Open your eyes, clean out your ears, and have a mind like Christ!

19. *Spiritual Dropouts*

"Let us not become weary in doing good, for at the proper time we will reap a harvest if we do not give up" (Gal. 6:9).

The definition of a dropout would be a student who leaves a school for any reason except death before graduation or completion of a course of study, and without transferring to another school. The definition of a spiritual dropout would be a Christian who leaves a church for any reason except death before completing their course on earth without transferring to another church. Many of us know spiritual dropouts. They struggle with their purpose in life without finding their proper place. We need to be aware of spiritual dropouts (Gal. 1:6-8, 4:8-9, 5:7-8).

Jonah was a prophet who became a spiritual dropout when God sent him to Nineveh. He tried to skip out and go to Tarshish, and wound up in the belly of a great fish. He finally repented and finished his course. Jonah's prayer is in the book of Jonah 2:1-10, with him praising God after being spit out onto dry land and admitting that God brought him up from the pit. He sang a song of thanksgiving and said that what he vowed he would make good.

Elijah became a spiritual dropout because of a combination of exhaustion, loneliness, and fear (1 Kings 19). Elijah was one of the greatest prophets in the Old Testament. He brought down idols and he brought down rain. He performed miracles and wonders throughout the land, as the Spirit of the Lord carried him from pillar to post. Through Elijah, God displayed His power, and then Elijah sat under a bush and said, "I have had enough, Lord" (1 Kings 19:4). Ever been under a bush?

John Mark was a spiritual dropout who later returned to his mission and became a profitable and efficient servant of the Lord Paul gave him a charge in the presence of the Lord to preach the Word, be prepared in season and out, correct, rebuke, and encourage with great patience and careful instructions (2 Tim. 4:1-2).

And who can forget David? A man after God's own heart (Acts 13:22) but he dropped out so many times that we feared he would not get up at times, and at other times we feared for his very life.

Spiritual conduct is a struggle. God knew this would be, so He gave us Ephesians 6:11, the full armor of God. He knew He knew we would strive for financial success, so He wrote 1 Timothy 6:5-10, warning us not to think of godliness as a financial gain, but godliness with contentment as great gain. He knew we sometimes would be unwilling to forgive others, so He left these words from Matthew 6:14-15: If you forgive men when they sin against you, your Father in Heaven will forgive you. We suffer when we neglect God's will (1 Tim. 4:14-16; Heb. 2:1-3). God is not looking for a reason to hurt you, but the devil is. The devil and his demons would love to lure you outside of God's protection so they can beat on you. When you get outside of God's protection, He has a Word for you. He will say, "Now where are their gods, the rock they took refuge in, the gods who ate the fat of their sacrifices and drank the wine of their drink offerings? Let them rise up to help you and give you shelter (Deut. 32:37-38). Stay within the protective service of God, and He has these words for you: "Surely I am with you always, to the very end of the age" (Matt. 28:20).

There is a cost to others when we become spiritual dropouts. Consider those who could have been blessed by your life and the ministry that you could render (Prov. 31:28, 20:7). Consider how your family will be deprived and even robbed by your neglect to be the person that you are capable of being with God's help (1 Cor. 8:9-13). A dropout will cost you the Kingdom of God (Matt. 9:37).

To prevent spiritual dropout, we must accept personal responsibility for ourselves. Many people think God should do everything for them while they just sit! Remember the man stranded on the flooding river, asking God to send help. He refused a jeep passing by, a boat, and a helicopter, saying that God would take care of him. Well, he drowned and then blamed God for not sending help in his time of need. The first thing we need to do is learn to recognize God's help when He sends it. Recognize that God has saved you, in order that you might be of service to others (Matt. 28:18-20), respond to the inward witness of the Spirit and His lead toward spiritual maturity (Isa. 11:12), and let the Spirit do his work as divine comforter and guide (John 14:26). We need to be attentive to His leading in our lives (Luke 12:12) and let Jesus help us become mature, competent, and productive Christians, so that we might have life and that we might have it more abundantly (John 10:10).

20. *Lord, Revive Us Again*

Do we have a need of a revival today in our churches and Christian lives? A revival is not a group of special evangelist meetings but a sovereign move of God. The word *revival* means a spiritual awakening or a refreshing from being out of the presence of the Lord. The word *revival* does not appear in the King James Version of the Bible, but is picked up from the combined translations of the scriptures, such as the word *Rapture*, to express the outpouring of the Holy Spirit in Acts 2. This is the beginning of the first church and the gathering together the sermon of Peter, and the Lord added to their number daily those who were being saved. A revival is the Lord God of heaven becoming real to His people. The prophet Habakkuk was conscious of something unusual in the air around him. He felt that he was on the brink of some manifestation of God, and he was afraid. Habakkuk said that he heard what the Lord had to say, and his heart pounded, his lips quivered at the sound. He felt like God was drawing near, and he did not wish to fight against God. Then the prophet cried out: "I stand in awe of your deeds, O Lord. Renew them in our day; in our time, make them known." Just as we cry out for rain when we see the grass beginning to burn, this should be our cry when we see our church and our Christian brothers becoming spiritually dry and stagnant.

In 2nd Chronicles 7:14, we have the call of God to His people to return to Him in repentance, forsaking their sins, that He may heal them, save their souls, and bless them in mercy. Our prayer should be as the psalmist: "Will you not revive us again" (Ps. 85:6). He promises that He will do just this in Isaiah 44:3: "For I will pour water on the thirsty land and streams on the dry ground; I will pour out my Spirit on your offspring and blessings on your descendants." Jeremiah prayed for the backslider (14:7) and asked the Lord to let us return to Him; and Hosea tells us that it is time to return to the Lord so He will revive us and to seek the Lord. The psalmist again asked the Lord to restore us that we may be saved (Ps. 80:3). In Revelation 3:20, we have the picture of Christ standing at the door of the church, knocking for entrance. The church has become unaware of Christ knocking, and that He is often outside of the church and hearts. Do we talk about Christ in the church, or do we talk about what happened this past week? Have we let the gathering together of the saints become a habit instead of worship?

A revival is the Lord Jesus living again in the midst of His people. Have we abandoned the authority of God's Word? Does the average church member mold his life by the Word of God? Are we reading the Word or reading the words? The religious world made much of the Word, but still they crucified Christ. Are we the same today? Are we so self-willed that we border on rebellion against the Word? Do we who claim to believe God's Word tend to add our opinion and said that you do not think that God really meant it the way the Bible reads? Or perhaps when a passage is read, someone will speak up and say that this really means...

Do we sit in church and mentally criticize the ones in front of us? "The sinful mind is hostile to God. It does not submit to God's law, nor can it do so" (Rom. 8:7). Maybe we need an evangelist like John the Baptist (Matt. 11:12). Our evangelism is not a violent assault on the kingdom of darkness, and surveys show that 99 percent of those who respond in an evangelic service turn back to their old life.

Have we lost our compassion for the lost? Jonah was angry at the Lord's compassion for the lost. He cared more for nature than he did the souls, and the scripture says he was very happy about the vine. When God dried up the vine, then Jonah was angry enough to die. The argument ends with God asking Jonah if He should not show concern for the people of Nineveh. Do we put more store in things than we do the salvation of lost ones? Have we lost our prayer chamber and the knowledge of power of prayer? We have substituted suppers, youth parties and banquets for prayer meetings. The Samaritan people would not welcome Jesus, and when the two disciples saw this, they asked if they might call fire down from heaven and destroy the disbelieving (Luke 9:54). This may seem like it does not apply today, since none that I know can call fire down from heaven, but I will tell you that a non-compassionate heart can be plenty fiery against a lost person. Carnal nature can be strong. Instead of having a heart of love for man, we put ourselves in place of God and pronounce judgment. Have you said that they brought it on themselves?

Have we lost Holy Spirit conviction and forgotten what the altar is for? "Everything that touches the altar shall be holy" (Ex. 29:37). Every sinner who, by faith, lays hold of Christ and is cleansed. The horns of the altar were for binding of the sacrifice and a symbol of strength and protection if truly repenting. Woe be unto the one who misused the horns of the altar. We still pray unceasingly to find the manifestations of the convicting power of God's Spirit come upon a humble man kneeling at the altar. This is the Holy Spirit's job, to humble man and hide pride from him, and then we will realize that we are wretched, pitiful, poor, blind, and naked (Rev. 3:17). When we humble ourselves, then we will once again pray like our lives depended on it. Then revival will come within each heart and spread out into the congregations of the churches. We will see that revival is an excitement created and sustained by God through His Holy Spirit. It is an excitement promoted by prayer that becomes an intercession with groaning which cannot be uttered. It is such a refreshing from the presence of God in which souls are quickened or made alive unto God. It is the Lord Jesus Christ walking in the midst of His people until hearts are broken down with weeping and brought to the place of repentance, realizing that some are going to hell.

God will live with the one with the contrite heart and the lowly in spirit, and revive them. He will esteem him who is humble and contrite in spirit and trembles at His Word. He is close to the brokenhearted and saves those who are crushed in spirit. Our sacrifice to God should be a broken spirit and contrite heart, and like Jeremiah, our bones should tremble because of His Holy Word. When the Spirit is allowed to stir things up, then the devil will also be stirred up and will put forth every effort in his power to keep the sleeping church from awakening and to keep unconverted souls from fleeing from the wrath to come. The devil is filled with fury because he knows that his days are numbered and his time here is short, but so is ours. If invited into your revival, God will break down all opposition to the progress of His own work. Are you ready for a revival? Will you pray for a revival in my heart as I pray for one in your heart? Pray that we no longer play church but be totally committed to the work of the Lord. Lord, revive us again!

21. *Questions and Answers*

Q: How do I deepen my relationship to God?

A: Faith! "Faith comes from hearing the message and the message is heard through the Word of Christ" (Rom. 10:17). Paul compares the game of an athlete to the following of Jesus (1 Cor. 9:25) and to become a great athlete and win, you must be in shape and train. We must train for our relationship with God, and our competition, of course, is Satan (James 4:7). Daily Bible readings, prayer, Sunday school, and Bible studies are all training to deepen God relationships.

Q: Why does it seem like God is always saying wait?

A: Elisha was told repeatedly that his master would leave him, but he waited and stuck close to Elijah, not wanting to miss the double blessing he had promised if he saw his master leave (2 Kings 2:3, 5, 11). David was anointed king three times before actually being accepted as king of Israel (1 Sam. 16:13; 2 Sam. 2:4; 1 Chr. 12:39). Waiting may mean we do not believe that God will answer (Mark 11:24; James 1:5-7), we may have sin in our heart (Ps. 66:18) and believe that we have received what we prayed for (1 John 3:22). Jesus, while praying in the Garden of Gethsemane, was told to wait (Matt. 26:39). Jacob waited all night and was wrestling with God the whole time (Gen. 32:24-28). Daniel waited twenty-one days (Dan. 10:2-3) and we are told to wait and see how God answers (Hab. 2:1).

Q: Why do people take sin so lightly?

A: Justification! People can always justify why they sin. However, the scriptures can always counteract these justifications. In Luke 10:25-29, the expert in the law questioned Jesus about eternal life. When Jesus said to love our neighbor, the expert justified himself by asking who was his neighbor. Another excuse is saying that we are living better than someone else and they are Christians. 2 Corinthians 5:10 counteracts this type of comparison, saying each one will be judged for the things we do wrong. The god of this world, Satan, has blinded the minds of the unbelievers so that they might not see the light of the gospel (2 Cor. 4:4). Jesus said that if they did not believe Moses and the prophets, they will not believe Him, that He actually is coming again in judgment (Luke 16:31).

Q: Do I need Bible verses regarding fellowship with other believers?!

A: Christians are the Body of Christ, and each one is a part of God's Body (1 Cor. 12:27, 12:12-31, 14:26, 1:10-17). Some plant the seed, some water, but God makes it grow (1 Cor. 3:4-9). Christians are being built together (Eph. 2:19-22); we should live holy lives (Heb. 12:14-15) and learn to serve and be eager to keep unity (Eph. 6:7-8, 4:1-3). Jesus prayed that we all should be one (John 17:20-21) and brought into complete unity (John 17:23).

Q: What does the Bible say about integrity?

A: Integrity means honesty, soundness, completeness, sincerity, and unimpaired condition. God's Word is in itself integrity. "And the Words of the Lord are flawless" (Ps. 12:6). A liar has no integrity and Jesus says that he is a child of the devil (John 8:44); integrity does not sell the Word for profit (2 Cor. 2:17), thus corrupting the Word. Persons with integrity love their neighbors (Rom. 13:8-10), have a spirit of unity (Rom. 15:5), and carry each other's burdens (Gal. 6:2).

Q: My five-year-old granddaughter asked how God speaks to you, that she cannot hear Him. What is the best way to explain?

A: Read the Bible to her and explain that all scripture is God-inspired (2 Tim. 3:16), in other words, the Bible is like a letter written to her from God. Take her for walks and show her nature, explaining how God created us and the earth and the heavens and is showing Himself to her through all things (Rom. 1:20). "And He took the little children in His arms and blessed them" (Mark 10:16). Each time you take her in your arms and tell her you love her, tell her Jesus loves her too.

Part X Balance

1. Balance

When you were small, did you ever try to walk on top of a narrow fence? Unless you were very agile or walking on a short fence, you would quickly lose your balance and tumble off. After a few unsuccessful tries, maybe an older friend or parent would extend a balance hand and walk along the ground beside you. This is the principle of Christian living. This balance is what John is speaking of in his letter in 2 John. Generally supposed to be in his nineties, John used the term *elder* in reference to himself, not as a name of office, but designating his advanced age. The other apostles had all passed on years before, and John alone was left, the surviving companion of Jesus.

Second and third John were personal little notes to friends whom John expected soon to visit. He wrote other letters, possibly many of them. Personal letters such as these, on account of their brevity and private nature, would be less generally read in Christian assemblies than church letters, and consequently less widely known. These two little epistles, under the guidance of God's Spirit, were rescued from oblivion and preserved for the church, possibly being attached to a copy of 1 John in the churches where they had been received. 2 John is a letter that urges a balance between bold loving and cautious thinking. Teaching the truth without adding love can be too harsh and ineffective. Love without a proper regard for truth can lead to weak sentimentality.

The key is the truth and genuineness of the gospel. The word *truth* is used five times in the first four verses. False teachers had already been referred to in 1 John, going from church to church, teaching in the name of Christ. They taught doctrines that were utterly subversive of the Christian faith. This letter seems to have been written to caution the elect lady to be on her guard and refuse hospitality to such teachers. The warning is prefaced with the exhortation to love, as if to indicate that the practice of Christian love does not mean that we should give encouragement to enemies of the truth.

The letter is addressed to a woman and her children. There is some debate as to whether this letter is written to an actual woman and her kids, or whether the woman is actually a church and the children the congregation. John tells the woman that he has found some of the children walking in the truth. He is not necessarily accusing the others of not walking in faith, but may imply that only the ones he has met are doing so and the rest may be. He teaches two ways God wants us to practice the truth. Love God! When we obey God's commands, we show that we love, trust, and honor and respect Him. It is easy to say "I love you," but proving that love takes action on our part. We should not see obedience as a burden, but as a delight. Love each other! John did not give this as a new commandment, but was reminding the believers of the Words of Jesus: "A new command I give you; love one another. As I have loved you, so you must love one another. By this all men will know that you are my disciples, if you love one another" (John 13:34-35). When you see those who are difficult to love, try to understand rather than criticize; recognize their bad days; be sensitive to the hurts, insecurities, and disappointments in their lives; extend forgiveness; see the best and forget the rest, and listen when they need to talk. Balance your narrow-fence thinking!

John revealed in his first letter how a number of false teachers have broken from the church. 2 John addresses some of the problems associated with these erroneous teachers who travel through the area at the expense of both the church's material and spiritual welfare. At the heart of these heresies is a false belief called Gnosticism, which claims a hidden knowledge for its followers. The Gnostics profess they are a special, spiritual elite, which keeps them from being accountable for right or wrong behavior. The root word of gnostic is the Greek term *gnosis*, which means knowledge. The Gnostics believe they were the owners of secret information about how things really were. John's reference to the Son of the Father showed he still kept in view the miraculous conception of Jesus, a doctrine which is the groundwork of our salvation, and which the Gnostics denied. They did not believe that God actually became a man. Jesus was either not God or He was not truly human. There may not be true Gnostics today, but there are those who diminish the person of character of Jesus. Some say Jesus was a good man, did not live a sinless life, did not die for our sins, but was simply a martyr. And the most subtle of all is the statement that we are all just trying to get to heaven but just choose different ways of getting there! These are false teachings! Check out anything that stirs your spirit with the true Word of God, the Bible, and guard your hearts (Pro. 4:23).

John continued warnings about those who do not teach the truth about Jesus, speaking of his joy for those walking according to the commands of God. What is the danger of listening to false teaching? A story is told of a man who, because he did not like the cost of oats, decided to gradually substitute sawdust in the diet of his mule. Everything went fine for a while, but by the time the mule was satisfied with the sawdust, he died! The danger is that we are being fed sawdust. We barely notice a difference, but as the error sinks into our spirits and hearts, we lose our intimacy with God. John's lesson for then and now? The relationship believers have with those of the world must be discerning. False teachers should not be encouraged in any way. John was very serious about this, as we should be. "Do not take him into your house or welcome him" seems a bit unchristian, doesn't it? False teachers are in the world and they seek to deceive us, and when we show hospitality to them, we give them the idea that their teachings are acceptable. We lower our defense and open our minds to their teaching, and we give them an opportunity to enter the next person's home by using our name.

How do we recognize false teachers? The Treasury Department trains their agents to spot counterfeit bills not by giving them counterfeit bills to study but by giving them the real thing, making them so familiar with the true currency that the false currency is easy to spot. We need to be so familiar with the truth of the gospel that we can easily identify what is false. John calls us to be balanced in our living. This balanced diet must include daily Bible reading with understanding. Without balance, we may lose our joy and the intimacy of God's presence in our lives, and even cause others to be hindered from finding the grace of God.

2. Let's Take a Trip

Salvation is one of the most important words in the entire Bible, and is used 164 times, in most versions. In the Old Testament, the word comes from a Hebrew word which means deliverance and victory. In the New Testament, it comes from a Greek word that means deliverance, preservation, and safety. Salvation is what we receive when we trust Jesus as our Savior, and is the greatest gift we will ever receive. It is not a thing that we will get someday, but a present possession of every person who believes (Rom. 10:9-13). If we study the scripture closely, we will find that salvation always takes you somewhere, moving you from the place where you are to a higher ground. This elevation has nothing to do with altitude, but rather attitude and trust in God will take you from glory to glory (Isa. 62:2-3; 2 Cor. 3:18). Throughout the Bible, salvation and trust in God were glorious, although sometimes grueling, trips. Calling out to God brought Israel out of bondage (Ex. 14:13),

Jonah out of the big fish (Jon. 2:9), David out of the pit (Ps. 40:1-3), Paul out of a lost condition (1 Tim. 1:12-15), and every nonbeliever out of darkness (1 Pet. 2:9).

Salvation is the key to the Kingdom of God, and will take all believers to live in that glorious city by and by (Rev. 21:4, 21:9-22:6). It will alter your life, since no man can receive Jesus and remain the same, and the one mark of true repentance unto salvation is a drastically changed life (1 John 2:9; Col. 3:10). There will be a recognizable difference in the believer's lifestyle (Gal. 5:22-23) and a noticeable desire to serve God (Eph. 2:10). Salvation will take you on the harvest of souls (Mark 16:15), and you will have power to share the gospel and be a witness for Jesus (Acts 1:8). Jesus never called us to be lazy, but to be about the business of our Father, just as He was when He lived on this earth (Luke 2:49). Every Christian takes a fisherman's trip (Mark 1:17), letting their light shine before men, that they may see good deeds and praise our Father in heaven (Matt. 5:14-16). A Hindu trader in India once asked a missionary what he had put on his face to make it shine. With a surprised look, the man of God answered that the secret was that it was not something he put on the outside but something that came from the inside. That being the reflection of the light of God in their hearts.

Many Christians lack the shine of joy on their faces, and the reason for this is what they allow into their inner being through the eyes. Whatever image you allow your eyes to see is therefore received into your heart, making it inevitable that evil thoughts, murder, adultery, sexual immorality, theft, false testimony, and slander will dull your eyes (Matt. 15:19). We should look to the Lord to save us (Isa. 45:22) and our eyes should always be on the Lord (Zech. 9:1). "Your eye is the lamp of your body. When your eyes are good, your whole body also is full of light. But when they are bad, your body is full of darkness (Luke 11:34), therefore see to it that you always travel in the light" (Luke 11:35). The heart which receives the impulses of the eye directs the practices and well-being of the body. Therefore, in order to guard our hearts against leading our bodies into destructive practices, we must keep a close watch over what enters our eyes (Prov. 4:23). Turn your heart totally over to God, and He will guard it for you (Phil. 4:7) and furnish salve for your eyes, that you may see (Rev. 3:18).

As you journey along the trails of salvation, make a covenant with your eyes as Job did, not to allow lust to enter your mind and heart (Job 31:1). "Does He not see my ways and count my every step" (Job 31:4) and the lust of a sinful man's eyes comes not from the Father, but from the world (1 John 2:16). On our trip, we will encounter darkness, but we should strive to keep it from entering into our heart and soul through our eyes (Ps. 101:3). God's eyes are too pure to look on evil (Hab. 1:13), and we are called to be holy as He is holy (1 Pet. 1:16). Even the angels watch our progress toward that goal of glories that will be revealed in the last times, when we come into our inheritance (1 Pet. 1:3-12). God has rescued us from the dark paths (Col. 1:13), brought us into the light of the Lord, and now this light shines in our hearts to light our way. Jesus told us that the road that leads to life is a narrow one, and only a few find it, however, there are instructions throughout the scripture to guide our walk with Jesus. "Let your eyes look straight ahead, fix your gaze directly before you. Make level paths for your feet, and take only ways that are firm. Do not swerve to the right or the left; keep your foot from evil" (Prov. 4:25-27). Now some us will have trouble with our eyesight while trying to keep on the straight and narrow, but not to worry. Just open your ears and listen to the voice of God, and He will tell you whether to turn to the left or to the right (Isa. 30:21).

I would like to remind you and myself that God knows where all of His children are today. No believer is traveling alone, for He has promised that He will always be with us. He knows what we are going through and will not forsake us, but will faithfully keep us and bring us out in His time. Another reminder is that we can have a joyous time on this trek and enjoy our salvation. There are ways listed in God's Word that will help. Most of us would just as soon forget our pasts, since probably none are anything to brag about. However, it is the very past that we wish to forget that makes the present and the future so wonderful. Because of our pasts, we receive redemption with the great price the Lord paid to save our souls (Rev. 1:5). We have renewal when God calls us by name, implying He knew who we were in the past. When God knew the people of the Bible, He changed their name because He had changed their character. When we came to Jesus, carrying our past on our shoulders, He did the same thing for us. We were called lost, children of the devil, sinners, the wicked children of wrath, and the damned. After salvation, we are called saints, children of God, the redeemed, and Jesus's friend.

We can rejoice in the fact that at the very moment of our salvation, Jesus took possession of our lives, and now we belong to Him and nothing can change that status (2 Tim. 2:13). We were the sinners whom Jesus died for, demonstrating His love for us, and that fact should cause us to have joy and to walk with our head held high on our journey to the Promised Land. We are reminded to look to the pit from which we were dug. God met the needs of His people in the history of the nation by letting them pass through the waters of the Red Sea, pass through the Jordan River, and walked Shadrach, Meshach, and Abednego through the fire. What He did for Israel, He can be counted on to do for you and me. After all, He is no respecter of persons. There is not an area of your walk with God in which He will not work to fulfill His promises. As you face the storms, walk through the valleys, and endure the dark nights, remember that He is the same God now as He was then, and He will never fail you. He will, however, meet every need you have for His own glory. He is able, He is willing, He is faithful to His Word, and He is always near.

There will be a gathering at the end of this journey (1 Cor. 15:51-52). One day, Jesus will return in the clouds and receive His people unto Himself. There is no need to pack a bag, since all you need to clothe yourself is Christ (Gal. 3:27). He has clothed you with garments of salvation and a robe of righteousness (Isa. 61:10) that will by your responsibility to keep clean. You will finish this trip, wearing white, walking into glory with Jesus Himself, and He will acknowledge your name before His Father and His angels (Rev. 3:4-6). Are you ready for the trip?

3. *How to Present the Plan of Salvation*

The Lord does not want anyone to perish (2 Pet. 3:9), and has commanded us as Christians to "go and make disciples of all nations, baptizing them in the name of the Father and of the Son and of the Holy Spirit, and teaching them to obey everything I have commanded you" (Matt. 28:19-20). How you present the plan of salvation to another person may mean life or death to that person. The suggestion is that you first get acquainted with the person whom you are led to witness. An encounter with a stranger on the street or at your front door most times is a turnoff, and you will likely get the door slammed in your face. Meeting those who are not believers is the work of God and He will guide you, through the Holy Spirit's nudging. Salvation is the work of God and conviction is the work of the Holy Spirit (John 16:8); however, the Spirit needs a voice to speak to the ones who He convicts, and that is where Christians come in.

Christians are to be prepared in season and out of season to preach the Word of God, with great patience (2 Tim. 4:2) and have ready answers for everyone who asks you to give reasons why you are saved and the hope that you have in salvation. But do it with gentleness and respect, defending the gospel as Paul did, even though it put him in chains. Always be honest, because the ones who are not will be recognized immediately as wolves in sheep's clothing (Matt. 7:15). Believers and nonbelievers alike are recognized by their fruit, remembering that fruit is not what you do but what you are. Jesus did not say go and do witnessing, but go and be my witness. James 1:22 tells us that we are not merely to read the Word, but do what it says, while Ephesians 5:17 instructs us not to be foolish but understand what the Lord's will is. The will of God is that everyone be saved and that we as believers see to it. You may say that you do not know anyone who is not saved, but Jesus says to "open your eyes and look at the fields. They are ripe for harvest for eternal life" (John 4:35-36).

Millions of lost people live in our country, yet some of us cannot name one of them. Develop sensitivity to the spiritual condition of people you know and meet. Compile a list of lost people or perhaps those you think to be lost, and pray for them daily. These people need personal relationships with ones who care, share, and give. They are waiting for you to reach out to them, many times feeling insecure and shy about coming to you. Most lost people do not even realize they are lost, and do not understand the helpless feeling they have deep inside. Look for opportunities to begin cultivating relationships, and watch for the receptivity of the person. Open doors through the Bible, since they do not know the righteousness of God and are ignorant of the mystery of the gospel (Rom. 10:3, 11:25). Show your love to these people with patience, encouragement, and above all, honesty. Prove you can be trusted, understanding, nonjudgmental, and a good listener. Never miss an opportunity to answer the person's questions with the Bible.

Always have your Bible with you. Don't leave home without it! If it is within your budget or the church's budget, take a simple-to-read Bible to give to the person with whom you are witnessing, provided they do not have one. How do you know if they have one or not? Ask them! Guide them to John 3:16-18, Romans 3:23, 6:23, 10:134, reading with them because how can they hear without someone like you reading to them? Always remember that preaching is not the in-your-face, condescending attitude of the pious Christian. "Woe to you experts in the law because you have taken away the key in knowledge; you yourselves have not entered and you have hindered those who were entering" (Luke 11:52). After sharing the scripture, ask if they understand what the two of you were reading. If the answer is yes, then ask if they agree with the reading. If again the answer if yes, then ask if there is any reason why they would not be willing to receive God's gift of eternal life by accepting Jesus as their Savior, believing that everyone who calls on the name of the Lord will be saved (Rom. 10:13). Prayerfully, the third answer will also be yes, and now it is time to lead them in what is commonly known as the sinner's prayer or the believer's prayer. Pray your own words as the Holy Spirit leads you, using the guide below, and ask the person to pray after you line by line. Dear Father, I believe you are the Son of God and that you died on the Cross and was raised from the dead. I know I have sinned and need forgiveness. I turn from my sins and receive you as my Savior and Lord. Thank you for saving me!

Welcome this loved one into the family of God, saying they have just made the most important decision of their life. "The Spirit himself testifies with our spirit that we are God's children" (Rom. 8:16). Assure them that as a newborn babe in Christ, they will find direction for living a Christian life, and live eternally with Jesus in heaven. Now back off! Give them time to let all this soak in, call a friend, or just ask more questions concerning the Bible. Next, it is time to call a pastor, preacher, or deacon of the person's choice of church, and set up preparations for baptism (Mark 16:16) and fellowship or membership in a church body (Heb. 10:25). Now listen carefully and maybe you can hear the "rejoicing in heaven over one sinner who repents" (Luke 15:7). This sound of rejoicing is not necessarily hidden from human ears, and I believe we can hear it in the crying of a mother whose lost child has just been saved, in the singing of a choir as their godly emotions carry their voices higher than their expectations in praise of our Lord, through a sermon that we have heard numerous times but this time there is a word that awakens our spirit. It is my belief that during these reverent, awe-filled moments, some soul has been rescued, even if we do not have the privilege of being a witness.

Leading a person to Christ is the most rewarding, exciting, and refreshing experience that I have ever had as a Christian. To some, this may seem a bit frightening, but remember that when Jesus commanded us to save the nation, He also assured us that He would be right there with us. Follow the lead of the Holy Spirit, and "as soon as you hear the sound of marching in the tops of the balsam trees, move quickly, because that will mean the Lord has gone out in front" (2 Sam. 5:24). The end of our time is near and Jesus is coming soon (Rev. 22:20), and there are some who are not ready to meet the Lord. He is coming and will not be silent about the coming, and warned us if we were silent about Him that the stones would cry out (Ps. 50:3; Luke 19:40). Do you really want the stones to be your voice?

4. How to Accept Christ

Do you know for certain that you have eternal life and that you will go to heaven when you die? God wants you to be sure! He wrote things in the Bible to you who believe in the name of the Son of God, so that you could know that you can have eternal life. Suppose you were standing before God right now and He asked you why He should let you into heaven. Do you have an answer? You may not know what to say, but you do know God loves you and has a purpose for your life, and that He made a way for you to be saved eternally. His main purpose is that you have eternal life, and you can receive this life as a free gift (Rom. 6:23). You can live a full and meaningful life while here on earth, through Jesus Christ, who came that you may have this life (John 10:10). You can spend eternity with Jesus in heaven, for He promised to go and fix up a place for you and come again to take you there (John 14:3).

Our need is to understand our problem of not understanding God's purpose for us, and that we have meaning in life as we direct our lives and hearts toward Him. Why is it that people seldom find true meaning in life? Our sinful nature keeps us from fulfilling God's purpose for us, and since we are sinners by nature and by choice (Rom. 3:23) we cannot save ourselves. We deserve death and hell, for the wages of sin is death (Rom. 6:23), however we can receive what we do not deserve through salvation. God is holy and just, and must punish sin, yet He loves us and has provided forgiveness for our sin. He sent His Son Jesus to become the way and the truth and the life, and we can come to the Father through Jesus (John 14:6). Jesus is God and became human, becoming flesh, dwelling among us and dying on the cross for sins once and for all, the righteous for the unrighteous to bring you to God (John 1:1, 14; 1 Pet. 3:18). Jesus was resurrected from the dead, raised to life for our justification (Rom. 4:25). The only way Jesus can affect our lives is for us to receive Him, believe that He is the risen Son of God, and call on His name to save us, and then He will give us the right to be called His children (John 1:12).

We receive Jesus by realizing that Jesus is the solution to our rebellion against God, and we find a desire to establish a relationship with Him. We must repent of our sins, meaning to turn away from the evil things we are doing (Acts 3:19). Repentance is not just feeling sorry for our sin, but truly having a contrite and broken heart for the things we have done and a willingness to turn away from the world and turn to God through Jesus, placing our faith in Him (Eph. 2:8; James 2:19). To trust Jesus totally is to confess with your mouth that He is Lord, and believe in your heart that He is the Son of God raised from the dead, and you will be saved (Rom. 10:9-10). As evidence of this, you will want to identify with Him by confessing He is your Savior publicly, and following Him into baptism and church fellowship (Matt. 10:32-33; Acts 2:41).

Three important questions you need to be asked upon making the decision to accept Jesus as your Savior are: Do you understand what you have been read on the subject and does it make sense to you? Is there any reason you would not be willing to receive God's gift of eternal life as opposed to the alternative? Are you willing to turn from your sin and place faith in Jesus right now? If there is any part of this statement that you do not understand, please get some more help and counseling before making this decision. This is not a game or a part you will be playing, but a lifetime commitment to Jesus Christ as your Savior. All you have to do is ask and God will save you and stay with you in the form of the Holy Spirit, who now will come and live within you. The Spirit will guide, counsel, and even pray for you when needed. Welcome to the family of God and the beginning of your Christian growth.

5. Obadiah Versus Pride

Big things come in small packages! This small package is the shortest Old Testament book, called Obadiah. The big part of this book, with only twenty-one verses, contains a powerful message about the justice of God. This is a prophecy directed against the nation of Edom.

Edomites were descendants of Esau, but were always bitter enemies of the Jews, perpetuating the enmity of Esau and Jacob (Gen. 25:23, 27:41). They refused passage to Moses and were always ready to aid an attacking army. God's righteousness demanded vengeance on Edom, who was Israel's antagonist from the earliest days. Judgment against Edom is mentioned in more Old Testament books than any other foreign nation. This short book speaks of the danger of the great sin of pride and arrogance, and the feeling of superiority that results from taking advantage of others (Prov. 16:18). Edom's pride led them astray and caused God to bring them down.

Edom was in a great location, and the people were proud of their security. The land was hilly and the cities were built high up in the rocks. The chief city of Sela was part of a fortress known as Petra. The only way to get into the city was by a winding canyon about a mile long and quite narrow. Any soldiers coming through could be held off by a dozen or so men. Edom was one of the most secure places in the world, however, her pride deceived her into thinking that no one could conquer her. The word *pride* translates *Z'don'* from Zid, meaning to boil up. Jacob boiled up the stew that Esau bought with his birthright (Gen. 25:29).

Edom was the center of a copper industry, and major trade routes of the world went through. Anyone wanting to trade in Egypt had to travel through Edom; therefore, they were able to control and tax all the commerce, making Edom a very wealthy nation. The surrounding nations had to have a good relationship with Edom to have passage through their country, but these allies would be the ones God would use to bring down Edom (Ps. 41:9).

Everyone has a measure of pride, and most pride becomes a vice that everyone hates to see in others. People hardly ever see pride in themselves, especially false pride. This is a fault which makes us very unpopular, and we are very unconscious of it in ourselves. The problem is that we do not see pride as a problem. We call it an unfortunate personality trait. Perhaps we encourage pride when we should simply encourage striving for excellence. Pride in its simplest manifestation is the feeling that we do not need God (2 Cor. 12:1-20). Pride destroys your character, and Edom's pride kept them from helping when Israel was under attack. There was a sense in which Edom felt Israel got what was coming to them, and they rejoiced and celebrated the defeat of their brother Israel, and perhaps worst of all, they took part in the attack.

Another point of irony in Obadiah 7 is that Edom, known for her wise men, would be totally unaware of her allies' deception and schemes. The downfall referred to here probably occurred in the late sixth century B.C., when the northern Arabian worshipers of gods of fertility and the celestial bodies were active. They were renowned stone carvers of Petra and went to Edom's banquet, and once welcome inside Edomite territory, the idol worshipers turned against them and killed the guards.

Edom's arrogance led to her complete humiliation, and her security and wealth would be gone, and her wise leaders, soldiers, and others would all fall under God's mighty hand. Nothing could save her—not her position, military, wisdom, or wealth. Within four years after Jerusalem was burned, Edom was raided and desolated by the same Babylonians whom they had aided against Jerusalem. What false hope pride gives unbelievers who try to find security in their own strength apart from God.

My guess is you see evidence of pride in your own life, and I know I see it in mine. The message of Obadiah reminds us of the words of Solomon: "pride does come before the fall." To save our church body from the fall of pride, we must change one individual at a time, beginning with ourselves. Ask the question to your mirror: "Do I have a problem with pride?" Are we much different from the Edomites? The message of Obadiah is not archaic and outdated. It is as powerful and pertinent today as then. It is a call for you and me to remember who we belong to and what we came out of.

6. Take a Seat

There are things in this world that no one wants, and worse yet, there are people in this world whom no one wants. It is human nature to want the best and most, and most do not mind the pushing and shoving it takes to get it. When it comes to the best seat in the house, we pay top dollar, except for the best seat in the church being the back row, and it is free as long as you get there first, and woe unto the poor fellow who beat you to it.

The disciples James and John were not above asking Jesus for the best seat, and more or less demanded that He do for them whatever they asked (Mark 10:35). Now, when the other ten disciples heard about what James and John were up to, they became indignant with them. Remember, woe to the one who beat you to it. I cannot decide here if the others were indignant out of shame and embarrassment for their friends or the fact that they did not think to ask Jesus this question first. Jesus explained to all of them that this request was not His to grant, and they had some growing and serving to do before they would qualify to sit anywhere near His Father. Jesus knew that they had already argued about who was the greatest in Mark 9:33-35 and had explained then that "if anyone wants to be first, he must be the very last and the servant to all," but some take just a little time to catch on.

Jesus was invited to the house of a prominent Pharisee for dinner, and there noticed how the guest picked the places of honor at the table. He explained in parable form that if they were asked to move from the place of honor, they would be humiliated. However, if their host invited them to move up to a better seat, then they would look important to the other guests. At this high-class Pharisee banquet, there was a man suffering from dropsy. It is unlikely that this poor, afflicted man was a friend of the Pharisee, but instead was probably invited to put Jesus to yet another Pharisee test. Jesus never fell into their traps—and they set many of them—but turned to them and asked if it was lawful to heal on the

Sabbath or not. Upon healing the man, Jesus answered His own question with another question, which He often did. "If one of you has a son or an ox that falls into a well on the Sabbath day, will you not immediately pull him out?" And again, the Pharisees were speechless in the presence of righteousness (Luke 14:1-14).

There are lots of seats in the scripture, starting with God's instructions for making the tabernacle and everything in it. They were to make a mercy seat of pure gold and place it above the Ark. "And there I will meet with you, and I will commune with you from above the mercy seat" (Ex. 25:17-22)   By this, we understand that the best seat is for God also understanding that our seat is bowing before the mercy seat in the presence of our Lord. Two of Aaron's sons offered unauthorized fire before the Lord. His fire consumed them and they died there before the Lord (Lev. 10:1-2). God sent a message through Moses to Aaron that he was not to enter the Most Holy Place whenever he pleased, or he too would die; "for I will appear in the cloud upon the mercy seat" (Lev 16:1-2). The message to us for today is to be careful how we approach God. Job, at one time, occupied the seat of honor in the public square before his afflictions. Even though Job was blameless and upright, this seat of honor did not last (Job 29:7).

There are seats listed in the scripture that you do not want to sit in. "Do not sit in the seat of mockers (Ps. 1:1), pass quickly by the woman Folly who sits on a seat at the highest point of the city (Prov. 9:13-18) or the seat of violence (Amos 6:3-7). The Pharisees sat in Moses's seat, but only to weigh down men with burdens, thus bringing on Jesus's pronouncement of woe. We do not want to be caught in the judgment seat against our brothers, or we will stand before the judgment seat of Christ, and for sure we do not want to sit in the seat of Satan (Rev. 3:13). "God will put down the mighty from their seats and exalt them of low degree" (Luke 1:52). Ezekiel was shown the seat of the image which provoked jealousy, and Jesus went to the temple and overturned all the tables and the seats of those who were making it a den of thieves. Nor do we want to be in the seat of favoritism, giving the well-dressed man the best seat in the house and the poor man a place to stand (James. 2:1-9).

So, you want to do something really big for the church and God, and you believe you are well-prepared for the first chair. I read a story about a young seminary graduate who had these thoughts. He came up to the pulpit very self-confident and smug, knowing he had what it took. He began his well-prepared sermon in his first church before his first congregation, but when he started to speak, the words simply would not come out. Humiliated, he burst into tears and ended up leaving the platform, obviously humbled. There were two old ladies on the front row; you know them. One remarked to the other, "If he had of come in like he went out, he would have gone out like he came in!" Start humbly and God will move you up. Start arrogantly and God will move you down. When you get that move upward, remember the one whale's warning to the other: "When you get to the top and start to blow, that is when you get harpooned!"

"Do not think more highly of yourself than you ought, but rather think of yourself with sober judgment; in accordance with the measure of faith God has given you" (Rom. 12:3). Jesus took the humble seat, hanging out with criminals, enduring persecution and false accusations. Because He humbled Himself, God exalted Him to the right hand of His Father.

The Pharisees and the teachers loved the best seats everywhere they went. Jesus said they were showoffs and they were in for trouble. Actually, He asked them how they would escape being condemned to hell (Matt. 23:33). I do not know why people choose the seats they sit in, but I do know that a certain seat can get to be a habit. I see nothing wrong with sitting in the same pew each and every time you go to worship, if you are not hindering or being a stumbling block to others. Just a couple of questions that you may ask yourselves are, would you give up your seat to someone with poor dress code and poor hygiene? Would you move over and let them sit beside you? Would you talk to them about Jesus, or talk about them to your neighbor after you went home? Do you notice that a first-timer is sitting alone and casually join him? Maybe a young mother with more than one child could use a little help! Perhaps a handicapped person needs to sit on an aisle seat, and there are none available! Be sensitive, alert, and ready to lend a helping hand, and when you finally find your seat, wherever it ends up being, you will feel good about yourself.

Jesus in now sitting on the only seat that matters, in the position of our High Priest. The only way for us to reach Him as He sits there is on our knees in prayer. He will sit on the Judgment Seat of Christ when this old world ends and the scripture says that all knees will bow! I do not see any mention of chairs, seats, or pews here, first or last, good or bad. I am going to step out and declare that there will not be a bad seat in the house of God, and I surely hope none of us are fighting over where the best seat is when He comes (Rom. 14:11; Rev. 1:7; 1 Cor. 15:52).

7. *God Didn't Cause it to Happen and the Devil Didn't Make You Do It*

The most asked question in history is "Why did God allow this to happen?" Why does God cause bad things to happen to good people? runs a close second. Jesus said there was no one good except God alone, and the psalmist said there is no one who does good because they have all turned aside and become corrupt, and there are none who seek God (Luke 18:19; Ps. 14:1-4, 53:1-4). Why is there no one good? Because they have all sinned and turned away and have become worthless. God made a perfect world, but through the disobedience of mankind, it became corrupt and filled with sin. God did not like what He had made, and was grieved that He had ever made man, and His heart was filled with pain, so He wiped man off the face of the earth, with the exception of Noah and his family. Noah was spared because he was blameless among the people and did everything God had commanded. However, even Noah was not good, as shown in Genesis 9:21. Again God looked for someone He could trust, and turned to Abraham. Abraham could not find anyone worth saving in Sodom, but was allowed to warn his family and lead them out before God destroyed the city of sin. Lot's wife disobeyed orders and looked back after being warned not to, and was turned into a pillar of salt. God did not cause these events, the devil did not make them happen, and Adam and Eve are not to blame for all the bad things we do. From cover to cover, the Bible is filled with rebellious people causing their own destruction, and we continue to do the same in spite of numerous warnings (Gen. 6:3; Heb. 3:10).

The only thing required of us is faith, but understand that faith is not an insurance policy, but a blanket assurance that God will be with us no matter what we encounter. In our world of pain and hardship, we find God in the loving act of sending someone to stand in the gap for us. There are those who stand by us when we suffer the loss of a loved one, those who stand in prayer for us, the medical profession that attends our aches and pains, and these are all instruments of God. Goodness and faith does not make us immune from suffering, because God did not promise to prevent pain and tragedy, only to be with us through it all. Throughout scripture, God has searched for those who would stand in the gap to prevent His wrath (Ezek. 22:30), and He sought to strengthen those whose hearts were fully committed to Him (2 Chr. 16:9), to no avail. I believe He still searches today and is still having trouble finding anyone.

God did everything He could in the Old Testament to get things ready for us. He looked everywhere for someone to save the world from His fiery judgment. He finally found one person to commit fully to Him in order to bring Jesus into the earth. Her name was Mary! Did this miraculous birth and ministry change minds? For a while, when Jesus walked on earth healing and feeding, everyone clamored around Him, believing. Yet, some of the very ones He healed and fed crucified Him. God stayed honorable and strove to help mankind, even though we turned on Him. He has healed and fed multitudes today, and still we are turning on Him and yet wondering why bad things happen to us. He is wondering why we do not use our faith, the Word, and the power of the Holy Spirit. Many do not know the stories about people doing evil in the Bible and God staying true, because they have never read the Bible. "You are in error because you do not know the scriptures or the power of God" (Matt. 22:29).

God does not punish, but He does discipline. We, man, did not establish the standards of what is right. We need to settle it in our minds and hearts that whatever God does is right, whether we understand it or not. Seek ways in which we can profit spiritually from suffering and trials, as well as the blessings we receive in life. Do not be a fair-weather friend to God. The world is now under God's curse because of man's rebellion against God's Word. I am hesitant to say that this includes the very young. You see, there is no one born innocent, because just as sin entered the world through one man, then all men are born into sin (Rom. 5:12-14), not to forget that one must reach the age of accountability for salvation. God does not wish any of the little ones to perish, and "the little ones that you said would be taken captive, your children who do not yet know good from bad, they will enter the land" (Deut. 1:39), and David said that he would go to him, meaning the baby who died at birth. God knows the end from the beginning, and it is appointed a time for each man to die once. Maybe, just maybe, those who die so very young are being spared from evil and find rest as they lie in death (Isa. 57:1-2). God did not create the world this evil way, and one day will set it free (Rev. 21:14, 21:1-6; Acts 3:21; Isa. 65:17).

Does God want you to know His plan? The God who has shown Himself to be for us wills also to be with us. He is infinitely capable and desirous of relating Himself to you and me and anyone else who freely opens himself to such a relationship. God wills this as the means of fulfilling His purpose in us, enabling us to become the kind of persons He intends us to be. Wisdom does not come to us naturally, but we gain it by respecting God and making careful choices. Surely you have heard of God; He does not hide from us and will tell us His secrets, but He is in control. He sends death and brings life, and the people who do right will have problems, but the Lord will solve them. He will catch you when you stumble—and stumble you will—but the good will not be defeated. Through faith, nothing can harm you and God, but much can bother you until the day the Lord has set to judge all the world with fairness (Acts 17:31).

Evil acts and events are not part of God's plan. He loves us, feels our sorrow, takes no pleasure in death, and does not afflict. He offers us a choice between life and death, blessings or curses, and if we choose life, we have chosen to love the Lord, obey Him, and stay close to Him. The ability to have and use personal freedom is what is called image of God in humans. Only humans are given this personal freedom of choice. Other creatures are governed by the peculiarities of their species to which they belong. We may ignore, disobey, or be disrespectable in spite of bad consequences. Jesus told His disciples to pray for strength against temptation because "the spirit is willing but the flesh is weak" (Matt. 26:41).

We have an enemy of our souls that we cannot see, but he is prowling around, trying to devour each and every one he can catch off guard. Satan is not the opposite of God, as if he had an equal standing with God, because God has no counterpart. God has no equal. Satan is merely an angel under God's judgment. Satan attempts to have power over Christians, but we are not to give in to Him, but to cling to the higher and greater power of God. Satan's main goal is to tempt us to sin and keep us from believing in God. Knowing the weakness in us, Jesus prayed that the Father would keep us from the evil one. Paul warns us not to be ignorant of Satan's schemes, but to recognize the lies as lies and believe totally on God, in God, and with God, and that old serpent can do nothing but hiss. He hits you when you are down and tells you that God could never love a loser like you or you would not be having so many problems. Jesus said that as the Father loved Him, He loved us, and called us children of God. Satan tells you that your mistake is so bad that God will never forgive you, but God says all we have to do is confess that sin and He is faithful and will forgive us.

Although Satan cannot force you to sin, he delights in taking the credit, clouding your thinking that God is depriving you of something. He will try to convince you that this present temptation is too much for you to resist, but God says no temptation is too much and that we will all be tempted, and also that He will provide us a way out of it. Satan cannot read our minds, but he can plant negative thoughts about yourself or others, so capture those thoughts and give them up to God, and He will clean up your mind. Check out these lies against the Bible, and if they are not in line with God's Word, you know they are from the devil, and now you must resist him and he will flee from you. "The one who loves us will guide us into all truth" (John 16:13).

God's angels were active in the lives of believers in the Bible. In Daniel 6:22, we read that an angel shut the lion's mouths when Daniel was in their den, they ministered to Elijah in 1 Kings 19:5, and more than once they delivered Peter from prison (Acts 5:19, 12:8-11). Fallen angels, with Satan as their leader, will copy anything that God's angels do. They will falsely comfort you by telling you what you have done is not bad. If the devil and his angels can get you to believe this, they can deceive you into continuing to live in sin. He can program you to be defeated (John 8:44-47), and you have allowed him to outwit you with his scheme. The functions of God's Word and prayer are to change mindsets. When we walk in truth, righteousness, salvation, and faith, there are no gaps in the armor. Guard your heart, yourself in your spirit, so the devil cannot fill your heart and spirit with lies (Acts 5:3).

Satan and his demons can do only what God allows (Job 1:12, 2:6) but they will take full advantage of this leeway. Satan will blind you to the truth, lead your minds astray, take you captive to do his will, and harden you with sin. He does not force you to do any of these things, but rather talks you into it. No one is tempted by God, but on occasion He will hand you over to the devil and let you do as you please (Rom. 1:28-32). This is God's discipline, which is painful at the time, but later produces a harvest of righteousness and peace for those who have been trained by it (Heb 12:11). Jesus suffered when tempted, so therefore He understands our temptation and will help us. Death and trials are facts of life here on earth, but we are never alone. "Even though I walk through the valley of the shadow of death I will fear no evil for you are with me" (Ps. 23:1-6). Jesus told us we would have troubles, but also told us to take heart, for He has overcome the world and neither the world nor humans will last very long because: "You are a mist that appears for a little while and then vanishes" (James 4:14). Jesus is coming soon!

8. Judging Versus Judging

"Judge not, and you shall not be judged. Condemn not, and you shall not be condemned. Forgive and you will be forgiven" (Luke 6:37).

There are different types of judgment; one involves discernment, not allowing harm to come to you or others from those who cause harm. And along with that comes sensitivity to potential trouble, attempting to prevent the bad actions of others. We should be vigorous, fearless, and undaunted in our efforts to keep the church pure and free from the corrupting influences of evil. We should seek the restoration of those who will listen and repent, but we must separate ourselves from those who remain hard-hearted. Warn such men twice, but after that, have nothing to do with them. Not even a cup of coffee (1 Cor. 5:11; 2 Tim. 3:1-5; Titus 3:10).

State the facts! Let the facts stand on their own. Slander, insult, and sarcasm may strengthen emotions, but they weaken sound arguments. Purge false doctrine and false ministers from your churches. Once the source of impurity is successfully removed from your congregation, it is the Lord's responsibility to bring judgment (Rom. 12:19). Warn whom you can, purge whom you can, rebuke those you can rebuke, but leave their destruction to the Lord (James 5:19, Ezek. 3:17-19).

Jesus said to not judge, or you would be judged, so then what is Paul talking about when he says that the saints will judge the world (1 Cor.

6:2-3)? What did Paul mean when he commanded the Corinthians to expel the immoral brother and deliver such a one to Satan for the destruction of the flesh that his spirit might be saved in the day of the Lord? Paul used this strong language because the man had chosen to follow Satan. The church was merely recognizing and finally making official what the man had openly decided and declared by his conduct. There was no thought to consign him to the devil, but rather to register on a temporary basis that the man preferred Satan's path to the path of Jesus. Perhaps the shock of being expelled from the fellowship of the church would turn the sinner to repentance and cause him to crucify the flesh, and he could be restored to the church fellowship and saved at the coming of Jesus.

We have not only the right but also the responsibility to judge the immoral, ungodly, and wicked behavior of those in the church. Paul rebukes us for failing to take matters in hand and deal with them. On the other hand, the Lord tells us, as do Paul and James in their epistles, not to judge. Contradictive? The dictionary defines judging as the sense of an impartial, non-emotional, dispassionate analysis of facts. The other meaning has to do with human nature and the need to use power. We love power! There are few things in all the earth that the average man or woman desires more than being number one, on top, and in control. This is called pride! Understanding a bit about personal power and the carnal nature's desire for it, we can immediately see the term "holier than thou" in a clearer light! We cannot tolerate arrogant, self-righteous, and holier-than-thou types, so we judge them. We will go on at length about all their faults and how sad it is that they are not as wise as we are. After all, only one died and put them on the throne that we know of. Self-directed sarcasm of this nature is okay, but it is when you turn it around and use it as a tool to slander others that it becomes a problem (James 4:11; Rom. 2:1).

We use judgment, criticism, and other thinly veiled forms of gossip to put others down so as to elevate ourselves. We judge the new convert who has not yet mastered his tongue, but we spew forth hatred. We judge the man who smokes while gorging our 300-pound carcass at an all-you-can-eat buffet. Our pride knows no boundary. We hide this kind of judgment behind doing what is right and what God told us to do. Remember the secrets of our hearts are judged by Christ (1 Cor. 4:5, 5:12-13).

We are not to judge in a pious and self-righteous manner, but rather as those who will stand before God ourselves. He gives us a pattern for moral judgment in John 5:30, and 8:16. We are to judge right and wrong in some things such as sin versus virtue (James 4:11-12). Church leaders are called to exercise discerning judgment as to the moral or spiritual condition of the people under their care. This is always done in the character of the fruits of the Spirit (Gal. 5:22-23).

Speck and plank in the eye refers to the need for eye surgery, and means we must correct our own faults by removing the beam from our eye, and then we will be able to see or discern and help others who are not dealing with their faults (Matt. 7:3-5). The right way to help someone with faults is to go to them privately with constructive criticism in love and offer gentle, humble criticism and help that would lift them up (Matt. 10:12-15; Acts 13:42-46; 2 Tim. 2:24-26). Jesus tells us, simply put, do not judge! This means we are not to be critical or have a measuring stick to which we compare everyone else. A Christian who is critical and condescending is a terribly destructive force to the Kingdom of God, as they exhibit the direct opposite behavior of what Jesus would do and what a Christian should be. May God help keep us all from such judging and enable us to be more useful in helping others with their problems. Try hard to keep your mind from thinking of another person when you read this, but perhaps clean out your own eyes, and above all keep them on Jesus.

9. *We, Like Sheep, Have Gone Astray*

Sheep are mentioned hundreds of times in the Bible, and many of the mentioned scriptures are comparing people to sheep. Wake-up call! This is not always a compliment! "I tell you the truth; I am the gate for the sheep" (John 10:7). In the ancient days of the Bible, the pens for the sheep had no gate. Often, the pens were rock formations with three sides, and the shepherd would stay in the gate all night to keep the sheep in and the predators out. Jesus also compared himself to the Shepherd and us to the sheep, and said that His sheep listened to His voice. An observation of shepherds showed that they might take a noon break together and their sheep would mingle. When the shepherds headed home, they each had a unique voice or whistle or song, and the united flocks would divide up and follow their own shepherd. Jesus told Peter to feed His sheep! A test of sheep showed that the owner put a pan of grain under the sheep's nose and he ate his fill. When the sheep came back for seconds, the owner had moved the pan just six inches from the original spot, and the sheep could not find it. If your seat were moved form its spot in the church, could you find it?

Sheep are followers! To move a flock, the shepherd only had to lead one sheep away and the rest would quickly follow (Mark 6:32-34). Sheep pay no attention to where they are going and can get so intent on eating that they will walk right off a cliff, and if the sheep behind him does not look up, he too will fall off the side of the cliff (Matt. 12:11). Sheep are always on the move, even if they have enough food where they are, and will wander away from the protection of the flock and cannot find their way home (Matt. 18:12-14). Sheep do not sense danger and sometimes are too trusting to follow anyone who wants to lead them away (Matt. 7:15; Acts 20:29-31).

The twenty-third psalm is possibly the most-quoted scripture in the Bible. The shepherd David wrote it in tribute to his Godly Shepherd. He compared his caring for the earthly sheep to how the Lord cared for him and for all of us today. Sheep can do nothing on their own, and without a shepherd, they would die. The shepherd led the sheep up to the high land in the spring to feed on green grass. Sheep would wade into rushing water and get dragged down by the weight of their wet wool and drown or get swept away by the current; thus, verse three, the shepherd led them beside still waters. The shepherd led the sheep over rocky, thorny, steep, and narrow trails, and these trails were infested with predators. The shepherd's staff was a long cane with a crooked end, to pull the sheep out of the water or to retrieve him from a bush or an incline. The rod was a twelve-inch bat that the shepherds could accurately throw for fifty yards and kill predators.

The shepherd used an oil concoction to doctor the sheep. The sheep would come to the shepherd, head down, and he would anoint them with the oil mixture for healing. Parasites would embed in the soft membrane of the sheep's face and work their way to the eyes and cause blindness. They were continually getting torn and scratched from the brush and the animals that attacked them. Sheep have no way to protect themselves, no claws, sharp teeth, or antlers. They do not watch out for one another; they scatter, they spook easily, and they have a hard time sleeping because they are a nervous lot.

Do you see the parallels? When Jesus offered to be our Good Shepherd, He was offering to be our friend and offering to stay with us through thick and thin. In the Old Testament, the word for *shepherd* and for *friend* came from the same root. When Jesus offered to be our Good Shepherd, He was saying that He would lead us. He knows our needs, the pitfalls of life, the hurts we experience, the agonies we suffer, and the doubts we feel. Nowhere are we promised by the Good Shepherd that life's journey will be free from wilderness experiences or that all danger will be abolished and that all rocks, thorns, and slippery places removed. What the Good Shepherd promises is that He will be with each sheep in every experience that comes upon them. Best of all, what He promises is that they will not lose their way, and that at last, they shall arrive where He wants them to be (Luke 12:22-24; John 10:11-15).

Jesus, the Good Shepherd, knows what we are like. We are like sheep. We can be stupid, roam all over looking for meaning, inclined to follow the wrong people, do not sense danger, and we all have our own sounds and our own individual needs. Despite all this, He promises that we will dwell in the house of the Lord forever (Ps. 23:6).

10. *Questions and Answers*

Q: What does the Bible say about dealing with stress?

A: Actually, the Bible does not teach how to deal with stress, but rather teaches not to deal with stress. Matthew 6:25-34 is the best lesson on trusting God and not worrying about your life situations and what you will do with tomorrow. 1 Peter 5:7 tells us to cast all or our anxieties on the Lord, Luke 21:34 advises us not to let our hearts be weighed down by the anxieties of life, and Matthew 13:22 explains that worry makes us unfruitful. When you are afraid and feel stress coming into your life, call upon the name of the Lord (Ps. 56:3), be still (Ps. 37:7-8), let the joy of the Lord replace stress (Neh. 8:10), and do not be dismayed (Isa. 41:10).

Q: How can God help me to be organized?

A: You can do all things through Jesus Christ who strengthens you (Phil. 4:13). God did all that He did through a plan, and is not a God of disorder but of peace (Ex. chapters 25-30; 1 Cor. 14:32). Paul, too, was teaching order (1 Cor. 14:40), and Proverbs has a lot to say about organization (Prov. 13:16), including committing everything you do to the Lord (Prov. 16:3).

Q: Does the Bible say anything about people who knowingly wrong others? Does it actually say what goes around comes around?

A: What goes around comes around is actually an Italian proverb: "*Ci Cento Ne Fa, Unane Aspetti.*" The Biblical Proverb says, "Do not say, I will pay you back for this wrong; Wait for the Lord and He will deliver you" (Prov. 20:22). Romans 12:14-19 tells us not to repay evil for evil, because it is the Lord's to avenge.

Q: Can you separate spiritual from secular leadership? Should you?

A: We do not separate spiritual from secular; God does. "For if their purpose or activity is of human origin, it will fail. But if it is of God, you will not be able to stop these men" (Acts 5:38-39). As for combining the two, there are many scriptures against this: "Do not conform any longer to the pattern of the world" (Rom. 12:2); "Bad company corrupts good character" (1 Cor. 15:33); and "do not be yoked together with unbelievers" (2 Cor. 6:14-17).

Q: How can we not do anything without God, yet when we do something wrong, is it still God's fault?

A: Why would we ever want to try to do anything without God when "He is able to do immeasurably more than all we ask or imagine" (Eph. 3:20)? "A man without God is trusting a spider's web" (Job 8:14). The book of Job best explains things happening to an upright guy. Job's friends tried to help him figure this out, and whose fault it was, his or God's. God never explained to Job the reasons for his suffering, but instead He questioned Job, and after this Job said, "Surely I spoke of things I did not understand" (Job 42:3).

We do not always understand why things go wrong or even why we do wrong, but we need to understand that God knows what is best (Isa. 46:10; Rom. 8:28) and will forgive us our wrongs when we confess, ask forgiveness, and repent.

Q: Our church is big into praise and worship and I think they carry it too far. I am uncomfortable with this. Can you help?

A: Praise is an expression of worship which recognizes and acknowledges God as the ultimate source and giver of all good gifts and can be expressed in many ways (Ps. 113:1, 117:1, 70:4, 16:7; Rom. 15:6; Ex. 15:1) just to name a few. Praise and worship are not preludes to the sermon but the sermon that comes from your heart. It is not what you get out of it but what you bring into it. If, however, you are uncomfortable, you should talk to the pastor, and maybe you could be assigned to a "behind-the-scenes" prayer that would lift up the Church Body and take you out of the sense of being watched.

Part XI
Good, Better, Best

1. You Are Extraordinary

Everybody knows about fingerprints. Of all earth's billions, no two people have the same pattern. Each of us is unique. But did you know that no two hearts are alike? Or stomachs, eyes, livers, nerves, blood vessels, or brains? You are, in fact, extraordinary! On physical examination, it is quite apparent that each of us in a very special way is a unique person. Even the shape of the liver differs from one person to another. So, too, its color and how it reacts inside its special environment and its size. One mature liver, for example, can weigh four times as much as another, and the same is true in principle for every organ.

Our brains also differ. The functions of this growing and vital organ can be mapped out in rough on the cortex, yet no neurosurgeon can have an accurate knowledge of a particular brain without careful and detailed pre-investigation, using all manner of scans and psychological tests. As one research neurologist points out, Individuals start life with brains differing enormously in structure. Its diversities within the species are of the same general character as are the differences between related species. As that successful and very human psalmist, King David, exclaimed, "For you created my inmost being; you knit me together in my mother's womb. I praise you because I am fearfully and wonderfully made; your works are wonderful, I know that full well" (Ps. 139:13-14).

Did you ever wonder why your partner feels pain or cold or heat more acutely or less acutely than you do? It is because of the striking variation in the sensitivity of our pain or other receptors. Some have little or no pain sensation, a fact which might influence your choice of occupation. Of ninety-seven prizefighters tested in New York, all but ten had a low pain sensitivity. Then there is color vision. You might say that curtain is green but your spouse's perception is blue. Who is right? Both of you are right, for we each see colors in a special way.

We are each a bundle of nerves. In the Bible, it is described as the spirit in man that is capable of great development, whatever our age. The brain consists of a billion interconnecting neurons mostly present from birth; the most complicated machine in the entire universe. But the numbers decrease with age, for millions of cells die daily. Is there no hope for us then? Not so! Your brain can grow whether you are seven or seventy. Whether we are young or old, neurologists now tell us that any learning activity actually increases the size and weight of the brain, and not from eating fish but from mental effort. King Solomon said, "The heart of the discerning acquires knowledge; the ears of the wise seek it out" (Prov. 18:15). The successful human being is one who forever questions his views and looks constantly to improve him- or herself.

That old, but ever new book, the Bible is a rich vein of practical business wisdom. So grasp firmly what Paul said in his letter to the Roman Christians: "We have different gifts according to the grace given us" (Rom. 12:6). Einstein said we use only .02 percent of our capacity. We each have a storehouse of unused talent in a combination that is unique to us. So accept yourself for what you are: a special blend of strengths and weaknesses. The servant who hid his talent, the only failures are those who die without taking advantage of their inborn capabilities and those who do not recognize and offset their weaknesses (Matt. 25:25). On the other hand, do not accept yourself as you are. Our present attainments are but a step along the way. What we knew as children is probably no longer true, and what we learned about God in Sunday school is just as likely not to be true. Jesus warned us about tradition (Mark 7:6-9). This is not to say that you have received false teachings all your life, but rather to say that if Jesus seems the same to you today as He did when you were a child, then you have not done much spiritual growing.

Even though we are of dust from the ground, we have the potential through repentance and the indwelling of the Holy Spirit to become a part of the divine family of God. We can truly become children of God (Rom. 8:12-17). Man does not have immortality, only God (1 Tim. 6:16). We do not have dwelling within us some kind of immortal soul freshly dished out at our birth. We are not, as human beings, godlike. But we can become, through Jesus Christ, in God's image, just as He originally planned. You have an undiscovered and unused talent. Use it in the service of God and of humanity and of yourself. You are indeed extraordinary. Be proud of yourself.

2. Who Is to Blame?

A young mother and father stood weeping over the still form of their son, and if that were not enough to weigh them down with heartache, it was his own brother who, in a fit of rage and jealousy, had lifted the weapon that brought death to their second son. Where did this terrible scene take place? Just outside the Garden of Eden (Gen. 4:3-8). Eve could have asked the same question that many other mothers have asked through the centuries. "Why, God?" She may, for an instant in her grief, have forgotten that it was through her disobedience that the flood of sickness, trouble, and death poured into the world. Let us check the biblical reasons for suffering, lest we, in an instant of grief, forget. Let us remember that God's love never fails (Heb. 13:5) when you or those dear to you come face-to-face with the inevitable suffering, loneliness, and grief in the lot of humanity.

Jesus once healed a woman who had been ill for eighteen years, but He did not take the blame for her illness. In fact, God has never accepted the blame for the problems of this life. Jesus pointed out the guilty party, Satan, in this woman's illness (Luke 13:10-16). Who afflicted Job with boils (Job 2:7)? Satan leads men to inflict pain. Bethlehem's boy babies were slain because Satan determined to kill baby Jesus. Consider it an honor that God believes you capable to bear a difficult experience as he did Paul. Paul could rejoice in tribulation because he knew God would give him grace to bear it, and at the same time use it to develop his character (2 Cor. 12:7-10).

Sometimes we have a tendency to assume that those who suffer are being punished for their sins. God is not in the business of dealing out punishment. Evil men will do their terrible deeds despite God. Those crushed in the tower of Siloam (Luke 13:4-5) or the ones from Galilee whom Pilate had killed while they were worshiping (Luke 13:1), were they worse sinners than others? The scripture says, "No, I tell you. But unless you change your hearts and lives, you will be destroyed as they were." Jesus was not saying that being killed was a sign of a person's unrighteousness. Death will come to us all, and His point is that unless we repent, we will not live again, but perish eternally.

Even the best of us have sometimes brought problems upon ourselves. A man dies if he violates the law of gravity by leaping from a high building. Disregard the laws of health and you become sick. Man has polluted the air and water and bulldozed away the countryside. We are to blame for most of our sicknesses due to neglect (Gal. 6:7), and or our mistakes of choice which violate natural, moral, and physical laws. God does not step in and stop things of nature. When Eutychus fell asleep on a windowsill, God did not work a miracle to prevent him from falling out of the window (Acts 20:9); rather the miracle came when Paul threw himself on him and he was revived. Victims of selfishness—our own or others'—cause disaster (1 Kings 21:1-16); Naboth, through innocence, was killed because of Ahab's selfishness.

Does God cease to love us during the suffering? Does He not care? We cannot forget that the Father shared with the Son the suffering of Calvary (2 Cor. 5:19). God alone can fully know the sum of what Satan introduced into the universe, and He alone knew that there was only one solution, which to counteract sin's deadly influence. There is nothing to indicate that Satan was aware of God's plan of salvation for man. No doubt, it came to him as a surprise when Christ promised to appear on the world scene in the form of man against him. No doubt, he had expected God to destroy man after he sinned, and this would have given him an opportunity to accuse Him of being a merciless executioner. But instead, Christ promised Adam and Eve that He would come and die in their places (Gen. 3:15).

Through Jesus, every man is given an opportunity to make his own choice between two lords, Jesus or Satan, truth or falsehood (Deut. 30:19-20). The enemy of God has so successfully conditioned men's minds that most people do not even bother to investigate the matter (Hos. 4:6). God did not destroy Satan as soon as he rebelled, for there was no way to explain sin to a universe that had never experienced it, and God would not have a kingdom in which His subjects served Him from fear rather than love. Even knowing that we were sinners, Jesus died for us (Rom. 5:8).

Let us not forget that the Father shared with the Son the suffering of Calvary. God suffered for us and with us, and will not allow it to continue one moment longer than it is necessary to fulfill the prophecies. God does not shield His own from the stern realities of life, and may permit the test as He did Job to prove Himself true. "He is faithful and will not permit you to be tempted above that which you are able to bear" (1 Cor. 10:13).

Can troubles or problems or sufferings or hunger or nakedness or danger or violent death separate us from Christ's love? "I am sure that neither death, nor life, nor angels, nor ruling spirits, nothing now, nothing in the future, no powers, nothing above us, nothing below us, nor anything else in the whole world will ever be able to separate us from the love of God that is in Christ Jesus our Lord" (Rom. 8:38-39) and this statement is worth living for God.

3. God's Umbrella of Protection

Is God's protection everywhere you are? The question really should be: Are you everywhere God's protection is? Habakkuk 1:13 assures us that God's eyes are too pure to look on evil, and He cannot tolerate wrong. According to this statement, we should be careful where we go and what we tolerate if we expect God's protection. The psalms are filled with the promises of God's protection, such as Psalms 91:4, 10; "He will cover you with His feathers and no harm will befall you; no disaster will come near your tent." However, read the passages before and after carefully and in their entirety. God's blessings, promises, and protections come with conditions that we dwell in this shelter and that we love Him. We can compare God's protection to an umbrella. When you are under the physical umbrella, you are protected from the downpour of rain. When you stay under God's umbrella, then you are protected from the downpour of dangers and snares that the devil throws at you. Do not take this protection for granted or misuse it. Remember, the Scripture warns "not to put the Lord our God to the test, but do what is right and good in the Lord's sight so that it may go well with you" (Deut. 6:16-18). Even Jesus did not test His Father's protection when the devil was tempting Him (Matt. 4:7).

God promises to protect you from your biggest enemy, sin, which no longer has the power to enslave you or determine your eternal destiny, provided you have accepted Jesus as your Lord and Savior (John 3:16-18).

This protection goes beyond your idea of bodily protection from sickness, disease, and distress. You have an eternal life insurance bought by the blood of Jesus. Notice, Jesus tells us not to fear those who can destroy only our bodies, but to fear, stand in reverent awe of the one that can destroy both soul and body (Matt. 10:28-31). Again, carefully examine the passage and understand that you will have injuries, trials and tribulations as you live this life. There is a most encouraging clause in the policy that states that Christ is able to guard what you have entrusted to Him for the Day of the Lord (2 Tim. 1:12). What He is guarding is your eternal life that He has given you and no one can snatch this out of His hand (John 10:27-29).

The protection that Jesus prayed over His disciples that God would protect them (John 17:9-12), He also prayed for you and me (John 17:20-26). This protection is for you to resist the devil that is out to destroy you. Satan may win a few battles by making you sick or hurt, or taking a loved one, but he will never win your soul that you have given to Jesus Christ. This protection is for judgment (Rom. 2:1-11) and if you are right with Him, then you will follow His laws (Rom. 5:9) and will be safe from the wrath of God's judgment. The insurance policy is free, but God expects you to follow the psalmist in expressing your love to God because you realize how great God's love is for you (Ps. 86). Everything was written down as scripture for our learning, and we have the same hope in God as the men who were inspired to write them.

One of the most precious gifts of protection comes in the form of the Holy Spirit. Jesus promised to send a counselor to be with us forever, to live within all of us, to teach everyone the truth and remind believers of everything Jesus promised. Once more I caution you to read and study each passage, and find that this love, teaching, and protection comes through obedience and love for the Father. The Lord does not want anyone to die and go to hell, but to be prepared for the day of His coming by living holy and godly lives. Peter reminds you of Paul's writings, which he says are hard to understand, and which ignorant and unstable people distort, as they do the other scriptures, to their own destruction (2 Pet. 3:8-16). Do not be found guilty of pulling out one or two passages to justify your actions, expecting God to protect you in your sinful follies. "Do not be arrogant, but be afraid. For if God did not spare the natural branches, He will not spare you either" (Rom. 11:20-21). Reading the entire chapter of Romans 11, you will find that this is speaking of the remnant of Israel, but God is speaking to us today with this strict warning. Therefore, as Paul warns, do not be conceited, do not act like the world, do not think more of yourself than you should, and do not be overcome by evil.

Remember in John 9:2-3, the power of God is seen in suffering. When faced with tragedy or disability, try not to ask why God did not protect you, but instead ask God to give you strength for this trial and a clearer perspective of what is happening. You know that such troubles are going to a Christian and they are not always caused by sin or lack of faith. Experiencing problems and persecutions can build character, patience, and sensitivity toward others who also face trouble. God will not give you more than you can stand and His protection still covers you. His protective love is strongly expressed in 2 Corinthians 4:8-9: "We are hard pressed on every side, but not crushed; perplexed, but not in despair; persecuted, but not abandoned; struck down, but not destroyed."

Living for God protects you from shame so that Christ will be exalted, whether by life or death (Rom. 9:33). The Lord is near, and we do not have to be anxious about anything and will have peace that God is guarding our hearts and minds. You have been anointed and He has set His seal on us and His Spirit lives within us and we are guaranteed eternal life. Now, for the price we pay, that is one great insurance policy. You see, Jesus paid the premiums for us in one lump sum on the cross, and it is paid in full for eternity.

4. Stress Relief

We live in a town with two blinking lights and a few city-enforced stop signs that no one pays any attention to. We do, however, pay attention to who is on the other side of the sign, in case we have a back fence tidbit for them. On my morning jaunt to the post office and Allsup's for my daily caffeine fix, I managed to encounter only one of the caution lights and a couple of the slow-down-and-look-both-ways signs. My husband bypasses the hazards of small town and manages to find his winding way to and from his work on the farm to market roads. From this enlightenment, you can understand the cautious apprehension of changing lanes and finding turning points in the neighboring city. However, the overzealous fellow bumper-car drivers are not so considerate of their country cousins, as shown by screeching brakes, sounding horns, and a friendly wave! An old philosopher—that would be me—penned: "rushing through the cities of life, causes dissension between husband and wife!"

We have tried bringing some of the city-bred folks to our home to show them the way to relax and encourage them to enjoy God's scenery, only to learn that they quickly become bored. Their cars sputter and stall when driven under sixty miles per hour, and they live in constant fear of getting lost and never being found on the lonely dirt roads. Then there is the disappointment of no one to crowd off of the lane which they consider theirs. That is life among humans! But is this the way it should be or the way God intended? Not according to John 14:27: "Peace I leave with you" and Romans 12:18: "If it is possible, as far as it depends on you, live at peace with everyone!"

This world of drivers and pedestrians lives by the philosophy of hurry up and stop—a standard that, in a short time, wears out the brakes of caution, and all is bulldozed over with thin-treaded tires of inconsideration. As we rush to our self-appointed destination, we should glance into the rear view mirror and discover who and what we have laid low, causing permanent scars. Perhaps we might even see a blessing striving to rise up, only to be left behind in a cloud of exhaust, grieving the Holy Spirit in the process. "And do not grieve the Holy Spirit of God, with whom you were sealed for the day of redemption. Get rid of all bitterness, rage, and anger, brawling and slander, along with every form of malice. Be kind and compassionate to one another, forgiving each other, just as in Christ, God forgave you" (Eph. 4:30-32).

We are changing our course now and we are out of the city, passing through a string of small towns and farmland. To my right, I spot a herd of goats acting much like what I observed in a large department store a short time ago. Two of them have rushed over to the same spot, butting heads in a battle for the same clump of grass in a twenty-acre spread. There are at least 150 scriptures concerning goats, and most of them speak of sacrifice. However, one jumped out at me from Isaiah during the prophecy of Babylon. "Babylon will be overthrown by God and jackals will fill her houses and there the wild goats will leap about." The fact that we still see goats leaping upon any- and everything that is in their path tells us that their nature has never changed. Just to throw in a side lesson here, I will add that Jesus's prophecy said that the goats and the sheep will be separated when He comes again. The goats that will be on His left will be told they are cursed and condemned to eternal fire prepared for the devil and his angels (Matt. 25:31-46). It is time to change our goatish nature and stop leaping around?

The cattle in the adjoining field have a different approach than the goats. They, although in a congregational herd, seem to be oblivious of each other. More human characteristics? You will have to get out your King James Version of the Bible to read these next scriptures. "Seemeth it a small thing unto you to have eaten up the good pasture, but ye must tread down with your feet the residue of your pastures? And to have drunk of the deep waters but ye must foul the residue with your feet? And as for my flock, they eat that which ye have trodden with your feet and they drink that which ye have fouled with your feet. Therefore thus saith the Lord God unto them, behold, I, even I, will judge between the fat cattle and between the lean cattle. Because ye have thrust with side and with shoulder, and pushed all the diseased with your horns, till ye have scattered them abroad. Therefore will I save my flock and they shall no more be a prey and I will judge between cattle and cattle" (Ezek. 34:17:22). In other words, pay attention to those around you who may need some of what you have.

Now we see the pen of sheep, clustered together, knowing there is safety in numbers and warmth and protection within a huddle. These little guys depend totally on their shepherds for guidance, food and drink, medical treatment, and protection. We have a Good Shepherd who laid down His life for us (John 10:11). He oversees our souls and will come and gather us one day. He is the Shepherd who equips us with everything we need for doing His will, and we live securely in our Shepherd's strength. Born-again believers listen to the Shepherd's voice and follow the ways of the Lord. We sheep have been promised eternal life and will never perish. This sheep huddle is the Body of Christ, and we should make every effort to cluster together and keep the unity of the Spirit through the bond of peace (Eph. 4:3-4) and do not give up meeting together (Heb. 10:25).

Phew! There is a pigpen! Now these little stinkers, if not contained, can cause havoc. They can root up a crop row by row and destroy a well-planned garden, much like Satan destroyed God's plan for the Garden of Eden and uprooted it. The pig, which wallows in the mud, has come to symbolize the complete enjoyment of almost all sins of the flesh, including sloth (Prov. 19:15), selfishness (Prov. 15:27), lust (Matt. 5:28), wrath (James 1:20), pride (Prov. 16:18), and gluttony (Prov. 23:21). He enjoys the mud he is covered with, and instead of washing it away, grows sleek with sin. The Lord warned His disciples not to give what was holy to the dogs, nor cast their pearls before swine, or they might trample them under their feet and turn on you, tearing you to pieces (Matt. 7:6). The swinish person enjoys wallowing in his sin and will destroy anything in the way of that enjoyment, even the truth. Paul said that he, and all of us, were just this wretched but thanks be to God, through Jesus Christ our Lord, we have been rescued from this sinful mud bath.

We can learn a lot from God's creatures! Remember the command from Jesus not to worry about what we wear, eat, or drink because of the birds. They are beautiful, as are the lilies of the field, and God provides for them all. He goes on to tell us that first we must seek the Kingdom of God and these provisions will be given to us as well. Jesus also compares us to good trees and bad trees, saying that we should bear good fruit, because this is how we will be recognized as God's. God sent His messenger ahead of Jesus to prepare the way for Him, and then sent His Son to prepare the way for all who would follow. This way that Jesus prepared will of course include trials and tribulations, but can be stress-free if we allow Him to do all that He offers. "Come to me, all you who are weary and burdened and I will give you rest" (Matt. 11:28-30).

5. Good Seed and Bad Seed

You will notice that on every application, questionnaire, medical form, etc. there will be questions with multiple choice answers. I do okay with these, but then a question will pop up with one of the options being "other"! This confuses me somewhat, especially if it appears after the choice of male or female! Assuming that one was a typo, I ignore it and go to the next question. On some forms, hospital admittance mostly, there will be a list of denominations and "other." This is totally acceptable; however, when it comes to God and Christianity, there should be no "other," as stated in the First Commandment (Ex. 20:3). When it comes to God, there is only one choice (Deut. 6:4; Mal. 2:10).

Should Christians be concerned with life outside of the Christian faith? Absolutely! Paul spoke to the crowd, telling them about the time on the road to Damascus when Jesus explained to him his assignment (Acts 22:8-10). God sent a man named Ananias to further explain that God had chosen Paul to know His will and to see the righteous one and to hear words from His mouth. He was appointed to be a witness to all men about everything that he had heard and seen. Now we all will not be knocked flat by a blinding light from God to get our attention, but He has called all Christians to be His witnesses. Even if God did knock us down, we would probably react as the Apostle Paul by asking, "Who are you and what shall I do?" The question, how do we know when God is speaking to us, has been asked throughout the ages. Samuel heard the voice of God but did not recognize it until he was instructed by Eli

(1 Sam. 3:1-10). Gideon, the doubting Thomas of the Old Testament, asked for a sign to prove God was speaking, not once but three times (Jud. 6:37-39).

We have something the Old Testament people did not have, which is the completed Bible, and it is filled with written instructions. Even though He has called all to be His witnesses, we can hardly tell others what we have seen if we have seldom or never opened the instruction book. In order to hear God, you have to know God through His revelation found in the Bible. One of the instructions is to study so we will be approved by God and to God. Do not be ashamed to work for and say we work for God and be prepared to answer the questions that people ask about God and His holy Word. Discipline yourself to spend time daily reading the Bible and praying. To know someone, you must spend time with them; otherwise, they are just a casual acquaintance. The more time you spend with God and reading the Bible, the easier it will be to recognize His voice. God speaks to us so that we may understand the truth, primarily through the Bible as we read, and the Holy Spirit points out the truth to us. Do you have a problem? Ask God! Do you have a solution? Ask God if it is the right one! He does not lie (Titus 1:2) and will comfort you in time of trouble (1 Cor. 1:4).

Let us take a look at the parable of the Sower in Matthew 13:3-23. After you are told about God and Christianity, you must root yourself in the Word of God, or the new plants will wither. If you do not understand the Word, the devil comes and snatches them away from your mind. Once the devil has taken hold of the Word, he can twist it to make it non-understandable to you. Jesus bluntly explained that you do not understand His language and ask why it is not clear to us. And then, as He often does, He answered His own question, saying that nonbelievers belong to their own father, the devil, and wish to work for him instead of God. He who belongs to God hears the Word of God. The reason nonbelievers do not hear God's voice is because they do not belong to God (John 8:42-47). The devil will use what interests you the most to snatch the Word from your heart. This day in time, the new religious interest appears to be the occult and idol worship that is as widespread now as in the earliest days of the Old Testament. This generation, if they are thinking they invented these new interests, will be surprised to learn that God knew it would come. "The Spirit clearly says that in later times, some will abandon the faith and follow deceiving spirits and things taught by demons" (1 Tim. 4:1).

We can read about these deceiving spirits from Genesis to Revelation. All forms of the occult, divination, necromancy, astrology, hypnotism, fortune telling, and magic are forbidden by God (Lev. 19:26-28; Deut. 18:9-14). Witchcraft was openly and widely practiced in the Old Testament times, and it was still rampant in the early church. Not all miracles were from God. Satan can also perform lying signs and wonders. The Bible clearly states that it is in the realm of deception that these workers of iniquity operate (Jer. 14:14). Fortune tellers can reveal much but their power is limited (Dan. 2:2, 5:7-8). God challenged the people to see if the power of their astrologers was greater than that of God. Is this really a serious offense? The scripture says that they shall not escape judgment, and they shall be refused entrance into the Kingdom of God and their end shall be the lake of fire (Mal. 3:5; Gal, 5:19-21; Rev. 21:8, 22:14-15).

These practices are not only an abomination in God's sight, they have a bad influence on others. Christians must separate themselves from all forms of these detestable practices, including choosing carefully the people we spend time with. The book of Proverbs teaches against believers hanging out with nonbelievers, as does the New Testament (2 Cor. 6:14). Close relationships are not recommended, but neither does scripture say to ignore them or think Christians are better. James writes that friendship with the world is hatred toward God; however, he goes on to teach us to pray, because there is great power in the prayer of a righteous person. We have God's promises that prayers are not in vain. "Delight yourself in the Lord and He will give you the desires of your heart" (Ps. 37:4). It is the desire of God that all might be saved! Is this your desire? Get to know the God that loves you and let His desires become so real to you that your prayer becomes His answer. Eliminate the competition and turn all your attention on God and His will for your life (Matt. 6:24). My prayer for you is that He will fill you with hope and joy and peace as you trust Him, and that you fear the Lord and serve only Him faithfully. Do not associate with anything or anyone or any message that is not from God, and hold to the commitment of Joshua: "As for me and my household, we will serve the Lord" (Jos. 24:14-15).

6. *Pardon*

Have you accepted from the King of the universe, the pardon for your sins which He came all the way down from heaven to this prison house of sin to give you? No one on this earth needs to be lost, because He has broken God's law and committed crimes against the government of heaven. Jesus Himself paid the death penalty for us at the cross. Everyone who is lost will be so because he has refused God's pardon.

Salvation is a gift, yet Jesus says that those who obtain it must sacrifice all (Luke 24:33). Jesus loved us so much that if there had been just one person to be born on this earth that sinned, He would have still have died for that one person. In turn, He asks us to make Him number one in our affections above every other person or thing.

Faith is an act of the will in receiving Christ as our Savior. However, this involves more than a mere intellectual belief that Jesus is the Son of God and died for our sins. The Bible tells us that the devil believes and his demons believe in God and tremble (James 2:19). Well may he tremble, for who knows better than he the reality of God and the certainty of his punishment? Paul says that we are saved by grace through faith and we cannot save ourselves because salvation is a gift that cannot be bought or earned. Faith is a work we use to describe a relationship with God, as with a person well known. The better we know Him, the better our relationship with Him may be. Faith implies an attitude toward God of love, trust, and deepest admiration. It means having enough confidence in Him, based on the more-than-adequate evidence revealed, to be willing to believe whatever He says, to accept whatever He offers and to do whatever He wished, without reservation, for the rest of eternity.

Peter said we had to repent and turn to God and be baptized in the name of Jesus. Repentance involves a genuine sorrow on the sinner's part that his sins crucified the Son of God. As he realizes this, he will turn from his sins to follow the Savior. Sin is disobedience to God's revealed will, and the wages of sin is death. God worked out a solution to this problem whereby both His mercy and His justice could be maintained. His justice would be satisfied in a twofold way: (1) the penalty of sin would be paid and (2) no man could say God treated him unfairly, for God would give every person the opportunity to choose for himself which side he would be on.

Only by adoption can a person change his family. The same applies to the spiritual life. Only through a new birth can one transfer from Adam's family to God's family. This new birth is the Christian's adoption into His new family (Gal 4:4-7). God's children become heirs of God and the promise to Christ's heirs is eternal life. Our inheritance is a gift of God and is being kept in heaven, awaiting our arrival (1 Pet. 1:4).

7. Does Grace Contradict the Law?

You name it and there is a law for it or against it. In the Bible are found the laws of God's government. Some were temporary, such as a detour, twenty-miles-an-hour sign near highway construction. One law towering high above all others was translated into ten "thou-shall-nots," carved in stone, that even sinful man could not fail to understand. Four specific laws are described in the Bible, usually under the general term law or statute. No distinction among them was necessary in the Old Testament, since they were all in force. By Christ's time, Roman civil laws had largely replaced the Jewish civil statutes, and after Christ's death, the sacrificial laws became obsolete.

The moral law or the Ten Commandments were written by Moses on stone tablets given to him by God (Ex. 24:12). These were the first tablets which Moses broke in a fit of anger because of the rebellious people. The second set of tablets was given to Moses and placed into an ark that Moses built (Ex. 32:19). The ceremonial or worship laws are comprised of most of the books of Exodus and Leviticus. The ceremonial laws may be compared to the scaffolding of a building, to be removed when they have served their purpose. When the death of the real Lamb of God, Jesus, rendered the sacrificial laws pointless, they were replaced by ordinances and ceremonies Christ Himself commanded: baptism and the Lord's Supper. The civil laws are scattered throughout the books of Exodus and Leviticus. These laws were set up, then Israel became a nation and covered sanitation, crime, court procedures, etc. They ceased to exist when the Jews ceased to be a nation. An example of a civil statute is found in Exodus 21:33:34. The health laws found throughout the Bible start in the Garden of Eden. After man sinned, he was not permitted to eat of the tree of life. This necessitated the first modification in his diet, and consisted of the addition of vegetables (Gen. 3:18). The principles of healthful living are in God's Word, and if followed, will still maintain optimum health, even in today's degenerated society.

We know of no written Ten Commandments before Sinai, but there is much evidence that those who lived back then knew God's law. No doubt it was passed from one to the other in oral form. If sin existed before Sinai, law also had to exist. Before Cain killed his brother Abel, God said to him, "If you do things well, I will accept you, but if you do not do them well, sin is ready to attack you. Sin wants you, but you must rule over it" (Gen 4:7). There are recorded instances of every commandment being broken before Sinai. No one disputes that the Tem Commandments were in effect from Sinai until Christ's day. David wrote a song of praise for God's law, Isaiah regarded the law in testing all religious teachings, and Solomon knew that it was impossible to please God while despising His law.

Some claim the law has been done away with, for Christ fulfilled it. To learn what the word fulfilled means, let us see how it is used elsewhere.

Jesus came to John the Baptist to be baptized, saying, "Let it be so now, it is proper for us to do this to fulfill righteousness" (Matt. 3:15); and in Matthew 5:17, Jesus said that he had come to fulfill the law, not to abolish it. Paul said the law is holy; James said a person who follows the law but fails to obey even one command breaks them all; John calls a professed Christian who does not keep the law a liar and also says that God's people must obey God's commands.

Since breaking God's law separates us from God (Isa. 59:2) and only in His presence is there joy, it follows that the lawbreaker is the unhappy person. Jesus told us that He was the door, and all who entered would be saved, and that He came to give life. Man seeks for the abundant life in a shorter work and more things, but Jesus says that He will give life more abundantly. So is man searching in the wrong places? Christ summarized the Ten Commandments in saying to love the Lord your God and your neighbor like you love yourself. All the law and writings of the prophets depend on these two commandments. Some think these two commandments replace the original ten, but have misunderstood Jesus's meaning, because He went on to say that these two hang on all the law and the prophets.

Does grace free us from keeping the commandments? "We are not under the law but grace" (Rom. 6:14); however, Paul considered the law to be holy, just, and good, and quickly covered his sometimes-called contradiction with: "What then? Shall we sin because we are not under the law but under grace? God forbid!" (Rom. 6:15). So we do not destroy the law by grace and following the way of faith, because faith causes us to be what the law truly wants. Did Calvary demonstrate that now, since the cross, it is safe to toy with sin, or does the fact that sin took the life of God's Son demonstrate for all time it is a deadly nature? We cannot suggest that God could not change the law, even to save the life of His Son, but then would turn around and tell us that we need no longer keep it. If the law could have been changed or set aside, Jesus would never have needed to die, and Calvary was nothing more than a meaningless drama. It is not the Law versus Grace, but the Law *is* Grace. Both are vital to the plan of salvation. Jesus said, "If you love me keep my commandments." Only that obedience which is promoted by love is acceptable to God. He said He would put the teachings in our hearts and minds and be our God, forgive us our sins, and remember them no more (Heb. 8:10-12).

8. Health

Jesus was not totally understood to the people of His day on earth. Not only did He freely associate with tax collectors and other outcasts, but He showed no interest in overthrowing the Roman government. Sometimes it seemed that He was more interested in healing people than anything else, for He spent more time doing this than preaching. Didn't He know that physicians care for the body, while preachers look after the soul? Why didn't He stick to saving the lost and leave the sick bodies to those professionally trained?

Until very recently, it was believed that if the body was sick, you should go to a physician. If the mind was confused, you should see a psychiatrist, and if your soul was in trouble, you should seek out a minister. Today, there is a growing interest in total health, the well-being of the total man. Modern medicine is beginning to realize that it is impossible to heal the body without treating the mind; they are calling this therapy. However, the mind refuses to recover if the body needs additional treatment.

Jesus knew this! He knew how man was made. He Himself had made man, formed him of the dust of the earth, and then into his nostrils breathed His own life-giving breath (Gen. 2:7). He knew that illness, even fatigue, acts like a drug and dulls the mind. And whatever dulls the mind weakens willpower. He knew that conscience operates through the mind, therefore the conscience is affected by the quality of the brain tissue and the health of the nerves. And the quality of the brain tissue is affected by the food man eats. Jesus knew that a sick body means a mind that is not functioning at its best. He wanted those that came to be healed in the body to also have a sound mind. Jesus treated the whole man (Matt. 9:2-6).

Recently, the owner of a self-portrait looked at the painting he had purchased and was horrified. The colors of the features had begun to run downward, and bled together like a white shirt on a bad wash day. He turned the canvas upside down, trying to coax the features into place like a "sand under glass" puzzle, but to no avail. A restorer tried to push the features back, but the oozing paint refused to return to its original place. Evidently, the young painter had mixed his paints with too much cheap oil, and now the portrait was worthless. The canvas on which we paint is heredity, the health, the intellect, and the talents we are born with. The paints and oils are what we add throughout our lifetimes.

God wants to be a tube of paint in our portrait, and He is anxious that we reflect His likeness so perfectly, with no addition of cheap oil, that seeing us, men may see Him, and seeing Him, love Him. This is the purpose of redemption, to restore God's image in His creation (Rom. 8:29). Glamour refers to the world of emotional being and of desire in which all forms dwell. It is this glamour which colors all our lives and produces false values, wrong desires, needless so-called necessities, worries, anxieties, and cares, cheap oil. Since the Holy Spirit communicates with us through our minds and thoughts, the health of our minds becomes very important to God. The more alert our minds, the better condition of our bodies, the more surrendered our will, the more fully Christ can achieve His purposes through us.

God wants us to enjoy health. Man's original diet came from seed-bearing plants, and every tree that had fruit with seed in it, nuts, and grain. Seems we are trying to get back to the original diet today with supplements, vitamins, and health foods. It is amazing how smart God was and is. Like the old saying about your mom and dad getting smarter as you grow older. We are sons of God and are entitled to good health and well-being. "By His stripes we were healed" is past tense. We are not being healed but were healed, and now by faith, we can claim our health through Christ. The healing of the physical body would be enough for most, but the healing of our spirit and soul is more important. When we live spiritually and emotionally healthy, our inner live is oriented to God, not because of what we can receive, but because we seek total relationship with God. Then the forces of divine life will pour thorough us and produce what is needed. That this kind of life will produce a sound body and freedom from physical ills is quite possible. A truly spirit-filled life puts the concerns of others before himself and this freedom from self-centeredness is one of the first laws of good health.

Holistic health from a Christian viewpoint emphasizes the importance of the whole person, physical, emotional, and spiritual. Holistic health sees a person not only as an individual, but as someone living in relationship with God, other people, and the whole of creation. Jesus's ministry was holistic. "The Spirit of the Lord is upon me because He has anointed me to bring the good news to the poor. He has sent me to proclaim release to the captives and recovery of sight to the blind, to let the oppressed go free, to proclaim the year of the Lord's favor" (Luke 4:18-19). Jesus ministered to the whole person. He healed physically, emotionally, spiritually, and socially.

In the Hebrew tradition, a human was a unity of body and soul, and when in a right relationship with God, they were in a state of *shalom*, health-wholeness-peace. In the Christian Greek tradition, persons who were whole had *soteria*, salvation, viewed not just as a spiritual state or physical state, but in its whole context. Get right with God and ask to receive your healing from your head down to your toes in the name of Jesus.

9. The End of the Rainbow

Have you looked for that elusive pot of gold at the rainbow's end? Did you know that the rainbow has no end? If the earth were not in the way, a rainbow would be a complete circle. It is also a three-dimensional cone, which puts me in mind of the Trinity. In this light, there really is a pot of gold at the end of the rainbow. A rainbow resembling an emerald encircles the throne of God in heaven, and the one who sits on it has the appearance of jasper and carnelian. The Bible is a beginning, an end and a beginning. The rainbow around the throne may signify the completion of the covenant that God made with Noah when he promised the earth would never again be destroyed with rain. Noah's rainbow showed old life destroyed and a beginning of new life on earth, and the rainbow around the throne shows old life destroyed and a beginning of an eternal life with God.

There was a gold rush in Colorado in 1859, and the town of Auraria was built. In Latin, the word *Auraria* means City of Gold. When the ground ran out of gold, the miners left for California with the '49ers and left the golden city a ghost town. There is an eternal city of gold at the end of God's rainbow of life in that new city that will never exhaust its supply of gold or time. As John gazed at the wall, he saw that it was made of jasper, and that the city was made of pure gold, as pure as glass. John was using the language of appearance, for apparently both the jasper and the gold differ from these metals as they are known today. For certain, this is not the gold God put in His earth, but a very precious purified gold, just as we too will be purified. John saw that the altar before God was gold, and the twenty-four elders around the throne wore crowns of gold. The crowns were similar to those given to victors in Greek games, in contrast with the crown of a sovereign ruler. The crowns seem to indicate that the elders had been purified and rewarded. The church of Laodicea was urged to buy not ordinary gold, but refined gold, referring to that which would glorify God and make them truly rich. Through its banking industry, the city had material wealth. The church lacked spiritual richness. Though they had beautiful clothes, they were urged to wear white clothes, symbolic of righteousness, which would cover their spiritual nakedness (Revelation).

Gold is used through the Bible not only literally but figuratively. Peter compared faith to gold and contrasted purified faith with purified gold.

Faith is more precious and of greater worth than gold. Even refined gold, though it lasts a long time, eventually perishes. It will be valueless in the marketplace of eternity, but faith purchases an inheritance that can never perish. Paul had laid a foundation in Corinth with the message of the cross. Apollos too had labored beneficially in Corinth, and apparently so also had Peter, whom Paul here called Cephas (1 Cor. 1:12, 3:22). But as Paul wrote, someone else was ministering in Corinth, and Paul's message to him and others like him was a warning. Jesus alone was the foundation and the basis of salvation, but others had come to Corinth and preached a different gospel (2 Cor. 11:13). Perhaps such a one was present in Corinth when Paul wrote this letter to the Corinthians. Paul described three kinds of builders or ministers: the expert, the unwise, and the destructive.

The materials used in the building may be interpreted in as least four ways: (1) The gold, silver, and costly stones refer to the enduring quality of the builder's work, and the wood, hay, or straw suggest work that is temporary and valueless. This view is supported by work and what he has built. (2) The three expensive materials suggest sound doctrine which the builder builds into people's lives, and the three valueless materials are false doctrines. (3) The first three materials refer to the worker's worthy motives and the other three point to his unworthy motives. (4) The gold, silver, and costly stones refer to the believers who constitute the church, that is supported by similar uses of the metaphor in Ephesians 2:22, and the wood, hay, or straw represent unregenerate, not spiritually reborn, stubbornly defiant people present in the church (1 Cor. 3:10-12).

At the Beautiful Gate, when the beggar asked Peter and John for money, Peter told him he did not have any silver or gold, but would give him what he had, and healed him in the name of Jesus (Acts 3:1-8). When all the people stood amazed that the lame man could walk, Peter assessed the situation and used it as an opportunity to preach. "Change your hearts and lives! Come back to God and He will forgive you sins." He may have reminded them that on the day that God will show His anger, neither their silver nor gold will save them (Zeph. 1:18).

In Lamentations, Jeremiah described the people's fate (4:1-3) and Isaiah told of a land filled with silver and gold, but also filled with idols. He said they would bow low with shame and God would not forgive them (Isa. 2:7-9). God promises to guide those who obey and trust Him. Those who obey must actively explore God's Word, searching for the silver and gold of wisdom which brings them profit. The commands of the Lord are worth more than gold, even the purest gold, and the psalmist stated he loved them more than the purest gold (Ps. 119:27). Job told his friends that God would test him and he would come out of his trials like gold, but added he had not put his trust in gold (Job 31:24).

"The Kingdom of God is like treasure hidden in a field. When a man found it, he sold all he had and bought the field" (Matt. 13:44). This parable illustrates the value of the heavenly treasure and the effort that should be made to secure it. Count no sacrifice too much or labor too hard in order to gain the treasures of truth. The gospel is interlaced with golden veins of wisdom, and filled with the knowledge of God. In the gold fields, a man might pass over the place where the treasure is concealed. So it was with the Jews, and when Christ came, they did not recognize Him as the Messiah. They held this pot of gold in their hands, but the tradition that had been handed down from generation to generation and the human interpretations of the scripture hid from them the truth as it is in Jesus. "If the gospel is hid, it is hid to them that are lost" (2 Cor. 4:3-4).

We cannot expect to gain spiritual knowledge without earnest toil. Those who desire to find the golden treasures of truth must dig for them, just as the miner digs for gold in the earth. Everyone who competes in a race goes into strict training, and Bible study needs to be strict in order for us to find the gold. "If you call out for insight and cry aloud for understanding, and if you look for it as for silver and search for is as for hidden treasure, then you will understand the fear of the Lord and find the knowledge of God" (Prov. 2:3-5). David loved God's commands more than gold, and we should too!

10. He Won, We Win

We cannot always see sin or touch it or feel it. Every man, woman, and child stands helpless before it. Helpless, were it not for the selfless act of the Son of God, who dared to touch sin and death for every man.

Adam and Eve were created innocent and holy; however, they were not placed beyond the possibility of doing wrong. They were created with the capacity to appreciate the wisdom and benevolence of God's character and the justice of His command, and were free to obey or disobey. The tree of knowledge would test their loyalty and love to the one who had created them. It was obey and live, disobey and die. Rather than follow God's instructions, Eve followed the temptations of the serpent and ate of the tree. When she saw that it was good for food, pleasant to the eye, and a tree to make her wise, she ate the fruit and gave some to her husband, and he ate also. Satan spoke through a serpent in the garden, a creature God had created. This is the first recorded scripture of Satan entering into a body to cause deception.

Because of man's disobedience, God drove man out of the Garden to till the ground from where he came. Originally, immortality was promised to man only on the condition of obedience; the day they disobeyed, they would forfeit eternal life and be doomed to death. When the connection between God and man was cut by Adam's sin, man was cut off from the source of life and immediately began to die. That death would have been permanent, had not God immediately put into operation His plan for saving man. "Sin came into the world because of what one man did and with sin came death. This is why everyone must die, because everyone sinned" (Rom. 5:12). "All have sinned and fall short and the wages of sin is death" (Rom 3:23, 6:23).

Christ said that the hate in men's hearts, the lust in their eyes, and even the idle words they speak are considered sin by God. If you and I were to commit only those sinful acts each day, there would be a thousand sinful acts each year of which we were guilty! Multiply your age by 1,000 to see how many that would be in your lifetime!

Man cannot save himself from his sinful condition, no more than the person from Cush can change the color of his skin or a leopard can change his spots. In the same way, Jerusalem could not change and do good because they were accustomed to doing evil. Man is helpless before the power of sin because he is a creature of the flesh, having been sold into slavery under the control of sin. Paul's reaction when he realized his sinful nature was "what a wretched man am I," but his next comment gives up the hope he had: "I thank God for saving me through Jesus Christ our Lord" (Rom 7:24-25).

One day, as a painting crew was working at the top of a lighthouse, an accident occurred that hurled one of the painters through space to certain death on the rocks below. The workmen hurried down the ladders to the foot of the lighthouse, and you can imagine their shock when they discovered a dazed but apparently unharmed painter sitting on the ground. Beside him was the broken body of a soft, wooly sheep. Instead of being dead, the man was only stunned, but the sheep was dead! The stricken painter represents you and me, and the dear sheep portrays Jesus, the Lamb of God, and what He did to save us from death. "Look! The Lamb of God who takes away the sin of the world" (John 1:29).

Jesus actually took my sins upon Himself as if they were His own. He died in my place! He became my substitute and took my death penalty. He had no sin but made Himself sin because He loved the world and gave His life for each of us. This is more than the human mind can understand. What did Paul mean when he said that Jesus was made to be sin for us? It can mean only one thing: that the Lord did in reality lay my sins on Jesus. It was the same as if He had committed that sin which I did, and not I. Christ was treated as we deserve, so we could be treated as He deserved. He was condemned for our sins in which He had no share, that we might be justified by His righteousness in which we had no share. He suffered the death which was ours that we might receive the life which He gave up. When we realize and fully understand what happened at Calvary, how can we help but exclaim, Oh, what a Savior; Oh, hallelujah.

Adam was the father of the human race. The laws of heredity state that one cannot pass on to his offspring any characteristics which his own genes do not possess. So with Adam and Eve. When they sinned, they no longer possessed a righteous nature; therefore, they could pass on to their offspring only that which they themselves possessed: a sinful nature and to be carnally minded, which is death. The human race was doomed as the result of this one man's disobedience, and now mankind needed a new father, who was perfect and had never sinned. And here lies the wonder, the marvelous beauty and simplicity of God's plan! Jesus would become man, live a perfect life, pay man's death penalty, and offer to adopt all the children of Adam. He would take Adam's place as head of the human family and become our new Father. "The first man came from the dust of the earth. The second man came from heaven" (1 Cor. 15:47).

Have you ever been to a ball game where the opposing team was leading by one run, but your team was at bat with one on base? This was their last chance to score the winning two runs. The windup for the crucial pitch was thrown, a connection of bat and ball was heard, and the ball soared over the fence and the fans went wild. *We won! We won!* they screamed. We? Now really! Who won? Did the fans play? Did the fans hit the ball? Of course not! Yet we claim the victory along with the team, even though all we did was to cheer them on. Jesus came to earth to take our place in the arena of life and death on my behalf. He ran to the finish line to win for me an eternal victory. "It is finished!" He cried from the cross. And in that cry, He destroyed sin, crucified my old sinful nature, provided righteousness for me that I could never secure myself, and defeated the devil forever. Looking to Christ, our substitute, we can triumphantly cry, we have won! His victory is ours! Get as excited over your eternal salvation as you do at a ball game.

11. *Questions and Answers*

Q: Does the devil have the power to take your life from you?

A: The devil has no power except that which God allows (Job 1:8, 2:6; Luke 22:31). Satan's purpose here on earth is to kill, steal, and destroy (John 10:10). Jesus destroyed the one who holds the power of death, that is the devil, and freed us from that power (Heb. 2:14-15). You must enforce Jesus's victory and lordship in the situations of life or the devil will take control by default (Eph. 4:27, 6:11; James 4:7). If the devil can get us to operate in fear and doubt, he gains the advantage over us, distorts our thoughts, and takes us captive to do his will (2 Tim. 2:26). If one continues down the devil's path, he may cause enough harm, sickness, or disease to take your life from you.

Q: Should Christians let others take advantage of them?

A: Christian humility has nothing to do with being a doormat that others can walk on with impunity. We are to forgive those who wrong us (Matt. 6:14) and love our enemies (Matt. 5:44), but I see nowhere in scripture where Christians are to let others take advantage. The wisdom to discern when it is appropriate to turn the other cheek comes from God (James 1:5), as does the power to discern spirits (1 John 4:1-6). If someone sins against you by taking advantage, talk to him, take this to the church, and if he refuses to listen, "treat him like you would a pagan or a tax collector" (Matt. 18:15-17).

Q: A non-believer just asked a believer what serving God looks like. How would a believer answer?

A: "The reason the world does not know us [Christians] is that it did not know Him [Jesus]" (1 John 3:1b). The non-believer does not know what serving God looks like because he does not know God. The believer should answer with John 3:16-21, and continue with "so that it may be seen plainly that what he has done has been through God" (John 3:2b). Let them see what serving God looks like through you (Matt. 25:40, 20:32; Prov. 3:28; Phil. 2:3-5; Ps. 100:2; Rom. 13:13).

Q: How does one block one's blessings?

A: Blessings are conditional and are blocked by the largest little word in the Bible: IF! "If you fully obey the Lord then you will receive the Lord's blessings" (Deut. 28:1-6, 28:15-19). If you seek first His Kingdom (Matt. 6:33), you will receive His blessings. Love Him and His commands and receive blessings (John 14:15-21) and do not sin against the brethren (1 Cor. 8:12). Going against any of the Bible's commands will block your blessings.

Q: Where would I find scripture that relates to talent, meaning skills, not money, in the Bible?

A: When building the Tabernacle, the Lord chose Bezalel, filled with the Holy Spirit and with skill, ability, and knowledge in all kinds of crafts (Ex. 35:30-35). God gave men special skills (Ex. 36:8-38, 38:23). Paul was a tent maker (Acts 18:3), Peter, Andrew, James, and John were fishermen (Matt. 4:22), and Matthew a tax collector (Matt. 9:9). Remember that it is the Lord who gives the ability to produce wealth (Deut. 9:17), so He is also the one who hands out the talent. If you are speaking of talent as in gifts, then they are listed in 1 Corinthians 12:27.

Q: Does God punish you physically for your terrible thoughts?

A: You cannot always control what comes into your mind; however, you can and are expected to control what stays there (Col. 3:1). The devil is always striving to put evil thoughts into your mind (Rev. 12:9, 13:14, 20:10) but we must equally strive to keep pure thoughts (Phil. 3:4-8). God does not punish, but rather He disciplines. He does not send sickness to punish, but allows pain to master you if you continue to harbor evil in any way. We need never do this, as God offers immunity from the snare of the devil (Ps. 91). Romans 2:5-6 and Ephesians 5:5-6 speak of God's wrath coming on stubborn hearts and the disobedient, but I believe these refer to the end of the world, when Jesus comes again in judgment and then everything will be laid bare before Him, and we must give account. In the meantime, take every thought captive and give it up to God (2 Cor. 10:5).

Part XII facts

1. Facts of Life, Truths of the Bible

People say this is their life and they will live it the way they please. The Bible says that God's hands made us and formed us, knew us before we were formed in our mother's womb, and created every inch of us. Our bodies are the temple of the Holy Spirit, who lives within each Christian, and God sent Him to us. We are not our own, since we were bought at a price, that price being that Jesus died on the cross that we might be saved (Ps. 119:73, 139:13-14; 1 Cor. 6:19-20).

We can know if something we do is a sin by checking with the scripture. There are numerous issues that are not specifically mentioned in the Bible, but when they are not covered, we have some general principles in His Word to live by. We must evaluate our actions, not only in relation to God, but also in relation to their effect on our family, our friends, and other people in general. 1 Corinthians 10:31 says that whatever we eat or drink, or whatever else we do, do all to the glory of God. Not having faith in Jesus and going against God's will is a sin (Rom. 14:23), and it is not good to eat, drink, or do anything that causes others to stumble (Rom. 14:21, 15:1).

Many have questioned if homosexuality is a sin. The Bible consistently tells us that it is (Gen. 19:1-13; Lev. 18:22; Rom. 1:26-27). Romans teaches specifically that homosexuality is a result of denying and disobeying God. When a person continues in sin and disbelief, God gives them over to even more wicked and depraved sin, in order to show them the futility and hopelessness of life apart from God. However, homosexuality is not a greater sin than any other. All sin is offensive to God. God's forgiveness is just as available to a homosexual as it is to an adulterer or murderer.

To drink alcohol and say you do not get drunk is trying to justify your actions. We are commanded to avoid drunkenness (Eph. 5:18), and the Bible condemns drunkenness and its effects (Prov. 23:29-35). We are also commanded to not allow our bodies to be mastered by anything. In light of these principles, it would be extremely difficult for any Christian to say they are just drinking for fun or to say drinking can be to the glory of God (1 Cor. 10:31).

All sin is equal in God's eyes. Jesus does equate committing adultery with having lust in your heart, and committing murder with having hatred in your heart. God judges a person's thoughts as well as his actions. He says that we will be judged for every deed we do, whether good or bad, so in view of this, I say that all sins are equal in God's eyes. Even though we see murder as a worse sin than to simply hate, they are both sinful in God's eyes. There are sins and there are things that go against the commands that people try to separate. The New Testament does not say anything about a believer getting a tattoo or not, but the Old Testament commands against it (Lev. 19:28), saying do not put tattoo marks on yourself. If there is room for doubt as to whether it will please God or not, then it is best to give it up.

Christians continue to sin after they are saved, because it is human nature and we have not reached perfection and will not until we die and go to heaven. So how badly can a Christian sin and get by with it? If you are asking this question, then you need to rethink your Christianity. This is not a pass to do anything we please and still get to heaven just because we are saved. A Christian should have a changed life and be producing the fruits of the Spirit (Gal. 22:23) given by the Spirit which lives within the saved. You were washed, you were sanctified, you were justified in the name of the Lord Jesus Christ, and by the Spirit of God. Can a person who is saved continue to live in sin and still be saved? Yes, but you are treading on thin ice. Read the book of 1 John and decide for yourself.

It is a sin to do drugs, although the Bible does not address drug use. It does tell us to avoid anything that is harmful to our bodies (1 Cor. 6:20) and to not get involved with anything that is addicting (1 Cor. 6:12; 2 Pet. 2:19) and drugs fail both these blood tests. The Bible tells us to obey the law of the country we live in, and drugs are illegal, so therefore we should stay away from them (Rom. 13:1-4). The same goes for gambling. Gambling can be defined as risking money in an attempt to multiply the money on something that is against the odds. The Bible does warn us to stay away from the love of money (1 Tim. 6:10). It also encourages us to stay away from attempts to get rich quick (Prov. 13:11, 23:5).

The sin unto death is deliberate, willful, continuous, unrepentant sin. God, in His grace, allows His children to sin without immediately punishing them. However, there comes a point when God will no longer allow a believer to continue in unrepentant sin. When this point is reached, God sometimes decides to punish a Christian, even to the point of taking his or her life (Isa. 57:1-2; Gen. 6:3). Pornography is another sin that is not listed in the Bible, but is highly insinuated throughout. The three main categories of this sin are lust of the flesh, the lust of the eyes, and the pride of life (1 John 2:16). Pornography definitely causes us to lust after flesh, and it undeniably is a lust for the eyes. Pornography definitely does not qualify as one of the things we are to think about: "Finally brothers, whatever is true, whatever is noble, whatever is right, whatever is pure, whatever is lovely, whatever is admirable, if anything is excellent or praiseworthy, think about such things" (Phil. 4:8). Pornography can be addictive (1 Cor. 6:12; 2 Pet. 2:19), destructive (Prov. 6:25-28; Eph.

4:19), and leads to ever increasing wickedness (Rom. 6:19). Lusting after other people in our minds, the essence of pornography, is offensive to God (Matt. 5:28).

2. Definitions

Christians many times wonder why they cannot get through to others about their faith, hope, and love for Jesus Christ as their Savior. The frustration could be eased with more knowledge as to where these people live in their thoughts and ideas. I have here a list of different beliefs that might help you to find the reasons needed to counteract these ideas when leading someone to Jesus.

Atheism is the disbelief in and negation of the deity, so an atheist is one who does not believe in God. Usually, a practical atheist is one who has been disappointed because of Christianity and does not believe in God. A dogmatic atheist is one who teaches the principles of the nonexistence of a deity. A virtual feels that belief in God is inconsistent with the principles of truth. An agnostic believes it is impossible to know anything for certain, because all knowledge is relative. Since you cannot know anything, one cannot know the existence of God. Polytheism is the belief in the multiplicity of many gods. Henotheism recognizes one god is supreme among many gods. Tritheism believes there are three gods, co-equal in every respect, yet distinct deities, each with its own personality.

Dualism is the view that there are two distinct and irreducible substances or principles that have always existed. Some explain this by saying that good and evil have always existed. Some explain it by saying that God and Satan have always existed. Some say mind over matter has always existed. Pantheism says everything in the world is part of one eternal self-existent being, which is God. A pantheist views all material objects, including mind, as a part of the infinite single substance that is God. Deism teaches that God created the world by His power, and endowed the world with laws that govern the oversight of nature. God has also created people and left them to work out their destinies by their own power within the laws of the universe. All Christians are monotheists, believing in one true God, however not all monotheists are Christians. "Hear, O Israel, the Lord our God, the Lord is one!" (Deut. 6:4). When we acknowledge that the Father, Son, and Holy Spirit are each part of the triune God, we still hold to the unity of one God. Mormonism believes that God the Father was once a man, but progressed to godhood. He has a physical body, as does his wife, heavenly mother. No Trinity since the Father, Son, and Holy Spirit are three separate gods. Worthy men may one day become gods themselves. Jehovah's Witnesses say that Jesus is not God. Before he lived on earth, he was Michael the archangel. Jehovah made the universe through him. On earth, he was a man who lived a perfect life. After dying on a stake, not a cross, he was resurrected as a spirit. His body was destroyed. Jesus is not coming again. He returned as an invisible spirit in 1914. Very soon, he and the angels will destroy all non-Jehovah's Witnesses.

To Armstrongism, Jesus is God incarnate, in human form. Armstrong suggested that Jesus would return to earth in 1975, that Jesus was not resurrected physically, and that he is the only one who had been born again. There are two views of Armstrongism. Perhaps when Jesus did not return in 1975, some changed their doctrine. Unification Church says that Jesus was a perfect man and not God. He is the son of Zechariah, not born of a virgin. His mission was to unite the Jews behind him, find a perfect bride, and begin a perfect family. The mission failed. Jesus did not resurrect physically. The second coming of Christ is fulfilled on Sun Myung Moon, who is superior to Jesus and will finish Jesus's mission.

Islam says Jesus is one of up to 124,000 prophets sent by God to various cultures. Abraham, Moses, and Muhammad are others. Jesus was born of a virgin, but not the son of God; not divine or God himself. He was not crucified, but ascended to heaven without dying. Jesus will return in the future to live and die. Christianity believes, "God so loved the world that He gave His only begotten Son, that whoever believes in Him will not perish but have everlasting life" (John 3:16). "Believe in the Lord Jesus Christ and you will be saved" (Acts 16:31). "If you confess with your mouth the Lord Jesus, and believe in your heart that God raised Him from the dead, you will be saved" (Rom. 10:9).

"Now fear the Lord and serve Him with all faithfulness. Throw away the gods your forefathers worshiped beyond the river and in Egypt and serve the Lord. But if serving the Lord seems undesirable to you, then choose for yourself this day whom you will serve, whether the gods your forefathers served beyond the river or the gods of the Amorites in whose land you are living. But as for me and my household, we will serve the Lord" (Joshua 24:14-15).

3. Got Questions? The Spirit Has Answers!

Have you ever heard a sermon that you wondered about? Are there religious rules you observe but do not understand? Did God command them or did man create them? Do they help you feel close to God, or are they just confusing? Are you timid about posing your questions to the minister, teacher, or anyone you deem more knowledgeable than you about the scripture? It is your right and duty to ask questions. "For God did not give us a spirit of timidity, but a spirit of power, of love, and of self-discipline" (2 Tim. 1:7). "Therefore brothers, we have an obligation, because those who are led by the Spirit of God are sons of God" (Rom. 8:12-15).

The Spirit is in tune with God and will speak His Words to all who will listen. If you are confused, stay with the scripture and whomever you have chosen to talk to, until you are satisfied in your mind and heart that you understand what God is saying through ministers or through your reading the Bible. All of the scripture was inspired by God, and He has sent the Holy Spirit to help us to understand what is written. John tells us not to believe everything we hear, but to test the spirits to see if they are from God. The best way to do this is to see if what you heard lines up with what is written in the Bible. The Holy Spirit, sent to be our Counselor, will teach you all the things you need to know, and remind you of the things you have already been taught, because He lives within each and every Christian (2 Tim. 3:16; 1 Cor. 14:33; 1 John 4:1-3; John 4:17).

Gain knowledge of the Bible and you gain wisdom about God and His Spirit. God says to look and search for His wisdom as though it were hidden treasure, and then you will understand the reverent fear of the Lord. This fear is the beginning of knowledge, and again, if you need help, all you have to do is ask for wisdom, and God will generously give it to you. The Spirit within you and the wisdom of God are partners, but you must believe this and not doubt the Spirit or God (James 1:5-6; Acts 6:3-4).

An angel told John in the book of Revelation a riddle of sorts, requiring great wisdom to comprehend. Unless the Lord gives spiritual sense, you will not be able to unfold the mysteries of the scripture, and will be missing some of the greater blessings that God has for you. In the Old Testament, the Spirit of God enabled the people to follow God, and will do the same for you today. The only difference is that in the Old Testament, the infilling of the Spirit was given to a few, and on a temporary basis. After the death and resurrection of Jesus, the Spirit was given to whoever believed in the only Son of God for salvation as a permanent indwelling. God says if we follow His decrees and be careful to keep His laws, He will give us a new heart and put a new spirit inside of us (Ezek. 36:26-27).

The Spirit that indwells the Christian will help you to pray and make intercessions for us (Rom. 8:26). He will also speak through Christians so we might have something tangible, which some insist on, to help understand the scripture (1 Cor. 8:13). He, of course, lives inside of each Christian so we have a continuous, warm, loving, and knowledgeable friend to call on, night or day. He will enable you to speak the Word of God accurately and with boldness, which is needed to win souls and to be God's witness (Acts 18:24-26). The Holy Spirit will also testify for us that we truly are children of God (Rom. 8:16), and opens people's hearts to hear the Word that God sends down to us (1 John 4:6). He will allow you to have true Christian love, including the ability to share willingly (1 Pet. 1:22-23; Phil, 2:1-4). The Spirit will search out the secrets of God and share them with us, showing the mysteries that are hidden there among the treasures of the Bible (1 Cor. 2:10-11), and watches over us to dissuade us from doing wrong things (Rom. 8:13).

We live in an atmosphere of antagonism, yet Christ calls us to follow the Spirit and produce peace (Gal. 5:22-26). We have been given the power of the Holy Spirit, and He was sent for all Christians to use in all His fullness, if we choose to do so. The Holy Spirit is a gentleman and will not come unless you ask, however, as it is written: "No eye has seen, no ear has heard, no mind has conceived what God has prepared for those who love Him, but God has revealed it to us by His Spirit" (1 Cor. 2:9; Gal. 4:6). What a sad waste that some choose never to allow the Spirit to work in their lives!

4. Genesis: The Beginning

Genesis is a book of beginnings. God wants us to know from where we came, and learning this will give great insight about the place we are going. Before Genesis, God was and always will be. Billions of dollars have been spent on research, trying to figure out who God is and where He came from, and some of these billions were spent trying to prove that He could not possibly even be! However, all theories remain just man's guess, and the only true and lasting Word is the one God wrote for us. "I am that I am" (Gen 3:14)! "I am" brought the cosmos out of the chaos, turned darkness into light, made divisions between them, transformed cursing into blessings, and moved from what was evil to what was holy. The apostles wrote of this change: "He who caused light to shine out of darkness made His light shine in the hearts of believers" (2 Cor. 4:6), "so that they became new creations" (2 Cor. 5:17). This chaos was waste and void and darkness, and was over the surface of the deep, the abyss, or bottomless pit.

In the myths of the Creation, there was nothing but a water chaos called Nun, and from that came the god Atum, who created himself. He made the earth-god, Geb, and his sister who was also his wife, Nut (appropriate name for a false god) and she was goddess of the sky. To hold up and fill the sky, they had two kids, god of the air and goddess of the moisture and rain. This family of four was the very foundation upon which the world existed as they represented earth, water, and sky.

Some see a separation between verses 1 and 2 of Genesis 1, allowing for the fall of Satan (Isa. 14:12-15) and entrance of sin into the world that caused the chaos. They feel this formless earth was here before creation week. We may see support for this idea in a statement of Jesus speaking of a time "before the world was" (John 17:5).

God's Word produced light, showing the power of the Word and moving Israel to trust and obey Him. Light is symbolic of good and victory, leading us to the age to come, where there will be no darkness (Rev.22:5). Separating the waters below from waters above, meaning God's work involved making divisions and distinctions. Vegetation is part of the ordered universe of the true God. Pagans believed in deities of the deep, but have no myth to explain the foundation of plant life and could not contradict that God controlled the boundaries of the sea (Job 38:8-11). The sun was created to rule the day, and the moon and stars to rule the night. These heavenly bodies were to serve as signs for seasons, days, and years. In astrology, non-believers use stars and planets for guidance, but the Bible says they merely displayed the handiwork of God (Ps. 19:1). However, many humans reject the Creator to worship the creation (Rom. 1:25).

Another myth tells us the stars were fixed on the surface of a crystal hemisphere which made a daily rotation around the flat earth. The great creatures of the sea and of the air were created, and these too were worshiped in the ancient world. Golden and wooden images were made in their likeness, and prayers and sacrifices were offered up to them. Man was the last creature mentioned in the account. Man did not evolve, but was created in the image of God. The term "in our image" was used in Creation only for humans. Since God does not have human form, the term means that humans share, though imperfectly, in God's nature, that is His communicable attributes, which include life, personality, truth, wisdom, love, holiness, and justice, and therefore have the capacity for spiritual fellowship with Him. The Egyptians later in idolatry made statues of themselves in imitation of in our image statement of God.

God made man to tend His perfect Garden, and to have someone to fellowship with. Man was formed from earth; the word *formed* describes the work of an artist. Man was made from earth and remains earthy in spite of hopes of becoming like God. The Hebrew name *Adam* is the same as the word for ground. Man's obedience was tested in the Garden when God explained the difference between the trees planted there. Everything Adam and Eve could ever want or need was provided, still they chose the forbidden. In self-confident pride, they tested the knowledge of God and attempted to pilot their own destination. If they ate from the tree, God said they would surely die! Satan said they would not surely die, adding only one word, and causing destruction to come into the Garden. After digesting the fruit, they did not drop dead; therefore Satan was successful in planting doubt in their minds about God's true Word. They did not understand spiritual death, and assumed God had misled them. Big mistake! The serpent also took away the peace of the Garden and the ease between male and female. He cast doubt on God's character, insinuating He was jealous and did not care to share His knowledge of their destiny. Man and woman mistrusted each other and were alienated from one another and God, and hid from Him in fear and embarrassment. Satan's promise of wisdom never came about, and his promises today are just God's Words twisted out of context. Wisdom is never gained by disobedience, but from the fear of the Lord that came into the Garden (Prov. 9:10). Sin caused them to fear, fear caused them to understand and find wisdom, wisdom caused then to have faith. Adam's faith was shown in naming his wife Eve, meaning living, looking to the future and not death. Eve showed faith in naming her firstborn Cain, because he was from God.

The number seven often represents the covenant, and it is no surprise that God chose the seventh day as the Sabbath, and it became the sign at Sinai. The number seven also represents completion or perfection. His creation was perfect, sanctified and at rest on the seventh day. Today, believers enter into the Sabbath rest spiritually (Heb. 4:8-10).

5. *Genesis: Myth? History? Fact?*

Genesis provides a dramatic account of the origins of mankind and his universe, introduces sin into the world, the effects of its curse on the race, and the beginning of God's plan to bless the nations through His seed. This book has been a stumbling block for many who have approached it with preconceived notions against its supernatural truth. But for those who recognize it as the true Word of God, Genesis is a source of comfort and edification. Both scripture and tradition agree that the author of Genesis is Moses, and no one would have been more qualified to write the book. Since Moses was educated in all the wisdom of the Egyptians (Acts 7:22), his literary skills would have enabled him to collect Israel's traditions and records and to compose the work. His communion with God throughout his lifetime would have given him direction for the task. The traditional view is that Genesis and the Pentateuch possess unity, and is the work of Moses that has not been destroyed. The evidence points more and more to the antiquity and unity of the work. Over time, the book has been edited by his successors, guided by the Holy Spirit's inspiration, with no unfounded or unnecessary reshaping. Any reshaping of the traditions of Genesis would have been done by Moses under divine inspiration, with the result that the book reports actual events and gives correct theological interpretations of them.

Many writers describe the contents of Genesis as myth, or attribute its origin to myth. Mythological literature seeks to explain the origins of things in symbolic forms. Myth records so-called sacred history, rather than actual history. It reports how reality came into existence through the deeds of gods and supernatural creatures. Myths were not merely symbolic language or reflections of primitive mentality; they were ancient man's expressions of the view of reality. The Old Testament makes a radical break with this philosophy of the ancient world. One does not do justice to the Old Testament by saying that Israel borrowed myth or used mythological language to describe its faith. To the Hebrew, an absolutely sovereign God brought them into existence as a nation. Their ritual at the temple was not magical, but an enactment of their redemption. Therefore, Genesis is not myth. The Hebrew faith was a radical departure from the characteristic mythical thought of the pagans. If the Old Testament preserves any traces of myth, it is to show that such were done away with through Yahweh. The Old Testament in general, and Genesis in particular, is a cemetery for lifeless myths and gods.

Some writers say that Genesis is etiology, stories to explain some given phenomenon. Etiological themes do occur in general in the Bible, especially in Genesis, which explains the beginning of many things. But these accounts cannot be referred to as etiological tales that came into being to answer certain questions. For many, the evidence of events from Genesis is not reliable as history. Without outside sources to verify the events, historians must depend on the biblical records themselves. Even the findings of archaeology, though confirming the culture, do not actually prove the existence of an Abraham or a Joseph, so critical scholars do not designate Genesis as factual history. They may be forgetting that the Bible is a unique book. Genesis was not intended to be a mere chronicle of events, a history book, or a complete biography of the nation. It is a theological interpretation of selected records of the ancestors of Israel. Genesis explains the causes behind the events, but its causes are divine as well as human. It is part of the revealed Word of

God; therefore, the events and the explanations are true. God's people could look back and see what God had done, and they could look forward to the fulfillment of the promises.

All the traditions, oral and written, could have been preserved in Egypt by Joseph, along with his own records. Moses could have then compiled the work in essentially the same form in which it exists today, being preserved from error and guided in truth by the divine inspiration of the Holy Spirit. Whether the stories in Genesis are called tradition or history, they record God's true revelation, and therefore correspond with what actually happened. Throughout Genesis, one may understand that Moses was preparing his readers for the revelation of the law. The moral deterioration of mankind was connected with the growth in civilization, and when it was corrupted beyond repair, it had to be destroyed by the Flood. After the cleansing flood, man's vices were multiplied, and the revolt against their Maker was increasing with every generation. Rebellious man was left looking for a solution to his dilemma. After the judgment at Babel, when people scattered throughout the world, was God's relationship with the human race broken? No! God came up with another program, focusing on one man and his seed to bring about the blessings to the human race. God's saving will was extended to the scattered nations through Abraham, who through total obedience became the father of many nations.

The creation of man, made in the image of God, enjoying sovereignty over the creatures of the earth, and observing the Sabbath rest of God, had a blessed beginning. Then up jumped the devil, and man fell into sin, and God cursed sin. No longer at rest, mankind experienced flight and fear, making his way in the world, surviving and developing civilization. God sent down a threefold curse on man, the ground, and the serpent. Yet there is a token of grace and a ray of hope, as man began to call on Yahweh. From Adam to Noah, the downward spiral continued, and God's intense displeasure over man's existence increased. One exception to the curse of death, Enoch, provides a ray of hope that the curse was not final. God would not leave the world to a growing and divided population under the curse without hope and help. He would select a man and build a nation that would provide blessings for the earth. The Genesis writer would deal with Abraham, who was blessed above all men.

Several stories meld into one book here, as we read about Abraham's son Ishmael, born to the servant girl, and what became of him. We meet Isaac, the promised son, the story of Jacob, his son, the struggle within the family, and the emergence of the people of Israel. The blessings given to Abram were now transferred to Jacob, and although Jacob was faithful, he was not the man his grandfather was; yet Israel was born. God moved through the evil of Joseph's brothers to bring him into power in Egypt. When the land of promise was cursed with famine, blessings were provided through Joseph's power and wisdom.

The final events and the closing words of Genesis anticipate the Exodus: "God will surely come to your aid and take you up out of this land to the land He promised on oath to Abraham, Isaac, and Jacob" (Gen. 50:24). This statement was quoted by Moses when he took the patriarch's bones out of Egypt. The Israelites recognized that they had indeed become the great nation promised in the blessing to Abraham, and would also realize there was no future in Egypt or Sodom or Babylon. They needed to go forward into the land they were promised. Genesis portrays God as the sovereign Lord over the universe, who will move heaven and earth to establish His will. He seeks to bless mankind, but will not tolerate disobedience and unbelief. "Without faith, it is impossible to please God" (Heb. 11:6).

6. *Genesis According to the Psalmists*

Seventy-three of the psalms are ascribed to David, and twelve to Asaph. Asaph was put in charge of the service of the song by David (1 Chr. 6:39). He was appointed by David as the chief minister before the Ark of the Lord in Jerusalem, and is referred to once as the seer. Eleven of the psalms were ascribed to the sons of Kareah, and two were written by Solomon. Chapters 90-100 are believed to have been written by Moses, who lived some 400 years before David. Regardless of the identities of the authors, the psalms mimic the works of God through the Old Testament prophets and give us a preview into the life of Jesus, the majority being songs and poems of praise exalting God.

The psalmists praise the Lord, declaring that He founded the world and all that is in it. These psalms bring out that God created north and south (89:11-12; Gen. 1:1). They praise the Lord for His remarkable attributes and marvelous works. God, the psalmists write, is faithful, incomparable, fearful, and mighty. His great words include His ruling over the sea, crushing Rahab with His power, creating the heavens and earth, and even the mountains were personified as if they rejoiced in the Lord's creative power. David gave credit and praise to the Lord for protection, referring to Him as the Lord, the Maker of heaven and earth (124:8; Gen. 1:1-6). Songs for festivals are introduced, with causes for praise summarized as wonders that come from God's love. The same God that made the heavens and earth created the great lights, the sun, the moon, and the stars (136:4-9; Gen. 1:1-6).

Psalm 104 is a glorious psalm in praise of God's marvelous creation and of His sustaining of that creation. It portrays the Lord's power, wisdom, and goodness to all creation. The psalmist spoke of God stretching out the heavens in light, His sovereign control over the deep, His adorning the earth as a dwelling place for man, arranging night and day for life, and preparing the sea for its life. He then praised God, who gloriously reigns over creation and renews it by His Spirit. He prayed that God would purge sinners, Adam and Eve, who are out of harmony with creation. The Lord spread out the heavens like a tent and arrayed His messengers, angels, with physical phenomena similar to ways He often manifested Himself. God gathered the waters into rivers and oceans, creating boundaries that they could not go beyond, suggesting that the waters were a force to be conquered.

Psalm 105 traces some aspects of the history of Israel, from Abraham to the wilderness wanderings. The Lord moved His people miraculously in fulfillment of His covenant promises. The psalmist praised the greatness of the Lord's love for His own. His covenant made with Abraham was confirmed in Isaac's presence, and also given to Jacob. Then the history of Israel was traced, in which the Lord fulfilled His promise to make Israel a great nation. The Lord protected them while they traveled to other lands. This may refer to Abraham's trips from Ur in Chaldea to Haran, Canaan, Egypt, and his living in Negev. The Lord led the Israelites into Egypt and exalted Joseph. The Lord remembered His Word, brought the people out of Egypt, and led them to the Promised Land, where they were redeemed from bondage so they might obey the Lord.

"You turn men back to dust, return to dust O son of men" (Ps. 90:3), "from dust you are and to dust you will return" (Gen. 3:19). The word for dust, *dakka,* meaning "to crush," used only here in Psalms in the Old Testament, means something pulverized like dust. Man is like grass that withers in the heat; God sweeps them away to death. Human life is frail and brief compared to the everlasting God. While here on earth, you will work the dust. "They sowed fields and planted vineyards, and He blessed them and their numbers greatly increased and God parceled out land to the offspring", are phrases found in both Genesis and Psalms.

Psalm 11 looked to a sudden and swift judgment on the wicked with the mentioned burning sulfur reminding us of God's judgment on Sodom and Gomorrah. Fiery coals could be translated as snares, a fitting judgment for the wicked, since they would be trapped because of their sin. Psalm 51 is agreeing with God that all have sinned, and He is justified in His judgment. The psalmist sings of the Lord's justice in Psalm 101, and vows to be careful to lead a blameless life. The Lord worked righteousness and justice for all the oppressed, and made His ways known to Moses and David (Ps. 103:6-10). Along with justice for the wicked, God showed love to those who feared Him, and showed His righteousness with their children's children (Ps. 104:17; Gen 48:11).

In conclusion, the fear of the Lord is the beginning of wisdom (Ps. 111:10), and the man finds great delight in God's commands who has wisdom. His children will be mighty in the land, wealth and riches are in his house, this wise man's heart will be secure, and he will have no fear. I do wish the people back in Moses's day would have learned this and followed the Lord sooner and without question. I wish the people in David's day would have listened, stopped fighting, and praised the Lord more as He deserved. As for us living today, well, my wishes and prayers are the same! What are we waiting for? Let us learn the fear of the Lord, that we might sing the song of Moses (Rev. 15:1-5; Ps. 111:2).

7. Exodus

The Hebrew people lived in Egypt for about 400 years (Ex. 12:40; Gen. 15:13). They went from being honored and welcomed guests when they first came to Egypt, to being demoted to the level of feared foreigners. From a pharaoh who elevated Joseph to second in command, the Egyptians had come to have a king who did not know Joseph. Living in the northeast part of the country in the Nile delta called Goshen, the Israelites were at the doorway where foreign armies would enter to conquer, pillage, rape, and kill. Nationalistic rulers saw these non-Egyptians as a possible threat to their national security. Thus, the Egyptians felt a need to change the Hebrews' status and to stop their population growth. Discrimination and oppression came upon the Hebrews in Egypt.

How do people keep their identity intact, their religion vital, and their heritage precious in an alien country and culture? Israel, with its shepherding heritage and simple faith in the God of Abraham, Isaac, and Jacob, faced sophisticated culture and an enticing religious system in Egypt. Deities abounded, and religious pluralism flourished. Polytheism—belief in more than one god—was broad-minded and inclusive. New gods and religions could be accommodated alongside the old ones. Polytheistic thinking expressed itself in a variety of ways.

From the sacred Nile to the sun deity, from sacred monkeys and baboons to the deified Pharaoh, from sacred beetles to sacred bulls, all forms of life took on a mystical and magical meaning. Music and ceremony were beautiful and attractive, and temples were well-furnished and attended by numerous priests administering magnificent rituals polished by centuries of aesthetic refinement. All of life was saturated and regulated by religion, and the pharaoh himself was regarded as a god. Everyone in the land had to give respect to him, and not to do so was not only sacrilege, it was considered treason.

How did a simple people maintain their own simple faith in an unseen, invisible God, with no pompous ceremony or system of priests, in a situation like Egypt? When that faith teaches covenant and promise, how long could people believe it when they became subjugated by others? How did enslaved people keep on believing in their God, when they were not the victors? The Israelites had several options in Egypt. Through the centuries, they could have given up their faith in the God of Abraham, Isaac, and Jacob and become polytheists like the Egyptians, and some must have done just that. They could hold to henotheism, letting the God of their fathers be only one of many gods, or they could opt for monotheism. By living apart from the main culture of Egypt in their own enclaves, they could keep traditions and customs unique. There were people in all three of these categories when Moses came back into their lives.

With great God-given gifts, a brilliant mind, and a courageous spirit, a rich heritage, and a life-transforming experience at the burning bush, Moses sought to bring a renewed concept of the covenant-making, covenant-keeping God of their fathers to an oppressed people. Some of them must have wondered if He really existed at all, and if He would not or could not help them. Moses faced incredible problems convincing his own people, to say nothing of the pharaoh, that they should leave Egypt. He overcame opposition, resentment, misunderstanding, and all the problems associated with leading a slave people. He led them through some of the most desolate country on the earth, and faced rebellion and apostasy by his fellow Israelites. He received the most famous and far-reaching code of laws the world had ever known. He would become for the Hebrew people, the most influential person of the entire Old Testament.

The book of Exodus would remind the Hebrews as they entered and settled in Canaan, and also in later years, how the God of their fathers had delivered them from bondage when they were an oppressed people, how He kept His promise to Abraham, how He covenanted with them at Sinai, and how He "tabernacled" in their midst. It would remind them that He was a holy God who demanded first place in their lives with no images or idols. It would remind them of His might and power to cause plagues, divide the sea, and bring water from a rock, and shake a mountain with His awesome presence. Because He acted in such a mighty deliverance, He had the right to demand their utmost loyalty and obedience.

The God who acted in history to deliver Israel from Egypt is the same God who acted in history during the Roman Empire, in the person of Jesus, to redeem us today. We are slaves to sin, and He set us free by His grace and power. It was no accident that Jesus chose to use the two elements of the Passover meal to institute the Lord's Supper. Both observances symbolize death and deliverance, and both reflect mankind's plight and God's mighty deed of grace and love in redemption.

Exodus leads us to recognize that people are oppressed today, that God cares and is working to redeem us, to be open to hear His calling, and to be willing to obey Him whenever and wherever He wants us to serve. It helps us to understand that He is still a covenant-making God and a covenant-keeper, and our part in the covenant is obedience. It teaches us to trust God to lead, to guide, and to provide for us. It shows a holy God that calls for a holy people. He is just and demands punishment for the disobedient, instructing everyone to live with deep gratitude and in genuine humility because of His deliverance from our bondage of sin.

8. *Questions and Answers*

Q: What is the proper way, according to the Bible, to confess sin?

A: There are many ways listed in the Bible to confess one's sins. The point, however, is that we confess and ask forgiveness, and not to be too concerned in the proper position and the right place. We are told to confess with our mouth that Jesus is Lord (Rom. 10:9), confess to each other and our sins will be forgiven (James 5:13-20). Ezra led an entire congregation of people in confession (Ezra 10:10-12), Daniel prayed for Jerusalem, confessing their sins (Dan. 9:4-19), and the Israelites stood and confessed for a quarter of a day (Neh. 9:1-37). The psalmist said he moaned all day to acknowledge his sin (Ps. 32:3-5), and John says only to confess (1 John 1:9).

Q: What scriptures point to the fact that there are different levels of the Holy Spirit in us?

A: There is a new birth, salvation where we are born of the Spirit (John 3:3-8), baptism in the Holy Spirit (Acts 1:5), being endued with power (Luke 24:49). The Spirit dwells with you and in you (John 14:17), receiving power (Acts 1:8) and walking by faith; therefore, the Holy Spirit is in each Christian, whether we "use Him" or not (2 Cor. 5:7). Like an auto that will run 120 and the speed limit is 70, but you only drive 35, you have the power to drive the limit, and so it is with the Holy Spirit. You as a believer have the power to bring the level up to full speed in your Christian power. Why not do it?

Q: Can you give me some Bible support that there is no such thing as coincidences?

A: This statement is not actually in the Bible, however, it is implied throughout scripture. He created us, knows all about us, and wrote the number of our days in His book (Ps. 139:1-16). He formed us in our mother's womb (Isa. 44:2, 44:24) and set us apart for His service (Jer. 139:1-5). He knows the end from the beginning (Isa. 46:24, 55:1).

Sovereign means absolute control and rule. Our God who decreed His whole plan before the first creature was created (Rev. 4:11), for everything there is a season (Ecc. 3:10-8) are just a few scriptures that indicate there are no coincidences where God is concerned.

Q: Is there anywhere in the Bible where we are guaranteed certain human or inalienable rights?

A: The American way is the divine concept of personal freedom, equality, honesty, and liberty. The Bible was the political textbook of the patriots. They publicly acknowledged that the concept of freedom is divinely guaranteed as non-negotiable human rights, equally granted directly to all people by our Creator. There would be no inalienable rights without a Creator. They are guaranteed in the Ten Commandants listed in Exodus 20:3-17.

Q: What does it mean, "where their worm dieth not" (Mark 9:44)?

A: The worm is the internal torment in hell and the fire is the external torment. This quote from Isaiah 66:24 vividly portrays the unending, conscious punishment that awaits all who refuse God's salvation. The essence of hell is unending torment and external exclusion from His presence.

Q: In Revelation 2:9 and 3:9, reference is made to Jews who call themselves Jews but are the synagogue of Satan. Who is this referring to?

A: These were the Jews who opposed the believers' Christian testimony. These are the same Jews from the book of Acts where the hatred certain Jews had toward believers was revealed (Acts 13:50, 14:2, 14:19, 17:5). "Even after Jesus had done all these miraculous signs in their presence, they still would not believe in Him" (John 12:37).

Part XIII Life and Death

1. Life After Death

Every person has an appointment with death (Heb. 9:27), an appointment that looms before us like a wall we cannot see around. If only we knew someone we could talk to who knows what awaits us. Good news! There is one who knows, who has passed through the portals of the tomb, and His Word can be depended on and that Word if life. Jesus Christ met death head on and defeated it! The book of Revelation describes someone among the lamp stands who was like the Son of Man. He wears a long robe and His hair is white like wool, and His eyes are like flames of fire. His voice is like the noise of flooding water, and he holds seven stars in His right hand, and a sharp, double-edged sword comes out of His mouth, which is the Word of God. He shines like the sun at its brightest, and He holds the keys to death and to the place of the dead.

Jesus destroyed death, and through the gospel, He showed us the way to have life that cannot be destroyed. Paul said that he was chosen to be an apostle and a teacher to tell this good news (2 Tim. 1:10-11). The Greek word for death is *thanatos*, and a prefix added to it makes *athanasia,* meaning the opposite of death, which is often translated life, immortality, and not subject to death. We are to seek glory, honor, and life that have no end, and would God tell us this if we already had it? We only seek for something we have lost or never had. Many honest-hearted people believe that man is immortal, but if this is the case, why does scripture urge us to seek for it? We seek this eternal life in God's Son, and whosoever has the Son has life (1 John 5:11-12). Eternal life is ours only if we have Jesus, and everywhere the scriptures proclaim that the moment we accept Christ as our personal Savior, eternal life is ours. We have it, present tense, now! Nothing is as certain as death, and nothing should be as certain as eternal life.

We die to Christ when we are saved, and now live a new life which is kept with Christ in God until upon His return we will share in His glory (Col. 3:3). You can be assured that your eternal life is safe, since Jesus now is seated at the right hand of God, and is keeping your inheritance in heaven for you (1 Pet. 1:3-4). Paul writes that our life was hidden with Christ who sits on the right hand of God, while Peter states it is reserved in heaven. I will take the word of either of these guys.

We will take possession of our inheritance of life eternal when Jesus raises us up in the last days (John 6:54). The Lord will come for us from heaven, and everyone will be able to hear the voice of the angel and the trumpet call, and the dead in Christ will rise first (1 Thess. 4:16-17). Paul describes this climactic moment when the dead are raised as changing, in a flash, in the twinkling of an eye, at the last trump, saying that the dead will be raised imperishable and we will all be changed. We will have glorious bodies and leave behind these worn, sickly ones that we are wearing now and we will be like Jesus. And we will have a new name written on a white stone (Rev. 1:17).

The saved will live again here on earth; however, this will not be the earth in its present deformed, sinful condition, but a new earth (Rev. 21:1). The saints will be ruptured, caught up in the air to meet Jesus, and Christ promised to come again and take us to our mansions He is preparing for us. This is true that Jesus will come and gather the saints in the air, but this will be a round-trip space flight. After spending a thousand years with God, we will return to the Holy City, which will become the capital of the new earth that God will create for our permanent home. This will be a perfect place just like the Garden of Eden that God planned for man to live in and before sin crept in.

There will be no sea in heaven, no tears, death, mourning, crying, or pain. No more hunger or thirst, as we will be eating from the tree of life and drinking the crystal-clean water of life. We will not toil in vain or bring forth children doomed to misfortune. The blind will see, the deaf will hear, and the lame will be walking or probably running and leaping for joy. The tongue that was once stilled will be singing, and the weary will run and not grow tired.

We can never fully explain or understand death and heaven, because the scripture still holds mysteries, but we can know that Jesus paid our death penalty, died on Calvary, and has abolished our greatest enemy, death. There is life after death and life in abundance. We may not escape the sleep of natural death here on earth, but Jesus made it possible for everyone to face it with a heart full of hope and assurance. Because He lives, we too shall live and come forth in that resurrection morning. Because He lives, I can face tomorrow.

2. Loud and Clear

Last message! Last call! Last appeal! The last message of a dying father to his children; the last warning to evacuate a hurricane-threatened city; the last appeal to jump from a burning building into the net. There is something strangely fascinating and sobering about last words, and something that rivets our thoughts and attention like nothing else.

God has never failed to warn of impending judgments, and His message is loud and clear. "Before the Lord does anything, He tells His plans to His servants, the prophets. The lion has roared" (Amos 3:7-8). Have you been in a zoo and heard a lion roar? You can hear him for blocks, and his roar echoes all around him. There is nothing quiet about his warning, and there is nothing quiet about God's! No one will ever be able to say God failed to give adequate warning.

Nearly 600 years before the birth of Jesus, Daniel was given special prophecy to help Israel prepare for her Savior. He heard the lion roar for standing up for his Savior (Dan. 6:16-23). Noah warned the people for 120 long years that they would hear the roar of the thunder clouds when the flood came to destroy them (Gen. 6:8-9, 17). And who can forget Moses and the burning bush (Ex. 3:1-3). Scripture does not say that this bush was loud, but it was surely clear.

Zechariah's loss of speech and its subsequent restoration at John the Baptist's birth was loud. "They were noised abroad throughout all the hill country of Judea" (Luke 1:65). God's people knew his mission was to prepare the way for their Messiah. When His Son was born of a virgin and wrapped in swaddling clothes, God sent heaven's choir down to honor this greatest of all events (Luke 28:13). Through the shepherds, the word spread like wildfire. There was nothing secret, quiet, or obscured about the birth of Jesus, and there will be nothing quiet about His second coming.

Dignitaries from the East appeared, seeking Israel's king! Travel in the ancient East was a dangerous and difficult affair, due to weather, wild animals, and roving bands of robbers. Caravans provided protection, and a king could afford to provide an armed escort, maintain fortresses at strategic points along the way, and guard the vital oasis water supplies. Many caravans were remarkably large and could move substantial quantities of goods, such as gold, frankincense, and myrrh (Matt. 2:11). The average caravan numbered 100 to 300 animals; however, one record testifies to a caravan of 3,000 donkeys. We do not know for sure what size caravan carried the wise men and their treasures to Baby Jesus, but surely it had to be noticed. They also told where they were going and why, so they were not only clear but loud (Matt. 2:3-5).

The work and ministry of Jesus were God's final appeals to the Jewish nation. Nothing hidden here! Jesus taught in the synagogues that were built to seat the important people on the main floor and would hold up to 300 people in the upper levels. "When the people in the synagogue heard these things they became very angry" (Luke 4:28), leading us to believe that not only Jesus's message was loud and clear, but also the rejection of Christ by the people. "In the synagogue a man who had within him an evil spirit shouted in a loud voice" (Luke 4:33). When Jesus cast out the demon, the demon was angered and threw the man down on the ground. Now, this must have caused people to pay attention. The message Jesus gave about His temple being a house of prayer was anything but quiet, but He was very clear when He overturned tables and upset the benches of those who were selling God for a profit.

By the time the crucifixion week rolled around, the name of this great teacher and healer from Nazareth was on every tongue. The message of the cross was no secret. Each year, people came from miles around to Jerusalem for the Feast of the Passover. This was the time of the year that Jesus was crucified, so He had a great audience. The soldiers walked Him through the narrow streets of Jerusalem to the Hill of Calvary known as Golgotha, which means "the place of the skull" (Matt. 27:32-33). The leading priest, the teachers of the law, and the older Jewish leaders were also making fun of Jesus, and I am sure they were loud and clear. When Jesus gave up His Spirit, He too was loud and clear: "Jesus cried in a loud voice, Eli, Eli, Lama Sabachthani?"

The Bible teaches that before the great and terrible day of the Lord, the announcement will go forth: "Blow the trumpet in Jerusalem; shout out a warning on my holy mountain. Let all the people who live in the land shake with fear, because the Lord's Day of judging is coming; it is near" (Joel 2). That great and terrible day is explained to the Apostle John in the book of Revelation. This is the last message! The last call! The last appeal! The last message from the Father to His children! It reveals what must soon happen (Rev. 1:3), and unlike the book of Daniel, which was sealed until the time of the end (Dan. 12:4), Revelation was not sealed, for the time is at hand (Rev. 22:10). The time the righteous have looked forward to since all that was lost in Eden will be restored.

God's angel in Revelation is preaching the everlasting gospel one last time (Rev. 14:6), to every nation, kingdom, tongue, and people. The message is not whispered! "He preached in a loud voice" (Rev. 14:7)! From God's first promise to Adam after he sinned to Jesus's second coming, all men were and always will be saved by believing in the gospel of Jesus. It was preached by ceremonies to the patriarchs and through the temple services to the Israel of old. It was proclaimed by Jesus to His disciples. The everlasting gospel is not new! It is God's original gospel! His true gospel! The only gospel! God reminds us that the highest of all goals, eternal life, is not the product of human abilities. Jesus said, "Without me, you can do nothing" (John 15:5). "Here I am! I stand at the door and knock! If you hear my voice and open the door, I will come in and eat with you, and you will eat with me" (Rev. 3:20). Will you open your door to Him?

3. Locusts

Scientists classify locusts and grasshoppers among the *locustidae* family of insects. They have been known from very ancient times, just as they still are today all around the world, as being extremely destructive to agriculture. Locusts were well-known throughout the Bible history.

According to the Levitical dietary laws, locusts were classified as clean for food (Lev. 11:20-22). I do not recommend this, although in New Orleans, they dip the little creatures in chocolate and they become a high-priced delicacy. John the Baptist, preaching in the wilderness of Judea, wore a garment of camel's hair, a leather girdle around his waist, and his food was locusts and wild honey (Matt. 3:1-4). The locust tree grew wild in the wilderness of Judea and produced a pecan-like nut. I choose to believe this is what John ate, since the scripture does not specify that he ate the jointed-legged hoppers. "There is nothing new under the sun" (Ecc. 1:9), so if John's diet was nuts and honey, then the cereal company is not too original.

Locusts' plagues were used as agents of God's wrath against those who opposed Him. Locusts' plagues were also used as agents of God's wrath against His own people when they were disobedient to Him. They were used as symbols of the end-time, armor-plated, missile-firing, flying war machines that were not known to writers of the Bible (Rev. 9:1-11). Swarms of locusts were used as a symbol of great multitudes of people (Jud. 7:12).

With the burning south winds of Syria there came from the interior of Arabia and from the most southern parts of Persia, clouds of locusts whose ravages to these countries are as grievous and nearly a sudden as those of the heaviest hail in Europe. Those who witnessed this find it difficult to express the effect produced by the sight of the whole atmosphere filled on all sides and to a great height by an innumerable quantity of these insects, whose flight was slow and uniform and whose noise resembled that of rain. The sky was darkened and the light of the sun considerably weakened. In a moment, the terraces of the houses, the streets, and all the fields were covered by these insects, and in two days they had nearly devoured all the leaves of the plants. Happily, they lived but a short time and seemed to have migrated only to reproduce themselves and die. Five months is the time that locusts live and are in their strength and power—from April to September, the five hottest months of the year. The good news is that they appear only every seventeen years. Some kinds of locusts are beautifully marked and were sought after by young Jewish children as playthings.

Locusts appear in great numbers and sometimes obscure the sun (Ex. 10:15; Jer. 46:23). Their voracity is alluded to in Exodus 10:12-15 and

Joel 1:4-7, and they are compared to horses in Joel 2:4 and Revelation 9:7. They make a fearful noise in their flight (Rev. 9:9), their irresistible progress is referred to in Joshua 2:8-9, and they enter dwellings and devour even the woodwork of houses (Ex. 10:6; Joel 2:9-10). They do not fly at night (Nah. 3:17), the sea destroys the greater number of them, and their dead bodies taint the air (Joel 2:20).

"What the locust swarm has left the great locusts have eaten; what the great locusts have left other locusts have eaten" (Joel 1:4). They swarm, and the palmerworm, cutting locust, cuts the leaves off and eats the tender shoots. The great locusts, swarming locusts, eat upon the dropped leaves and the young locusts, cankerworm, hopping locusts, dripping locust licks up all the leftovers. The other locust, caterpillar, destroying locust, finally came and stripped the bark from the trees and totally destroyed or devoured all that is left.

The New John Gill's Exposition of the Entire Bible interprets it this way: Palmer worms were the Assyrians, Babylonians, and Chaldeans who—coming from one climate of the world—destroyed the people of Israel. The locusts they interpret to be the Medes and Persians, who—having overturned the Chaldean empire—carried the Jews captive. The canker worm is the Macedonians, and all the successors of Alexander, who—like the canker worm—sat in Judea and devoured all the remains of the former kings. The caterpillar refers to the Roman Empire that drove the Jews out of their borders.

"Cry, because the Lord's Day of judging is near; the Almighty is sending destruction" (Isa. 13:6). Locusts play a part in the end times (Rev. 9:11). An Arabic proverb compares the antennae of locusts to the hair of girls (Rev. 9:8), and again in Revelation, it is said the locusts had a king over them whose name in Hebrew is Abaddon and in Greek is Apollyon, meaning a destroying angel. Calling on God supposes knowledge of Him, faith in Him, desire toward Him, dependence on Him and as evidence of the sincerity of all this, conscientious obedience to Him. Those only shall be delivered in the great day, who are now effectually called from sin to God, from self to Christ, from things below to things above. Locusts have wings but hop instead of flying. The devil tells you that you have to hop. God says you can fly (Isa. 40:28-31). Do you want to hop with the locusts or fly with the eagles?

4. Do You Believe It?

The life, death, and the resurrection of Jesus occurred in history, on earth, and were recorded by men who witnessed the events. In the first century, much less writing took place than does in our time. Many were illiterate, few could read, much less write, and paper or parchment to write on was expensive. The incentive to fabricate was not as it is today, and a high regard was given to writing. The luxury to create fictional material was non-existent; for instance, there was no such thing as a novel or a newspaper. Although the Bible has artistic poetry form in places, it was not written as a poem or story. It was, for the most part, written as history, and is intended to communicate truth throughout.

Luke was not an apostle, but a companion of Paul, and probably dictated some of his letters. He writes: "Many have tried to report on the things that happened among us. Since I myself have studied everything carefully from the beginning, most excellent Theophilus, it seemed good for me to write it out for you" (Luke 1:1, 3).

Can we be sure that Luke and Paul existed? There is no scientific proof. We believe the history books that are presented to us without question, but there is no scientific proof that any of the historical figures actually existed. Why, then, do the scientists question the birth, death, and resurrection of Jesus Christ?

The Jewish historian Josephus, writing for the Roman government in the '70s AD, records some incidental things regarding Christ and the church. He confirms that John the Baptist died at the hand of Herod.

This same incident is recorded in the gospels, as well as the death of the brother of Jesus, who was called James. He delivered them to be stoned. Josephus, who was probably alive during the time of Jesus, is attesting to the reality of His existence.

The Jews believed that adding any mistake to the scripture would be punishable by hell, therefore, great care was exercised with scripture when someone held a conviction such as this. Some think with the copying and recopying of the words that errors came into the manuscripts and built up over time, so that our copies look nothing like the originals. In 1947, the accuracy of these documents was confirmed by the Dead Sea Scrolls. The manuscripts, discovered in caves dated from 250 BC to shortly after the time of Jesus, confirmed that the copies we have were almost precisely the same as those which date over 1,000 years earlier. In the days of Jesus, there was in the literature of the Jewish nation a group of writings called "The Scriptures," now called the Old Testament, which the people commonly regarded as having come from God (Deut. 10:4-5). They called it The Word of God, and Jesus Himself so recognized it. As the writings of the apostles appeared, they were added to these Jewish scriptures, and were held in the same sacred regard. The Council of Carthage, AD 397, gave its formal ratification to the twenty-seven books of the New Testament as we know them, expressing what had already become the unanimous judgment of the churches, and accepted for itself the book that was destined to become man's most precious heritage.

The Bible is a reliable document, and its accuracy has been proven numerous times. We need to come to terms about what the Bible claims and not dismiss it out of hand, because we were not there, regardless of the difficulty of what is said. "I tell you the truth, whoever hears what I say and believes in the one who sent me has eternal life" (John 5:24). This promise alone is worth believing that the Bible is true.

5. *Evidence of the Resurrection of Christ*

Jesus died by crucifixion. He was buried in a tomb known to the authorities. His disciples were distraught because of His death; His tomb was found empty, and the disciples believed that they saw Jesus risen from the grave. This experience changed their lives; the message was central to early church teachings, and it was preached in the very city in which Jesus died. The few arguments against the facts of the resurrection of Jesus did not and will not hold up.

Crucifixion was a most painful and certain means of death. Jesus was whipped by Roman soldiers before His crucifixion, and the Roman method for this was to give thirty-nine lashes on the back with a cat-o'-nine-tails, a most destructive weapon. Forty lashes were considered legally dead, after which point an individual could no longer be punished, so they stopped short with thirty-nine lashes to Jesus. The effect of this was to induce considerable blood loss using this whip that had many ends to it and usually had pieces of bone, glass, and metal shards attached to it, which would rip open the flesh. After being whipped, Jesus was forced to carry His own cross to the place of crucifixion in His weakened state. The soldiers forced a man standing along the road to carry it for Him, although this was not out of compassion.

Jesus was then nailed to a Roman cross, at which point His death came within hours. The Jews were concerned that no bodies would be left on crosses at sundown that evening, because it was the beginning of the Sabbath. "The Jews therefore, because it was the day of preparation, so that the bodies should not remain on the cross on the Sabbath, asked Pilate that their legs might be broken, and that they might be taken away" (John 19:31). Crucifixion could last days on a cross, and victims die primarily through blood loss, dehydration, and suffocation. In order to breathe when on a cross, it is necessary for the victim to push up with his legs to release the pressure on the lungs. This is a painful process because of the nails in both hands and feet or ankles. The purpose of breaking the legs was so that they would be unable to push themselves up to breathe, and die more quickly.

When they came to Jesus, the Roman guards realized He was already dead (John 19:32-34), so they did not break His legs, but pierced His side with a spear, and immediately there came out blood and water. Joseph of Arimathea, being a secret disciple of Jesus, asked for the body in order to take it to a tomb, and Pilate granted permission. Nicodemus came and brought a mixture of myrrh and aloes (John 19:38), and the two of them took Jesus's body, wrapped in a clean linen, and laid Jesus in his own new tomb. And Mary Magdalene and the other Mary were sitting there opposite the grave (Matt. 27:59-61).

The next day, the authorities decided they had better secure the tomb, since they were almost to the point of believing what Jesus had said about rising on the third day, and were concerned and probably afraid after what they had done to Him. So Pilate ordered the tomb to be sealed and guarded, and to break this seal was punishable by death, so they felt a little safer once this was done. The disciples were disillusioned by Jesus's death, for they had never really understood that their promised Messiah who would live to be king, not a criminal to be convicted and killed in the most humiliating way was really dead. They scattered when Jesus was arrested in the Garden of Gethsemane, and Peter, although following Him, denied ever knowing him. The disciples were ready to return to their lives as fishermen, because they thought it was over (John 21:3). But the tomb could not hold our Lord and Savior, and three days later, the women and the disciples found the grave empty.

Did the Jews steal the body? No! The Jews would not want to steal it since it was they who posted the Roman guard, and they had the most to gain if Jesus stayed in the tomb and His teachings died with Him. Did the disciples steal it? No! They were depressed and afraid and would need to overpower the Roman guards, and they had no courage to stay with Jesus, so not likely the courage to carry out such a plan. Did He really just faint on the cross and somehow crawl out of the tomb? Come on now! Really, no one could think that after the beating and being wrapped in cloth like a mummy—and do not forget the large stone in front of the tomb—that Jesus in His weakened condition and human form could crawl out of that grave.

A group of women were the first to see Him as the risen Christ and ran to tell the apostles, who considered women unreliable sources of information and did not believe them. Thomas's response was, "Unless I see the imprint of the nails and put my finger into the place in His side I will not believe" (John 20:25). If this story of the risen Savior were false, then why choose women, whose testimony no one would accept, since they had no legal right as witnesses, to be the first witnesses? Perhaps this was the reason, since they already doubted, so Jesus used the only ones who showed up at the grave other than the Roman guards. Now, since Thomas asked, Jesus showed up where the disciples were locked in a room and walked right through the closed door and stood in their midst and said, "Peace be with you!" Then He turned directly to Thomas and offered to let him touch and feel his scarred hands and side. Now, I think that seeing Him walk through a closed door would have convinced me to fall on my face in repentance, but Thomas touched Him and answered, "My Lord and my God" (John 20:26-28)!

The resurrection of Christ is central to the Christian faith, and without it, there would be no Christianity. Paul said, "If Christ has not been raised then our preaching is in vain and your faith also in vain" (1 Cor. 15:14). Christians stake their entire faith and hope of eternal life on the resurrection of Jesus, for it is only because of this that forgiveness can come. The gospels and the historical evidence bear out this claim that Jesus rose from the dead, so the question is what will you do with the evidence? It has been God's practice to give evidence to those willing to accept and respond. Christ appeared to His disciples because they were willing to respond, and because they were willing to believe when given evidence. Thomas was willing to accept the evidence he saw, and Jesus told him that he believed because he saw him. "Those who believe without seeing me will be truly happy" (John 20:29). That's us, folks! How much evidence will it take for you to believe?

6. Zion

"I have installed my King on Zion, my Holy Hill" (Ps. 2:6). Throughout scripture, both Old and New Testament, Zion is used to represent the people of God. Many Old Testament prophecies fulfilled in the New Testament in the church are, in fact, prophecies of Zion (Acts 2:17-21; Rom. 9:33). Zion was a literal place, a small fortress hill jutting out from the south of Jerusalem. Yet the concept of Zion was in the mind of God long before the natural hill of Zion was ever created. Before the creation of man, Lucifer defied God with five statements of intent, one of which was "I will sit upon the mount of the congregation in the sides of the north" (Isa. 14:13). Why did Satan covet this location so much? "It is high and beautiful and brings joy to the whole world. Mount Zion is like the high mountains of the north; it is the City of the great King" (Ps. 48:2). The Hebrew word *zaphon* is used in the King James Version and can refer to the direction north or has a root meaning hidden, to esteem, or to keep secret. Since Zion is located on the south of Jerusalem, I believe the second meaning fits here. Zion is spoken of as one of the mysteries of God, a place not easily obtained, since the word *Zion* itself means "fortress." The first mention of Jerusalem and Zion is found in Genesis 14:17-20, when Melchizedek, the priest of the most high God, blesses Abraham. Melchizedek is king of Salem, the old name for Jerusalem, which is used interchangeably with Zion (Ps. 76:2). Though only mentioned once historically, Melchizedek made a great impact in scripture as a foreshadow of Christ Himself (Heb. 7:1-17).

The Lord chose Zion as His desired dwelling place and resting place forever and ever, and He says He will sit enthroned there (Ps. 132:13-14). When the Israelites conquered Canaan, they took Jerusalem, but failed to take Zion (Jude 6) and David who had grown up in Bethlehem, six miles to the south, obviously loved Zion, not only for its position, but also for its history. The first thing he did when he became king of all Israel was to take Zion (1 Chr. 11:3-9). Zion was conceived in the mind of God and never changed, but the people marred that image (Jer. 18:1-321). An angry God became like an enemy to Israel. The representative of Zion, the church, has likewise marred the ideal image God had for us, since the church has become a place of spiritual desolation. Do not despair, because God offers hope both for Zion and the church. "The Lord will surely comfort Zion, and will look with compassion on all her ruins; He will make her deserts like Eden, her wastelands like the Garden of the Lord. Joy and gladness will be found in her, thanksgiving and the sound of singing. The ransomed of the Lord will return, and they will enter Zion with singing; everlasting joy will crown their heads" (Isa. 51:3, 11).

Scriptural Zion represents unity, God's presence, the spring of living water, righteousness, and victory. It also represents rest, praise, perfection, glory, and God's promises and requirements. "Walk about Zion, go around her, count her towers, consider well her ramparts, view her citadels, that you may tell of them to the next generation. For this God is our God for ever and ever; He will be our guide to the end" (Ps. 48:12-15; Micah 4:2). I'll meet you in the City.

7. Second Coming

There is only one second coming, but it occurs in two phases that I can find in the scripture. The first phase is only for His church, that is, all living and dead believers since the church was founded in AD 33 (Acts 2:1). The second phase is for all those living on the earth at the end of the Tribulation. That the Glorious Appearing will take place at the end of the Tribulation just before the millennium I do not question, for Jesus predicted that His Glorious Appearing would come immediately after the distress of those days (Matt. 24:29). Those Tribulation saints in Revelation are individuals who do not receive Christ until after the church has been taken up. Revelation 7:9 indicates that during the first part of the Tribulation, the greatest soul harvest in all history will take place. In fact, it is my belief that more people will accept Christ during the early months of the Tribulation, before the Antichrist really has a chance to consolidate his one world government and set up his on world religion of self-worship (Rev. 13:5-7) than have been converted in the nearly two thousand years of the church age. "The Multitude are they who have come out of the great tribulation; they have washed their robes and made them white in the blood of the Lamb" (Rev. 7:13-14).

The work of the two witnesses will be helping those who receive the Lord to return to normal thinking. It is probable that they will be the special witnesses of God to the Holy Land, whereas the 144,000 are witnesses throughout the entire earth (Rev. 7:9). We find further that they will testify, for we are told that they have finished their testimony (Rev. 11:7). There is indication that the Antichrist will make a covenant with Israel for seven years, which as we have already seen, will be broken in the middle of the Tribulation when it suits his purposes (Dan. 9:27). This covenant will only serve to keep the Children of Israel from seeking God; just as they looked at Egypt in the Old Testament, they will look for help and alliance from the Antichrist for the first three and one half years of the Tribulation.

The False Prophet will use the numbers 666 as a means of forcing people to worship the Antichrist. He will demand that everyone have this mark on his forehead or on his hands in order to buy and sell. Physically speaking, it will be necessary for every human being to have the mark of the beast. Spiritually speaking, it will be fatal. For we have repeatedly seen that those who are redeemed by the Lamb, those who have the seal of God, do not have the mark of the beast. But those who receive the Antichrist's mark will have made the fatal decision for eternity go reject Christ and worship his archenemy.

The 144,000 are offered as first fruits to God and the Lamb (Rev. 14:4). This suggests that these 144,000 are the outstanding believers of the Lamb and have been given a special position, as indicated in Rev. 14:1, in standing with the Lamb on Mount Zion before the throne and before the four living creatures and the elders. We may think of some famous people who were put to death standing up for Christ as being among these 144,000. We can expect to see many heroes of the faith who were totally unknown during their lifetime. They may have missed rewards on this earth, but this and other passages of the Word indicate they will receive just reward in the next life, and that will last for eternity.

The armies of God, riding on white horses, following Jesus and dressed in fine linen, consist of the angelic hosts, the Old Testament saints, the church, and Tribulation saints. Military men are issued uniforms for battle dress, but here the Commander-in-Chief of the heavenly forces clothes His army in white. The reason should not be overlooked! No member of the armies of Christ that come with Him in His Glorious Appearing will do battle! Not one of us will lift a finger, for the battle will be consummated by the spoken word of our Lord (Rev. 19:16). On His robe and on His thigh, He has this name written: "King of Kings and Lord of Lords." A warrior goes into battle with his sword on his thigh, but Christ's sword will be His spoken Word. The same way He created this heaven and earth will be the same way He takes them out, with His spoken Word.

8. He Is Coming

You probably know how you would react if someone told you your house was on fire or that you had just won the Irish Sweepstakes. But how would you react if someone told you that the Son of God is about to return personally to this earth? Would you take it seriously? Would you smile it off? Would you question the emotional balance of the one who told you? Check your present reaction with the comments below.

Would you not believe it at all, say that it is not scientific or intelligent people know better? Maybe you would say that you have never given this a serious thought, or that the thought depresses or frightens you. Do you perhaps think that that day is getting closer but will not happen in your lifetime, or do you think it could be any day or hour or minute? Do you dread the thought of it happening in your lifetime, or can you hardly wait?

Or you may be thinking that you believe Jesus will return and sometimes think it will be soon, but are confused and have many questions. Is the coming of Christ really literal or does it simply imply that He comes into your heart? We have heard that He is coming back for so many years, and nothing has happened yet, so why should we believe it ever will? Some people say that when Jesus comes, only the Christians will know it, so how will the unsaved know and what will happen to them?

The second coming of Jesus is the greatest theme in the Word of God. It is referred to 380 times in the New Testament an average of one verse in every twenty-five. Below are listed a few scriptures that should answer the above questions.

1. I will come again (John 14:2-3).

2. You will in the future see the Son of man seated at the right hand of the Almighty and coming on the clouds of the sky (Matt. 26:64).

3. The same Jesus who was caught away and lifted up from among you into heaven will return in just the same way in which you saw Him go into heaven (Acts 1:9-11).

4. The Lord Himself shall descend from heaven with a loud cry of summons and with the blast of the trumpet (1 Thess. 4:16).

5. He will come with power and great glory (Rev. 5:11).

This shout is so penetrating that it awakens the righteous dead. Surely there is nothing secret or quiet about this. Jesus came to earth the first time rather quietly, but not so the second coming (Rev. 1:7). Only the Father knows the day and the hour of the second coming (Matt. 24:36), so all the predictions are just guesswork and should be ignored. We must be ready at any time for this glorious event (Matt. 24:24). Watch, give strict attention, be cautious and active (Matt. 24:42). Take heed to yourselves, be on your guard, keep awake, watch at all times, and pray for strength that you may be accounted (2 Pet. 9:14, 18).

You see, when Jesus comes back, no longer beaten and crucified, but as the King in His glory, He will look for you. If you are not there waiting for Him, He will be disappointed. Thousands of others will be waiting and He will be glad, but His joy will be incomplete if you are missing. It was you He had in mind when He first thought of Calvary, and you that He came to earth to save. He took your place on the cross, but no one else can take your place when He comes for you. Why not, just now, wherever you are, tell Him you will be waiting when He comes, and that you are ready anytime He chooses to come for you?

9. *Life With the Goats*

"When the Son of Man comes in His glory and all the angels with Him, He will sit on His throne in heavenly glory. All the nations will be gathered before Him, and He will separate the people one from another as a shepherd separates the sheep from the goats. He will put the sheep on His right and the goats on His left. Then He will say to those on His left, depart from me, you who are cursed into the eternal fire prepared for the devil and his angels" (Matt. 25:31-34, 41).

All people fall into two categories regardless of your race, size, or shape; you are either a sheep or a goat. Your category determines your destination. There will be a day of separation when the Lord will divide the sheep from the goats. The sheep will enter eternal life, and the goats are condemned to eternal punishment. I want to be on the right side of God, not only in this life here on earth, but especially on Judgment Day. I do not want to be among the goats, even though we are to put up with the goats here until we are divided on that great day.

Do you know what goats are best known for? Their hard heads! Goats are well-known for butting heads. They stand on their hind legs and come down and butt one another, or you, if you happen to be in the way. You would think they would knock each other out cold, but somehow they survive. Why? Because they are hard-headed! Goats will butt heads with anything, and have been known to butt heads with a bull, a much stronger adversary, in a battle they are not likely to win. People-goats are equally hard-headed and will butt heads with any opposition that comes their way. Whether they be right or wrong makes no difference, as long as there is someone to butt heads with. There are goats outside the church, and we all know a few by other names. They are the ones who say they would go to church, but they have other things to do, and besides, there are people there they do not agree with. They would give their hearts to Jesus, but refuse to give up the things of their lives, so their head and heart remain hard.

There are goats inside the church. They say they would come to the ongoing revival, but they are too tired; they would pay their tithes, but they have spent their money elsewhere, usually at the local mart or bowling alley. They would praise the Lord, but they are not the emotional type and their heads are just too hard for anything to penetrate. They are butting heads with the scriptures, where it tells us to bring a tenth to the storehouse (Mal. 3:10), I cannot afford extra offerings (Lev. 23:38) and praise the Lord with trumpet blasts, with harps, with tambourines and dancing, with instruments and flutes, and with loud cymbals. Let every thing that has breath praise the Lord (Ps. 150). These hard-heads save all their praise for ballgames.

Goats eat all the wrong things. They do not eat weeds in the yard, but the flowers, shrubs, small trees as far up as they can stretch. They will eat the siding from the house and everything else in their path except the weeds. People-goats are not satisfied with the sincere milk of the Word (1 Pet. 2:2), but search out false doctrine and false teachings. Whatever fits their lifestyle and does not ask them to change, they love to feed on. Paul writes about this, saying that they were babies in Christ. He gave them milk teachings but thought they should be old enough and mature enough in their faith to chew on a piece of spiritual meat and solid food. Why? Because of their hard heads causing jealousy and quarreling among them, causing them to act like the people of the world.

Goats can keep you busy repairing the fence. They will break out of the enclosure at all hours of the day and night, regardless of the fact that you may be sleeping and must get up and retrieve the wandering goats. People are this way with church. They will come awhile and then break out because they are mad at the preacher and too hard-headed to reconcile. If there is not a hole in the fence, a goat will make one. If some people cannot find a reason to leave church, they will make one up. When you go out to get one of these escapees, he will just look at you and turn his head from side to side. The same with a goat that has escaped! He will just stare at you while you talk softly to him, turning his head from side to side; then he will either come at you to butt you or run away. When you visit a missing goat-person for leaving the church, the old goat (sorry) will stare at you or avoid your eyes, and then he will either charge you or walk away (James 5:19-20).

Be a good and faithful sheep (John 10:27), but do not shun the goats, remembering that it is not your decision to determine who the goats are. Allow the Holy Spirit to guide you, do not be a stumbling block, gently teach in order to change their minds to save them from the devil's snare (2 Tim. 2:25-26). You will notice that this judgment is between the sheep and goats, and not between sheep and wolves. Jesus is not choosing between the obviously bad and the obviously good. There is no division here between the opponents of the gospel and the believers in it. That separation is to be made the very hour of the appearing of Jesus in power and glory. But in the judgment of the sheep and goats, Jesus is distinguishing sharply among persons, all of whom profess to be Christians and claim to belong to Him as members of the family of God; but some are deceivers. This is the separating of the hypocrites from the real!

Some goats honestly think they are sheep, and they point with pride to a moment when they made a profession of belief. This is sometimes described as having your conscience saved, but not your soul. The issue is really one of faith, and the sheep take their place on the right side because their genuine faith has been producing fruit (Matt. 7:17; Gal. 5:22-26). The goats are shocked that they have been rejected, because they are remembering all the good deeds they had done on earth. They have forgotten what Jesus said in the Sermon on the Mount. Deeds to be seen by men already have their reward (Matt. 6:2; Col. 3:23; Eph. 6:8). This is not to say that works gets you saved and into heaven, but to say that you must believe in the Son of God and confess that He is Lord and Savior and do like Jesus does. If you were saved, then you still are saved but every word and thought will be judged by God. Wouldn't it be safer to live like a sheep and go where His voice leads, and never allow your heads and especially your hearts to harden (Heb. 3:15)?

10. Questions and Answers

Q: What does the Bible mean by dead works?

A: Dead works are acts performed in disobedience to God's law. If a person does not have salvation, the works he does are dead. He who does what is sinful is of the devil. The devil and unsaved people produce dead works. The reason the Son of God appeared was to destroy the devil's work (1 John 3:1-10). Everyone who does what is right had been born of God, believed in the Lord Jesus Christ as his Savior (1 John 2:29). The man of God is prepared through scripture to complete the good works (2 Tim. 3:16-17).

Q: In Matthew 7:23, Jesus says "I never knew you." I take this to mean that to sinners, Jesus can say "I never knew you" but to backsliders, He could not. Did He mean that He did know them at one time but now He does not because they are living in sin?

A: The parables in Matthew 7 and 25 are for the lost, non-believers, those who have never accepted Jesus Christ as their Savior. We all have sinned (Rom. 3:23) and we all must accept Jesus as our Savior in order that Jesus know us (John 6:44, 47). Throughout the Sermon on the Mount, the Lord explains the divine standards of His Kingdom. Entrance into the Kingdom is dependent upon righteousness through salvation. The Pharisees and scribes were as righteous as they could be on their own, but the Lord requires a righteousness that is beyond man's capacity to attain, and it can only come from the Lord (Rom. 5:19). Backsliders did not fall so far as to recover (Rom. 11:11) and Jesus will not lose those the Father gave Him (John 6:37, 39, 40; Rom. 8:38-39).

Q: Referring to 1 Corinthians 3:14-15, wouldn't this apply to someone who had not done much in the way of good works?

A: The image of fire associated with the coming of Christ is used elsewhere in the Bible (2 Thess. 1:7; Rev. 18:8). What the reward for the expert builder consisted of was not detailed, though praise is certainly a part (1 Cor. 4:5). The inept builder will see the loss of his labor, but he himself will be saved like a burning stick snatched from the fire (Amos 4:11; Jude 23). The Day of Judgment is when Christ will judge the quality of His servant's work (2 Cor. 5:10). It is not a question of salvation, which is a gift (Rom. 6:23) or a matter of individual deeds (Eph. 2:8-9), but of service, which is judged on the basis of quality, not quantity. Considerable apparent success can be had by human effort and wisdom (1 Cor. 2:4), but unless it is empowered by God in accordance with His plan, it cannot last (Ps. 127:1).

Part XIV Happy Ending

1. A Little Story

This story came entirely from imagination, because we have no knowledge or our Savior's childhood or teenage years. We do not even know for sure if the apostles, prophets, and saints had sons and daughters. But we can be sure that the Good News of Salvation will still set you free. The added scriptures will guide you to the ancestors of the characters in this little fictional story.

Somewhere near Jerusalem, on a hillside, children gathered for their weekly Bible study meeting. Their ages ranged from three to nine, and their number on occasion reached beyond one hundred. They were the descendents of the saints of old. Some were great-grandchildren, and some stemmed back through many generations, with lineage connected to the Old Testament believers. Simon and Andy (Mark 1:16) were there, sitting together, pulling, tugging, and knotting fishing strings together. Joey (Luke 23:50-53) and Simmy (Matt. 27:32) were picking at what seemed to be splinters from their little hands. They could never resist picking up pieces of old, rugged wood. Jamie and Jon-Jon were wishing the class was over, so they could run down to the river and try out their new toy boats (Matt. 4:21). Little Mattie (Matt. 9:9) and her brother Levi (Mark 5:27) were dropping some shiny new coins in and out of a leather pouch. They had brought them for the collection plate, of course. Eshterlina (Esther 2:17, 5:2) sat twisting her long dark hair into ringlets and daydreaming about becoming a great queen some day. Johnny (Matt. 3:4) was nursing a bee sting on his hand, and Jordan (Jos. 3:16), well, he was just trying to keep it together.

An elderly lady with white hair, stooped shoulders, and piercing eyes, walked onto the scene and sat on a large rock padded with sheepskin. In her hand, she held a small wooden cross that had become smooth and thin from age, and saturated with oils from her own hands. She was never without it. You see, it was the last gift her son ever made for her. With a wave of her wrinkled hand, she silenced the kids, saying, "I will be your teacher today. My name is Mary" (Acts 1:4). Little Tommy, full of doubt, was the first to speak (John 20:25). "What can you teach us? You are really old!"

With a twinkle in her eye and a patient smile, she answered, "I can teach you about unconditional love and unprecedented sacrifice." For a mother knows unconditional love for her first born and unprecedented sacrifice when her son takes a bride (Rev. 21:9-10, 19:7).

Mary began her story about a baby born in a manger (Luke 2:6-7). Again, little Tommy contradicted by stating that only lambs (John 1:29) were born in a stable. Tears of remembrance filled Mary's eyes. She gently caressed the lamb's skin beside her and nodded. "You are right!" Going on with her story, she told of the dedication of the baby boy (Luke 2:22-24) and of the poor man's sacrifice (Lev. 5:7) made at the temple. The law required a lamb and a dove, but if a lamb could not be afforded, they were to bring two young doves or pigeons. The young couple brought to the temple a pair of doves, but unknowingly they also brought the purest of the Lambs (1 Pet. 1:19).

Although Joseph provided well for his family, he was only a carpenter (Matt. 13:55), not a man of wealth. The couple had other children, seven in all. Half-brothers James, Joseph, Simon, Judas, and some sisters, the scripture says (Mark 6:3). Being a large family, there was no opportunity for the special child to be pampered or doted on. He was expected to do his share of the chores. Perhaps sweeping up sawdust, peeling bark from logs, maybe he even had to cut down a few trees. We know he planted at least one. He helped his mother tend to the smaller children, becoming their protector, leader, and sometimes teacher. Mary recalled a time when little brother Simon got himself penned behind some rocks. After his brother, Jesus, pulled him free and took him home to safety, Mary saw that his palms were pierced and bleeding from the sharp rocks. Another time, some town bullies pushed Jesus down an incline into some briars, causing his brow to be scratched and bleeding from the thorns. There were a couple of times when his brothers got into some mischief and blamed him, and he, without a word in his own defense (Isa. 53:7), took their punishment. But there were good times. His mother was a devout and sensible woman who taught him Old Testament stories. She told the story of Moses; she remembers the smile on his face as he picked up a staff (Ps. 23:4). When ask to fill the water jars (John 2:7) at a very young age, was there just a moment's hesitation.

Mary took a short break from the class to reflect. Did "He" know then what she knows not?

There were schools connected with the synagogue and city square teachings from scrolls, and of course, the handed-down teachings. Then too, along with his human education, there must have been a gradual interjectory of reincarnation knowledge, for at the age of twelve, on his first trip to Jerusalem, He was utterly engrossed by the teachings (Luke 2:46-47). No doubt, at an early age, the wicked splendor, corruption, and ungodliness burned into his soul and filled him with a holy zeal to stop it! When his family returned homeward, they were unaware that their son had stayed at the temple. Returning to find him, his surprised answer, to their concern, was, "Didn't you know that I must be in my Father's house?" (Luke 2:49). These words must have started the separation pains in Mary's heart.

Returning to the class, Mary began to tell each child present about their ancestors. How Peter walked on water (Matt. 14:29). You should have seen little Simon beam with pride. Little Johnny forgot his bee sting when Mary mentioned the Baptism (Matt. 3:3-17). Mattie leans over and reminds Levi to put his coins in the collection plate. All of them! (Matt. 9:9). Danielle raised her stuffed toy lion in victory (Dan. 6:16-23). Jerry is moved to tears; his ancestor was known as the weeping prophet Jeremiah. Joelie (Joel 2:28-32) is trying to get attention, but to no avail, for all eyes were on little Davie and his latest dance (2 Sam. 6:14). Jonahanna leaves in a rush, because it seems she is a little sick to her stomach (Jon. 1:17). As Mary continues, they can almost smell the cooking fish and taste the fresh-baked bread. Judy (Luke 22:47-48) was the only one to sit in silence. She had heard all these stories all her young life. The shame and mistrust had been passed down through the ages. In her mind, these beautiful stories did not pertain to her, and she wished she had stayed away from the meeting. Mary, sensing her rejection and pain, reached out her hand and pulled her up beside her to sit on the snowy white lamb's skin (Matt.19:14). Then she continued with the Good News and the story of salvation (John 3:16). She offered the little lost girl the wooden cross she held in her hand.

Judy was born the victim of fear and guilt, but upon hearing the truth, she was set free (John 8:31-32). Free from the punishment of an ancestral sin. Free to choose life over death. Being filled with the love of Jesus Christ left no room in her heart for bitterness or confusion (1 Cor. 14:33). The light of the world was now shining through her little face. She could almost hear his voice: "Your sins are forgiven" (Luke 23:24). You can hear it too!

THE END

Printed in the United States
66895LVS00003B/1-48

9 781425 961800